VARIORUM COLLECTED STUDIES SERIES

The Medieval Antecedents of English Agricultural Progress

For Kate and Rebecca Nye

Bruce M.S. Campbell

The Medieval Antecedents of English Agricultural Progress

Published in the Variorum Collected Studies Series by

Ashgate Publishing Limited
Gower House, Croft Road,
Aldershot, Hampshire
GU11 3HR
Great Britain

Ashgate Publishing Company
Suite 420
101 Cherry Street
Burlington, VT 05401–4405
USA

Ashgate website: http://www.ashgate.com

ISBN 978–0–7546–5919–8

British Library Cataloguing in Publication Data
Campbell, B. M. S.
    The medieval antecedents of English agricultural progress.
    – (Variorum collected studies series; no. 872)
    1. Agriculture – England – History – To 1500 2. England –
    Economic conditions – 1066–1485
    I. Title
    338.1'0942'0902

    ISBN 978–0–7546–5919–8

Library of Congress Control Number:
Campbell, B. M. S.
    The medieval antecedents of English agricultural progress /
    by Bruce M.S. Campbell.
    p. cm. – (Variorum collected studies series; 872)
    ISBN 978–0–7546–5919–8 (alk. paper)
    1. Agricultural productivity–England–History. 2. Agriculture–
    Economic aspects–England–History. 3. England–Economic
    conditions–1066–1485.
    I. Title. II. Series: Collected studies; 872.

    S455.C27 2007
    630'.942–dc22   2006034269

Printed by TJ International Ltd, Padstow, Cornwall

VARIORUM COLLECTED STUDIES SERIES CS872

CONTENTS

This volume contains xiv + 348 pages

INTRODUCTION

At the height of England's medieval economic expansion, at the opening of the fourteenth century, probably more people were directly involved in agricultural production than at any subsequent time in the nation's history. Nor would the country again be so exclusively dependent upon domestic agriculture for food, fuel, draught power, raw materials, and export earnings. It was an impressive achievement given that gains in agricultural production within organic and animate production systems were hard won and ever prone to reversal. In economies thus constituted the capacity of agriculture to produce the essentials of life effectively set a ceiling to economic and demographic expansion. For as long as there was an abundant supply of potential agricultural land capable of being brought into production the problem was not acute. Once all available land was in use, however, further increases in output were contingent upon raising the productivity of agriculture through greater investments of labour and capital, adoption of better technology, and increased specialisation. Because progress along these lines involved much trial and error it was slow in delivering results. Hence, as the Rev. T.R. Malthus reasoned in his *First Essay on Population*, published in 1798, there was an innate tendency for the natural increase of population to outpace the growth of agricultural output, with potentially grave economic and demographic consequences.

Malthusian pessimism impregnates much that has been written about the medieval English economy and 'The manorial system of farming' in particular. After all, the national population at least doubled and may even have trebled between 1086 and 1315 without any commensurate increase in agricultural area. Much of this growth in numbers is now thought to have taken place during the thirteenth century and would thereby account for a halving in the real wages of building and agricultural workers which Gregory Clark estimates to have occurred between the 1210s and 1310s.[1] Over the same period subdivision and subletting similarly eroded the size of holdings, creating a sub-class of indebted and often rack-rented small holders and cottiers.[2] To exacerbate matters, from

---

[1] G. Clark, 'The long march of history: farm wages, population, and economic growth, England 1209–1869', *Economic History Review Online Early*, 2006.

[2] B.M.S. Campbell, 'The agrarian problem in the early fourteenth century', *Past and Present*,

the 1290s a general de-stabilisation of weather conditions set in, exposing this congested, poorly paid, under-employed, and immiserated population to a heightened incidence of harvest failure. Although the conspicuous difficulties of this troubled period owed much to the exceptional nature of these exogenous environmental shocks – which delivered massive triple harvest failures in both 1315–17 and 1350–52 – there can be no doubt that the economic vulnerability of the population did much to magnify their impact. That vulnerability was further heightened by war – with the Welsh, Irish, Scots, and French – with its attendant destruction of capital stock, disruption of markets, purveyancing of provisions, and increased burden of taxation.[3]

Had agriculture performed better, population growth been less headlong, and land hunger less acute, it is argued, society would not have been in such dire straits. Yet, according to Ricardian theory, diminishing returns were inherent to the very process of agricultural expansion. Thus, the drive to produce more food, raw materials, and draught power for an expanding population resulted in the reclamation and cultivation of land of ever decreasing inherent fertility, leading, ineluctably, to diminishing returns to first land and then labour. Only investment in better soil management, improved methods of cultivation, and greater specialisation according to the comparative advantage of individual farms might have averted this trend, but these developments had little real effect before the so-called agricultural revolution of the seventeenth and eighteenth centuries. Instead, in M.M. Postan's view, during the course of the thirteenth century the combination of over-cultivation and under-investment progressively jeopardised the fragile ecological equilibrium upon which production depended.[4] The stored fertility of newly colonised land (much of it marginal for tillage) was rapidly depleted, while the progressive conversion of grassland to tillage drove down stocking densities and starved even good grain lands of the manure necessary to maintain yields. This hypothetical scenario of output per unit of land declining absolutely as well as relatively is worse even than that envisaged by Malthus. On this diagnosis it was the inability of medieval producers to maintain let alone raise existing levels of land productivity that impelled both population and economy on their crisis-bound course. Such reasoning has exercised a powerful appeal and has recently been revived by the American environmental historian, Brian Donahue, for whom population growth and market penetration were the twin enemies of sustainable organic farming systems based upon essentially

---

188, 2005, 3–70.

[3] The problems of this period are explored in a third collection of essays: *Land and People in Late Medieval England* (forthcoming 2009).

[4] M.M. Postan, 'Medieval agrarian society in its prime: England', in *idem*, ed., *The Cambridge Economic History of Europe, I, The Agrarian Life of the Middle Ages*, 2nd edition, Cambridge, 1966, 549–632.

medieval methods of production, since each was likely to promote a dangerous imbalance between tillage and grassland, resulting in too little pasture and hay, too few animals, a deficiency of manure, and depressed yields.[5] Marxist historians have been similarly attracted by the thesis that the medieval English economy succumbed to a failure of agricultural productivity but prefer to explain that failure as the consequence of systematic underinvestment in agriculture rather than the pressure of population or limitations of available technology *per se*. Robert Brenner, for instance, has contended that prevailing feudal socio-property relations privileged lords relative to tenants and endowed them with coercive powers of rent extraction.[6] Thus, serfs were unable to invest, or discouraged from doing so, by the excessive and arbitrary exactions of lords, while lords, preoccupied with power and status, preferred conspicuous consumption to constructive investment. Both socio-economic groups therefore tended to extract more from the land than was compatible with the long-term sustainability of production. On this diagnosis, there could be no prospect of productivity growth in agriculture until the arbitrary powers of feudal lords were curbed, serfdom was eliminated, customary replaced with contractual tenures, and competitive market rents substituted for exploitative feudal rents. In short, the full potential for agrarian development could not be achieved until the institutions and socio-property relations of agrarian capitalism had been put in place. Creation of this new and more productive agrarian order was, however, a protracted process which only began in the aftermath of the Black Death, did not begin to deliver sustained productivity gains until the eighteenth century, and was concerned less with the adoption of better technology than the improvement of incentive structures via reform of property rights and tenures.

Told in this way, the story of English agricultural development echoes that earlier narrated by Lord Ernle in his influential and much reprinted *English Farming Past and Present*, first published in 1912. By stressing the limitations of medieval agriculture, much of it conducted by servile peasants producing for subsistence in commonfields without the technological benefit of either clover or root crops, Ernle was the better able to extol the virtues of the era of parliamentary enclosure, enlarged and commercialised tenant farms, stock breeding, new crops and improved rotations. His is an essentially Whiggish account of when, why, and how medieval 'backwardness' was transformed

---

[5] B. Donahue, *The Great Meadow: Farmers and the Land in Colonial Concord*, New Haven and London, 2004.

[6] R. Brenner, 'Agrarian class structure and economic development in pre-industrial Europe', *Past and Present*, 70, 1976, 30–75; reprinted in T.H. Aston and C.H.E. Philpin, eds., *The Brenner Debate: Agrarian Class Structure and Economic Development in Pre-industrial Europe*, Cambridge, 1985, 10–63.

into modern 'progress' and it has been qualified by recent research in four main ways. First, the onset of sustained agricultural productivity growth has now been dated to the mid-seventeenth century, if not earlier, well before the era of parliamentary enclosure. Second, it has been established that the pastoral rather than the arable sector led that growth. Third, within arable husbandry it is clear that much of this growth was initially based upon essentially medieval methods and techniques of production. And fourth, it has been recognised that medieval agriculture was itself more dynamic and far more commercialised than Ernle and many others realised.

The ten essays assembled in this volume contribute to this process of revision. They provide clear empirical evidence that, when and where economic, environmental, and institutional circumstances were ripe, medieval cultivators were as capable of securing high levels of land productivity as their early modern successors and did so without compromising the ecological sustainability of production. In fact, it was where population densities were greatest and land was scarcest that yields per arable acre were highest. This was not merely because of the adoption of a whole range of labour-intensive techniques – fodder cropping with oats and legumes, stall feeding of livestock, systematic manuring and marling, multiple ploughings, virtually continuous cropping, and regular weeding – it was also because integrated mixed-farming systems had been developed which ensured that crop and livestock production were complementary rather than competitive, thereby ensuring sufficient recycling of nutrients to preserve soil fertility. Such systems would eventually become the corner stone of the advanced organic husbandry of the seventeenth and eighteenth centuries and already existed in more than embryo by the mid-thirteenth century. Tracking trends in crop and livestock production within a single English county – Norfolk – over the course of six centuries further highlights the strong continuities between medieval and early modern agriculture within the county most closely associated with the improved husbandry of the eighteenth century. As late as the end of the seventeenth century, Norfolk farmers still cultivated their land and managed their livestock in much the same ways as their medieval forebears and obtained results that were only marginally better. This highlights the merits of testing generalised historiographic claims against consistently gathered and systematically analysed data.[7] Nor was thirteenth-century agriculture significantly less commercialised than that of the sixteenth century. As several of these essays demonstrate, the production decisions of medieval demesne producers were shaped by the prices of inputs and outputs and transaction costs. The strength or weakness, dispersal or concentration, of market demand

---

[7] This historiographical and methodological theme is developed further in a second collection of essays: *Field Systems and Farming Systems in Late Medieval England* (forthcoming 2008).

therefore exercised a powerful influence upon the commodities produced and methods of their production. In these respects, medieval cultivators were little different from those in later centuries, except that medieval market demand was less concentrated and hence the incentives to intensify, innovate, invest, and specialise were correspondingly weaker, which is why the bulk of medieval producers opted for extensive rather than intensive methods of production.

All of these essays relate primarily to the seigniorial sector whose large, surplus-producing farms collectively comprised perhaps a quarter of all agricultural land. As such, they draw upon the exceptionally rich and detailed seam of agricultural information contained in manorial accounts, augmented by data on demesne land-use and land values contained in extents attached to *inquisitiones post mortem*. Seigniorial and non-seigniorial producers drew upon a common pool of knowledge, technology, and labour and were exposed to the same fluctuations in harvests and variations in prices. Nevertheless, they were differently endowed with land, labour, capital, and enterprise and engaged in production on entirely different scales and probably with differing objectives. The similarities and dissimilarities between these two sectors invite closer investigation. The seigniorial evidence deployed here can also be taken much further. Thus, E.I. Newman and P.D.A. Harvey have tested whether key soil nutrients – nitrogen, potassium, and phosphorus – were being depleted or replenished by reconstructing nutrient flows on a single well-documented demesne.[8] This agronomic approach has much potential and can usefully be extended to the livestock sector in order to establish how adequately animals were fed where pastures and meadows were scarce. Detailed case studies have also been used by Christopher Thornton and David Stone to evaluate the quality and efficiency of demesne management and estimate the relative productivities of servile and hired labour.[9] Similarly, Eona Karakacili has pioneered a method of calculating labour productivity in grain production for demesnes with detailed work accounts, which suggests that output per task in the fourteenth bore favourable comparison with that prevailing in the eighteenth century.[10] It remains to be seen whether these results are replicated when tested against the evidence of larger and more representative samples of demesnes.

---

[8] E.I. Newman and P.D.A. Harvey, 'Did soil fertility decline in medieval English farms? Evidence from Cuxham, Oxfordshire, 1320-1340', *Agricultural History Review*, 45, 1997, 119–36.

[9] C. Thornton, 'The determinants of land productivity on the bishop of Winchester's demesne of Rimpton, 1208 to 1403', in B.M.S. Campbell and M. Overton, eds., *Land, Labour and Livestock: Historical Studies in European Agricultural Productivity*, Manchester, 1991, 183–210; D. Stone, *Decision-Making in Medieval Agriculture*, Oxford, 2005.

[10] E. Karakacili, 'English agrarian labor productivity rates before the Black Death: a case study', *Journal of Economic History*, 64, 2004, 24–60.

Most of the key ingredients of English agriculture's later success – integrated mixed farming systems, fodder cropping with legumes, careful on-the-farm recycling of nutrients, specialised production of crops, animals, and livestock products, impressive levels of labour output per task, and close involvement with the market – can in fact be documented well before the Black Death. Seemingly, medieval cultivators were as capable of being progressive and productive and were as alert to market opportunities as their capitalist successors. Why, then, did demographic and economic expansion fail so spectacularly in the fourteenth century? Plainly, the answer has less to do with the lack of appropriate technology than the limited adoption of that technology. Low labour productivity was undoubtedly a problem but this owed more to the want of sufficient tasks to keep the bulk of the working population gainfully employed than to any intrinsic inferiority in the performance of those tasks. And although the agrarian economy was already highly commercialised, urbanisation in the form of a large and rapidly expanding metropolis had yet to materialise as a powerful motor of agrarian change. Until the economy as a whole became more developed, with larger and more dynamic secondary and tertiary sectors, there could be little prospect of realising agriculture's latent potential for productivity growth.[11] Agriculture, in fact, was a victim of its own overwhelming economic dominance.

BRUCE M.S. CAMPBELL

Belfast
Michaelmas 2006

---

[11] These issues are discussed more fully in *Land and People in Late Medieval England.*

ACKNOWLEDGEMENTS

Grateful acknowledgement is made to the following journals, institutions and publishers for their kind permission to reproduce the essays included in this volume: Snoeck-Ducaju & Zoon, Ghent (for essay I); Blackwell Publishing, Oxford (II); Cambridge University Press, Cambridge (III, IX); Manchester University Press, Manchester (IV, VIII); Oxford University Press, Oxford, (V); Elsevier, London (VI); Service des Publications Scientifiques, Muséum national d'Histoire naturelle, Paris (VII); *NEHA-Jaarboek*, Amsterdam (X).

PUBLISHER'S NOTE

The articles in this volume, as in all others in the Variorum Collected Studies Series, have not been given a new, continuous pagination. In order to avoid confusion, and to facilitate their use where these same studies have been referred to elsewhere, the original pagination has been maintained wherever possible.

Each article has been given a Roman number in order of appearance, as listed in the Contents. This number is repeated on each page and is quoted in the index entries.

I

PROGRESSIVENESS AND BACKWARDNESS IN THIRTEENTH- AND EARLY FOURTEENTH-CENTURY ENGLISH AGRICULTURE: THE VERDICT OF RECENT RESEARCH

The belief that medieval English agriculture was characterised by static technology, low productivity, and a tendency towards productivity decline dies hard. For almost as long as historians have been writing seriously about the history of English agriculture the story told of the Middle Ages has been a predominantly pessimistic one. Lord Ernle, for instance, (in many respects the father of English agricultural history) considered that "large improvements in the medieval methods of arable farming were impossible until farmers commanded the increased resources of more modern times".[1] Since he was concerned to highlight agriculture's dynamism in the post-medieval centuries it obviously suited his purpose to emphasise the inertia of medieval agriculture. If, as he believed, technological progress was hampered during the Middle Ages by the predominance of communal agriculture in subdivided fields, it follows that the enclosure of those fields – especially during the parliamentary enclosure era of the eighteenth and nineteenth centuries – opened the way to rapid change. Similarly, where medieval farmers had to rely upon a simple two- or three-course rotational system, with bare fallowing every second or third year, husbandmen from the seventeenth century on were able to avail themselves of a variety of new crops which served both to diversify rotations and raise vital nitrogen levels in the soil. On this reasoning, it was not until the institutional environment changed and agricultural know-how improved that English farmers were able to escape from the low productivity trap which had been their lot during the greater part of the Middle Ages. In fact, the difficulty of maintaining, let alone improving, soil fertility under medieval technological conditions has led a number of writers – Ernle among them – to claim that soils became progressively exhausted during the Middle Ages, eventually leading to falling yields, demographic decline, and the abandonment of land.[2] The

---

[1] Lord ERNLE, *English farming, past and present*, London, 1912, 3rd edition, 1922, p. 33.
[2] This hypothesis was first advanced in W. DENTON, *England in the fifteenth century*, London, 1888, and has since been adapted and employed by a number of historians. For a discussion of the relevant historiography see N. HYBEL, *Crisis or change. The concept of crisis in the light of agrarian structural reorganization in late medieval England*, tr. J. Manley, Aarhus, 1989.

problem was not just that farmers lacked efficient nitrogen-fixing crops, such as clover and sainfoin, it was also that mounting demand for bread grains led to over-expansion of arable at the expense of pasture thereby driving down stocking densities and starving the land of manure.[3]

This generally pessimistic school of thought found its most powerful and influential advocate in M. M. Postan. In the 1950s and 60s he refashioned many of the existing but often disparate lines of argument into a comprehensive overall interpretation of medieval agrarian development which also incorporated ideas culled from German historians who had drawn attention to the widespread colonisation of marginal lands during the demographic upturn of the High Middle Ages.[4] That interpretation has determined the agenda of discussion and research ever since. In brief, Postan argued that sustained population growth during the twelfth and thirteenth centuries under circumstances of low and near static technology progressively eroded the ecological basis of agrarian reproduction. On the one hand – much as Ricardo had envisaged – the extension of cultivation onto soils of increasingly inferior natural fertility drove down mean yields per acre.[5] On the other, the relentless expansion of arable at the expense of pasture resulted in such a deficiency of animals and manure that yields began to fail even on soils well suited to arable cultivation.[6] Moreover, since lords enjoyed privileged access to land and capital he inferred that yields obtained on their demesnes – dismal as these often were – must nevertheless have been superior to those on the holdings of the dependent peasantry. It was the latter who bore the brunt of the mounting agrarian crisis, as manifest in land hunger, falling living standards, and rising mortality.

To claim that population growth eventually outstripped available food supplies is to argue much as did Malthus in the first edition of his *Essay on the principle of population*.[7] But Postan gives his version of this familiar scenario an additional grim twist by claiming that output per unit of land as well as output per worker succumbed to the pressure of numbers, leading to a permanent contraction in

---

[3] V.G. SIMKHOVITCH, "Hay and history", *Political Science Quarterly*, 28, 1913, pp. 385-404; Lord ERNLE,"The enclosures of open-field farms", *Journal of the Ministry of Agriculture*, 27, 1920, pp. 831-841.

[4] The most seminal and influential of his various writings is: M.M. POSTAN, "Medieval agrarian society in its prime: England", in ID. (ed.), *The Cambridge economic history of Europe*, 1, *The agrarian life of the Middle Ages*, Cambridge, 2nd edition, 1966, pp. 549-632. These ideas are developed further in M.M. POSTAN, *The medieval economy and society: an economic history of Britain in the Middle Ages*, London, 1972. The principal German source on marginal lands is W. ABEL, *Die Wüstungen des ausgehenden Mittelalters*, Stuttgart, 2nd edition, 1955.

[5] Ricardo's ideas are usefully summarised in D.B. GRIGG, *The dynamics of agricultural change: the historical experience*, London, 1982, pp. 50-51; see also, M. OVERTON and B.M.S. CAMPBELL, "Productivity change in European agricultural development", in B.M.S. CAMPBELL and M. OVERTON (eds.), *Land, labour and livestock: historical studies in European agricultural productivity*, Manchester, 1991, pp. 18-19.

[6] A view strongly endorsed by J.Z. TITOW, *English rural society 1200-1350*, London, 1969, pp. 52-54, and, ID., *Winchester yields: a study in medieval agricultural productivity*, Cambridge, 1972, pp. 24-33.

[7] D.B. GRIGG, *Population growth and agrarian change: an historical perspective*, Cambridge, 1980, pp. 11-13.

total agricultural output and corresponding downward adjustment in population levels, a trend already set in train a full generation before the devastating visitation of plague in 1348-1349 and not reversed until a century or more thereafter.[8] The contrast with subsequent phases of population growth – in the sixteenth and early seventeenth centuries, and the eighteenth and nineteenth – could not be starker, for although declining marginal labour productivity in agriculture may have recurred, no one has suggested that land productivity suffered in the same way. On the contrary, increases in output per unit area – won partly at the expense of output per worker – made a significant contribution to overall rises in total agricultural output. The ultimate challenge, of course, was to raise total output in conjunction with rising land *and* labour productivity. It is this that constituted the agricultural revolution and in England the breakthrough does not appear to have been achieved until the eighteenth century.[9] As far as the Middle Ages are concerned, however, the issue for historians to resolve is whether land as well as labour productivity suffered as population pressure mounted.

Postan's population-resources model of medieval agrarian development never commanded complete acceptance, not least among those historians who attach prime importance to the socio-property relations of feudalism. For them it was the adverse impact of those socio-property relations upon capital accumulation and investment levels that deprived farmers of the capacity to match rising demand with rising output. The most forceful recent exponent of this view has been Robert Brenner.[10] But although Brenner differs fundamentally from Postan in the general thrust of his interpretation, he nevertheless accepts Postan's basically negative assessment of the technological proficiency of medieval agriculture. Thus, he stresses low investment levels, inadequate and inert technology, over-expansion of the arable at the expense of the pastoral sector, the inferiority of peasant as compared with seigneurial production, and the primacy of ecological over economic considerations. For him, too, agriculture displayed a secular tendency towards productivity decline, although the root cause of this lay less in the growth of population *per se* than the progressive erosion of the means of production via the institution of feudal rent.[11]

The problem with these overwhelmingly negative verdicts on medieval agriculture, however, is that they have proved increasingly difficult to square with a mounting body of empirical evidence. As early as 1915 H. L. Gray drew attention to the intensity and productivity of arable rotations in certain parts of south-

---

[8] Current knowledge of population trends between 1300 and 1348 is reviewed by R.M. Smith, "Demographic developments in rural England 1300-48", in B.M.S. Campbell (ed.), *Before the Black Death: studies in the "crisis" of the early-fourteenth century*, Manchester, 1991, pp. 25-78.

[9] M. Overton and B.M.S. Campbell, "Productivity change...", pp. 41-45.

[10] R. Brenner, "Agrarian class structure and economic development in pre-industrial Europe", *Past and Present*, 70, 1976, pp. 30-75; R. Brenner, "The agrarian roots of European capitalism", *Past and Present*, 97, 1982, pp. 16-113. Both reprinted in T.H. Aston and C.H.E. Philpin (eds.), *The Brenner debate: agrarian class structure and economic development in pre-industrial Europe*, Cambridge, 1985, pp. 10-63 and 213-327.

[11] R. Brenner, "Agrarian class structure...", reprinted in *The Brenner debate*, pp. 31-34.

I

eastern England and thirty years later R. A. L. Smith documented a comparatively progressive and productive system of husbandry on the Kentish estates of Canterbury Cathedral Priory.[12] Similarly productive systems of husbandry have since been identified in several other parts of eastern and south-eastern England, thus demonstrating that the central problem of medieval agriculture was not that methods of raising and maintaining productivity levels were unknown but, rather, that there were insufficient incentives to encourage their adoption outside a few favoured localities.[13] Moreover, unless farmers during the twelfth and thirteenth centuries succeeded in producing more from the land it is difficult to account for the doubling or trebling of total population that appears to have occurred over these two centuries. Indeed, on the most generous estimates England *c.* 1300 may have supported a national population of 6.0 million or more, a figure not exceeded until the second half of the eighteenth century.[14] Patently, the population could not have grown to this level without the means to feed itself. In part, of course, the increased food supplies were obtained by bringing more land into agricultural use and devoting a larger proportion of the farmed area to the production of food for humans rather than animals. Nevertheless, active though reclamation and colonisation may have been during the twelfth and thirteenth centuries, on the evidence of the extent of cultivation in 1086 as recorded by Domesday Book it is difficult to see how the farmed area could have doubled let alone trebled over these two centuries.[15] By implication, therefore, productivity must have risen.[16] This in turn implies that medieval English agriculture was more dynamic than it has hitherto been given credit, which would certainly accord with what is known of contemporary developments in northern France and the Low Countries where the late thirteenth and early fourteenth centuries

---

[12] H.L. GRAY, *English field systems*, Cambridge, Mass., 1915, pp. 301-303; R.A.L. SMITH, *Canterbury Cathedral Priory: a study in monastic administration*, Cambridge, 1943, pp. 128-165.

[13] J.A. RAFTIS, *The estates of Ramsey Abbey*, Toronto, 1957; P.F. BRANDON, "Demesne arable farming in coastal Sussex during the later Middle Ages", *Agricultural History Review*, 19, 1971, pp. 113-134; M. MATE, "Profit and productivity on the esates of Isabella de Forz (1260-92)", *Economic History Review*, 2nd series, 33, 1980, pp. 326-334; B.M.S. CAMPBELL, "Agricultural progress in medieval England: some evidence from eastern Norfolk", *Economic History Review*, 2nd series, 36, 1983, pp. 26-46; M. MATE, "Medieval agrarian practices: the determining factors?", *Agricultural History Review*, 33, 1985, pp. 22-31; P.F. BRANDON, "Farming techniques in southeast England", in H.E. HALLAM (ed.), *The Agrarian History of England and Wales*, 2, *1042-1350*, Cambridge, 1988, pp. 312-325; M.P. HOGAN, "Clays, *culturae* and the cultivator's wisdom: management efficiency at fourteenth-century Wistow", *Agricultural History Review*, 36, 1988, pp. 117-131.

[14] R.M. SMITH, "Human resources", in G. ASTILL and A. GRANT (eds.), *The countryside of medieval England*, Oxford, 1988, pp. 189-191. But see also B.M.S. CAMPBELL, J.A. GALLOWAY, D. KEENE, and M. MURPHY, *A medieval capital and its grain supply: agrarian production in the London region c. 1300*, Historical Geography Research Series, 30, London, 1993, pp. 43-45 and 172.

[15] R.H. BRITNELL, "Commercialisation and economic development in England, 1000-1300", in R.H. BRITNELL and B.M.S. CAMPBELL (eds.), *A commercialising economy: England 1086-1300*, Manchester, 1994, pp. 11-12.

[16] Titow, in contrast (*English rural society*, p. 72), infers that mean living standards fell significantly over this period, presumably from a relatively high level in 1086.

are regarded as representing a peak both in total agricultural output and output per unit area.[17]

In England, where a more pessimistic assessment of agricultural proficiency has prevailed for so long, the empirical foundation of that assessment has been provided by the rich archives of several major ecclesiastical estates, above all the extraordinary records of the bishopric of Winchester – possibly the fullest compendium of detailed agricultural information ever compiled – whose lands were concentrated in southern England.[18] Over the past twenty-five years or so, however, investigation has been extended to other classes of estate and to different parts of the country, to such an extent that knowledge and understanding of medieval agriculture have been transformed and something of a sea-change has occurred in interpretations of the period.[19] There is now a far greater awareness both of the diversity of agrarian experience and of the potential for progress provided by available technology.[20] New and more rigorous methodologies have been developed for analysing farming systems and measuring their productivities, and the task has commenced of subjecting the critical and voluminous Winchester material to more systematic and searching scrutiny.[21] Controlled comparison with the evidence of later periods, particularly the sixteenth and seventeenth centuries, has also enabled medieval developments and levels of performance to be seen in clearer perspective.[22] Overall, this is transforming assessments of the agricultural

---

[17] H. VAN DER WEE, "Introduction - the agricultural development of the Low Countries as revealed by the tithe and rent statistics, 1250-1800", in H. VAN DER WEE and E. VAN CAUWENBERGHE (eds.), *Productivity of land and agricultural innovation in the Low Countries (1250-1800)*, Louvain, 1978, pp. 1-23; E. LE ROY LADURIE, "The end of the Middle ages: the work of Guy Bois and Hugues Neveux", in E. LE ROY LADURIE and J. GOY, *Tithe and agrarian history from the fourteenth to the nineteenth centuries: an essay in comparative history*, Cambridge, 1982, pp. 71-92. Although for a more negative assessment see G. BOIS, *The crisis of feudalism: economy and society in eastern Normandy, c. 1300-1550*, Cambridge, 1984, pp. 264-267.

[18] Among the many studies based on the Winchester Pipe Rolls are W. BEVERIDGE, "The yield and price of corn in the Middle Ages", *Economic History* (a supplement of *The Economic Journal*), 1, 1927, pp. 155-167; J.Z. TITOW, *Winchester yields*; D.L. FARMER, "Grain yields on the Winchester manors in the later Middle Ages", *Economic History Review*, 2nd series, 30, 1977, pp. 555-566; D.L. FARMER, "Crop yields, prices and wages in medieval England", *Studies in Medieval and Renaissance History*, 6, 1983, pp. 117-155.

[19] For example, R.H. BRITNELL, *The commercialisation of English society, 1000-1300*, Cambridge, 1993.

[20] Much fresh knowledge is summarised in H.E. HALLAM, *Agrarian history...*, and E. MILLER (ed.), *The agrarian history of England and Wales, 3, 1348-1500*, Cambridge, 1991.

[21] J.P. POWER and B.M.S. CAMPBELL, "Cluster analysis and the classification of medieval demesne-farming systems", *Transactions of the Institute of British Geographers*, new series, 17, 1992, pp. 227-45; B.M.S. CAMPBELL, "Land, labour, livestock and productivity trends in English seignorial agriculture, 1208-1450", in B.M.S. CAMPBELL and M. OVERTON, *Land, labour and livestock*, pp. 144-182; K. BIDDICK, "Agrarian productivity on the estates of the bishopric of Winchester in the early thirteenth century: a managerial perspective", in B.M.S. CAMPBELL and M. OVERTON, *Land, labour and livestock*, pp. 95-123; C. THORNTON, "The determinants of land productivity on the bishop of Winchester's demesne of Rimpton, 1208 to 1403", in B.M.S. CAMPBELL and M. OVERTON, *Land, labour and livestock*, pp. 183-210; B.M.S. CAMPBELL, J.A. GALLOWAY, D. KEENE, and M. MURPHY, *A medieval capital...*

[22] P. GLENNIE, "Continuity and change in Hertfordshire agriculture, 1550-1700: II - trends in crop yields and their determinants", *Agricultural History Review*, 36, 1988, pp. 145-161; M. OVERTON and

response to the demographic and commercial challenge of the twelfth and thirteenth centuries. In particular, technological change, the status and performance of the pastoral sector, the experience of marginal regions, the range and character of farming types and farming regions, and levels of productivity and trends in yields have all now been cast in a fresh light.

Technological change

A central theme of the success story of post-medieval English agriculture as it is commonly told is the innovation and diffusion of new technology, especially in the form of new crops, better breeds, improved methods, more rational management, new tools and implements, and above all new systems of husbandry.[23] In all these respects change – and therefore progress – can be explicitly observed and measured. An apparent absence of correspondingly conspicuous innovations in the Middle Ages has therefore been taken as synonymous with technological stagnation and inertia.[24] True, the range of crops and animals available to husbandmen changed little during this period compared with later centuries, but it does not necessarily follow that the period was bereft of fresh technological opportunities nor, in particular, that systems of husbandry were unchanging. On the contrary, several potentially significant technological innovations can now be dated to this period and in certain areas these helped bring about important changes in farming systems.

To judge from the foundation of markets and fairs, from price trends, and from the volume of money in circulation, the pace of economic activity appears to have quickened c. 1180 and it is at almost precisely this point in time that the windmill has recently been shown to have made its first appearance in England.[25] Watermills had long been in existence but in the drier and flatter parts of the country, where sites suitable for watermill construction were limited, there was a serious deficiency in milling capacity. The windmill made good this deficiency and, as Richard Holt has recently demonstrated, after some initial hesitation its diffusion was remarkably rapid. Since windmill construction required capital in larger

---

B.M.S. CAMPBELL, "Norfolk livestock farming 1250-1740: a comparative study of manorial accounts and probate inventories", *Journal of Historical Geography*, 18, 1992, pp. 377-396; B.M.S. CAMPBELL and M. OVERTON, "A new perspective on medieval and early modern agriculture: six centuries of Norfolk farming c. 1250-c. 1850", *Past and Present*, 141, 1993, pp. 38-105.

[23] For example, Lord ERNLE, *English farming...*; J.D. CHAMBERS and G.E. MINGAY, *The agricultural revolution 1750-1880*, London, 1966; E. KERRIDGE, *The agricultural revolution*, London, 1967; R.C. ALLEN, *Enclosure and the yeoman: the agricultural development of the south midlands 1450-1850*, Oxford, 1992.

[24] Most notably, G.E. FUSSELL, "Social change but static technology: rural England in the fourteenth century", *History Studies*, 1, 1968, pp. 23-32.

[25] P.D.A. HARVEY, "The English inflation of 1180-1220", *Past and Present*, 61, 1973, pp. 3-30; R.H. BRITNELL, *Commercialisation...*, pp. 79-151; R. HOLT, *The mills of medieval England*, Oxford, 1988, pp. 20-21.

quantities than most peasants were able to muster windmills from the outset were a largely seigneurial innovation.[26] They were also essentially ancillary to agriculture, aiding the processing rather than the production of grain, and are an important example of how productivity was raised by substituting mechanical for human energy.

A similar purpose was served by the progressive substitution of horses for oxen, since equipped with the right harness horses are capable of working longer, faster and harder than oxen (although at a far higher running and depreciation cost). The diffusion of horse haulage and especially horse traction, as John Langdon has shown in a detailed and comprehensive study, was an altogether slower and more drawn-out process than the diffusion of the windmill, beginning earlier and at the time of the Black Death remaining geographically much more circumscribed.[27] In part, of course, this is because it was contingent upon the supply of suitable animals and hence could proceed no faster than biological rates of reproduction. But purpose-bred carthorses were an expensive investment and hence the decision to employ them was also heavily influenced by commercial considerations.[28] That their diffusion was as widespread and rapid as it was – Langdon has described horse haulage as constituting "a revolution in vehicle transport in twelfth- and thirteenth-century England" – bears testimony to the expanding commercial opportunities of the age.[29] By contrast, the incentive to adopt horses for ploughing was weaker. It was strongest in areas of light or stoney soils where the horse's advantage over the ox was most conspicuous, and especially where economic advantage was to be gained by developing alternative forms of pastoral husbandry with the grassland resources thereby released.[30] Thus, there is a particularly close association between the partial or complete substitution of horses for oxen and the commercial development of cattle-based dairying. Since horses were heavily reliant upon fodder crops and helped maximise the ratio of non-working to working animals, they were an essential ingredient of the most intensive and developed mixed-farming systems.[31] Significantly, too, diffusion of the horse provides the clearest example of a technological innovation whose adoption was more rapid among peasant than seigneurial producers.[32]

Windmills and horses both show up in the records of the period as innovations which were already well under way before the thirteenth century opened. With several of the other technological innovations of the age the timing of their intro-

---

[26] R. Holt, *The mills of medieval England*, pp. 20-35.

[27] J.L. Langdon, *Horses, oxen and technological innovation: the use of draught animals in English farming from 1066-1500*, Cambridge, 1986.

[28] K. Biddick, *The other economy: pastoral husbandry on a medieval estate*, Berkeley and Los Angeles, 1989, pp. 116-121; B.M.S. Campbell, J.A. Galloway, D. Keene, and M. Murphy, *A medieval capital...*, pp. 56-59.

[29] J.L. Langdon, "Horse hauling: a revolution in vehicle transport in twelfth- and thirteenth-century England", *Past and Present*, 103, 1984, pp. 37-66.

[30] B.M.S. Campbell, "Towards an agricultural geography of medieval England", *Agricultural History Review*, 36, 1988, pp. 91-97.

[31] J.P. Power and B.M.S. Campbell, "Cluster analysis...", pp. 233-236.

[32] J.L. Langdon, *Horses, oxen and technological innovation*, pp. 172-253.

I

duction and spread is less certain, since most of the available evidence dates from last quarter of the thirteenth and first half of the fourteenth centuries when manorial accounts (a managerial innovation of the very beginning of the thirteenth century) and other associated records are most abundant.[33] On this evidence it was in the late thirteenth and especially the fourteenth century that the rabbit – an introduction of the twelfth century – first began to become a lucrative crop, converting to productive and profitable use some of the sandiest, poorest and agriculturally most marginal soils in the country.[34] Its modest and selective spread was mirrored within the arable sector by the diffusion of vetches, a nitrogen-fixing leguminous crop often specifically grown as fodder for horses.[35] Vetches, along with peas and beans, had in fact long been known but by the final quarter of the thirteenth century there are indications that they were being grown on a greatly increased scale in certain parts of the country, often as a partial or complete substitute for bare fallows. As both a fodder crop and a means of restoring soil nitrogen they anticipated the role that clover, sainfoin and the other nitrogenous grasses were to perform in later centuries.[36] Indeed, as late as 1740 in as innovative a county as Norfolk the area devoted to the old "medieval" legumes of peas, beans, and vetches still exceeded that devoted to clover and other recent introductions.[37]

As in the seventeenth century, the selective spread of legumes was a symptom of changes in rotational practices and the closer integration of arable and pastoral husbandry. Once manorial accounts begin to name the fields in which crops were sown, as became the practice on some estates from the late thirteenth century, it is possible to reconstruct cropping plans in considerable detail. Although in much of the country two- and three-course cropping tended to remain the norm (often conducted within the institutional context provided by the two- and three-field system) the range and combination of the actual crops grown became increasingly differentiated.[38] In the east midlands, where crop combinations became particularly diverse, there are signs that fields were subdivided into smaller furlong units

---

[33] P.D.A. HARVEY, "Agricultural treatises and manorial accounting in medieval England", *Agricultural History Review*, 20, 1972, pp. 170-182; P.D.A. HARVEY (ed.), *Manorial records of Cuxham, Oxfordshire, circa 1200-1359*, Oxfordshire Record Society, 50, and Royal Commission on Historical Manuscripts joint publication 23, London, 1976..

[34] J. SHEAIL, *Rabbits and their history*, Newton Abbot, 1971; M. BAILEY, "The rabbit and the medieval East Anglian economy", *Agricultural History Review*, 36, 1988, pp. 1-20.

[35] B.M.S. CAMPBELL, "The diffusion of vetches in medieval England", *Economic History Review*, 2nd series, 41, 1988, pp. 193-208.

[36] G.P.H. CHORLEY, "The agricultural revolution in northern Europe, 1750-1880: nitrogen, legumes and crop productivity", *Economic History Review*, 2nd series, 34, 1981, pp. 71-93.

[37] B.M.S. CAMPBELL and M. OVERTON, "A new perspective...", pp. 54-60.

[38] Contrary to the view sometimes expressed, there appears to have been no widespread conversion of two- to three-field systems over this period: H.S.A. FOX, "The alleged transformation from two-field to three-field systems in medieval England", *Economic History Review*, 2nd series, 39, 1986, pp. 526-548.

in order the better to accommodate this diversity.[39] But it was outside the confines of the regular commonfield system that medieval rotations attained their greatest diversity. By the first half of the fourteenth century there are clearly documented examples of convertible husbandry systems in which land alternated between arable and grass as well as of highly intensive systems in which land was fallowed rarely if ever at all, thereby anticipating two of the key technological achievements of the seventeenth and eighteenth centuries.[40] Both are rotations which in their different ways relied for their success upon the close integration of arable and pastoral husbandry and hence on the carefully controlled recycling of nitrogen.[41] In the long run, until the development of artificial fertilisers, this was to prove the most revolutionary innovation of all.

The status and performance of the pastoral sector

Many writers on medieval agriculture have regarded trends in pastoral husbandry as the inverse of trends in arable husbandry: as population rose and more land, of necessity, was devoted to grain production so, it is argued, less was available to support flocks and herds and stocking densities must have fallen.[42] Such symmetry would only have prevailed, however, if arable and pastoral husbandry were conducted as largely self-contained enterprises, which was far from being the case. Without animals to supply traction and manure the arable could not have been cultivated; in return the arable contributed fodder crops and temporary pasturage. Perforce, most medieval farming systems were mixed, although the extent to which each sector was dependent upon the other varied according to the composition of available landuse resources and the character and intensity of the farming system in question. Historians have only recently begun to explore the detailed nature of this relationship, but already it is plain that it was far more complex, varied, and dynamic than envisaged by earlier writers, not least because rising pressure upon scarce land resources tended to drive up the intensity of their management and induce the evolution of more integrated mixed-farming systems. The latter were associated with a shift in the composition of flocks and herds and an enhanced emphasis upon fodder crops.

In thirteenth- and fourteenth-century England it was at the extensive margin of cultivation that the relationship between arable and pastoral husbandry approxi-

---

[39] B.M.S. CAMPBELL and J.P. POWER; "Mapping the agricultural geography of medieval England", *Journal of Historical Geography*, 15, 1989, p. 35; D. HALL, *Medieval fields*, Aylesbury, 1982, pp. 44-55; G. ASTILL, "Fields", in G. ASTILL and A. GRANT, *The countryside...*, pp. 75-80.

[40] T.A.M. BISHOP, "The rotation of crops at Westerham, 1297-1350", *Economic History Review*, 9, 1938, pp. 38-44; E. SEARLE, *Lordship and community: Battle Abbey and its banlieu, 1066-1538*, Toronto, 1974, pp. 272-291; B.M.S. CAMPBELL, "Agricultural progress...", pp. 27-29 and 41-42; B.M.S. CAMPBELL and M. OVERTON, "A new perspective...", pp. 62-63.

[41] R.S. SHIEL, "Improving soil fertility in the pre-fertiliser era", in B.M.S. CAMPBELL and M. OVERTON, *Land, labour and livestock*, pp. 51-77.

[42] For example, M.M. POSTAN, "Medieval agrarian society...", pp. 553-556.

mated most closely to the simple, direct relationship envisaged by Postan. This was especially so where environmental circumstances fostered a physical division between areas of arable and areas of grassland, as was the case in much of upland England. In parts of northern England, for instance, lowland arable farms which carried just enough working animals to satisfy the needs of cultivation were complemented by specialist pastoral farms on the upland margins which bred and reared replacement stock.[43] Here, therefore, the geographical separation of pastoral from arable husbandry underlined their functional independence. Elsewhere, in certain pasture-rich parts of lowland England, Kathleen Biddick has demonstrated that this separation was more functional than physical. In the first half of the thirteenth century, for instance, the demesnes of the bishops of Winchester in the downland country of southern England carried substantial stocks of animals, particularly sheep, but a negative correlation between livestock numbers and yields per acre "hints at the possibility that the bishop considered his pastoral farming as a parallel enterprise to his grain farming, rather than the two as an integrated enterprise".[44] Such practice may have been rational where there was no great pressure upon the arable and permanent grassland was available in quantity, but in the more populous parts of eastern and south-eastern England it was neither prudent nor practicable. In these regions, as the intensity of land-utilisation rose so the interdependence of arable and pastoral husbandry grew.

As the premium rose upon turning available pastoral resources to maximum advantage so demesne managers placed increased emphasis upon the more productive categories of livestock – horses rather than oxen, cattle rather than sheep, and dairying rather than rearing or fattening. Increasingly, too, that meant housing them temporarily or permanently – horses in stalls, cattle in byres, sheep in cotes, and swine in styes – and supplementing natural grazing with produced fodder. This was both more capital and labour intensive but transformed the character of pastoral husbandry and rendered it increasingly complementary rather than competitive with the arable sector.[45] As Biddick has observed of arable and pastoral husbandry on the estates of Peterborough Abbey in the east midlands: "The simple relations between pastoral and cereal husbandry posited by Postan do not adequately account for the comparative commercialisation of haulage, dairying, and wool production over the thirteenth century and the trade-offs made between producing such products and selling pastoral resources to others to produce them".[46] The upshot of these developments was a paradox, insofar as the pastoral sector attained its fullest development – as measured by the range and type of ani-

---

[43] See, for instance, I.S.W. BLANCHARD, "Economic change in Derbyshire in the late Middle Ages, 1272-1540", unpublished PhD thesis, University of London, 1967, pp. 168-174.

[44] K. BIDDICK, "Agrarian productivity...", p. 115.

[45] B.M.S. CAMPBELL, "The livestock of Chaucer's reeve: fact or fiction?", in E.B. DEWINDT (ed.), *The salt of common life: individuality and choice in the medieval town, countryside and church. Essays presented to J. Ambrose Raftis on the occasion of his 70th birthday*, Kalamazoo, 1995; B.M.S. CAMPBELL, "Commercial dairy production on medieval English demesnes: the case of Norfolk", in E. GRANT (ed.), *Animals and their products in trade and exchange, Anthropozoologica*, 16, 1992, pp. 107-118.

[46] K. BIDDICK, *The other economy*, p. 130.

mals stocked and the relative importance of working and non-working animals – in some of the least grassy parts of the country (where, on Postan's logic, the opposite might have been supposed to apply). These most developed pastoral regimes when married to correspondingly progressive arable regimes created integrated mixed-farming systems that were both intensive and productive, possessing in some measure all the elements exhibited by those mixed-farming systems which were to have such a revolutionary effect upon the output of English agriculture from the eighteenth century on.[47]

Of course, all this evidence – telling as it is – relates exclusively to the seigneurial sector, which Postan and Brenner agree was better placed to invest in pastoral husbandry than the dependent peasant sector.[48] Indeed, Postan has employed tax returns which record the goods upon which assessments were based to demonstrate that peasant producers were particularly deficient in animals and therefore susceptible to shortages of traction and manure.[49] A. R. Bridbury, however, has challenged this reading of the evidence and has drawn attention to the size of the national sheep flock as evidenced by wool and cloth exports, a very large part of which must have been in peasant hands.[50] Biddick, too, has demonstrated that the wealthier peasant taxpayers in Bedfordshire were alive to the commercial opportunities offered by pastoral husbandry.[51] This also ties in with Langdon's conclusion that peasants were more active than demesnes in their adoption of the horse.[52] None of this evidence is as yet conclusive but it does suggest that for the time being an open verdict should be returned on the scale and character of the pastoral activities of the peasantry.

Marginal regions

It was in ecologically marginal regions that Postan believed medieval cultivators ultimately paid the highest price for over-expanding grain production and neglecting sound management of the soil. Few regions were more infertile and marginal for cultivation than the arid, sandy Breckland of East Anglia and this is one of the regions which Postan cites in support of his hypothesis. Whether diminishing returns to land early manifest themselves here has recently been put to the test by Mark Bailey using the abundant documentation that survives for

---

[47] B.M.S. CAMPBELL and M. OVERTON, "A new perspective...", pp. 88-95.

[48] M.M. POSTAN, "Medieval agrarian society...", p. 554 and 602; R. BRENNER, "Agrarian class structure...", in T.H. ASTON and C.H.E. PHILPIN, The Brenner debate, pp. 31-33.

[49] M.M. POSTAN, "Village livestock in the thirteenth century", Economic History Review, 2nd series, 15, 1962, pp. 219-49, reprinted in ID., Essays on medieval agriculture and general problems of the medieval economy, Cambridge, 1973, pp. 214-248.

[50] A.R. BRIDBURY, The English economy from Bede to the Reformation, Woodbridge, 1992, pp. 16-17 and 185-186.

[51] K. BIDDICK, "Medieval English peasants and market involvement", Journal of Economic History, 45, 1985, pp. 823-31; K. BIDDICK, "Missing links: taxable wealth, markets, and stratification among medieval English peasants", Journal of Interdisciplinary History, 18, 1987, pp. 277-298.

[52] J.L. LANGDON, Horses, oxen and technological innovation, pp. 291-292.

I

many manors in the region from the late thirteenth century. His careful assessment of this evidence indicates that, far from manifesting the worst features of demographic pressure and overcultivation: "Within the bounds of medieval agrarian technology, farming practices in Breckland represented an innovative and highly adapted method of exploiting meagre soils".[53] Flexible rotations, periodic long fallowing, and the close integration of sheep farming and grain production via the systematic folding of sheep on the arable ensured that the ecological equilibrium of this essentially extensive mixed-husbandry system was maintained.[54] Significantly, Bailey could find no unequivocal evidence of land abandonment prior to the Black Death. Too narrow a dependence upon agriculture was also avoided by the development of a host of ancillary activities, including cloth-making, fishing, and a variety of rural crafts. As a result, poor though Breckland may have been physically, its population enjoyed higher levels of per capita wealth than some supposedly better endowed and more prosperous regions.

Such conclusions bring into question Postan's whole physically-deterministic concept of marginality. For, as Bailey points out, Breckland's inferior environmental resources were offset by certain advantages. In the first place because it was relatively weakly manorialised it was able to evolve the kinds of agrarian arrangements which made best use of its unusual physical circumstances. Secondly, and probably more crucially, it was advantageously located relative to regional, national, and international markets and hence was able to specialise in producing those agricultural and industrial products to which it was best suited. In an increasingly commercialised age, a location that was economically remote may have been far more disadvantageous and "marginal" than one characterised by inferior soils.[55] Perhaps it is in such regions, where the economic incentives to make the best of available opportunities were weakest, that evidence of environmental degradation should be sought.[56]

Farming types and farming regions

The more that the focus of analysis has been shifted from individual estates to specific regions the more it has become apparent that the old notion that farm enterprise was largely an expression of environmental and institutional factors –

---

[53] M. BAILEY, *A marginal economy? East-Anglian Breckland in the later Middle Ages*, Cambridge, 1989, p. 95.

[54] M. BAILEY, "Sand into gold: the evolution of the foldcourse system in west Suffolk, 1200-1600", *Agricultural History Review*, 38, 1990, pp. 40-57.

[55] M. BAILEY, "The concept of the margin in the medieval English economy", *Economic History Review*, 2nd series, 42, 1989, pp. 1-17.

[56] B.M.S. CAMPBELL, "People and land in the Middle Ages, 1066-1500", in R.A. DODGSHON and R.A. BUTLIN (eds.), *An historical geography of England and Wales*, London, revised 2nd edition, 1990, pp. 95-97; B.M.S. CAMPBELL, "Ecology versus economics in late thirteenth- and early fourteenth-century English agriculture", in D. SWEENEY (ed.), *Agriculture in the Middle Ages: technology, practice and representation*, State College, Pa., 1995, pp. 75-108.

soils, terrain, climate, field systems, manorial structure and estate structure – does not hold.[57] Neither Postan nor Brenner accords much importance to the growth and development of the market and neither considers medieval agriculture to have been particularly commercialised (especially at a peasant level). Like many others they have equated production for subsistence with self-sufficiency.[58] As recently as 1973, for instance, a survey of the then available literature led R. E. Glasscock to conclude that "technology and exchange had not progressed far enough by the early fourteenth century to allow much (agricultural) specialisation".[59] Today such a view can no longer be entertained. In the first place, it is apparent that the twelfth and thirteenth centuries witnessed a relative and absolute growth in the institutions, arteries, and overall volume of commerce and trade. Markets, fairs, and boroughs proliferated, towns and cities expanded (with particular gains being made by those at the head of the urban hierarchy), the per capita volume of currency in circulation at least doubled, communications improved, and on all the available evidence domestic and overseas trade grew significantly.[60] In short, the economy became more commercialised. Secondly, as this implies, a growing proportion of net production from all classes of producer was disposed of on the market. By c. 1300 lords in the London region were selling approximately half of net demesne production and the fact that by this date money rents exceeded rents in kind suggests that peasants were not backward in selling much of what they produced.[61] To take a single commodity; by the opening of the fourteenth century lords and peasants were directly or indirectly selling abroad the wool of over seven million sheep.[62] Yet in the London region wool accounted for only an eighth of gross seigneurial agricultural sales income.[63] Thirdly, not only did a significant proportion of production enter commercial exchange, but it is apparent from systematic analysis and classification of a representative range of information on crops and animals drawn from national and regional samples of manorial accounts that the choice of crops, animals, and animal products produced and the intensity of their production were strongly influenced by market demand.[64] Had

[57] For example, J.C. JACKSON, "Regional variations in agriculture in medieval England", *Northern Universities Geographical Journal*, 1, 1960, pp. 41-53.

[58] M.M. POSTAN, "Note", *Economic History Review*, 2nd series, 12, 1959-60, pp. 77-82; R. BRENNER, "Agrarian class structure...", in T.H. ASTON and C.H.E. PHILPIN, *The Brenner debate*, pp. 29 and 33.

[59] R.E. GLASSCOK, "England circa 1334", in H.C. DARBY (ed.), *A new historical geography of England*, Cambridge, 1973, p. 167.

[60] R.H. BRITNELL, *Commercialisation...*; R.H. BRITNELL and B.M.S. CAMPBELL, *A commercialising economy*.

[61] B.M.S. CAMPBELL, "Measuring the commercialisation of seigneurial agriculture c. 1300", in R.H. BRITNELL and B.M.S. CAMPBELL, *A commercialising economy*; E.A. KOSMINSKY, *Studies in the agrarian history of England in the thirteenth century*, R. KISCH (tr.), R.H. HILTON (ed.), Oxford, 1956, pp. 191-196.

[62] A.R. BRIDBURY, *The English economy...*, pp. 185-186.

[63] B.M.S. CAMPBELL, "Measuring the commercialisation...", pp. 148-149

[64] B.M.S. CAMPBELL and J.P. POWER, "Mapping the agricultural geography..."; J.P. POWER and B.M.S. CAMPBELL, "Cluster analysis..."; B.M.S. CAMPBELL, J.A. GALLOWAY, D. KEENE, and M. MURPHY, *A medieval capital...*

the market been unimportant, as R. H. Hilton surmised in 1954, everyone would have "had to produce (on the whole) the same type of crop and tend the same sort of domesticated animals for meat, wool, and pulling power".[65] In reality, however, it is now plain that this was anything but the case.

Market demand was translated into patterns of landuse and types of farming system via its effect upon economic rent. Other important influences upon economic rent were land quality and population density.[66] The most intensive, productive and innovative farming systems therefore tended to evolve in areas of good soil with high population density and strong market demand. Since c. 1300 the bulk of demand remained concentrated in the countryside there was a close association between the distributions of population and farming types.[67] But it is also clear that agriculture was selectively coming under the influence of expanding urban centres on both sides of the North Sea.[68] In England by far the most important centre of urban demand was London. It had a population of c. 80-100,000 by c. 1300 and as such was the second largest European city north of the Alps after Paris.[69] Aided by its excellent riverine and coastal communications, London drew upon an area of at least 4,000 square miles for its grain, and an even larger area for livestock and livestock products.[70] Within this wide hinterland the city was a powerful influence upon both the character of landuse and the nature of farming systems. Where, in northern and eastern Kent, its hinterland overlapped with those of other major urban centres and coincided with the kind of light to medium loam soils to which the best available technology was particularly well suited, those farming systems attained their peak of intensity and productivity, reflecting the corresponding peak in economic rent.[71] These are the progressive farming systems identified by Gray and described by Smith.[72] Significantly, few of the demesnes of the bishopric of Winchester fell within the hinterlands of either London or other major urban centres. Nor were mean population densities especially high in those parts of southern England where the Winchester manors were concentrated. Under these circumstances prevailing levels of eco-

---

[65] R.H. HILTON, "Medieval agrarian history", pp. 145-98 in *Victoria County History of Leicestershire*, 2, London, 1954, p. 145.

[66] M. CHISHOLM, *Rural settlement and land-use: an essay on location*, London, 1962, pp. 20-32; D.B. GRIGG, *The dynamics of agricultural change*, pp. 50-51 and 135-140.

[67] D.L. FARMER, "Marketing the produce of the countryside, 1200-1500", in E. MILLER (ed.), *Agrarian History* ..., pp. 328-330.

[68] For the effect of urban growth upon agricultural development in the Low Countries in this period see A. VERHULST, "The 'agricultural revolution' of the Middle Ages reconsidered", in B.S. BACHRACH and D. NICHOLAS (eds.), *Law, custom, and the social fabric in medieval Europe: essays in honor of Bryce Lyon*, Kalamazoo, 1990, pp. 17-28.

[69] D. KEENE, "A new study of London before the Great Fire", *Urban History Yearbook 1984*, pp. 11-21; D. KEENE, "Medieval London and its region", *London Journal*, 14, 1989, pp. 99-111.

[70] For evidence of the contrasting ranges at which crops, livestock, and livestock products were marketed see D.L. FARMER, "Marketing the produce...", pp. 324-430.

[71] B.M.S. CAMPBELL, J.A. GALLOWAY, D. KEENE, and M. MURPHY, *A medieval capital...*, pp. 46-77 and 179-182.

[72] H.L. GRAY; *English field systems*, pp. 301-3; R.M. SMITH, *Canterbury Cathedral Priory*, pp. 128-165.

nomic rent remained comparatively low, thereby discouraging technological innovation and ensuring that farming systems remained more extensive than intensive
in character.[73]

Yields and productivity

In England the intensity and progressiveness of husbandry in parts of Kent was
matched only in Norfolk, where agriculture was similarly advantaged by easily
cultivated loam soils, an abundant labour supply, favourable market access, irregular field systems, and a weak manorial structure.[74] At the close of the thirteenth
century these two counties stood in the van of English agricultural progress and
enjoyed a greater productivity lead over the rest of the country than at any subsequent point in time.[75] Indeed, it is the subsequent closing of that lead which
constitutes much of the post-medieval story of English agriculture.

Of the two counties, Kent was better placed to take advantage of the London
market but Norfolk was the more densely populated and in Norwich possessed
the country's largest provincial city.[76] It was also one of the counties in which the
frontier between grain and grass had shifted furthest grainwards.[77] Yet, with certain notable exceptions, its soils were not particularly fertile. Here, if anywhere, it
might be thought, signs of environmental degradation and evidence of falling
yields ought to be conspicuous. Certainly, many demesnes on the county's lightest and least fertile soils yielded at a pitifully low level, and yields on the stiffest
and coldest clay soils were subject to wide and unpredictable variation, but across
the county as a whole mean yields per seed and per acre actually rose between
1275 and 1349 (a trend paralleled by the populations of Norwich and at least one
rural manor).[78] Encouraged by a rising demand for food and an increasing supply
of labour, farmers on Norfolk's better soils employed a combination of technological innovation and involution to raise their husbandry to the peak of intensity
and productivity which it attained in the second quarter of the fourteenth century. Once the population fell, however, as it did dramatically in 1349, and
labour became more expensive the economic viability of these methods was un-

---

[73] K. BIDDICK, "Agrarian productivity...", pp. 95-98 and 119-120.
[74] J.P. POWER and B.M.S. CAMPBELL; "Cluster analysis...", pp. 239-242; B.M.S. CAMPBELL,
J.A. GALLOWAY, D. KEENE, and M. MURPHY, *A medieval capital...*, pp. 179-181; B.M.S. CAMPBELL,
"Agricultural progress...".
[75] M. OVERTON and B.M.S. CAMPBELL, "Productivity change...", pp. 41-42.
[76] E. RUTLEDGE, "Immigration and population growth in early-fourteenth-century Norwich: evidence from the tithing roll", *Urban History Yearbook 1988*, pp. 15-30.
[77] B.M.S. CAMPBELL, "The livestock of Chaucer's reeve..."; B.M.S. CAMPBELL, "Medieval land use
and land values", in P. WADE-MARTINS (ed.), *An historical atlas of Norfolk*, Norwich, 1993, pp. 48-49.
[78] B.M.S. CAMPBELL, "Arable productivity in medieval England: some evidence from Norfolk", *Journal of Economic History*, 43, 1983, pp. 379-404; B.M.S. CAMPBELL, " Land, labour, livestock, and productivity trends...", pp. 159-173; E. RUTLEDGE, "Immigration and population growth...";
B.M.S. CAMPBELL, "Population pressure, inheritance, and the land market in a fourteenth-century peasant community, in R.M. SMITH (ed.), *Land, kinship and lifecycle*, Cambridge, 1984, pp. 95-101.

dermined with the result that there was a return to less intensive methods and lower levels of productivity.[79]

Here, therefore, as in northern France and the Low Countries, a positive correlation existed between output per acre and population trends.[80] In Norfolk the evidence for this chronology is particularly robust on account of the exceptionally large number of extant manorial accounts. The earliest of these accounts demonstrate that all the essential technological elements of the intensive mixed-farming system which delivered the county's most impressive yields were already firmly in place on the estates of the abbey of St Benet at Holm in the east of the county by the late 1230s.[81] A hundred years later the most successful demesnes in this locality were obtaining mean gross yields per acre of 30 bushels for wheat (2,612 litres per hectare) and 25 bushels for barley and oats (2,177 litres per hectare). In the county as a whole at this time the corresponding yields averaged 15.6 bushels for wheat, 17.2 bushels for barley, and 15.0 bushels for oats (respectively, 1,358, 1,498, and 1,306 litres per hectare). Comparison of these yields with those estimated for Norfolk by Mark Overton from probate inventories of the sixteenth and seventeenth centuries leads to the startling conclusion that the best medieval yields were not consistently and significantly bettered until the first half of the eighteenth century. When yields rose in the late sixteenth and early seventeenth centuries they were, in fact, recovering to the level of three centuries earlier.[82] On this criterion medieval agriculture was performing significantly better than would once have been believed possible.

Nevertheless, yields *per se* are a very imperfect measure of arable productivity since they neither take account of the relative importance of the different crops nor of the frequency with which the land was cropped.[83] Yet for medieval farmers the simplest method of obtaining more from the same area of land was to substitute higher- for lower-value crops and to crop the land more frequently. In eastern Norfolk it was with this intention that more flexible and intensive rotations were developed in which wheat was substituted for rye and barley for oats, bare fallows were replaced with legumes, and greater effort was devoted to ploughing and fertilising the land and weeding and harvesting the crop.[84] The beneficial effects which all this had for output per acre of arable (in contrast to output per cropped acre) has been brought out by Christopher Thornton in a detailed comparison of the east Norfolk manor of Martham, the Oxfordshire manor of Cux-

[79] B.M.S. Campbell, "Land, labour, livestock, and productivity trends...", pp. 173-181.

[80] B.M.S. Campbell, "Land, labour, livestock, and productivity trends...", pp. 181-182; Van der Wee, "Introduction..."; E. Le Roy Ladurie, "The end of the Middle ages".

[81] Norfolk Record Office, Diocesan Est/1 and 2/1; Church Commissioners 101426 3/13.

[82] B.M.S. Campbell, "Arable productivity...", pp. 388-389; B.M.S. Campbell and M. Overton, "A new perspective...", pp. 66-76.

[83] M. Overton and B.M.S. Campbell, "Productivity change...", pp. 9-13.

[84] B.M.S. Campbell, "Agricultural progress...".

ham, and the Somerset manor of Rimpton (respectively, the properties of the prior of Norwich, Merton College Oxford, and the bishop of Winchester).[85]

In terms of yield per seed Cuxham performed best, followed by Rimpton in the case of barley and oats and Martham in the case of wheat. Differences in seeding rates, however, meant that apart from barley and legumes Martham's yields per acre were slightly better than those at Cuxham and significantly better than those at Rimpton. Moreover, at Martham cropping was virtually continuous, whereas Cuxham and Rimpton both adhered to a three-course rotation which left a third of the arable fallow, with the result that at Martham each arable acre produced per annum half as much again as at Cuxham and three times as much at Rimpton. This marked productivity differential is consistent with the relative market access of these three manors and hence their respective levels of economic rent. Martham, half a day's journey from the port of Yarmouth and an easy river journey from Norwich, was well placed to take advantage of regional, national, and international markets (an advantage reinforced by naturally fertile soils and an abundant labour force). Cuxham, a day's journey from the busy river port of Henley, lay just within the regular grain-provisioning zone of London.[86] Rimpton, however, was remote from major centres of concentrated demand and had to rely in the main upon local markets.[87] Nonetheless, different as were Martham and Rimpton's economic circumstances and wide as was the productivity gulf which separated them, Rimpton shared Martham's positive correlation between output per unit area and the trend of population, its yields rising as population rose and falling as population fell.[88] Since Rimpton was a possession of the bishops of Winchester and Thornton's analysis is the most detailed and rigorous yet made of any single English demesne, this is a finding of considerable significance, for it challenges traditional interpretations of the important Winchester evidence with their emphasis upon the adverse consequences for soil fertility of attempts to produce ever more from the land. It invites a similar reassessment of the productivity experience of other manors on this much debated estate.

The thrust of much recent research on medieval English agriculture has therefore been to demonstrate that it responded much more positively to the challenge of rising population than would once have been conceded. In fact, the population was able to grow and the economy to expand for the better part of two centuries

---

[85] C. THORNTON, "The determinants of land productivity...", pp. 191-193. See also B.M.S. CAMPBELL, "Arable productivity...", pp. 390-392.

[86] P.D.A. HARVEY, *A medieval Oxfordshire village: Cuxham 1240-1400*, Oxford, 1965, pp. 92, 97, 103; B.M.S. CAMPBELL, J.A. GALLOWAY, D. KEENE, and M. MURPHY, *A medieval capital...*, pp. 53-55.

[87] Compare the predominance of localised marketing at Longbridge Deverill and Monkton Deverill in Wiltshire, 20 miles to the north-east: D.L. FARMER, "Two Wiltshire manors and their markets", *Agricultural History Review*, 27, 1989, pp. 1-11.

[88] C. THORNTON, "The determinants of land productivity...", pp. 207-210.

because husbandmen specialised, intensified, innovated and thereby produced more from the land. The period therefore represents a formative stage in the long process of English agricultural evolution and deserves to be recognised as such. When improved systems of husbandry developed in the seventeenth and eighteenth centuries these tended to grow out of the medieval systems which had preceded them, often in the self-same areas which had been most innovative in the Middle Ages.[89] In these respects continuity was more apparent than change.

Technological progress nevertheless proceeded slower and remained geographically more circumscribed than in the post-medieval centuries. That was particularly true of the key technological breakthrough represented by the integration of arable and pastoral husbandry into a mutually supportive, intensive and productive mixed-farming system, which always remained confined to a few distinctive areas. Had this system been more widely adopted there can be little doubt that medieval husbandmen would have succeeded in producing yet more from the land. That it was not is consequently one of the key issues to be explained, although as argued above this probably had little to do with ignorance or backwardness and a great deal to do with a lack of sufficient incentives to justify the adoption of such an expensive system. It is in a similar light that the limited diffusion of other innovations should also probably be viewed.

This is not, however, to claim that medieval farming systems were everywhere ideal and equal to the range of environmental circumstances with which husbandmen had to contend. On the whole, available technology was better suited to the problems and opportunities presented by light to medium soils than to those presented by medium to heavy (especially those which later generations were to convert to grass). Certain environments like certain locations were discouraging, and effort when expended often went poorly rewarded.[90] Insofar as environmental degradation occurred and output per unit area fell this was undoubtedly the exception rather than the rule (and probably outweighed by gains made elsewhere), specific to certain types of cultivators and particular geographical situations only, and possibly triggered by circumstances exogenous to the farming systems in question.[91]

A more commercialised economy may have created new opportunities for agriculturalists but it also created new types of risk so that any contraction in or disruption to the market will undoubtedly have spelt ruin for many.[92] By the first half of the fourteenth century the economic climate was certainly changing and many in the countryside were facing increased difficulties. The one part of Post-

---

[89] B.M.S. CAMPBELL and M. OVERTON, "A new perspective...", pp. 62-63 and 91-93.

[90] For example, I. KERSHAW, *Bolton Priory: the economy of a northern monastery 1286-1325*, Oxford, 1973, pp. 38-43; D.L. FARMER, "Grain yields on Westminster Abbey manors, 1271-1410", *Canadian Journal of History*, 18, 1983, pp. 331-348; D.L. FARMER, "Crop yields, prices and wages...".

[91] B.M.S. CAMPBELL, "Ecology versus economics...", pp. 93-96.

[92] B.F. HARVEY, "Introduction: the 'crisis' of the early fourteenth century", in B.M.S. CAMPBELL, *Before the Black Death*, pp. 12-16; J. H. MUNRO, "Industrial transformations in the north-west European textile trades, c. 1290-c. 1340: economic progress or economic crisis?", in B.M.S. CAMPBELL, *Before the Black Death*, pp. 124-130; B.M.S. CAMPBELL, "Ecology versus economics...", pp. 93-96.

an's thesis that has stood intact, reinforced rather than refuted or qualified by recent research, is his observation that peasant producers were experiencing mounting land hunger and falling living standards from the late thirteenth century on. Since he wrote evidence has steadily accumulated on all sides which confirms the grim picture of an increasingly impoverished peasantry trapped in growing numbers upon the land and subject to increasingly heavy and often arbitrary taxation.[93] If this did not necessarily result in soil exhaustion and falling yields it may have led to some curtailment of production and almost certainly drove down labour productivity in agriculture, due to high and rising levels of rural underemployment. Whatever agricultural progress there may have been, this was patently no agricultural revolution for the central dilemma of how to avoid declining marginal labour productivity in agriculture remained unresolved. It is towards a fuller understanding of this critical issue that future research needs to be directed, since this bears upon whether the problems increasingly experienced within the agricultural sector were a cause or consequence of the general economic downturn apparent throughout so much of north-western Europe at this time.

---

[93] The range and volume of work is considerable, for example A.R.H. BAKER, "Evidence in the 'Nonarum Inquisitiones' of contracting arable lands in England during the early fourteenth century", *Economic History Review*, 2nd series, 19, 1966, pp. 518-532, reprinted in A.R.H. BAKER, J.D. HAMSHERE, and J. LANGTON (eds.), *Geographical interpretations of historical sources: readings in historical geography*, Newton Abbot, 1970, pp. 85-102; J.R. MADDICOTT, *The English peasantry and the demands of the Crown, 1294-1341*, Past and Present Supplement 1, Oxford, 1975, reprinted in T.H. ASTON (ed.), *Landlords, peasants and politics in medieval England*, Cambridge, 1987, pp. 285-359; Z. RAZI, *Life, marriage and death in a medieval parish: economy, society and demography in Halesowen, 1270-1400*, Cambridge, 1980; B.M.S. CAMPBELL, "Population pressure..."; pp. 87-134; R.M. SMITH, "Families and their land in an area of partible inheritance: Redgrave, Suffolk 1260-1320", in ID., *Land, kinship and life-cycle*.

Agricultural Progress in Medieval England: Some Evidence from Eastern Norfolk

Thirteenth- and fourteenth-century English agriculture is currently held in low repute. According to M. M. Postan "the inertia of medieval agricultural technology is unmistakable"[1] with the result that an agricultural system persisted in which the arable and pastoral sectors were competitive rather than complementary. As J. Z. Titow has observed, "a chronic state of under-manuring . . . would go a long way towards explaining the low level of productivity generally prevalent on the Winchester manors", and since stocking levels were probably even lower on peasant holdings, few would dissent from Postan's assertion that "we could not expect the villagers' output per acre to equal that of a well-managed demesne in the same locality".[2] When, as in the thirteenth century, agriculture of such a low level of proficiency had to feed a steadily increasing population it is hardly surprising that events eventually followed a Malthusian course. This interpretation of the crisis which terminated the demographic and economic upswing of the early middle ages has been stated most succinctly by J. D. Chambers:

> The medieval boom in population was associated with . . . pressure on agricultural resources to the point at which there was a severe cut-back of agricultural productivity through soil deterioration and falling yields. It was not merely that agricultural techniques were unable to respond to the challenge of increased demand; it was worse than this. The techniques that had sufficed to enable the population to reach the existing limit began to recede owing to the encroachment of arable upon the pasture . . . . Every condition of a Malthusian crisis appeared to be present here, in the thirteenth century. It is important to note them, as it is doubtful if another example of this magnitude or duration can be cited for the entire range of English history.[3]

In contrast, an altogether better opinion is held of contemporary agriculture in the Low Countries, owing to its evolution of a system of cultivation which combined high yields per acre with the virtual elimination of fallow.[4] The

---

[1] M. M. Postan, *The Medieval Economy and Society* (1972), p. 44: this view is most forcibly expressed in G. E. Fussell, 'Social Change but Static Technology: Rural England in the Fourteenth Century', *History Studies*, 1 (1968), pp. 23-32.

[2] J. Z. Titow, *Winchester Yields: A Study in Medieval Agricultural Productivity* (Cambridge, 1972), p. 30; M. M. Postan, *The Cambridge Economic History of Europe, I, The Agrarian Life of the Middle Ages,* (Cambridge, 2nd ed., 1966), p. 602.

[3] J. D. Chambers, *Population, Economy, and Society in Pre-Industrial England* (Oxford, 1972), pp. 24-5. This view has recently been reiterated by D. B. Grigg: see *Population Growth and Agrarian Change: An Historical Perspective* (Cambridge, 1980), pp. 81-2.

[4] B. H. Slicher Van Bath, *The Agrarian History of Western Europe, A.D. 500-1850* (1963), pp. 177-80; C. T. Smith, *An Historical Geography of Western Europe before 1800* (1967), pp. 208-9; N. J. G. Pounds, *An Historical Geography of Europe, 450 B.C.-A.D. 1330* (Cambridge, 1973), pp. 372-5.

II

technology which made this possible included the cultivation of fodder crops, bed-and-row cultivation, and heavy fertilization, and required high labour inputs. Not all the component elements of this technology can be dated but, as B. H. Slicher Van Bath has shown, many are first mentioned in the thirteenth, fourteenth, and fifteenth centuries.[5] The cultivation of beans and corn on the fallow, for instance, is first mentioned in 1328 in the coastal region of French Flanders, whilst the introduction of fodder crops—either in place of the original fallow year or as an after crop, following the harvest—mainly took place in the fifteenth century (with the exception of vetches, which are first recorded in 1278): thus, turnips are first mentioned in 1404, spurry in 1426, and broom in 1490. The agricultural system which resulted from these developments was remarkably intensive and reached its fullest fruition on small and medium-sized farms with less than 10 acres of arable land. On these holdings productivity per capita was sacrificed to productivity per unit area, and economic viability was maintained only by employing labour-intensive techniques—spade cultivation, careful weeding, and heavy fertilization—and by cultivating high value crops—cole-seed, madder, and hops (which are all mentioned in the fourteenth century).

Hitherto, it has been thought that English agriculture lagged behind that of the Low Countries until the age of the so-called "agricultural revolution" in the seventeenth and eighteenth centuries.[6] However, there is a mounting body of evidence which now suggests that within certain restricted localities agricultural methods were already well abreast of the best continental practice in the thirteenth and fourteenth centuries. Where this was the case, a sustained high level of productivity was maintained on both demesnes and peasant holdings, and agricultural technology differed in detail but not in essence from that of the late seventeenth century. Recognition of this state of affairs has important implications for interpretations of the fourteenth century economy in particular and for the evolution of English agriculture in general.

I

Striking evidence of agricultural progress in certain parts of medieval England is provided by the rural economy of eastern Norfolk. This area is endowed with significant environmental advantages: fertile and easily culti-vated loam soils, gently undulating terrain, extensive tracts of alluvial marsh-land with associated peat deposits, and good riverine and coastal communi-cations. It is also well served by extant demesne account rolls. During the period in question eastern Norfolk possessed a number of distinctive socio-economic characteristics.[7] Most notable was its level of population, which was

[5] B. H. Slicher Van Bath, 'The Rise of Intensive Husbandry in the Low Countries', in J. S. Bromley and E. H. Kossmann, eds. *Britain and the Netherlands*, I (1960), pp. 130-53.
[6] G. E. Fussell, 'Low Countries' Influence on English Farming', *English Historical Review*, 74 (1959), pp. 611-22; J. D. Chambers and G. E. Mingay, *The Agricultural Revolution, 1750-1880* (1966), pp. 59-60; H. C. Darby, 'The Age of the Improver', in H. C. Darby, ed. *A New Historical Geography of England* (Cambridge, 1973), pp. 315-16.
[7] For a more detailed description of the area see R. R. Rainbird Clarke, *East Anglia* (1960); J. M. Lambert, J. N. Jennings, C. T. Smith, C. Green, and J. N. Hutchinson, *The Making of the Broads: A Reconsideration of their Origin in the Light of New Evidence* (Royal Geographical Society Research Series, 3, 1960); B. M. S. Campbell, 'Field Systems in Eastern Norfolk during the Middle Ages: A Study with Particular Reference to the Demographic and Agrarian Changes of the Fourteenth Century', (unpublished Ph.D. thesis, University of Cambridge, 1975), pp. 11-23. The account rolls are listed in Appendix I.

probably the highest in the country and had been so since the end of the eleventh century. In the most populous parts of the area in the early fourteenth century the density probably approached 500 persons per square mile. Moreover, a substantial proportion of this population was of free or semi-free status, a state of affairs which reflected the relative weakness of the manorial nexus. A spirit of individualism thus tended to prevail and was reinforced by a commonfield system bounded by the minimum of rights and regulations.[8] This comparative freedom and looseness of social structure undoubtedly underlay the high density of population; together they fostered an advanced degree of economic development. The latter is manifest in the high value placed upon arable land (valuations per acre generally being in excess of 8 pence and, occasionally, as high as 36 pence)[9] and in the high level of assessed lay wealth recorded in the Lay Subsidy of 1334. It is also manifest in the size and importance of Norwich and Yarmouth, in whose hinterlands this area lay. By the early fourteenth century Norwich had become possibly the leading English provincial city, with a population of perhaps 18,000, whilst Yarmouth was at the zenith of its prosperity as a mercantile and naval port and may have had a population of about 11,000.[10] Eastern Norfolk thus represents a socio-economic extreme and its level of agricultural development was correspondingly precocious.

Perhaps the most striking indication of the progressive nature of agriculture in this locality is the relative infrequency of fallowing. Explicit references to fallowing are rare before the middle of the fourteenth century but are nevertheless sufficient to demonstrate that it had already been eliminated on several demesnes by the last quarter of the thirteenth century. The earliest recorded instance of the total elimination of fallowing is on the Earl of Norfolk's demesne at South Walsham and dates from 1268-9; similar references from the Earl's other demesnes at Halvergate and Hanworth follow soon after.[11] Other instances, dating from the first half of the fourteenth century, derive from demesnes at Brandiston, Martham, and Flegg:[12] in addition, an Inquisition Post Mortem of 1324-5 for Filby states that arable land was worth 12 pence per acre because it was capable of being sown every year.[13] Such

[8] B. M. S. Campbell, 'The Regional Uniqueness of English Field Systems? Some Evidence from Eastern Norfolk', *Agricultural History Review*, 29 (1981), pp. 16-28.

[9] Examples of high arable valuations include Acle, Halvergate, and South Walsham—12d. per acre—P.R.O. C132 File 38, 54 Hen. III; Horsey—14d. per acre—C133 File 29, 10 Edw. I; Cawston, Knapton and Plumstead—18d. per acre—P.R.O. SC 11 Roll 471, C132 File 37, 53 Hen. III, N.R.O. DCN *Proficuum Maneriorum*; Catfield, Fishley, Herringby, Ingham, and Mautby—24d. per acre—C133 File 29, 10 Edw. I, File 23, 7 Edw. I, C134 File 67, 14 Edw. II; Alby, Brandiston, and Thwaite—24-30d. per acre—N.R.O. Diocesan Est/2, Magdalen College, Oxford: Estate Papers 130/16; Hemsby and Martham—36d. per acre—N.R.O. DCN *Proficuum Maneriorum*.

[10] The figures most usually quoted of 13,000 for Norwich and 5,000 for Yarmouth (J. C. Russell, *British Mediaeval Population* (Albuquerque, 1948), pp. 292-3; A. Saul, 'Great Yarmouth in the Fourteenth Century: A Study in Trade, Politics and Society', (unpublished D.Phil. thesis, University of Oxford, (1975), p. 1) are probably underestimates. See, for instance, T. H. Hollingsworth, *Historical Demography* (1969), pp. 363-4.

[11] P.R.O. SC 6/944/21 & 936/4 & 27.

[12] Magdalen College, Oxford: Estate Papers 166/3 & 130/16; N.R.O. DCN R 233C 4956; N.R.O. Diocesan Est/9.

[13] *Item iiij^{xx} acras terre arrabilibus que possunt seminari per annum et valent iiij libras pretium acre xijd.* (P.R.O. C134 File 83, 18 Edw. II). On the neighbouring manor of Ormesby 102¾ acres of arable (also valued at 12d. per acre) were described as *ad seminandum* (P.R.O. C135 File 66, 16 Edw. III).

total elimination of bare fallows was, however, neither usual nor desirable, since fallowing remained one of the most effective methods of cleansing land of weed growth. Throughout the last quarter of the thirteenth century and the first half of the fourteenth century, therefore, all demesnes fallowed a small amount of land (about 7 per cent of the total) in most years.[14] Whilst fallow, this land was subject to repeated ploughings in order to destroy weed growth. At least three, and sometimes as many as six, ploughings were the norm in the second half of the fourteenth century, by which time fallowing seems to have increased somewhat in frequency as part of a general lessening in the intensity of demesne production.[15] Even so, the average area fallowed on 18 demesnes in the 80 years after 1350 was only 13·5 per cent of all arable.[16] Plainly, reduced fallowing meant increased cropping with consequent gains in productivity. On eleven demesnes for which pre-1350 figures are available fully three-quarters of the total arable area was annually devoted to grain, a proportion which represents a significant increase over that normally possible under a three- or even a four-course rotation.

Such an intensive cultivation scheme made considerable demands upon the soil and there was a potential danger that any gain in productivity thus achieved would have been offset by a deterioration in fertility. The problem lay in the fact that livestock depended upon fallow land for temporary pasturage, so that a reduction in the amount of fallow was liable to have an adverse effect on livestock, thus depriving the arable of essential traction and manure.[17] A crude measure of the ratio of livestock to arable has been devised by Titow.[18] According to this measure, it is possible, by counting all equine and bovine animals as a single livestock unit, and all lambs and sheep as quarter units, to derive a single aggregate figure from the stock totals recorded in each Michaelmas account. The so-called animal ratio is then represented by the number of livestock units per hundred sown acres. This ratio has been calculated for 30 demesnes scattered through eastern Norfolk using data drawn from the period 1255-1350. The results are set out in Table 1. As can be seen, the individual demesne ratios were extremely low in the majority of cases: only four demesnes had a mean animal ratio in excess of 50, and on only two demesnes—Acle and Halvergate—did the animal ratio ever exceed 100. Overall, the median and mean animal ratio of all 30 demesnes were a mere 30·6 and 34·8 respectively. This average ratio is barely half that prevailing on the manors of the Bishop of Winchester, which, at 72·7, is considered by Titow to have been too low to have ensured adequate manuring.[19]

Notwithstanding this low animal ratio, productivity was not depressed. On the contrary, the case of eastern Norfolk casts doubt on the equation of a low

[14] See Table 1 in Campbell, 'Regional Uniqueness', p. 21. The bailiffs' accounts upon which this and subsequent observations are based are listed in Appendix I.

[15] Fallow was ploughed three times at Newton in 1366-7, Plumstead in 1395-9, and Taverham in 1367-8; four times at Lakenham in 1366-7, Martham in 1355-89, Plumstead in 1359-92, Scratby in 1360-3, and Taverham in 1362-3 and 1370-4; five times at Martham in 1392-8, Plumstead in 1404-5, and Taverham in 1364-5, and six times at Martham in 1390-1.

[16] Campbell, 'Regional Uniqueness', and Appendix I (B).

[17] Postan, Cambridge Economic History, pp. 553-9; J. Z. Titow, English Rural Society, 1200-1350 (1969), pp. 52-4; Titow, Winchester Yields, pp. 30-1.

[18] Titow, Winchester Yields, p. 136.

[19] See also D. L. Farmer, 'Grain Yields on the Winchester Manors in the Later Middle Ages', Economic History Review, 2nd ser. xxx (1977), pp. 563-4.

Table 1. *Animal Ratios on Various Demesnes in Eastern Norfolk, 1255-1350*

Demesne	Period	No.	Animal Ratio Min	Animal Ratio Mean	Animal Ratio Max
Acle	1269-1280	7	46·0	87·8	135·9
Halvergate	1269-1306	16	20·8	83·6	187·6
Attlebridge	1307-1315	2	45·4	58·1	70·8
Lessingham	1290-1298	2	42·2	51·5	60·8
Hevingham	1327-1347	3	18·7	47·0	99·7
Eaton	1263-1350	28	30·8	43·4	64·6
Saxthorpe	c. 1300-1337	3	36·4	41··6	45·1
Scratby	1296-1344	9	31·4	41·3	47·8
Newton	1274-1328	4	28·4	37·3	52·2
Ormesby	1294-1338	3	33·6	33·7	33·8
Aylmerton	1345-1346	1		33·3	
Knapton	1345-1348	2	30·3	32·8	35·3
Hanworth	1272-1306	21	25·6	32·5	43·8
Taverham	1255-1350	31	20·5	31·3	58·9
Wicklewood	1337-1338	1		30·7	
Intwood	1308-1334	3	24·3	30·5	35·6
Brandiston	1316-1348	4	15·9	30·1	45·7
Arminghall	1347-1348	1		29·6	
Lakenham	1295-1296	1		29·6	
Suffield	1292-1300	3	22·3	29·4	37·6
Framingham	1271-1303	14	15·2	29·0	45·3
Hemsby	1266-1335	18	17·3	25·4	35·1
Monks Grange	1266-1335	25	13·4	24·8	39·9
Worstead	1273-1321	3	22·1	24·7	26·0
Plumstead	1264-1350	23	14·4	24·4	46·7
Martham	1261-1350	27	11·1	23·9	32·5
Keswick	1274-1320	4	6·8	22·3	26·9
Gresham	1306-1307	1		12·4	
South Walsham	1268-1297	11	9·5	11·0	15·0
Heigham-by-Norwich	1302-1307	2	7·6	10·3	13·0
	maximum			87·8	187·6
30 demesnes:	mean			34·8	
	median			30·6	
	minimum		6·8	10·3	

Table 2. *Eastern Norfolk: Estimated Gross Yields per Statute Acre prior to 1350*

Crop	Number of Demesnes	Yield per Seed Number of Harvests	Yield per Seed Demesne Mean	Yield per Seed Demesne Maximum	Yield per Seed Harvest Maximum	Yield per Acre (bushels) Number of Harvests	Yield per Acre (bushels) Demesne Mean	Yield per Acre (bushels) Demesne Maximum	Yield per Acre (bushels) Harvest Maximum
Wheat	20	141	5·6	7·1	10·0	139	14·8	20·1	30·2
Rye	11	114	4·4	6·7	7·8	110	10·9	18·4	22·4
Maslin	7	42	4·4	6·8	10·5	40	11·9	18·0	29·5
Barley	21	207	3·4	4·5	5·7	202	15·1	20·8	23·6
Oats	20	199	2·8	4·1	7·4	195	13·2	19·9	29·8
Peas	20	197	2·8	4·4	10·7	194	7·4	11·8	20·8

animal ratio with low yields. Table 2 contains a summary of the gross yields of the principal crops grown in the area during the 90 year period ending 1350. From these figures it will be seen that the high frequency of cropping was matched by an equally high level of productivity, with yields per acre which were exceptional by the standards of the day. Wheat, for instance, which enjoyed pride of place in the prevailing rotational scheme, yielded an average of 14·8 bushels per acre prior to the deduction of tithe and on the most productive demesnes yielded considerably higher. Thus, late eighteenth-century levels of productivity were attained on the Prior of Norwich's twin demesnes of Martham and Hemsby, where wheat returned 20 bushels per statute acre in an average year and 30 bushels per statute acre on occasion.[20] At 6·4 the mean yield ratio of wheat on these two demesnes was also high, as it was throughout the area. Other types of winter corn—rye and maslin (a wheat/rye mixture)—were quantitatively much less important: they rarely occupied such a privileged position in the cropping schedule and were usually sown on poorer soils so that they invariably yielded at a lower level than wheat. Yields as high as 18 bushels per acre were sometimes attained but the mean yield of both crops was generally lower, at 11-12 bushels per statute acre. As in the case of wheat, the mean yield per seed, at 4·4, was relatively high. Winter corn, however, was grown on a much smaller scale than spring corn. Together barley and oats accounted for over four times the area occupied by winter corn, and of this it was barley which occupied the lion's share. Spring corn nevertheless occupied an inferior position in the cropping schedule relative to winter corn with the result that heavy seeding rates were necessary to keep weed growth in check.[21] Indeed, the seeding rate of oats was often so heavy, between 6 and 8 bushels per acre, that it was clearly intended to act as a smother crop. The yields per seed of barley and oats were accordingly relatively undistinguished; the former averaged 3·4 and the latter 2·8. Yet these yields were sufficient, when combined with relatively high seeding rates, to ensure that the yield per acre of spring corn was comparable with that of wheat. Barley yields averaged 15·1 bushels per statute acre in the area as a whole, and on the most productive demesnes a mean yield of 20 bushels was sustained.[22] With a mean of 13·2 bushels per acre, the yield of oats was somewhat lower.

By contemporary standards the yield of all these corn crops, and of wheat in particular, was high and especially so since fallowing was very infrequent. But the clearest vindication of the productivity of the agricultural methods employed in this locality is provided by the fact that some of the most impressive corn yields were obtained on demesnes with the least favourable animal ratios. The neighbouring Norwich Cathedral Priory demesnes of Hemsby and Martham provide the best illustration of this. These two demesnes had mean animal ratios of 25·4 and 23·9 respectively, yet their yields of wheat and barley are amongst the highest known in medieval England. Here, as elsewhere in the area, legumes were the only crop to yield poorly, both per seed and per acre, but this was largely because of the special function which they served in the prevailing course of husbandry.

II

The large-scale field cultivation of legumes was in fact the most prominent of a number of technological innovations which made it possible to maintain

---

[20] "Nathaniel Kent considered average wheat yields in Norfolk to be around 24 bushels per acre in the 1790s, a figure too high according to other commentators including William Marshall, who reckoned 20 bushels to be the norm". M. Overton, 'Estimating Crop Yields from Probate Inventories: An Example from East Anglia, 1585-1735', *Journal of Economic History*, XXXIX (1979), p. 375.

[21] For the significance of seeding rates see P. F. Brandon, 'Cereal Yields on the Sussex Estates of Battle Abbey during the later Middle Ages', *Econ. Hist. Rev.*, 2nd ser. XXV (1972), pp. 406-10.

[22] This compares with a late eighteenth-century yield of 28-32 bushels of barley per acre: Overton, 'Estimating Crop Yields'.

32

eastern Norfolk's intensive and highly productive system of agriculture. Legumes fulfilled the twin functions of enriching the nitrogenous content of the soil and providing a protein-rich source of fodder. Black peas were the predominant legume grown until vetches were introduced in the late 1350s;[23] thereafter both crops were grown in roughly equal quantities. Small amounts of white peas were also grown for human consumption, but beans always remained a garden crop confined to demesne curtilages. Legumes were already a field crop of some importance by the 1240s, when they occupied approximately 9 per cent of the total sown area on eleven demesnes belonging to the Abbey of St. Benet at Holm, and their importance grew as demesne production expanded in scale and rose in intensity. The 1270s and 1280s seem to have witnessed a particularly sharp expansion in their relative importance, although it was during the early 1320s, when a succession of bad harvests placed agriculture under great pressure, that their cultivation reached a peak. Taking both the period (i.e. 1239-1350) and the area as a whole, legumes accounted for 14·0 per cent of the total sown area. Table 3 shows, however, that this average figure masks wide variations within the area, and that on a small but significant group of demesnes legumes accounted for as much as a fifth and, occasionally, even a quarter of the total sown area. Noteworthy are demesnes such as Hanworth, Brandiston, South Walsham, Martham, Knapton, Hemsby, and Ormesby, which cultivated above average quantities of legumes and sustained above average levels of productivity, but yet had below average animal ratios. In these cases an association between the large-scale field cultivation of legumes and high levels of productivity is very apparent.

An important concomitant of the expansion in legume cultivation and associated reduction of permanent and temporary pasturage, was a heightened emphasis upon the stall-feeding of livestock.[24] This led to an increase in the supply of farmyard manure which could systematically be spread upon, and then ploughed into, the soil, thereby reducing the losses from leaching and oxidization which occurred when manure was deposited at random by livestock foraging upon the fallow.[25] Adoption of this method of spreading manure incurred greatly increased labour costs but it was economically worth while when labour was cheap and grain dear since it ensured that scarce manure was literally spread as far as it would go. Indeed, at Martham and Hemsby strenuous efforts were made to maintain a commensurate supply of manure by expanding livestock numbers in step with arable production, with the result that cattle herds were largest in years when cultivation was at fullest stretch (e.g. 1296, 1306, 1318 and 1349). Hence, although animal ratios were absolutely low a complementary relationship nevertheless existed between pastoral and arable production. During the second half of the fourteenth century price changes meant that the manual spreading of manure became a less viable proposition, so much so that it was nearly abandoned altogether at Eaton and Plumstead, although in eastern Norfolk as a whole (see Table 4) about an eighth of all cornland continued to be fertilized in this way.

[23] Vetches are first recorded at Plumstead in 1359-60 (N.R.O. DCN R 233D 5127), 90 years after the first English reference to them, in eastern Kent.

[24] One reason sometimes given for the low yield of peas was that they were fed unthreshed (*in siliquis*) to the livestock.

[25] W. O. Ault, *Open-Field Farming in Mediaeval England: A Study of Village By-Laws* (1972), p. 17 n. 8.

Table 3. *Cultivation of Legumes on Various Demesnes in Eastern Norfolk,*
1239-1350

Demesne	Period	No.	Min	% Total Sown Area Devoted to Legumes Mean	Max
Flegg	1340-1341	1		30·6	
Lessingham	1290-1298	2	25·1	28·8	32·3
Hanworth	1272-1306	21	14·1	21·5	31·2
Scratby	1295-1343	9	18·9	21·1	25·0
Brandiston	1316-1348	4	19·5	20·9	22·4
South Walsham	1270-1297	9	13·0	19·9	29·1
Martham	1261-1340	26	10·5	19·7	24·9
Knapton	1345-1348	2	17·6	19·5	21·4
Burgh in Flegg	1330-1331	1		19·4	
Hemsby	1265-1335	18	13·4	19·0	24·9
Coltishall	1292-1315	2	13·9	18·6	23·3
Ormesby	1294-1338	3	13·3	17·1	19·8
Wicklewood	1337-1338	1		16·7	
Suffield	1272-1300	9	12·3	16·5	19·8
Hardley	1295-1296	1		16·5	
Aylmerton	1345-1346	1		15·7	
Framingham	1271-1308	15	7·9	13·9	23·4
Halvergate	1269-1306	15	8·5	13·6	32·9
Worstead	1273-1321	3	11·1	13·6	17·8
Heigham-by-Norwich	1302-1307	3	11·4	13·6	16·8
Acle	1268-1280	7	9·4	13·4	17·5
Lakenham	1295-1296	1		13·1	
Plumstead	1263-1350	22	0	13·0	22·2
Hoveton	1295-1329	2	8·8	11·6	14·4
Saxthorpe	c. 1300-1337	3	9·7	11·6	13·1
Keswick	1274-1320	4	1·5	10·2	12·9
Hevingham	1327-1347	3	8·5	10·0	11·8
Newton	1273-1328	5	7·2	9·8	14·0
Little Hautbois	c. 1290	1		9·5	
Arminghall	1347-1348	1		9·1	
11 St Benet's Manors	1239-1246	3	1·4	9·1	17·9
Monks Grange	1255-1335	25	3·4	8·6	17·5
Intwood	1308-1334	3	7·0	7·2	7·5
Taverham	1255-1350	31	2·3	6·6	15·4
Eaton	1263-1350	28	1·8	6·3	13·3
Gresham	1306-1307	1		5·0	
Attlebridge	1307-1315	2	2·3	3·4	4·5
Melton	1333-1334	1		0	
38 demesnes:	maximum			30·6	32·9
	mean			14·0	
	median			13·6	
	minimum		0	0	

Farmyard manure alone, however, was rarely adequate to satisfy the needs of arable husbandry, with the result that it was invariably augmented with other sources of "fertilizer". Of these marl was the most generally available and references to its use are widespread. The earliest certain reference to it dates from 1263-4 at Martham; within the next ten years it is also recorded at Hemsby, Plumstead, Hanworth, and Suffield, and it is subsequently mentioned at a further twelve places.[26] Yet, although incidental reference is made

[26] Attlebridge, Caister-cum-Markshall, Coltishall, Eaton, Flegg, Heigham-by-Norwich, Lessingham, Ludham, North Walsham, Ormesby, Postwick, and Taverham. Five centuries later William Marshall was to describe marl as "the grand fossil manure of (east) Norfolk" in *The Rural Economy of Norfolk*, I (1795).

34

to marling on a relatively large number of demesnes, it is consistently recorded on very few (Martham and Hanworth being notable exceptions). This is probably because it was an extremely laborious exercise and hence very expensive when undertaken with hired labour: at Hanworth in 1284-5 the initial digging of the marl cost 3 shillings per acre, and its spreading a further 4 pence, whilst at Postwick in 1277-8 and Lessingham in 1290-1 the combined operation cost 3 shillings 6 pence and 4 shillings respectively. As a general policy marling therefore seems to have been undertaken either by the *famuli*, as at Ludham in 1355, or by using the works of customary tenants, as at Taverham in 1291-2, with the consequence that it rarely appears as a separate item in account rolls. It is this comparative silence which makes it difficult to gauge the actual scale on which marling was undertaken, although in those few instances when the areas concerned are recorded they are invariably small: at Hanworth, between 1272 and 1306, an average of $5\frac{1}{4}$ acres were marled each year, and at Lessingham, in 1332, a seven-year lease of the demesne specified that 4 acres were annually to be spread with white marl. Such evidence suggests that marling normally took place on a limited but regular basis, with the whole exercise remaining very much ancillary to manuring.

Marl was by no means the only supplementary source of "fertilizer" commonly employed on demesnes in this area. For instance, on the demesnes of Catton, Monks Grange, Eaton, Lakenham, Newton, and Plumstead, all located within a five-mile radius of the populous city of Norwich, the purchase of night-soil was a regular item of expenditure throughout most of the second half of the thirteenth and first half of the fourteenth centuries.[27] The night-soil itself was far from cheap, an average of $2-2\frac{1}{2}$ pence per acre of cornland being spent at Eaton and Newton on this item alone, and its carriage added still further to the cost. In this context, it is significant that the use of night-soil figured most prominently on demesnes such as Lakenham and Monks Grange which were within a single short boat or cart journey from Norwich. Where, as in the case of Plumstead, the journey was longer and involved the use of both boats and carts, carriage could add at least another 50, or even 100, per cent to the final cost. As a result the amounts purchased on this demesne were correspondingly reduced, averaging only $\frac{3}{4}$d. per acre of cornland. Evidently, at a distance of only five miles from Norwich the cost of carriage was becoming prohibitive.

Elsewhere in the area another group of demesnes displayed a similar degree of resourcefulness in tapping an external supply of organic fertilizer. On the Earl of Norfolk's demesnes at Acle, Halvergate, and South Walsham, and the Prior of Norwich's demesne at Martham, the arable strips were spread with dung gathered from sheep-pens in the neighbouring Broadland marshes. The procedure of collecting the dung and transporting it back to the demesnes by a combination of boat and cart was extremely arduous, costing 14 shillings 8 pence at Martham in 1272-3, 12 shillings at Halvergate in 1273-4, and 8 shillings 3 pence at Acle in 1279-80.[28] But the flocks in question were so large,

---

[27] *In fimis emptis apud Norwycum xjs. iiijd. ob., Item in j batello empto ad cariendum fymi de Norwyco cum corda ad eundem empta vs. viijd. ob.* (Plumstead, 1277-8; N.R.O. DCN R 233D 5104). Such references first appear at Monks Grange and Eaton (both immediately outside the city gates) as early as 1255 and 1263.

[28] *In cariaconem fimorum de Fulholm ad Martham per aquam xiijs. vjd.* (N.R.O. DCN R 233C 4943); *In cariagio fimorum de quinque mariscis usque ad terram post autumpnum xijs.* (P.R.O. SC 6/936/5); *In cariagio fimorum extra mariscum super terram comitis viijs. iijd.* (P.R.O. SC 6/929/7).

some 1,800 head of sheep being present on the Earl of Norfolk's three manors in Michaelmas 1278, and the marshland grazings were so rich, that the dung of these sheep had a potential value which was too great to be overlooked. Other local magnates maintained similarly large flocks on these alluvial grazings, the Abbot of St. Benet at Holm having over 1,500 head of sheep in 1343, and it is likely that their dung contributed to the maintenance of arable fertility in much the same way.

It was presumably the relative inaccessibility of the arable fields from the marshland sheep-walks which precluded the more usual East Anglian expedient of folding the sheep on the arable. Yet elsewhere in eastern Norfolk folding comprised one of the most effective methods of fertilizing the land. Each year, from the beginning of May to early November, sheep fed on the pasture by day were penned on the arable by night, whose soil they "tathed" with their dung and urine. The use of moveable folds meant that the benefits of this process were distributed on a systematic basis and the whole exercise was especially beneficial to light soils since the treading of the sheep compacted the soil and thereby improved its structure. The tathe of the fold was accordingly highly prized (being valued at 20-30 pence per acre in the late fourteenth and early fifteenth centuries), so much so that on most manors the sheep of customary tenants were appropriated to the use of the demesne.[29] Folding nevertheless had to operate within certain constraints and it was these which determined the scale and distribution of this activity within eastern Norfolk. On the one hand, flock-size was limited by the amount of pasture available for its daily sustenance (the requirements of horses and cattle took first priority almost everywhere), and, on the other, the area that could be folded was limited by the amount of arable free from crops during the appropriate summer months. Since arable represented a very high proportion of total land-use in this locality, and a high proportion of that arable was cultivated each year, the importance of folding was correspondingly restricted. After 1350 the norm, on the evidence of fifteen demesnes, was for about 15 per cent of all cornland to be folded each year, the degree of conformity to this norm being determined by individual circumstances (see Table 4). Thus folding tended to make its greatest contribution in the vicinity of extensive sandy heaths, where light soils meant that fallowing was relatively infrequent, as in the case of Eaton, Heigham-by-Norwich, Lakenham, Plumstead and Hevingham. Conversely, at Scratby, Martham, and North Walsham, the intrinsic higher fertility of the soil was reflected in a greater intensity of cultivation and hence in fewer opportunities for folding.

When all these different methods of fertilizing land are taken together it becomes apparent how this area escaped the vicious circle of declining soil fertility and falling yields. Plainly, not all methods were available to all demesnes, nor were they always employed with the same diligence. Nevertheless, despite the lowness of prevailing animal ratios, all demesnes succeeded in fertilizing a substantial proportion of cornland each year. This can be seen clearly from the middle of the fourteenth century, when the areas sown with legumes, manured, marled, and folded, are all recorded for the first time on

---

[29] On the lords' 'liberty of the fold' see Campbell, 'Regional Uniqueness', pp. 23-5.

a consistent basis. Such information is no surrogate for equivalent data relating to the first half of the century, when the more labour-intensive methods of fertilizing land were at their zenith (marling, for instance, is rarely referred to after mid-century), but it does have the merit of allowing at least some assessment of the combined effect of all these methods. The relevant information is summarized in Table 4. As will be seen, no demesne failed to fertilize less than one-third, or succeeded in fertilizing more than two-thirds, of its cornland each year. On average, cornland was fertilized every other year. This is a considerable achievement and reflects both a genuine concern to maintain the land in good heart and a desire to derive maximum advantage from available resources.

III

The same desire underlay the adoption of the horse as the principal beast of traction. Once the changeover had been made from natural to produced fodder it became important to convert that fodder into work with maximum efficiency. Since horses are capable of working faster and for longer hours than oxen, and since their superiority shows to maximum advantage where soils are light and easily tilled, the horse became the natural choice both for ploughing and other farm work. Little is as yet known about the extent to which horse-ploughing

Table 4. *Fertilization of Cornland on Various Demesnes in Eastern Norfolk After 1350*

Demesne	Years	No.	Mean Area Sown with Corn (acres)	% Cornland sown with Legumes	% Cornland Folded	% Cornland Manured etc.	Total % Cornland "Fertilized"	% Cornland Fallowed
Heigham-by-Norwich	1380-1381	I	80·1	26·3	28·2	10·0	64·5	23·8
Ludham	c. 1354-1355	I	128·5	26·5	5·0	28·8	60·3	19·5
Ashby	1391-1392	I	109·1	25·2	24·7	6·9	56·8	15·6
Haveringland	1356-1365	3	85·1	16·6	23·0	13·7	53·3	13·6
Flegg	1354-1428	10	98·7	36·0	9·0	7·6	52·6	21·2
Martham	1363-1407	10	135·2	22·5	14·5	13·8	50·8	18·5
Plumstead	1359-1405	12	134·0	22·9	19·3	8·1	50·3	24·5
Eaton	1358-1407	7	93·7	6·1	35·9	8·1	50·1	17·9
Scratby	1360-1363	2	34·8	30·9	0	18·0	48·9	15·1
North Walsham	1367-1427	5	56·3	24·0	0	19·7	43·7	10·6
Hevingham	1357-1358	I	71·5	0	26·6	12·6	39·2	21·0
Lakenham	1366-1367	I	165·1	12·9	18·2	6·7	37·8	31·3
Newton	1366-1367	I	280·0	14·3	7·1	15·7	37·1	18·6
Hoveton	1393-1394	I	119·0	22·7	0	12·6	35·3	23·9
Taverham	1362-1418	11	99·8	8·9	15·1	9·5	33·5	15·5
	maximum		280·0	36·0	35·9	28·8	64·5	31·3
15 demesnes:	mean		112·7	19·7	15·1	12·8	47·6	19·4
	median		99·8	22·7	15·1	12·6	50·1	18·6
	minimum		34·8	0	0	6·7	33·5	10·6

was practised in medieval England[30] but its early prominence in eastern Norfolk is not in doubt. Several demesnes belonging to St. Benet's Abbey already carried significant numbers of working horses by the mid-thirteenth century (there were five, six, and eight horses, respectively, at Thurgarton, Hoveton, and Ludham, at Michaelmas 1240, and eight stots at Heigham-by-Norwich at Michaelmas 1246),[31] and by the end of the century no demesne was without at least a pair of horses. Nevertheless, it does not necessarily follow that ploughing was now being undertaken exclusively by horses. Indeed, one of the few explicit references to the size and composition of plough-teams in this area refers to the existence in 1291, at both Reedham and Lound, of mixed teams comprising two horses and two oxen.[32] In this context it is perhaps significant that both of these places had access to extensive alluvial pastures, a circumstance which would have favoured at least the partial retention of oxen.[33] Demesnes at Acle, Caister-cum-Markshall, Halvergate, and South Walsham were similarly placed, and here too the likelihood is that plough-teams comprised a combination of horses and oxen.[34] Away from the Broadland marshes, however, there was a much heavier reliance upon fodder crops, and oxen were accordingly less prominent. At Scratby, for instance, there were no oxen and only three horses in 1343; hence, as only 26½ acres had been sown in the spring and there was only one plough on this demesne, it would seem that two horses sufficed to pull the plough, with the third horse being required for harrowing.[35] Roughly contemporary evidence relating to demesnes at Saxthorpe, Worstead, Knapton, Martham, and Ormesby points to a similar conclusion. Still later, towards the close of the fourteenth century, the dominance of horse traction is apparent from the retention of horses in hand when all other livestock were let at farm, as at Flegg, Gimingham, Hoveton, Lakenham, Newton, North Walsham, and Plumstead.[36] That two-horse plough-teams were perfectly adequate on the light soils which prevailed in much of this area can be seen from the fact that teams thus constituted were in general use here in the late sixteenth century.[37] The existence of such teams in the early fourteenth century helps to account for the paradoxical combination of high arable productivity and low animal ratios.

Another factor of paramount importance to the maintenance of agricultural productivity was the intensive use of labour. Eastern Norfolk's exceptionally

---

[30] Hence the contradictory claims of L. White—"in late twelfth-century England, at least in some regions which cannot yet be defined, the horse was taking over the plough" (*Medieval Technology and Social Change* (Oxford, 1962), p. 65)—and Titow—"English documents make it clear, beyond any possibility of doubt, that there had been no general change-over from ox-ploughing to horse-ploughing", (*English Rural Society*, p. 38.)

[31] N.R.O. Diocesan Est/1 & 2.

[32] *Item lego eidem Galfrido carucam meam apud Redam ibidem junctam ij equis & ij bobus* (N.R.O. DCN Q 232C 4114). I am grateful to Mr Paul Rutledge for drawing my attention to this reference.

[33] E. Boserup, *The Conditions of Agricultural Growth: The Economics of Agrarian Change under Population Pressure* (1965), pp. 36-9; D. C. North and R. P. Thomas, *The Rise of the Western World: A New Economic History* (Cambridge, 1973), p. 42; J. Thirsk ed. *The Agrarian History of England and Wales, IV, 1500-1640* (Cambridge, 1967), p. 165.

[34] At Caister-cum-Markshall in 1279-80, there were two ploughs, 3 stots *ad carucas*, and 4 oxen (P.R.O. SC 6/932/24 & 17).

[35] N.R.O. DCN R 233D 5153.

[36] Thus at Flegg in the period 1406-21, 100-120 acres were cultivated using 4-6 stots (all other livestock having been farmed out).

[37] Thirsk, *Agrarian History*, p. 164; E. Kerridge, *The Farmers of Old England* (1973), p. 87.

high population density meant that labour was both abundant and cheap. Managers of demesnes took full advantage of this situation. The reduction in fallowing, changeover to produced fodder, stall-feeding of livestock, assiduous marling, and repeated ploughings all demanded, and received, substantial labour inputs. But the lavish use of labour did not end here; it was extended to a whole range of supplementary tasks. Weeding for instance, was one labour intensive but particularly necessary job, since weed-growth tends to be rife where cultivation is virtually continuous and, if left unchecked, will have an adverse effect on productivity.[38] Occasional fallows, repeated ploughings, heavy seeding rates, and the use of oats as a smother crop, all helped to contain weed-growth, but they could not eradicate it. Weeding therefore remained unavoidable if the full benefits of clean cultivation were to be derived. Accordingly, at Scratby, in 1296-7, 60 per cent of the corn crop was weeded, at Taverham, in 1292-3, the equivalent proportion was 72 per cent, and at Plumstead, between 1293 and 1300, it was 87 per cent. Moreover, at Acle, Brandiston, Halvergate, Hanworth, Ormesby, and South Walsham it was normal practice to weed the entire corn crop each year. The transforming effect that such unstinting use of labour could have upon medieval agriculture has rarely been recognized, but it was plainly fundamental to the high level of productivity attained in eastern Norfolk in the early fourteenth century.

Explicit evidence of the crucial importance of labour is provided by an analysis of production and productivity levels on the Prior of Norwich's demesne at Martham during the first quarters of the fourteenth and fifteenth centuries.[39] The relevant data are summarized in Table 5, from which it will be seen that although the basic nature and scale of production remained much the same in both these periods, by the early fifteenth century the actual

Table 5. *Martham: Demesne Production and Productivity, 1300-24 and 1400-24*

		Mean 1300-24	Mean 1400-24	% Change
Acreage Sown		190·75	177·23	− 7·09
% Sown with Legumes		20·24	19·39	− 4·2
Animal Ratio		25·2	25·7	+ 1·98
% Fallow		c. 6·95	15·13	+117·7
Total Man-days Worked by *Famuli*		1987·9	1455·1	− 26·8
Expenditure on Weeding (pence)		210·3	93·0	− 55·78
Wheat	Seed Sown per Acre (bushels)	4·0	3·33	− 16·75
	Yield per Seed	5·12	3·85	− 24·8
	Yield per Acre (bushels)	20·47	12·52	− 38·8
Legumes	Seed Sown per Acre (bushels)	3·99	3·03	− 24·1
	Yield per Seed	2·88	2·83	− 1·7
	Yield per Acre (bushels)	11·47	7·05	− 38·5
Barley	Seed Sown per Acre (bushels)	6·07	5·24	− 13·7
	Yield per Seed	3·15	3·08	− 2·2
	Yield per Acre (bushels)	19·11	16·65	− 12·9
Oats	Seed Sown per Acre (bushels)	7·81	5·37	− 31·2
	Yield per Seed	2·67	3·83	+ 43·4
	Yield per Acre (bushels)	20·84	21·77	+ 4·5

[38] W. Harwood Long, 'The Low Yields of Corn in Medieval England', *Econ. Hist. Rev.*, 2nd ser. XXXII (1979), pp. 464-9.
[39] N.R.O. DCN R 233C 4949-57 & NNAS 5905-16 20 D2 & 3.

intensity of production was very much reduced. Conspicuous among the changes which had taken place was a reduction in labour inputs: the number of man-days worked by the permanent staff of *famuli* was cut by 26·8 per cent and even greater economies were made in the use of casual, hired labour. Hence, despite a doubling in the frequency of fallowing, and a reduction from heavy to moderate seeding-rates (which, other things being equal, should have raised productivity),[40] yields fell. Yields per acre fell most, declining by 38·8 per cent, 38·5 per cent, and 12·9 per cent respectively in the case of wheat, legumes, and barley, but yields per seed were also affected; that of wheat—once the most consistently high yielding crop—fell by no less than 24·8 per cent.[41] Only oats showed any improvement in yield, but then its former use as a smother crop, sown at almost 8 bushels per acre, had hardly been commensurate with the attainment of a high level of productivity. Since the basic technology of production remained virtually constant, and it was the first quarter of the fourteenth century which experienced the worst weather, there can be little doubt that it was the reduction in the use of labour which was primarily responsible for this deterioration in productivity.

Nevertheless, intensive as was the use of labour on these demesnes, it may have been on the small-holdings of the peasantry that labour made its most telling contribution to agricultural productivity. In eastern Norfolk these holdings were so small by the close of the thirteenth century—the vast majority containing fewer than 5 acres—that labour could always be applied more lavishly than on even the most intensively cultivated demesnes in the same locality. To continue the example of Martham, it can be calculated from an extent of 1292[42] that the average ratio of labour to land on peasant holdings was at least six times greater than that currently prevailing on the demesne. Given this advantage, it can be presumed that labour—which was undoubtedly most efficient when self-employed—was substituted wherever possible for such other factors of production, notably land and capital, in which these holdings were deficient. In so far as unflagging zeal was the prerogative of peasant holdings it is thus safe to assume that no pains would have been spared in executing all those essentially manual tasks—manuring, weeding, and harvesting—upon which the productivity of this agricultural system so clearly depended. Certainly, the remarkable degree of economic and demographic resilience exhibited by the peasantry on the manor of Hakeford Hall in Coltishall, during the difficult half-century from 1300 to 1349, would seem to imply that holdings of less than 5 acres were anything but non-viable.[43]

Yet the precise nature of peasant agriculture is not entirely a matter of surmise. On most manors part at least of the demesne was inter-mixed with peasant land so that there is every reason to suppose that they were being cultivated in much the same way.[44] Indeed, the evidence of tithes shows that

[40] "Thinner sowing should result in better returns per seed and thicker sowing in poorer returns per seed": Titow, *Winchester Yields* (1972), p. 22.

[41] Farmer was puzzled by a similar phenomenon on the Winchester manors at this time: "with better fertilized arable now available, one wonders why the yield per acre of the most valuable cereal should have dropped in this way"; 'Grain Yields', p. 565.

[42] B. L. Stowe, MS 936: 846 acres of arable were held by no less than 376 tenants.

[43] B. M. S. Campbell, 'Population Pressure, Inheritance and the Land Market in a Fourteenth Century Peasant Community', in R. M. Smith, ed. *Land, Kinship and Life-Cycle* (forthcoming).

[44] At Martham the demesne actually incorporated open-field strips formerly held by the peasantry: Campbell, thesis, pp. 34-7.

this was so. For example, at Hemsby in 1335 tithe was received of the same crops grown in much the same proportions as on the demesne, namely 54½ quarters of wheat, 177 quarters of barley, 2 quarters of oats, and 16¼ quarters of legumes.[45] In a few fortuitous instances a record of the crops grown on individual peasant holdings has actually survived, as in the case of Ralph Lif of Coltishall, whose holding of 5 acres 20 perches was cultivated, in 1315, as follows: 7·3 per cent with rye, 58·5 per cent with barley, 19·5 per cent with oats, and 14·6 per cent with peas.[46] There is even direct evidence to suggest that the yield of these crops was high. Thus at Hemsby, in 1328, the tithe of the vill was assessed at 3·23 times the value of the tithe of the large and productive demesne;[47] whilst at Coltishall in 1305 the chattels of John Welleman, who died possessed of a mere 3¼ rods of arable, included 17½ bushels of barley and 9 bushels of beans.[48] Perhaps the surest evidence of high yields per acre on peasant holdings is provided by barley rents, which averaged 5·1 bushels per acre at Coltishall from 1322-31, 4·8 bushels per acre at Worstead from 1350-8, and 4·5 bushels per acre at Martham from 1363-4.[49] In fact, at Martham 2 acres and a messuage were demised for no less than 4 quarters of barley per annum in 1359-60.[50] Although such rents primarily reflect the competition for land it is plain that yields must have been high for them to have been paid.

It is also known that peasant holdings employed many of the same techniques as demesnes. References at Acle to peasant purchases of manure and at Coltishall and Hevingham to the amercement of tenants for illegally digging marl, suggest that peasant cultivators were actively seeking-out supplementary sources of fertilizer.[51] And although many of these cultivators held so little land that they may have relied upon spade cultivation, at least some of them kept and used working horses. Thus, at Acle 34 horses were aggisted in the Earl of Norfolk's park and marsh in 1272-3, whilst at Eaton a surviving tax schedule for the 1332 Subsidy records 6 mares among the moveable goods of 23 tax-payers (along with 21 cows, 11 calves, but no oxen).[52] But the most explicit evidence of peasant livestock comes from Coltishall, where a court roll for 1384 contains an inventory of the 7 acre holding of Richard Collys, the stock of which comprised 2 stots, 1 cow, 2 young milking cows, 1 yearling heifer, and a sow (i.e. an animal ratio of 85·7).[53] Relating to the keeping of horses was the peasant cultivation of oats, to which there are a number of references. It is also quite possible that, as in the Low Countries, the cultivation

[45] N.R.O. DCN R 223B 4664. At Martham tithe received in 1360 amounted to 41 qr. 1 bus. of wheat, 134 qr. of barley, 2 qr. and 12 qr. of oats and peas (part of the tithe of oats and peas having been expended in the autumn)—N.R.O. NNAS 5893 20 D1.

[46] King's College, Cambridge E 29. The equivalent proportions sown on the demesne that year were: wheat 2·6%, rye 9·3%, barley 43·1%, oats 21·6% and peas 23·3%.

[47] N.R.O. DCN R 233B 4663.

[48] His death is recorded in the court held on 25 January 1305: King's College, Cambridge E 31.

[49] King's College, Cambridge E 30-3; N.R.O. DCN R 232B 5429; N.R.O. NNAS 5894 20 D1.

[50] N.R.O. NNAS 5893 20 D1.

[51] The sale of manure from the Acle marshes yielded 18s. in 1271-2 and again in 1272-3 (P.R.O. SC 6/929/3-4). At Coltishall 15 tenants were prosecuted in two successive courts for causing damage by digging marl (King's College, Cambridge E 31). At Hevingham Richard Mariot was fined for committing a similar offence in 1292 (N.R.O. NRS 14634 29 D2).

[52] P.R.O. SC 6/929/4; Bodleian Library, Oxford MS Rolls, Norfolk 27.

[53] King's College, Cambridge E 37.

of commercial crops made an important contribution to the peasant economy.[54] In this case direct evidence is lacking, although account rolls testify to the cultivation of cole-seed, flax, teasels, madder, and hemp on several demesne curtilages.[55] Such crops were valuable (the sale of $55\frac{1}{2}$ stones of madder from Monks Grange in 1306 yielded 9 shillings 3 pence) and provided the basic raw materials for a number of ancillary activities (notably textile manufacture).[56] They also pioneered such techniques as bed-and-row cultivation. Indeed, it would be no exaggeration to claim that the scale, techniques, and productivity of peasant holdings in this locality bore a striking resemblance to those most usually associated with horticulture.

IV

It is thus possible to identify in eastern Norfolk an advanced and productive agricultural system which matches in every essential that described by Slicher Van Bath in the Low Countries. In fact, the first East Anglian reference to the successful elimination of fallowing ante-dates that available for the continent by over 50 years. On whichever side of the North Sea this intensive cropping system originated, it is clear that it was firmly established in Norfolk by the last quarter of the thirteenth century. Moreover, there is a mounting body of evidence to show that agricultural progress in England was by no means confined to Norfolk.

The virtual elimination of fallowing in medieval England first received comment in 1915, when H. L. Gray drew attention to the existence of continuous cultivation on the Kentish demesnes of Giles de Badlesmere.[57] Since then studies by T. A. M. Bishop and R. A. L. Smith have confirmed the existence of an advanced agricultural system in eastern and north-eastern Kent.[58] As in eastern Norfolk this system was associated with exceptionally high valuations per acre[59] and was geared towards extensive

---

[54] Slicher Van Bath, op. cit., (1963), pp. 179-80.

[55] Cole-seed is mentioned at Monks Grange c. 1255 (N.R.O. DCN R 233D 5027), flax at Halvergate in 1304 (P.R.O. SC 6/939/16), teasels at Catton in 1339 (N.R.O. DCN R 234D 4485), madder at Catton in 1274 (N.R.O. DCN R 234D 4454) and Monks Grange in 1305-6 (N.R.O. DCN R 233D 5037), and hemp almost universally (60 sheaves of hemp were sold at Halvergate in 1304—P.R.O. SC 6/936/16). Buckwheat, whose cultivation became ubiquitous in the sixteenth century, does not appear until 1480, when it is mentioned as part of the tithe received at North Walsham (N.R.O. Diocesan Est/12).

[56] The inventory of the goods and chattels of Richard Collys, made at Coltishall in 1384, also records 30 ells of cloth *de Wordeston' super le stodeles* (King's College, Cambridge E 37). At this time cloth manufacture was well established at Worstead, North Walsham, and, to a lesser extent, at Dilham, Honing, Witton, Ridlington, and several other places (P.R.O. E 179/149/57).

[57] "Most interesting and significant are the somewhat numerous Kentish manors on which in the middle of the fourteenth century all the acres of the demesne were sown yearly . . . under these conditions the value of an acre often became 12d.": H. L. Gray, *English Field Systems* (Harvard, 1915), p. 302.

[58] T. A. M. Bishop, 'The Rotation of Crops at Westerham, 1297-1350', *Econ. Hist. Rev.* 2nd ser. IX (1938), pp. 38-44; R. A. L. Smith, *Canterbury Cathedral Priory* (Cambridge, 1943); A. Smith, 'Regional Differences in Crop Production in Medieval Kent', *Archaeologia Cantiana*, 78, (1963), reprinted as pp. 37-50 in *Essays in Kentish History* (1973); A. Smith, 'Medieval Field Systems on Some Kent Manors', pp. 173-91 in *Liverpool Essays in Geography* (Liverpool, 1967).

[59] High arable valuations additional to those noted by Gray include All Hallows Hoo, Ifield, Ripley, Meresborough, Greenwich, Westwood, Melton, and Dunstall—all 12-17d. per acre (P.R.O. C133 File 48, 14 Edw. I, File 123, 34 Edw. I, C134 File 17, 3 Edw. II, File 48, 9 Edw. II, File 76, 16 Edw. II, File 83, 18 Edw. II, C133 File 13, 4 Edw. I): Blackmanstone, Dane in Thanet, and Chilton—all 18-23d. per acre (P.R.O. C133 File 92, 27 Edw. I, C134 File 17, 3 Edw. II, C133 File 107, 31 Edw. I): the lands of John Crul and Thomas de Morton, Ivychurch, Westgate in Thanet, and Elmerston—all 24-29d. per acre (P.R.O.

42

grain production. The means by which the latter was achieved included the large-scale field cultivation of legumes (including vetches, which are first recorded in 1268,[60] a decade earlier than across the Channel) and heavy fertilization with manure, marl, lime, and the tathe of the sheep fold. Although yields per seed were unexceptional, heavy seeding rates and annual tillage together ensured that output per acre was well above the medieval average.[61] Further round the coast, a very similar course of husbandry was followed in the fourteenth century on the Sussex estates of Battle Abbey.[62] Here too, as P. F. Brandon has shown, substantial portions of the arable were under a virtually continuous sequence of crops, a circumstance made possible by the incorporation of legumes into rotations along with assiduous fertilization. Again, unimpressive yield ratios disguise yields per acre which were bountiful by medieval standards.[63] Elsewhere, an intensification of arable production along broadly similar lines seems to have occurred on the Huntingdonshire and Cambridgeshire estates of Ramsey and Crowland Abbeys, as also on several of the Holderness manors belonging to Isabella de Fortibus.[64] Indeed, in the fourteenth century the yields obtained on some of these demesnes bear very favourable comparison with the best yields obtained in Norfolk and Kent.[65]

It is therefore clear that there were a number of localities in the thirteenth and fourteenth centuries in which agriculture was both progressive and productive.[66] As observed at the outset, this conclusion has several important implications, both for interpretations of the fourteenth century economy in particular, and for the evolution of English agriculture in general.

In the first place, the example of eastern Norfolk demonstrates that by the late thirteenth century there was in existence a technology capable of raising the gross output of English agriculture. Consequently, it is no longer sufficient to attribute the economic and demographic crisis of the fourteenth century, either in whole or in part, to the absence of the technology required to ward

---

C132 File 41, 56 Hen. III, C133 File 64, 21 Edw. I, C134 File 10, 2 Edw. II, File 17, 3 Edw. II): Flete and Wickham—both 30-35d. per acre (P.R.O. C132 File 31, 48 Hen. III, C135 File 23, 4 Edw. III): Preston and Overland—both 36d. per acre (P.R.O. C134 File 17, 3 Edw. II).

[60] M. M. O'Grady, 'A Study of Some of the Characteristics of the Holdings and Agriculture of Eastry Manor, East Kent from c. 1086-c. 1350' (unpublished M.Phil. thesis, University of London, 1981).

[61] Gross yields of wheat and barley averaged 14·6 and 15·8 bushels per acre at Adisham, Chartham, Eastry, Godmersham, Ickham, Lydden, and Monkton in 1291. At Eastry, over the period 1272-1347, the equivalent yields were 14·9 and 16·8 respectively (calculated from A. Smith, 'Regional Differences', and O'Grady, thesis).

[62] Brandon, 'Cereal Yields'; idem, 'Demesne Arable Farming in Coastal Sussex during the Late Middle Ages', Agric. Hist. Rev., XIX (1971), pp. 113-34.

[63] "The average gross yields at Alciston in the late fourteenth century were about 17 bushels of wheat, 26 bushels of barley, and 22 bushels of oats": Brandon, 'Cereal Yields', p. 419 n. 1.

[64] J. A. Raftis, The Estates of Ramsey Abbey: A Study of Economic Growth and Organization (Toronto, 1957); F. M. Page, The Estates of Crowland Abbey: A Study in Manorial Organization (Cambridge, 1934); K. Ugawa, Lay Estates in Medieval England (Tokyo, 1966); M. Mate, 'Profit and Productivity on the Estates of Isabella de Forz (1260-92)', Econ. Hist. Rev. 2nd ser. XXXIII (1980), pp. 326-34.

[65] At Warboys mean gross yield ratios of wheat and barley were approximately 6·5 and 8·8 from 1344-1413 (calculated from Raftis, Estates of Ramsey). At Oakington mean gross yields per acre of these two crops were approximately 16·7 and 23·8 bushels from 1271-1320 (calculated from Page, Estates of Crowland). At Little Humber the equivalent yields were 14·3 and 31·7 bushels from 1268-91: Ugawa, Lay Estates.

[66] A shift in attention from agricultural estates to farming regions should clarify this picture: in this context see D. Roden's pioneering study 'Demesne Farming in the Chiltern Hills', Agric. Hist. Rev. XVII (1969), pp. 9-23.

off declining agricultural productivity. Soil exhaustion was not an inevitable concomitant of attempts to intensify arable production, nor were the arable and pastoral sectors necessarily competitive rather than complementary. That being so, why was agricultural innovation confined to certain restricted areas apparently strung out round the east and south coasts of England, despite the problems experienced elsewhere of low, and possibly declining, yields and rising population?[67] Is it that agricultural progress of the type described here was feasible only where soils were light and fertile and where market influences were strong? It is certainly a striking coincidence that Holderness, Huntingdonshire and parts of Cambridgeshire, eastern Norfolk, northern and eastern Kent, and coastal Sussex all possessed naturally fertile and easily cultivated soils, all enjoyed coastal and/or riverine access to major urban markets both at home and overseas, and all supported above average population densities. Or is there more to it than this? Could it be that such institutional factors as a low degree of feudalization and flexible field systems—both of which applied in many of these areas—were decisive? A. H. John has observed that "for the arable farmer . . . the important factors were access to London and foreign markets and the ability to adopt new techniques. The position of the husbandman excluded from either of these, whether because of geographical, economic, or institutional reasons, was less satisfactory".[68] This dictum would seem to be as valid for the late thirteenth and early fourteenth centuries as for the early eighteenth century.

Secondly, it transpires that the Low Countries were not the only area in medieval Europe in which an intensive and productive agricultural system was being developed: parts of England were also in the van of agricultural advance. Indeed, side by side with the evolution of the intensive arable farming system documented here went the development of convertible husbandry. The dividends which could accrue from adoption of this system have for some time been known from H. P. R. Finberg's study of the Devon estates of Tavistock Abbey in the fifteenth century.[69] But what is only now beginning to come to light is that fully-fledged convertible husbandry was already in use on some demesnes at a much earlier date (in fact, before the earliest references to it on the continent): E. Stone has suggested that this was the case on several Norfolk manors in the thirteenth century, and Brandon and E. Searle have both demonstrated that convertible husbandry was firmly established in Sussex in the fourteenth century.[70] Both the major technological innovations of seventeenth century English agriculture had thus been anticipated some three centuries earlier. Indeed, there is a striking degree of continuity between those areas which were most active in the adoption of new crops and techniques in

---

[67] "The real problem of medieval technology is not why new technological knowledge was not forthcoming, but why the methods, or even the implements, known to medieval men were not employed, or not employed earlier or more widely than they in fact were": Postan, *Medieval Economy*, p. 42.

[68] A. H. John, 'The Course of Agricultural Change, 1660-1760', in *Studies in the Industrial Revolution* (London, 1960), pp. 125-56, reprinted in *Essays in Agrarian History*, I (Newton Abbot, 1968), p. 249.

[69] H. P. R. Finberg, *Tavistock Abbey: A Study in the Social and Economic History of Devon* (Cambridge, 1951).

[70] E. Stone, 'The Estates of Norwich Cathedral Priory, 1100-1300' (unpublished D.Phil. thesis, University of Oxford, 1956), p. 347; P. F. Brandon, 'Agriculture and the Effects of Floods and Weather at Barnhorne during the Later Middle Ages, *Sussex Archaeological Collections*, CIX (1971), pp. 69-93; E. Searle, *Lordship and Community: Battle Abbey and its Banlieu, 1066-1538* (Toronto, 1974) pp. 272-323.

44

both the thirteenth and the seventeenth centuries. When at the end of the eighteenth century, William Marshall praised the agriculture of eastern Norfolk, he was praising an area with a tradition of progressive agriculture which dated back to the second half of the thirteenth century, if not before.[71]

Finally, it follows from the last point that the essential difference between thirteenth and seventeenth century agriculture in the more progressive parts of England was structural rather than technological. When comparison is made, it is the units of production—the farms and fields—which emerge as having changed most. In eastern Norfolk in the thirteenth century a relatively small number of substantial seignorial demesnes existed alongside a plethora of tiny, fragmented peasant holdings. By the seventeenth century, however, everything had changed; holdings were greatly reduced in number, increased in size, and improved in layout.[72] In short, occupancy was no longer universal. It was this change, not the adoption of specific technical innovations, which was to be the mainspring of more general economic advance. Yet even the replacement of open-field peasant holdings by enclosed capitalist farms had its roots in the middle ages. In the fifteenth century, whilst Low Countries agriculturalists were occupied developing the cultivation of clover, turnips, and other new crops, English farmers were actively engaged in engrossing and consolidating their holdings. This trend is already apparent in eastern Norfolk in the middle decades of the fourteenth century.[73] A century and a half later it had wrought striking changes, not the least of which was to create the forebears of those Norfolk yeomen who were subsequently to be so much admired by William Marshall.

APPENDIX I
List of Bailiff's Accounts consulted

Demesne	Range of years	No. of Accounts	Reference
A) *To 1350:*			
Acle	1268-1280	7	P.R.O. SC 6/929/1-7
Arminghall	1347-1348	3	N.R.O. DCN R 232B 4092
Attlebridge	1307-c. 1330	1	N.R.O. R 232B 4096-8
Aylmerton	1345-1346	4	N.R.O. WKC 2/24
Brandiston	1316-1348	8	M.C.O. Estate Records 166/3-12
Bawburgh	1274-1338	1	N.R.O. DCN R 232B 3338-42, 4099-102, 4577
Burgh in Flegg	1330-1331	1	P.R.O. SC 6/931/27
Catton	1265-1350	46	N.R.O. DCN R 234D 4450-95
Caister-cum-Markshall	1269-1300	15	P.R.O. SC 6/932/11-26
Coltishall	1292-1315	2	K.C.C. E 29-30 (footnotes in court rolls)
Costessey	1278-1293	3	P.R.O. SC 6/933/13-4
Eaton	c. 1263-1350	28	N.R.O. DCN R 233A 4567-93 & 232C 5176; L'Estrange Collection I B 4; B.L.O. MS Rolls, Norfolk 21-3

[71] It was in eastern Norfolk that Marshall (*Rural Economy*) found "that regular and long established system of practice which has raised, deservedly, the name of Norfolk husbandmen: and which, in a principal part of this district, remains unadulterated to the present time".

[72] B. M. S. Campbell, 'The Extent and Layout of Commonfields in Eastern Norfolk', *Norfolk Archaeology* XXXVIII (1981), pp. 5-32.

[73] B. M. S. Campbell, 'Population Change and the Genesis of Commonfields on a Norfolk Manor', *Econ. Hist. Rev.*, 2nd ser. XXXIII (1980), pp. 188-91.

Demesne	Range of years	No. of Accounts	Reference
Flegg	1340-1341	1	N.R.O. Diocesan Est/9
Framingham	1269-1308	17	P.R.O. SC 6/935/20-37 & SC 6/1121/1
Gresham	1306-1307	1	P.R.O. SC 6/936/1
Halvergate	1268-1306	16	P.R.O. SC 6/936/2-17
Hanworth	1272-1306	22	P.R.O. SC 6/936/18-32 & 937/1-10
Hardley	1295-1296	1	N.R.O. Diocesan Est/2
Heigham-by-Norwich	1302-1307	2	N.R.O. Diocesan Est/2
Hemsby	1265-1335	18	N.R.O. DCN R 233D 5144 & 233B 4651-65; L'Estrange Collection I B 4; B.L.O. MS Rolls, Norfolk 47
Hevingham	1327-1347	4	N.R.O. NRS 14748 & 14751 29D4; DCN R 232B 4138; NRS 14664 29 D2
Hoveton	1295-1336	2	N.R.O. Diocesan Est/2
Intwood	1308-c. 1346	3	N.R.O. NRS 23350 Z 97
Keswick	1274-1320	4	N.R.O. NRS 23357 Z 98
Knapton	1345-1348	2	G.C.W. XV 53 98-9
Lakenham	1295-1296	1	N.R.O. DCN R 232B 4127
Lessingham	1290-1298	2	E.C.R. Vol 49 242-2
Little Hautbois	c. 1289-1290	1	N.R.O. Diocesan Est/2
Martham	c. 1261-1350	30	N.R.O. DCN R 233C 4940-64 & 232C 5176-7; L'Estrange Collection I B 4; NNAS 5889-91 20 D1
Melton	1333-1334	1	N.R.O. DCN R 233D 5015
Monks Grange	c. 1255-1334	27	N.R.O. DCN R 233D 5027-52 & 232C 5176-7; L'Estrange Collection I B 4
Newton	1273-1328	5	N.R.O. DCN R 233D 5053-7
Ormesby	1294-1338	3	N.R.O. DCN R 232B 4130-2
Plumstead	c. 1263-1350	24	N.R.O. DCN R 233D 5101-23 & 232C 5176-7
Saxthorpe	c. 1296-c. 1341	6	N.R.O. NRS 19652-62 42 D7 & 19691-2 42 E
Scottow	c. 1348-1349	1	N.R.O. Diocesan Est/11
Scratby	1296-1344	9	N.R.O. DCN R 233D 5145-53
South Walsham	1268-1297	11	P.R.O. SC 6/944/21-31
Suffield	1272-1300	11	P.R.O. SC 6/944/1-11
Taverham	c. 1255-1350	33	N.R.O. DCN R 232A 5307-36 & 232C 5176-7; L'Estrange Collection I B 4
Wicklewood	1337-1338	1	N.R.O. DCN R 232B 4136
Worstead	1273-1321	3	N.R.O. DCN R 232B 5428-30; L'Estrange Collection I B 4
15 St Benet's Manors*	1238-1246	23	N.R.O. Diocesan Est/1 & 2

* Ashby, Bastwick, Easton, Heigham-by-Norwich, Horning, Hoveton, Ludham, Neatishead, Potter Heigham, Shotesham, Swanton, Thurgarton, Thurne, North Walsham, and South Walsham.

B) *From 1350*:

Aldborough	1430-1431	1	P.R.O. SC 6/929/8
Antingham	1409-1410	1	N.R.O. MS 6031 16 B8
Ashby	1378-1392	2	N.R.O. Diocesan Est/9
Blickling	1410-1421	3	NRO NRS 10196 24 A1 & 10535 25 B5
Burgh in Flegg	1390-1391	1	P.R.O. SC 6/931/28
Eaton	1358-1423	15	B.L.O. MS Rolls, Norfolk 29-45
Flegg	1350-1432	18	N.R.O. Diocesan Est/9
Gimingham	1358-1398	10	P.R.O. DL 29 288/4719-20 & 4734, & 289/4744; N.R.O. MS 6001 16 A6 & N.R.S. 11331-2 26 B6; NRS 11058-60 25 E2 & 11069 25 E3
Hautbois	c. 1380-1368	1	N.R.O. Diocesan Est/2
Haveringland	1356-1377	4	B.L. Add. Charters 15199-202
Heigham-by-Norwich	c. 1380-1381	1	N.R.O. Diocesan Est/2
Hevingham			N.R.O. NRS 14762 29 D4, 13996 28 F3, & 14750 29 D4
Horsham St. Faith	1407-1408	1	N.R.O. NRS 19517 42 C6
Hoveton	1393-1394	1	N.R.O. Church Commissioners 101426
Intwood	1417-1426	2	N.R.O. NRS 23351-2 Z97
Keswick	1366-1377	9	N.R.O. NRS 23358 Z98
Lakenham	1366-1367	1	N.R.O. DCN R 232B 4128
Ludham	c. 1354-1355	1	N.R.O. Diocesan Est/2

46

Demesne	Range of years	No. of Accounts	Reference
Martham	1355-1423	26	N.R.O. N.N.A.S. 5891-903 20 D1, 5904-15 20 D2, & 5916 20 D3
Melton	1366-1370	2	N.R.O. DCN R 233D 5016-7
Newton	1366-1426	5	N.R.O. DCN R 233D 5058-62
North Walsham	1367-1427	5	N.R.O. Diocesan Est/12
Plumstead	1351-1420	20	N.R.O. DCN R 233D 5124-43
Potter Heigham	1389-1390	1	N.R.O. Diocesan Est/11
Reedham	1377-1395	11	B.L. Add. Charters 26,852-62
Saxthorpe	1350-1439	12	N.R.O. NRS 19647-61 42 D7, 19677-9 42 E3, & 19690 42 E4
Shotesham	1353-1369	1	N.R.O. Diocesan Est/11
Scratby	1356-1363	3	N.R.O. DCN R 233D 5154-6
Taverham	1351-1424	22	N.R.O. DCN R 232C 5337-58
Thwaite	c. 1386-1387	1	N.R.O. Diocesan Est/2
Tunstead	1358-1360	2	P.R.O. DL 29 288/4719-20

Abbreviations:

B.L.O.	=	Bodleian Library, Oxford
B.L.	=	British Library
E.C.R.	=	Eton College Records
G.C.W.	=	St. George's Chapel, Windsor
K.C.C.	=	King's College, Cambridge
M.C.O.	=	Magdalen College, Oxford
N.R.O.	=	Norfolk Record Office
P.R.O.	=	Public Record Office

III

Arable Productivity in Medieval England: Some Evidence from Norfolk

I

CONSIDERABLE ingenuity has recently been demonstrated in the development of a technique for estimating sixteenth- and seventeenth-century grain yields on the evidence of probate inventories.[1] This ought to serve as a salutary lesson to the medieval agricultural historian, for he, in spite of working in an earlier period, enjoys the privilege of a qualitatively superior data source. Medieval bailiffs' accounts represent one of the most remarkable compilations of agricultural data ever devised, and in respect of seignorial demesnes provide all the information necessary for the direct measurement of both arable and pastoral productivity.[2] Of course, the survival of account rolls is often fragmentary and uneven; but, even so, the potential of those that remain has yet to be fully realized.

Hitherto, students of medieval account rolls have concentrated almost exclusively upon arable productivity and have attached overriding importance to the measurement of yields per seed: the ratio of seed sown to grain harvested. This emphasis derives from a belief that

The author is a lecturer in the Department of Geography, The Queen's University of Belfast, BT7 1NN, Northern Ireland. He wishes to thank Jenitha Orr for assistance with the preparation of the data on which the paper is based and Anthony Malcomson for comments on the text.

[1] Mark Overton, "Estimating Crop Yields from Probate Inventories: An Example from East Anglia, 1585–1735," this JOURNAL, 39 (June 1979), 363–78.

[2] For examples of account rolls see Jan Z. Titow, *English Rural Society, 1200–1350* (London, 1969), pp. 106–36. On the calculation of crop yields see Jan Z. Titow, *Winchester Yields: a Study in Medieval Agricultural Productivity* (Cambridge, 1972), pp. 5–9.

medieval bushels and acres are too indeterminate in size to permit any absolute measurement of yield in terms of volume of grain produced per unit area.[3] Only the yield ratio, it is supposed, can place the analysis of arable productivity on a firm, objective footing thereby permitting direct comparison both over time and between different manors, estates, and regions. Nevertheless, medieval grain yields remain the subject of controversy.[4] The preoccupation with yields per seed is particularly unsatisfactory now that it has become possible to make comparison with yields per acre in the sixteenth, seventeenth, and early eighteenth centuries.

To compound the problem, productivity has largely been analyzed with reference to individual manors and estates, with the result that local and regional variations in yield have only emerged incidentally, according to the location of the manors and estates in question.[5] Not surprisingly, large gaps have been left in the agricultural map of England and, to exacerbate matters, certain types of estate have received a disproportionate amount of attention. Hence, whereas much is known about the productivity of the properties of such ecclesiastical magnates as the bishops of Winchester and Worcester, priors of Canterbury, Bolton, and Durham, and abbots of Battle, Crowland, Ramsey, Tavistock, and Westminster (largely because Church estates tend to be represented by the best archives), little is known of their lay counterparts.[6] Of the great lay fiefs of medieval England only the Duchy of

[3] "Any attempt to demonstrate what these were in bushels per acre is virtually frustrated by the prevalence of customary measures both of area and volume; it is therefore safer to look at yields in terms of the ratio between seed sown and the crop subsequently harvested." Edward Miller and John Hatcher, *Medieval England—Rural Society and Economic Change, 1086–1348* (London, 1978), p. 215.

[4] Meghnad Desai, "A Malthusian Crisis in Medieval England: a Critique of the Postan-Titow Hypothesis" (Paper read at the Cliometrics Conference at the University of Warwick, Jan. 1978); H. E. Hallam, *Rural England, 1066–1348* (Glasgow, 1981), pp. 10–16.

[5] A notable exception is David Roden, "Demesne Farming in the Chiltern Hills," *Agricultural History Review*, 17, part 1 (1969), 9–23.

[6] Titow, *Winchester Yields*; David L. Farmer, "Grain Yields on the Winchester Manors in the Later Middle Ages," *Economic History Review*, 2nd ser., 30 (Nov. 1977), 555–66; Christopher Dyer, *Lords and Peasants in a Changing Society: The Estates of the Bishopric of Worcester, 680–1540* (Cambridge, 1980); R. A. L. Smith, *Canterbury Cathedral Priory: A Study in Monastic Administration* (Cambridge, 1943); Ian Kershaw, *Bolton Priory: The Economy of a Northern Monastery, 1286–1325* (Oxford, 1973); R. B. Dobson, *Durham Priory, 1400–1450* (Cambridge, 1973); Peter F. Brandon, "Cereal Yields on the Sussex Estates of Battle Abbey during the Later Middle Ages," *Economic History Review*, 2nd ser., 25 (Aug. 1972), 403–20; Eleanor Searle, *Lordship and Community Battle Abbey and its Banlieu, 1066–1538* (Toronto, 1974); F. M. Page, *The Estates of Crowland Abbey* (Cambridge, 1934); J. A. Raftis, *The Estates of Ramsey Abbey: A Study of Economic Growth and Organization* (Toronto, 1957); H. P. R. Finberg, *Tavistock Abbey: A Study in the Social and Economic History of Devon* (Cambridge, 1951); Barbara F. Harvey, *Westminster Abbey and its Estates in the Middle Ages* (Oxford, 1977); D. V. Stern, "A Hertfordshire Manor of Westminster Abbey: An Examination of Demesne Profits, Corn Yields, and Weather Evidence" (Ph.D. thesis, University of London, 1978); David L. Farmer, "Grain Yields on the Winchester and Westminster Manors, 1270–1410" (Paper read at the seventeenth International Congress on Medieval Studies at Western Michigan University, Kalamazoo, Michigan, May 1982).

Cornwall, one manor of the Bigod lordship, and the far-flung lands of the Countess of Aumale have received the same degree of attention.[7] Middling and small estates have fared still worse: only the Merton College manor of Cuxham, Adam de Stratton's Wiltshire manor of Sevenhampton, and a handful of Essex and Sussex manors have so far been investigated.[8] This bias towards large ecclesiastical estates is unfortunate for, on the evidence of E. A. Kosminsky's analysis of the Hundred Rolls, the Church held only 26 percent of all manors and these tended to be the most heavily feudalized.[9]

Any general pronouncements about the level of arable productivity in the Middle Ages must therefore await a more systematic investigation of yields, as obtained both on all types of estate and in all parts of the country. What is required is a series of detailed regional studies which examines productivity using the widest available range of criteria. As a step in that direction, this paper discusses the results of an analysis of crop yields for 62 demesnes in the eastern half of Norfolk, derived from an examination of a total of 83 different demesnes belonging to a wide range of different estates.[10] Apart from being well-documented, eastern Norfolk lends itself to an exercise of this kind because it forms part of the area comprised in Mark Overton's East Anglian yield estimates for the period 1585–1735.[11]

II

Although bailiffs' accounts are preserved for a large number of demesnes within eastern Norfolk none retains a continuous series of annual accounts. In fact, the great majority of demesnes is represented by a total of less than 20 years' discontinuous record, and to obtain full coverage both of the area and of a range of different estates it is necessary to have recourse to a substantial number of demesnes for which the record of only one or two harvests is preserved. Such sparsely recorded demesnes have not as yet attracted much attention

---

[7] John Hatcher, *Rural Economy and Society in the Duchy of Cornwall, 1300–1500* (Cambridge, 1970); Frances G. Davenport, *The Economic History of a Norfolk Manor (Forncett) 1086–1565* (Cambridge, 1906); K. Ugawa, *Lay Estates in Medieval England* (Tokyo, 1966); Mavis Mate, "Profit and Productivity on the Estates of Isabella de Forz (1260–92)," *Economic History Review*, 2nd ser., 33 (Aug. 1980), 326–34.

[8] P. D. A. Harvey, *A Medieval Oxfordshire Village: Cuxham 1240–1400* (Oxford, 1965); M. W. Farr, ed., *Accounts and Surveys of the Wiltshire Lands of Adam of Stratton*, Wiltshire Archaeological Society Records Series, 14 (Devizes, 1959); Richard H. Britnell, "Production for the Market on a Small Fourteenth-Century Estate," *Economic History Review*, 2nd ser., 19 (May 1966), 380–87; Richard H. Britnell, "Minor Landlords in England and Medieval Agrarian Capitalism," *Past and Present*, 89 (Nov. 1980), 3–22; Brandon, "Cereal Yields," 419–20.

[9] E. A. Kosminsky, *Studies in the Agrarian History of England in the Thirteenth Century* (Oxford, 1956).

[10] For details see Appendix.

[11] Overton, "Crop Yields."

from historians, although, at least in this area, they dominate the record. Since consecutive accounts, which alone provide information on what was sown and what was harvested, survive in comparatively small numbers, considerable reliance has to be placed upon calculations of yield ratios made by the medieval auditors. Such calculations begin to appear as marginal notes in the accounts from the mid–1280s and relate to the crops planted during the year prior to that being accounted for. On the assumption (normally valid) that seeding rates remained constant from one year to the next, information given in the accounts of the next year's seeding rates can then be used to derive the yields per acre of these same crops. In this way the number of yield figures obtainable is greatly increased. Indeed, for the Prior of Norwich's demesnes, the remarkable document known as *Proficuum Maneriorum* provides a separate record of not only yields per seed but also yields per acre for 12 years at the turn of the thirteenth and fourteenth centuries.[12]

Coincidentally, account rolls are also most abundant at this time and the 1290s stand out as the best recorded decade in the generally well-recorded period 1270–1340. In contrast, the second half of the fourteenth century is less well recorded, although the accounts themselves become more detailed. This contraction in available data is associated with the farming out of demesnes; by 1430 direct cultivation had ceased virtually everywhere. Of course, piecemeal leasing began to affect the amount of land in hand quite early on in the fourteenth century but even when direct cultivation was at fullest stretch most of these demesnes were of comparatively modest size. Almost a third of the demesnes were less than 100 cultivated acres, three-quarters less than 200 acres, and none more than 400 acres. But what is particularly interesting is that the data assembled here relate to a wide variety of different landlords. These include important churchmen such as the Bishop and Prior of Norwich, Abbot of St. Benet at Holm, Abbot of St. Edmundsbury, Abbot of Wymondham, alien Abbot of Bec, and the Priors of the local houses of Aldeby and Horsham St. Faith; important lay proprietors such as the Crown, the Bigod Earls of Norfolk, and the Dukes of Lancaster; and small knightly families such as the de Unedales, Burnels, de Crungethorpes, de Verdums, de Playes, Cleres, de Hedersetes, and de Gyneys. Thus, although ecclesiastical landlords are the best represented, fully 40 percent of recorded demesnes were in lay hands. This is the largest body of data on lay estates yet collected and, indeed, the entire body of data is the most complete so far assembled for one area. As such it casts new light on several aspects of medieval agricultural productivity.

In the Middle Ages the yield ratios of all crops were generally unimpressive. The yields of 5.0 per unit of seed for wheat, 8.0 for

---

[12] Norfolk Record Office, DCN *Proficuum Maneriorum*.

barley, and 4.0 for oats anticipated by the anonymous author of the *Husbandry* seemingly represented an unattainable ideal for, on currently available evidence, wheat commonly yielded at a rate of 3.0 to 5.0, barley at a rate of 2.5 to 5.5, and oats at 2.2 to 4.0.[13] Crop yields in eastern Norfolk were no exception. Yields per seed can be obtained for 44 demesnes in eastern Norfolk before 1350 and 30 demesnes after 1350 (see Table 1), a temporal distinction necessary to draw because of changes in farming practice during the second half of the fourteenth century. A distinction is also drawn between those demesnes for which there are fewer than five recorded harvests and those with more, there being 21 of the latter before and 13 after 1350. The evidence shows that wheat was the only crop to yield above the medieval average elsewhere before 1350, with a mean yield ratio of 4.6, although this deteriorated to 3.9 thereafter. In contrast the yields of spring-sown crops tended to be rather below average. Barley, which generally dominated the sown acreage, yielded at a rate of only 3.0 before 1350, while oats and legumes yielded at 2.6 and 2.7 respectively. The yields of oats and legumes remained unchanged after 1350, but that of barley did at least improve marginally to 3.2. Average figures, however, mask wide differences in yields between demesnes, and on the most productive demesnes in this area yield ratios were often twice those on the least productive.

In order to classify demesnes according to whether their yield ratios were high, moderate, or low, a system of scoring has been used based upon the respective quartile divisions of the four principal crops: wheat, barley, oats, and legumes (see Table 1). For example, Hemsby, with yield ratios for wheat, barley, and legumes before 1350 of 6.4, 3.8, and 3.7 respectively, which all fall within the fourth quartile, and a yield ratio of 2.8 for oats, which falls within the third quartile, scores 15 out of a possible maximum of 16 (four for each yield in the fourth quartile, three for the third quartile, and so on) and thus falls into the high productivity category. In contrast, Wymondham, with yield ratios for wheat, barley, and legumes before 1350 of 3.3, 2.5, and 1.7, which all fall within the first quartile, and a yield ratio for oats of 2.4, which falls within the second quartile, scores only five, just above the absolute minimum of four, and thereby falls into the low productivity category. For the purposes of classification, therefore, a score of 12 to 16 has been used to indicate high productivity, a score of 8 to 11 moderate productivity, and a score of 4 to 7 low productivity. On these criteria Flegg, Brandiston, Forncett, and Hemsby emerge as the highest-scoring demesnes before 1350 and Potter Heigham and Hoveton as the highest-

[13] Dorothea Oschinsky, *Walter of Henley and Other Treatises on Estate Management and Accounting* (Oxford, 1971), p. 419. For a survey of medieval yields see B. H. Slicher van Bath, "The Yields of Different Crops (mainly cereals) in Relation to the Seed c. 810–1820," *Acta Historiae Neerlandica* (Leiden, 1967), vol. 2, pp. 78–97.

TABLE 1
EASTERN NORFOLK: YIELD PER SEED

	Yield per Seed, Pre-1350						Yield per Seed, Post-1350					
	Wheat	Rye	Maslin	Barley	Oats	Legumes	Wheat	Rye	Maslin	Barley	Oats	Legumes
Excluding Demesnes with Fewer than Five Recorded Harvests												
Total Number of Demesnes	20	14	4	21	21	20	11	4	1	13	12	10
Total Number of Harvests	257	204	43	324	319	306	124	48	9	154	132	105
Harvest Minimum[a]	0.9	0.9	1.6	1.1	0.5	0	1.2	1.2	1.0	0.2	0.9	0
Demesne Minimum[b]	3.0	2.6	3.5	2.5	2.0	1.7	1.8	2.6	4.6	2.3	1.8	2.3
Median	4.6	3.8	4.7	2.9	2.5	2.6	4.2	4.1	4.6	3.3	2.6	2.6
Mean	4.6	3.6	4.8	3.0	2.6	2.7	3.9	3.9	4.6	3.2	2.6	2.7
Demesne Maximum[b]	6.6	4.2	6.1	4.0	3.5	4.0	5.0	4.6	4.6	4.3	3.4	3.3
Harvest Maximum[a]	10.3	8.5	10.5	5.1	7.3	9.6	11.1	8.8	6.6	6.3	6.0	6.4
All Demesnes												
Total Number of Demesnes	44	27	9	43	42	39	27	11	3	30	30	28
Total Number of Harvests	301	229	53	366	357	340	152	62	14	183	162	138
Harvest Minimum[a]	0.9	0.8	1.5	1.1	0.5	0	1.2	1.1	1.0	0.2	0.9	0
Demesne Minimum[b]	2.3	2.2	2.8	2.1	1.1	0.8	1.8	1.6	2.5	1.1	0.9	0.9
Median	4.4	3.7	3.5	3.0	2.5	2.4	4.0	3.6	3.0	3.3	2.7	2.6
Mean	4.5	3.7	3.9	3.1	2.7	2.5	4.2	3.5	3.4	3.2	2.7	2.5
Demesne Maximum[b]	6.8	7.1	6.1	4.1	4.1	4.6	9.1	4.9	4.6	4.5	5.1	5.0
Harvest Maximum[a]	10.3	8.5	10.5	5.1	7.3	9.6	11.1	8.8	6.6	6.3	6.0	6.4
Quartiles of Average Yields: 1	2.3–3.5	2.2–3.1	2.8–3.1	2.1–2.6	1.1–2.1	0.8–1.9	1.8–3.2	1.6–1.9	—	1.1–3.0	0.9–2.3	0.9–2.3
2	3.5–4.3	3.2–3.7	3.2–3.3	2.7–3.0	2.2–2.4	2.0–2.3	3.5–4.0	2.6–3.1	—	3.0–3.3	2.3–2.6	2.4–2.6
3	4.4–5.5	3.8–3.9	3.5–4.3	3.0–3.4	2.5–2.8	2.4–2.9	4.1–4.8	3.6–4.5	—	3.3–3.5	2.7–3.0	2.6–3.1
4	5.6–6.8	4.0–7.1	5.1–6.1	3.4–4.1	2.9–4.1	3.0–4.6	5.0–9.1	4.6–4.9	—	3.6–4.5	3.1–5.1	3.3–5.0

[a] Harvest Minimum (or Maximum) is the lowest (or highest) yield in a year ever observed.
[b] Demesne Minimum (or Maximum) is the average yield over all years which was the lowest (or highest) of all the demesnes.
Source: Accounts listed in Appendix.

scoring demesnes thereafter: while Loddon, Wicklewood, and Wy-mondham are the lowest-scoring demesnes before 1350, and Melton, Hevingham, and Thorpe Abbotts the lowest after 1350. When the three categories are mapped a strong spatial pattern becomes apparent (see Figure 1A). To the north and east of Norwich high-yielding demesnes tended to predominate—in fact 13 of the 14 high-yielding demesnes lay within the area—whereas south of that city moderate and low-yielding demesnes were the norm and it was here that virtually all the very lowest yields were recorded.

Nevertheless, although the yield ratio may evade the problems that arise from measures of indeterminate size it is not necessarily a true guide to arable productivity. For instance, as P. F. Brandon has demonstrated, variations in the rate at which seed was sown were capable of producing markedly different yields per acre even where yields per seed were identical.[14] To take the example of the two demesnes of Caister-cum-Markshall and Halvergate, both of which belonged to the Earl of Norfolk: during the last 30 years of the thirteenth century the net yield ratio of wheat was much the same at Caister as at Halvergate—4.0 as compared with 3.9—and yet, because the seeding rate at Halvergate was almost twice that at Caister, Halvergate obtained a much higher yield per acre—14.7 bushels as compared with 8.3 bushels. Since to any farmer it is the absolute amount of grain harvested which is of paramount importance, differences in seeding rates and the variations in yield per acre to which they may give rise clearly merit investigation.

This raises the whole thorny issue of the sizes of acres and bushels in use in the eastern half of Norfolk. As far as the size of acre is concerned, a smattering of references in manorial extents provides at least some direct evidence. For instance, at Ketteringham and Wymondham, to the southwest of Norwich, a statute acre with a perch size of 16 1/2 feet was in use, whereas as Martham and Brandiston, east and north of Norwich, a customary acre equivalent to 1.25 statute acres prevailed with a perch size of 18 1/2 feet.[15] How representative these four demesnes are of the area as a whole remains an open question, although they do demonstrate that the acres in use on some demesnes in eastern Norfolk were on the large side. The same may also be true of the size of bushels. In this case valuable indirect evidence is provided by Lord Beveridge's unpublished analysis of Norfolk grain prices.[16] It reveals that until about 1350 at Aldeby, Catton, Eaton, Martham, Monks Grange, Newton, Plumstead, Scratby, and Taverham, grain prices were on average a

---

[14] Brandon, "Cereal Yields," pp. 406–15. It is Brandon's view that "the yield ratio can deceive as much as it informs" (p. 414).

[15] Public Record Office, C 134 File 2 (14 and 16) 1 Edw. II; British Library, Stowe MS 936, f. 37; Magdalen College Oxford, Estate Papers 130/16.

[16] London School of Economics, Beveridge Price Data Box G9.

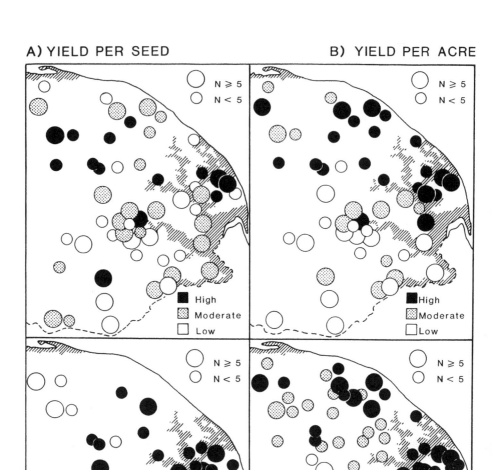

A) YIELD PER SEED

B) YIELD PER ACRE

C) FREQUENCY OF CROPPING

D) SEEDING RATES

FIGURE 1
ASPECTS OF ARABLE PRODUCTIVITY IN EASTERN NORFOLK, 1268–1427

Source: Accounts listed in Appendix.

Arable Productivity in Medieval England   387

sixth higher than elsewhere in the county, from which Beveridge inferred that a heaped or outsize bushel may have been in use on these demesnes. If the inference is valid then the outsize bushel will largely offset the outsize acre and there will be no serious exaggeration in the measurement of bushels per acre. In any case, the problem ceases to be of major moment if it can be ascertained that the differences in seeding rates and yields per acre are of a magnitude too great to be wholly or even largely explicable in terms of inconsistencies within Norfolk in the sizes of the units concerned.

In the case of seed sown per acre such real differences do emerge. Information on seeding rates has been obtained for 56 demesnes before 1350 and 43 demesnes after 1350 and is summarized in Table 2. As will be seen, in the earlier period seeding rates ranged between 2 and 4 bushels per acre for winter corn and legumes, between 3.7 and 6.6 bushels per acre for barley, and between 3.3 and 7.8 bushels per acre for oats. During the later period the range narrowed somewhat but the basic contrast between light and heavy seeding rates persisted. As with yields per seed a tripartite classification system has been employed, although in this case whether seeding rates were high, moderate, or low has been determined by means of terciles (see Table 2). When the three catego-

TABLE 2
MEAN SEEDING RATES IN EASTERN NORFOLK
(bushels per acre)

	Wheat	Rye	Maslin	Barley	Oats	Legumes
Pre–1350:						
Number of Demesnes	54	38	12	56	55	51
Mean Seeding Rate of Demesnes:						
Minimum	2.0	2.0	2.0	3.7	3.3	1.9
Median	2.7	2.4	2.7	4.9	5.0	2.8
Mean	2.9	2.6	2.8	4.9	5.2	2.9
Maximum	4.0	4.0	4.0	6.6	7.8	4.0
Lower Tercile	2.0–2.2	2.0–2.1	2.0–2.0	3.7–4.1	3.3–4.1	1.9–2.3
Middle Tercile	2.4–3.1	2.2–2.8	2.1–3.4	4.2–5.0	4.2–5.5	2.4–3.0
Upper Tercile	3.2–4.0	2.9–4.0	3.7–4.0	5.1–6.6	5.6–7.8	3.1–4.0
Post–1350:						
Number of Demesnes	38	15	3	43	41	40
Mean Seeding Rate of Demesnes:						
Minimum	2.0	2.0	2.0	2.7	2.7	1.8
Median	2.9	2.2	2.1	4.7	5.0	2.9
Mean	2.8	2.5	2.1	4.8	4.8	2.8
Maximum	4.0	3.1	2.2	6.2	6.6	4.0
Lower Tercile	2.0–2.4	2.0–2.0	2.0–2.0	2.7–4.0	2.7–4.0	1.8–2.3
Middle Tercile	2.5–3.0	2.1–2.5	2.1–2.1	4.1–5.2	4.1–5.5	2.5–3.0
Upper Tercile	3.2–4.0	3.0–3.1	2.2–2.2	5.3–6.2	5.6–6.6	3.1–4.0

Source: Accounts listed in Appendix.

ries are mapped, a spatial pattern emerges which is even stronger than that associated with yield per seed (see Figure 1D). Thus, stretching in an arc from Reedham in the southeast, via Hanworth and Gimingham in the northeast, to Hindringham in the northwest, lay a group of demesnes where seeding rates were invariably high: commonly up to 4 bushels an acre for winter corn and legumes, 6.6 bushels an acre for barley, and almost 8 bushels an acre for oats. Conversely, to the south and west of Norwich seeding rates were almost universally low, usually just 2 bushels an acre for winter corn and legumes and 4 bushels an acre for spring corn. Between these two extremes lay an intermediate zone where seeding rates were comparatively moderate: 2.5 to 3.0 bushels an acre for winter corn and legumes, and 4.0 to 5.5 bushels an acre for spring corn. What this pattern clearly demonstrates is that in the matter of seeding rates individual demesnes conformed to local practice and the practice was subject to wide variation within the area. The effect of the variation when combined with that already identified in yield per seed is therefore to produce marked contrasts in yield per acre, particularly where high seeding rates coincided with high yield ratios.

Accordingly, average yields per acre for wheat, barley, oats, and legumes of 10.8 to 13.6, 14.7 to 15.6, 12.2 to 13.1, and 7.2 to 7.5 bushels mask wide differences in the performances of individual demesnes (see Table 3). For instance, at Hemsby, Flegg, and Martham, the three highest-yielding demesnes before 1350, yields per acre averaged 22.5 to 25.1 bushels for wheat, 19.3 to 22.6 bushels for barley, 20.7 to 24.6 bushels for oats, and 10.7 to 18.9 bushels for legumes. Less than 25 miles away to the southeast, at Loddon, Wicklewood, and Wymondham, the equivalent yields were 4.6 to 6.7 bushels for wheat, 8.4 to 10.0 bushels for barley, 8.2 to 9.4 bushels for oats, and 3.5 to 4.2 bushels for legumes. Once again it has been found helpful to divide demesnes into three productivity groups according to whether yields per acre were high, moderate, or low (using the same system of quartile scoring as that first applied to yield per seed), and as with the previous two variables a geographical pattern emerges within the area (see Figure 1B). With rare exceptions all demesnes to the east and north of Norwich obtained yields per acre that are at least moderate and often high and it is within this area that all the highest-yielding demesnes—Hemsby, Flegg, Martham, Potter Heigham, Thwaite, Hoveton, and Blickling—are located. On the other hand, southeast and southwest of Norwich yields are everywhere lower, and it is in this area that yields per acre are generally at their nadir, as at Loddon, Bungay, Wicklewood, Wymondham, Intwood, Caister-cum-Markshall, Melton, Shotesham, and Thorpe Abbotts. That such sharp contrasts in yields per acre should exist within such a comparatively short distance of one another and in the absence of marked environmental variations is altogether remarkable. Moreover, the scale of the differences involved, often twofold in the case of

TABLE 3
EASTERN NORFOLK: YIELD PER ACRE

	Yield per Acre, Pre-1350						Yield per Acre, Post-1350					
	Wheat	Rye	Maslin	Barley	Oats	Legumes	Wheat	Rye	Maslin	Barley	Oats	Legumes
Excluding Demesnes with Fewer than Five Recorded Harvests												
Total Number of Demesnes	18	14	4	20	21	20	10	3	1	12	12	9
Total Number of Harvests	234	199	39	302	305	293	105	37	9	131	121	97
Harvest Minimum[a]	3.6	2.6	6.0	4.5	3.0	0	3.5	2.5	2.7	3.6	3.6	0
Demesne Minimum[b]	6.3	5.2	10.0	9.9	8.4	3.5	5.0	7.2	10.4	8.8	7.1	4.9
Median	13.4	8.4	18.4	14.8	12.3	7.3	10.3	9.3	10.4	14.4	11.7	7.5
Mean	13.6	8.8	17.0	14.8	13.1	7.4	10.8	8.9	10.4	15.1	12.2	7.5
Demesne Maximum[b]	25.1	12.7	21.4	22.6	21.8	14.7	15.0	10.1	10.4	24.0	19.0	10.0
Harvest Maximum[a]	34.0	24.0	33.2	29.5	33.5	26.0	22.2	22.0	15.5	29.0	40.0	22.8
All Demesnes												
Total Number of Demesnes	42	26	8	42	41	37	27	10	3	29	29	26
Total Number of Harvests	280	219	47	343	341	324	136	52	13	161	149	128
Harvest Minimum[a]	3.6	1.8	6.0	4.5	3.0	0	3.5	2.5	2.7	3.6	3.5	0
Demesne Minimum[b]	4.6	1.8	9.0	6.8	6.0	2.4	5.0	3.5	4.4	4.5	3.5	2.2
Median	13.4	8.1	12.0	14.8	12.3	6.7	11.2	7.8	5.0	15.6	12.1	7.5
Mean	13.3	9.3	13.8	14.7	13.0	7.2	12.0	8.0	6.6	15.6	13.2	7.5
Demesne Maximum[b]	25.1	23.0	21.4	23.4	24.6	18.0	36.4	12.2	10.4	24.0	25.3	13.8
Harvest Maximum[a]	34.0	28.0	33.2	29.5	33.5	26.0	36.4	22.0	15.5	29.0	40.0	22.8
Quartiles of Average Yields: 1	4.6–7.8	1.8–6.5	9.0–9.3	6.8–11.0	6.0–9.5	2.4–4.5	5.0–9.0	3.5–6.2	—	4.5–12.0	3.5–10.2	2.2–5.2
2	8.0–13.0	7.0–7.9	10.0–11.2	11.2–14.7	10.4–12.3	4.9–6.7	9.5–11.2	7.2–7.5	—	13.5–15.6	10.3–12.1	6.0–7.4
3	13.8–17.1	8.3–10.5	12.8–16.4	14.9–17.3	12.4–15.3	7.0–8.8	11.5–13.9	8.1–8.3	—	15.9–19.8	12.7–16.0	7.5–8.9
4	17.4–25.1	11.1–23.0	20.3–21.4	17.4–23.4	15.4–24.6	9.1–18.0	14.9–36.4	10.2–12.2	—	20.0–24.0	16.6–25.3	9.4–13.8

a Harvest Minimum (or Maximum) is the lowest (or highest) yield in a year ever observed.
b Demesne Minimum (or Maximum) is the average yield over all years which was the lowest (or highest) of all the demesnes.
Source: Accounts listed in Appendix.

yields of barley and oats and threefold in the case of yields of wheat and legumes, means that the pattern is unlikely to be a figment of the size of measures involved.

But not even yields per acre provide a true measure of productivity, for they do not take account of the frequency with which land was cropped, a factor no less significant than the rate at which it yielded when sown. For instance, with the same yield per acre, land cropped twice every three years will be one-third more productive than land cropped only every other year. To illustrate the difference that could in practice exist between output per sown acre and output per arable acre a comparison will be made between the Oxfordshire demesne of Cuxham and the Norfolk demesne of Martham.[17] These two demesnes have been chosen because they operated radically different rotational schemes which, in the case of Cuxham, produced some of the highest yield ratios yet documented in medieval England. Moreover, Cuxham has the merit of being one of the few demesnes for which sufficient relevant information is available in print to make such a comparison possible.

As will be seen from Table 4, yield ratios at Martham were in every case inferior to those at Cuxham and although a comparison between yields per sown acre is less one-sided, it still favors Cuxham. Whereas yields of wheat were much the same on both demesnes, Cuxham obtained by far the better yields of barley and legumes, and only in the case of oats were its yields worse than at Martham. If respective frequencies of cropping are taken into account, however, a very different verdict emerges. Cuxham employed a conventional three-course rotation of winter corn (exclusively wheat), spring crops, and fallow, while Martham employed a highly flexible and intensive rotational scheme in which cropping was virtually continuous. As far as can be judged, Martham fallowed only about 8 percent of all arable land each year during the late thirteenth and early fourteenth centuries, and devoted much of the rest to spring-sown crops, with barley predominating.[18] When these differences in the frequency and pattern of cropping are taken into account Martham's lower frequency of fallowing serves to give it the edge over Cuxham in terms of the net per acreage production of food. The relative figures are given in Table 4, and show that after allowance is made for the deduction of seed corn, an acre of arable was at least 17 percent more productive at Martham than at Cuxham. Moreover, this is very much a minimum figure, for there is a strong likelihood that the Cuxham yield statistics are not net of the

---

[17] Harvey, *A Medieval Oxfordshire Village*, pp. 39–58 and 164–65; also see Appendix to this article.

[18] For further details see Bruce M. S. Campbell, "Field Systems in Eastern Norfolk during the Middle Ages: A Study with Particular Relevance to the Demographic and Agrarian Changes of the Fourteenth Century" (Ph.D. thesis, University of Cambridge, 1975), pp. 79–95 and 105–17.

TABLE 4
COMPARISON OF MEAN ARABLE OUTPUT AT CUXHAM, OXFORDSHIRE (1289–1359)
AND MARTHAM, NORFOLK (1294–1340)

Crop	Mean Yield per Seed		Mean Yield per Statute Acre (in bushels)		Mean Percentage of Total Arable Acreage		Mean Output per 100 Acres Net of Seed Sown (in bushels)		Martham as Percentage of Cuxham
	Cuxham	Martham	Cuxham	Martham	Cuxham	Martham	Cuxham	Martham	
Wheat	6.4	5.7	16.0	18.0	33.3	16.5	449.5	244.2	54.3
Maslin		5.1		16.2		1.8		23.4	
Barley	5.8	3.2	22.0	15.4	4.1	52.9	74.6	555.5	744.6
Dredge	4.4		16.7		7.3		94.2		
Oats	3.1	2.8	10.2	16.6	16.2	2.9	111.7	30.5	27.3
Legumes	4.5	2.7	about 13.5	8.6	5.8	17.8	60.9	96.1	157.8
Winter Corn					33.3	18.3	449.5	267.6	59.5
Spring Corn					27.6	55.8	280.5	586.0	208.9
Cereals					60.9	74.1	730.0	853.6	116.9
All Crops Mentioned					66.7	91.9	790.9	949.7	120.1

Sources: Martham accounts listed in Appendix; P. D. A. Harvey, *Medieval Oxfordshire Village: Cuxham 1240–1400.*

deduction of tithe (whereas those for Martham are), and if Lord Beveridge is correct in supposing that a heaped or outsize bushel was in use at Martham, then the difference in Martham's favor would be greater by another 15 percent or so.[19]

Unfortunately, the frequency of cropping is the least satisfactorily recorded of the productivity variables, and information about it is particularly deficient for the period before 1350. Table 5 summarizes such information as can be garnered. From it two things would seem to be clear. First, Martham was by no means unusual in its high frequency of cropping. For the late thirteenth century there are several recorded instances of the total elimination of fallow, and throughout the period 1268–1427 it was quite exceptional for demesnes in eastern Norfolk to sow less than three-quarters of all arable each year.[20] After 1350, when account rolls begin to record the amount of fallow on a fairly consistent basis, the norm seems to have been to crop 80 to 90 percent of the arable each year, and there are grounds for believing that cropping had been even more intensive during the "high farming" years before 1350. Second, as with the other productivity variables, spatial differences in cropping practice appear to have prevailed within eastern Norfolk (see Figure 1C). Most significantly, the frequency of cropping appears to have been greatest in precisely the localities where yield ratios, seeding rates, and yields per acre were also highest. In other words, the productivity difference between demesnes such as Brandiston, Flegg, Martham, Hoveton, Newton, and Potter Heigham, on the one hand, and Lopham, Lakenham, Shotesham, Hevingham, and Eaton, on the other, was even greater than yields per acre would alone suggest. Thus, variations in the frequency of cropping served to accentuate still further the productivity differences to be found within the area.

This leaves one final aspect of productivity to be taken into account: the relative importance of the different crops being cultivated. Significant differences in productivity could exist, even where individual crop yields were the same, simply because high- and low-yielding crops were grown in different proportions. This factor has already been seen in operation in the comparison between Cuxham and Martham, where the very much higher yields of barley and legumes obtained at Cuxham were largely offset because the two crops occupied only a small proportion of the total sown acreage. Straightforward comparisons of yield, without reference to the relative importance of the different crops, are therefore of doubtful validity. What is required is a system of weighting yields, and this is most satisfactorily achieved by relating the

---

[19] "It seems clear that the rector's tenth part of the crop was taken straight from the field after harvest. This means that to find the amount actually reaped, one-ninth of the issue recorded in the rolls must be added to it." Harvey, *A Medieval Oxfordshire Village*, p. 52.

[20] This phenomenon is discussed in detail in Bruce M. S. Campbell, "Agricultural Progress in Medieval England: Some Evidence from Eastern Norfolk," *Economic History Review*, 2nd ser., 36 (Feb. 1983), 26–46.

TABLE 5
EASTERN NORFOLK: FREQUENCY OF CROPPING

| Demesne | Period | Number of Years | Percentage of Arable Cropped | |
			Mean	Range
Pre-1350				
Bressingham	1272–1273	1	73.3	
Lopham	1268–1306	18	83.3	71.1–92.1
Ditchingham	1269–1306	5	85.3	83.4–86.8
Thornage	1326–1327	1	89.3	
South Walsham	1270–1297	9	93.2	86.6–100.0
Acle	1268–1280	7	94.8	88.6–98.7
Heigham by Norwich	1302–1307	2	96.8	96.1–97.5
Brandiston	1316–1338	3	98.2	95.3–100.0
Halvergate	1268–1274	4	100.0	100.0–100.0
Flegg	1340–1341	1	100.0	
10 Demesnes:				
Minimum			73.3	
Mean			91.4	
Maximum			100.0	
Range			71.1–100.0	
Post-1350				
Thurning	1374–1375	1	74.5	
Lakenham	1366–1367	1	78.3	
Hindringham	1363–1416	5	80.5	77.1–84.0
Reedham	1394–1395	1	81.0	
Hindolveston	1358–1416	18	81.9	66.4–87.3
Shotesham	circa 1353	1	82.2	
Hevingham	1357–1358	1	82.7	
Plumstead	1359–1420	15	84.0	72.3–89.0
Eaton	1358–1410	9	84.1	68.4–90.8
Heigham by Norwich	circa 1381	1	84.1	
Aldeby	1403–1420	7	85.2	77.5–88.7
Burgh in Flegg	1390–1391	1	85.4	
Hoveton	1392–1422	2	86.4	83.7–89.2
Martham	1355–1420	19	86.6	72.1–97.1
Flegg	1351–1428	14	86.7	74.8–100.0
Ludham	circa 1355	1	86.7	
Ashby	1378–1392	2	86.8	84.8–88.9
Taverham	1362–1374	10	87.2	81.6–91.9
Newton	1366–1426	2	88.9	86.0–91.9
Scottow	circa 1365	1	89.4	
Thwaite	circa 1386–1387	1	89.6	
Haveringland	1356–1365	3	89.7	82.3–94.4
Scratby	1360–1363	2	90.2	86.1–94.3
Potter Heigham	1389–1390	1	90.6	
North Walsham	1367–1427	5	92.2	90.1–96.3
25 Demesnes:				
Minimum			74.5	
Mean			85.4	
Maximum			92.2	
Range			66.4–100.0	

Source: Accounts listed in Appendix.

yield per acre of each crop to the percentage it occupied of the total arable acreage (just as calculated for Cuxham and Martham in Table 4). Within eastern Norfolk the weighting has been done, not for each individual demesne but for two regional groupings: a group of 36 demesnes in the east and north of the area where high yields predominated, and a group of 26 demesnes in the southeast and west of the area where lower yields prevailed (see Table 6).[21] These two areas will be referred to hereafter as northeastern and southeastern Norfolk and were defined according to yields per seed and per acre and frequency of cropping. The data tabulated in Table 6 are mean figures calculated from the individual averages for each demesne within these two areas, both before and after 1350.

After what has gone before the contrasts revealed by Table 6—both between the productivity of the two areas concerned and in the results obtained by different methods of measuring that productivity—are hardly unexpected. By whatever criterion is adopted (yield per seed, yield per acre, or output per 100 arable acres) northeastern Norfolk emerges as by far the more productive of these two areas. Precisely how much more productive it was, however, depends upon how that productivity is measured. Thus, although yields per seed were consistently better for northeastern than southeastern Norfolk, the difference involved is on average only one-fifth. In the case of yields per acre the difference is very much greater; partly because of higher seeding rates, yields per acre in northeastern Norfolk were on average 70 percent higher than those in the southeast. But it is output per 100 arable acres which reveals the greatest and, arguably, truest contrast, for differences in both the frequency and pattern of cropping served to make arable land almost exactly twice as productive in the northeast. This contrast appears to have been equally pronounced both before and after 1350.

III

Although the results obtained by this analysis relate to a comparatively small area, they nevertheless hold valuable lessons for our understanding of demesne agriculture in the country as a whole. Not the least important of these lessons is that traditional approaches to the study of medieval arable productivity are capable of considerable refinement.

[21] The 36 demesnes in northeastern Norfolk are Acle, Aldborough, Antingham, Ashby, Blicking, Brandiston, Burgh, Flegg, Foxley, Gimingham, Gresham, Halvergate, Hanworth, Hautbois, Haveringland, Hemsby, Hindolveston, Hindringham, Hoveton, Knapton, Langham, Lessingham, Martham, Monks Grange, Newton, North Walsham, Plumstead, Potter Heigham, Reedham, Saxthorpe, Scratby, South Walsham, Suffield, Thurning, Thwaite, and Worstead.

In southeastern Norfolk the 26 are Aldeby, Arminghall, Attleborough, Bressingham, Bungay, Caister, Ditchingham, Earsham, Eaton, Forncett, Framingham, Heigham, Hevingham, Intwood, Keswick, Lakenham, Loddon, Lopham, Melton, Seething, Shotesham, Taverham, Thorpe Abbotts, Tivetshall, Wicklewood, and Wymondham.

TABLE 6
COMPARISON OF MEAN ARABLE OUTPUT BETWEEN NORTHEAST AND SOUTHEAST NORFOLK, 1268-1427

Crop	Mean Yield per Seed		Mean Yield per Acre (in bushels)		Estimated Percentage of Total Arable Acreage Devoted to these Crops		Mean Output per 100 Acres Net of Seed Sown (in bushels)		Northeast as Percentage of Southeast
	Northeast	Southeast	Northeast	Southeast	Northeast	Southeast	Northeast	Southeast	
Pre-1350									
Wheat	4.97	3.95	17.56	8.69	12.38	18.03	173.69	117.01	148.44
Rye	4.03	3.50	12.74	6.85	3.44	8.83	32.96	43.20	76.30
Maslin	4.09	3.20	14.49	9.0	0.55	0.33	6.02	2.04	295.10
Barley	3.19	2.91	17.44	11.73	48.05	30.56	575.16	235.28	244.46
Oats	2.56	2.51	15.46	10.40	12.47	15.56	117.47	97.35	120.67
Legumes	2.73	2.34	9.26	4.79	15.72	11.35	92.28	31.13	296.43
Winter Corn					16.37	27.19	212.67	162.25	131.08
Spring Corn					60.52	46.12	692.63	332.63	208.23
Cereals					76.89	73.31	905.30	494.88	182.93
All Crops Mentioned					92.61	84.66	997.58	526.01	189.65
Post-1350									
Wheat	4.48	3.66	14.28	8.02	12.62	13.14	139.99	76.59	182.78
Rye	3.67	3.44	8.70	7.71	1.24	7.21	7.85	39.43	19.91
Barley	3.50	2.67	18.33	10.49	46.84	39.35	613.27	258.18	237.54
Oats	2.93	2.21	16.04	7.79	10.37	12.55	109.57	53.53	204.69
Legumes	2.92	2.36	8.75	5.23	14.92	10.53	85.84	31.74	270.45
Winter Corn					13.86	20.35	147.84	116.02	127.43
Spring Corn					57.21	51.90	722.84	311.71	231.90
Cereals					71.07	72.25	870.68	427.73	203.56
All Crops Mentioned					86.0	82.78	956.52	459.47	208.18

Source: Accounts listed in Appendix.

396

In the first place the yield ratio stands revealed as a far from infallible guide to productivity levels prevailing on different demesnes and in different localities. As the comparisons between Cuxham and Martham and northeastern and southeastern Norfolk have shown, yield ratios may understate and even misrepresent the differences in relative output involved.[22] No study of arable productivity can therefore be complete which restricts itself to a consideration of the ratio of yield sown to grain harvested: if real differences in productivity are to be identified account must also be taken of the seeding rate, frequency of cropping, and relative importance of the different crops grown. J. Z. Titow has objected that the last variable is irrelevant "in so far as productivity as such is concerned," but this presupposes that the intrinsic fertility of the land is in some way measurable.[23] In fact it is not. Soil fertility was only one of a number of factors which determined the levels of output recorded in account rolls. Among the others are the weather, the incidence of pests and diseases, the techniques of husbandry, level of labor inputs, and efficiency of management. Since none of these variables ever remained constant, and explicit information is only available for some of them, the influence of soil fertility upon yields cannot be isolated.[24] Certainly, any claim that soil fertility was declining must be based on a great deal more than the evidence of yield ratios alone. *De facto*, therefore, it is the productivity of agriculture rather than the fertility of the soil of which the account rolls admit precise measurement and upon which, accordingly, it is most sensible to concentrate. Indeed, a keener understanding of prevailing levels of arable production has much to contribute to the debate concerning the economic consequences of thirteenth-century population growth.[25]

An essential corollary of improved methods of measuring arable productivity is that spatial variations in productivity should be given explicit attention. Only then will it be possible to evaluate the experience of particular demesnes and estates. For instance, in the virtual absence of other published yield figures, F. G. Davenport's classic study of the Earl of Norfolk's manor at Forncett has for long been taken as typical of productivity levels in the county as a whole.[26] Yet, as the foregoing analysis has revealed, Forncett was typical of neither its locality nor its estate, for its yield ratios were the highest obtained by

[22] This bears out Brandon's 1972 observation that "the use of yield ratios as indexes of medieval productivity is open to serious objections which bring into question their general validity." "Cereal Yields," p. 414.

[23] Titow, *Winchester Yields*, p. 11.

[24] For an examination of the relationship between changes in production methods and changes in yields, see Campbell, "Agricultural Progress."

[25] M. M. Postan, *The Medieval Economy and Society: An Economic History of Britain, 1100–1500* (London, 1972); Miller and Hatcher, *Medieval England*; Hallam, *Rural England*.

[26] Davenport, *A Norfolk Manor*. See, for instance, the table of yield ratios in Miller and Hatcher, *Medieval England*, p. 216.

any demesne in southeastern Norfolk or any of the 16 demesnes which made up the Earl's Norfolk property. Nevertheless, even this larger "sample" of 16 demesnes is unrepresentative of the area as a whole. The problem arises from the distribution of the demesnes, for two-thirds of them were located in the southeastern area of low productivity, where they included some of the lowest-yielding demesnes recorded. Similarly, the ten demesnes which the Prior of Norwich held in eastern Norfolk are no more representative of the area, for no less than seven of them were located in the northeastern area of high productivity, where two of them—Martham and Hemsby—rank among the most productive demesnes of all. Plainly, failure to recognize the contrasting distribution of the two estates within the area could foster false notions, not only about the productivity of the area as a whole and the variations within it, but also about the relative productivity of Church and lay estates. Yet, as has been demonstrated here, enough account rolls survive for the agricultural context of individual demesnes and estates to be reconstructed in some detail and a more valid evaluation thereby made of their respective productivities.

Perhaps the most significant conclusion which emerges is that no particular type of estate—Church or lay, great or small—was intrinsically any more productive than any other.[27] For instance, among the owners of the most productive demesnes are found the Prior of Norwich, Abbot of St. Benet at Holm, Earl of Norfolk, Duke of Lancaster, Roger de Gyney, and Richard de Playes; while among the owners of the least productive demesnes are found the Prior, Almoner, and Bishop of Norwich, Abbot of St. Benet at Holm, Abbot of St. Edmundsbury, Earl of Norfolk, Simon de Hedersete, and William Clere. The inference to be drawn would seem to be that where demesnes belonging to the greatest estates were highly productive this had more to do with the farming region within which they were located than with any supposedly superior command over resources, or greater commitment to the cause of agricultural progress, on the part of their landlord. This was undoubtedly why all but the highest-yielding demesnes of Prior Henry of Lakenham, a great and reputedly high-farming churchman, were surpassed in productivity by the demesne at Brandiston, the property of Roger de Gyney, a minor local lord.[28] Thus, in most practical aspects of husbandry individual demesnes apparently conformed to established local practice; insofar as their management was influenced by their landlord it was probably with regard to such matters of general estate policy as the taking-on or letting-out of land, fixed

---

[27] This would appear to comply with Britnell's observation that "in the important matter of their investments and improvements, the distinction between small estates and larger ones seems to be of no great moment." "Minor Landlords in Medieval England," p. 21.

[28] Eric Stone, "Profit and Loss Accountancy at Norwich Cathedral Priory," *Transactions of the Royal Historical Society*, 5th ser., 12 (1962), 25–48.

398

capital investment in land reclamation and building construction, marketing of produce, and concentration upon particular aspects of livestock production.[29] Since decisions as to which crops were grown and how they were cultivated were probably delegated to the local reeve or bailiff in charge of the demesne, it follows that the man who owned a demesne was probably less important than the man who ran it, who in turn was probably the creature of prevailing local husbandry practices. This inference prompts speculation as to the respective roles of demesne farms and peasant holdings in the evolution of farming regions.

How do the two very different productivity regions in eastern Norfolk compare with arable productivity elsewhere in medieval England? In the current state of knowledge it is only possible to give a provisional answer. The problem lies in the dearth of published studies giving information on both yields per acre and crop rotations. Cuxham remains the most fully documented demesne, and although its three-course rotation ranks as one of the most productive hitherto recorded, as has been seen, it was significantly less productive than the more intensive rotational scheme operated in northeastern Norfolk. Other farming regions did exist where rotations were similarly intensive and flexible, notably northern and northeastern Kent and coastal Sussex. Although yields per acre recorded on estates in these areas were high, in neither case did they match those obtained in northeastern Norfolk. Thus, in the early 1290s seven Kentish demesnes belonging to Canterbury Cathedral Priory obtained yields per acre on average 25 percent below contemporary yields in northeastern Norfolk.[30] Likewise, in the second half of the fourteenth century four of Battle Abbey's demesnes in coastal Sussex obtained yields per acre of wheat and barley which were on average 7.5 percent lower than equivalent yields in northeastern Norfolk.[31] Where yields per acre do bear much more favorable comparison, however, is on the Countess of Aumale's demesnes at Bovecumbe and Penne on the Isle of Wight (as also on her Holderness properties of Little Humber and Keyingham), and on the Crowland Abbey demesne at Oakington in Cambridgeshire.[32] On this last demesne, although yields per acre of oats were worse than in northeastern Norfolk, yields of wheat were about the same, and those of barley were much better; there was even some experimentation with the elimination of fallows. On available information it would seem that whereas a very few arable farming systems may have matched in productivity that of northeastern Norfolk, none exceeded it and most fell below it. In contrast, virtually

[29] For instance Dyer, *Lords and Peasants*, pp. 64–66 and 114–18.

[30] Ann Smith, "Regional Differences in Crop Production in Mediaeval Kent," *Archaeologia Cantiana*, 78 (1963), 147–60.

[31] Brandon, "Cereal Yields," p. 417.

[32] Mate, "Profit and Productivity," p. 332; Ugawa, *Lay Estates*, pp. 134–39; Page, *Crowland Abbey*, pp. 329–30.

the opposite holds true of arable productivity in southeastern Norfolk. In this area yields per acre of wheat, barley, and oats averaged fully 14 percent below the dismal level prevailing on the estates of the Bishop of Winchester.[33]

In view of the miserable performance of arable husbandry in southeastern Norfolk during the Middle Ages it comes as no surprise to find that by the seventeenth century "farms in this region consisted mostly of pasture and meadow, with a very small proportion of arable land."[34] This changeover from arable to pastoral farming seems to have occurred during the fifteenth and sixteenth centuries, and insofar as its antecedents may be traced to the thirteenth and fourteenth centuries, they are to be found in the low yields of grain rather than any embryonic specialization in livestock rearing. In the late thirteenth and early fourteenth centuries animal ratios on demesnes in the area averaged 32.1 (as compared with 33.3 in eastern Norfolk as a whole), which indicates a level of stocking both absolutely and relatively low.[35] Northeastern Norfolk, on the other hand, has maintained its regional identity as one of the premier arable districts of England until the present day. By the beginning of the nineteenth century, figures quoted by Arthur Young in his report to the Board of Agriculture show that there had been significant improvements in the yields of all crops and in those of spring corn in particular.[36] Thus, in the interval between the fourteenth and the nineteenth centuries wheat yields in northeastern Norfolk rose by two-thirds, barley yields doubled, and oats yields in some instances actually tripled (on the evidence of Overton's work on East Anglian grain yields the bulk of this improvement probably took place during the seventeenth and eighteenth centuries).[37] The vicinity of Hemsby, Flegg, and Martham seems to have maintained its position throughout as the highest-yielding district in the county, with yields of barley and wheat approximately 25 and 50 percent above the county average. By the time that Arthur Young was writing, this area's advantage over the rest of the county had perhaps been somewhat reduced.

Certain obvious explanations of the differences within eastern Norfolk suggest themselves. Plainly, soil type must have exercised considerable general influence. Within eastern Norfolk soils vary much more than the area's uneventful terrain might suggest, and a general relation-

---

[33] Farmer, "Grain Yields on the Winchester Manors," p. 565.

[34] Joan Thursk, ed., *The Agrarian History of England and Wales, IV, 1500–1640* (Cambridge, 1967), p. 47.

[35] Only 5 of the 38 demesnes belonging to the Bishop of Winchester had lower animal ratios than this, and the average for the estate as a whole over the period 1325–1349 was 72.7; see, Farmer, "Grain Yields on the Winchester Manors," p. 563.

[36] Arthur Young, *General View of the Agriculture of the County of Norfolk* (London, 1804), pp. 250–308.

[37] Overton, "Crop Yields," pp. 375–76.

ship can be seen between the distributions of best arable soils and most productive demesnes, and vice versa. It was these soil differences which underlay northeastern Norfolk's continued specialization in intensive grain production after southeastern Norfolk had changed over to dairying. Related to soils, and also exerting an important influence upon arable productivity, was agricultural technology. Again, significant variations may be recognized within the area. On the whole, northeastern Norfolk employed heavier seeding rates, cropped land more frequently, grew more spring corn, and sowed more legumes than the southeastern area.[38] Nevertheless, although a general relationship may be demonstrated between arable productivity, soil types, and agricultural technology, the relationship breaks down under closer inspection. Soils and technology alone, for instance, do not adequately explain why productivity on the Cellarer of Norwich's demesne at Scratby should have been so much worse than on other demesnes in Flegg, nor why the performance of the Earl of Norfolk's demesnes at South Walsham, Acle, and Halvergate should have been so disappointing. Similarly, it is puzzling that favorable animal ratios and the cultivation of large quantities of legumes should have produced high yield ratios at Forncett but not at Tivetshall, Earsham, and Bungay, just a few miles away. No simple explanation of productivity differences will therefore suffice. Apart from soil type and agricultural technology, account must also be taken of such human variables as the level of labor inputs, quality of labor, and efficiency of management, for they were capable of moderating environmental disadvantages and would have exerted a powerful influence upon the nature and efficiency of agricultural technology.[39] Since information on many of these variables may also be obtained from account rolls, it should prove possible for medieval agricultural historians to refine not only how they measure productivity, but also how they explain the results thus obtained.

---

[38] Agricultural technology in this area is discussed in detail in Campbell, "Agricultural Progress."

[39] Ibid.

APPENDIX

Demesne	Landlord	Number of Extant Accounts	Period Covered	Maximum Number of Recorded Harvests		References*
				Pre-1350	Post-1350	
Acle	Earl of Norfolk	7	1268–1280	4		PRO SC 6/929/1-7
Aldborough		1	1430–1431		1	PRO SC 6/929/8
Aldeby	Prior of Aldeby	12	1399–1424		8	NRO MS 21065-77 34 E5
Antingham		1	1409–1410			NRO MS 6031 16 B8
Arminghall	Obedientiary, Norwich Cathedral	1	1347–1348	1		NRO DCN R 232B 4092
Ashby	Abbot of St. Benet	2	1378–1392		2	NRO Diocesan Est/9
Attleborough	Earl of Norfolk	8	1274–1295	4		PRO SC 6/929/14-21
Attlebridge	Obedientiary, Norwich Cathedral	3	1307–c. 1330	4		NRO R 232B 4096-8
Aylmerton		1	1345–1346			NRO WKC 2/24
Bawburgh	Obedientiary, Norwich Cathedral	8	1274–1338	2		NRO DCN R 232B 3338-42, 4099-102, 4577
Blicking		3	1410–1421		2	NRO NRS 10196 25 A1 and 10535 25 B5
Brandiston	Lord Roger de Gyney	4	1316–1348	4		MCO Estate Records 166/3-12
Bressingham	Earl of Norfolk and Lord John de Verdum	6	1272–1402	2	2	PRO SC 6/931/21-23; BL Add. Charters 16535-38
Briston		1	1300–1301			PRO SC 6/931/24
Bungay (Suffolk)	Earl of Norfolk	13	1269–1306	7		PRO SC 6/991/16-28
Burgh in Flegg	The Crown	2	1330–1391		1	PRO SC 6/931/27-8
Burston		1	1384–1385			BL Add. Charter 26530
Caister-cum-Markshall	Earl of Norfolk	16	1269–1300	9		PRO SC 6/932/11-26
Catton	Prior of Norwich	6	1265–1281	1		NRO DCN R 233D 5052 and R 234D 4450-55; L'Estrange Collection I B 4
Cawston		1	1331–1332			PRO SC 6/933/11
Costessey		3	1278–1292			PRO SC 6/933/13-4
Crownthorpe	Lord William de Crungethorpe	4	1319–1348			NRO Kimberley Collection (7/5/74)
Diss		1	1351–1352			PRO SC 6/935/1
Ditchingham	Earl of Norfolk	17	1269–1306	11		PRO SC 6/933/20-9 and 6/934/1-9
Earsham	Earl of Norfolk	15	1269–1306	9		PRO SC 6/934/12-39
Eaton	Prior of Norwich	43	1263–1423	26	9	NRO DCN R233A 4567-93 and R 232C 5176; *Proficuum Maneriorum*; L'Estrange Collection I B 4; BLO Ms Rolls, Norfolk 20-45

APPENDIX

Demesne	Landlord	Number of Extant Accounts	Period Covered	Maximum Number of Recorded Harvests		References*
				Pre-1350	Post-1350	
Flegg	Abbot of St. Benet	17	1341–1428	1	11	NRO Diocesan Est/9
Forncett	Earl of Norfolk	15	1272–1309	8		PRO SC 6/935/2-17 and 6/1121/1
Foxley	Earl of Norfolk	1	1305–1306	1		PRO SC 6/935/19
Framingham	Earl of Norfolk	18	1271–1308	9		PRO SC 6/935/20-37 and 6/1121/1
Gimingham	Duke of Lancaster	10	1358–1398		7	PRO DL 29 288/4719-20, 4734, and 289/4744; NRO MS 6001 16 A6 and NRS 11331-2 26 B6; NRS 11058-60 25 E2 and 11069 25 E3
Gresham	Earl of Norfolk	1	1306–1307	1		PRO SC 6/936/1
Halvergate	Earl of Norfolk	16	1268–1306	10		PRO SC 6/936/2-17
Hanworth	Earl of Norfolk	22	1272–1306	18		PRO SC 6/936/18-32 and 937/1-10
Hardley	Abbot of St. Benet	1	1295–1296	1		NRO Diocesan Est/2
Hautbois	Abbot of St. Benet	3	c. 1290–1373		1	NRO Diocesan Est/2
Haveringland	Prior of Horsham St. Faith	4	1356–1377		3	BL Add. Charters 15199-202
Heigham by Norwich	Abbot of St. Benet	3	1302–1381		1	NRO Diocesan Est/2
Hemsby	Prior of Norwich	18	1265–1335	19		NRO DCN R233D 5144 and 233B 4651-65; *Proficuum Maneriorum*; L'Estrange Collection I B 4; BLO MS Rolls, Norfolk 47
Hevingham	Bishop of Norwich	7	1327–1418		1	NRO NRS 14748 and 14751 29 D4; DCN R 232 B 4138; NRS 14664 29 D2
Hindolveston	Prior of Norwich	54	1255–1416	24	20	NRO DCN R 233C 4739 and *Proficuum Maneriorum*; L'Estrange Collection I B 4
Hindringham	Prior of Norwich	33	1255–1423	24	6	NRO DCN R 233C 4883-920 and *Proficuum Maneriorum*; L'Estrange Collection I B 4
Hingham		2	1271–1304			BL Campb. IX 8; NRO Kimberley Collection
Horsham St. Faith	Prior of Horsham St. Faith	1	1407–1408			NRO NRS 19517 42 C 6

APPENDIX

Demesne	Landlord	Number of Extant Accounts	Period Covered	Maximum Number of Recorded Harvests		References*
				Pre-1350	Post-1350	
Hoveton	Abbot of St. Benet	3	1295–1422		2	NRO Diocesan Est/2; Church Commissioners 101426
Intwood	Sir Simon de Hedersete	5	1308–1426	3		NRO NRS 23350-2 Z 97
Keswick	Lord William Clere	13	1274–1377		7	NRO NRS 23357-8 Z 98
Knapton	Lord Richard de Playes	2	1345–1348	2		GCW XV 53 98-9
Lakenham	Obedientiary, Norwich Cathedral	2	1295–1367		1	NRO DCN R. 232B 4127-8
Langham	Bishop of Norwich	4	1326–1354	1	2	NRO MS 1307-8 2 B3 and 1554-5 1 C 1
Lessingham	Abbot of Bec	2	1290–1298	1		ECR Vol. 49 242-3
Loddon	Earl of Norfolk	5	1282–1296	2		PRO SC 6/937/22-6
Long Stratton		1	1410–1411			BL Add. Charter 18554
Lopham	Earl of Norfolk	18	1268–1306	11		PRO SC 6/937/27-33 and 6/938/1-11
Ludham	Abbot of St. Benet	1	c. 1354–1355			NRO Diocesan Est/2
Martham	Prior of Norwich	56	c. 1261–1423	30	24	NRO DCN R 233C 4940-64 and 232C 5176-7; *Proficuum Maneriorum*; L'Estrange Collection I B 4; NNAS 5889-903 20 D1, 5904-15 20 D2, and 5916 20 D3
Melton	Obedientiary, Norwich Cathedral	3	1333–1370	1	2	NRO DCN R 233D 5015-7
Monks Grange	Prior of Norwich	27	1255–1335	26		NRO DCN R 233D 5027-52 and 232C 5176-7; *Proficuum Maneriorum*; L'Estrange Collection I B 4
Newton	Prior of Norwich	10	1273–1426	13	4	NRO DCN R 233D 5053-62 and *Proficuum Maneriorum*
North Walsham	Abbot of St. Benet	5	1367–1427		4	NRO Diocesan Est/12
Ormesby		3	1294–1338			NRO DCN R 232B 4130-2
Plumstead	Prior of Norwich	44	c. 1263–1420	24	19	NRO DCN R 233D 5101-43, 232C 5176-7 and *Proficuum Maneriorum*
Potter Heigham	Abbot of St. Benet	1	1389–1390		1	NRO Diocesan Est/11
Reedham		11	1377–1395		8	BL Add. Charters 26, 852-62
Saxthorpe		8	c. 1296–1386	2		NRO NRS 19647-61 42 D7, 19677-9 42 E3, and 19690 42 E4
Scottow	Abbot of St. Benet	1	c. 1364–1365			NRO Diocesan Est/11

APPENDIX

Demesne	Landlord	Number of Extant Accounts	Period Covered	Maximum Number of Recorded Harvests		References*
				Pre-1350	Post-1350	
Scratby	Obedientiary, Norwich Cathedral	12	1296–1363	3	3	NRO DCN R 233D 5145-56
Seething	Earl of Norfolk	2	1283–1290	1		PRO SC 6/943/10-11
Shotesham	Abbot of St. Benet	1	1353–1369		1	NRO Diocesan Est/11
South Walsham	Earl of Norfolk	11	1268–1297	5		PRO SC 6/944/21-31
Suffield	Earl of Norfolk	11	1272–1300	4		PRO SC 6/944/1-11
Tacolneston	Formerly Lord Peter de Unedale	1	1354–1355			Pomeroy & Sons, Wymondham
Taverham	Prior of Norwich	55	c. 1255–1424	29	19	NRO DCN R 232A 5307-36, 232C 5337-58, and 5176-7; Proficuum Maneriorum; L'Estrange Collection 1 B 4
Thornage	Bishop of Norwich	1	1326–1327			NRO DCN R 232B 4143
Thorpe Abbotts	Abbot of St. Edmundsbury	18	1336–1379	7	11	NRO WAL 478-95 274 x 6
Thurning	Lady Aline Burnel	3	1319–1375	1		NRO NRS 2796-8 12 E2
Thwaite	Abbot of St. Benet	1	c. 1386–1387			NRO Diocesan Est/2
Tivetshall	Abbot of St. Edmundsbury	13	1335–1380	3	9	NRO WAL 1245-9 288 x 1, 1250-2 288 x 2, and 451-5 274 x 3
Tunstead	Obedientiary, Norwich Cathedral	2	1358–1360			PRO DL 29 288/4719-20
Wicklewood	Obedientiary, Norwich Cathedral	1	1337–1338	1		NRO DCN R 232B 4136
Worstead	Obedientiary, Norwich Cathedral	3	1273–1321			NRO DCN R 232B 5428-30; L'Estrange Collection 1 B 4
Wymondham	Abbot of Wymondham and Lord Peter de Unedale	22	1290–1363	22	2	NRO NRS 10107-8 22 F5; 11277-80 26 B 1; 18508-22 33 D3; 14038 28 F6; 18523-30 33 D4; 8811-2 21 E4; 18534 and 18544-5 33 D5; 18565-6 33 D6

* Abbreviations:
BLO   Bodleian Library, Oxford
BL   British Library
ECR   Eton College Records
GCW   St. George's Chapel, Windsor
MCO   Magdalen College, Oxford
NRO   Norfolk Record Office
PRO   Public Record Office

IV

Land, labour, livestock, and productivity trends in English seignorial agriculture, 1208–1450

I The historiography of pre-industrial agricultural productivity

Accounts of agricultural productivity change on opposite sides of the English Channel during the pre-industrial centuries present an historiographic contrast. In northern France and the Low Countries, for instance, analysis of tithe data has suggested a predominantly positive relationship between population trends and output per unit of land, but an essentially negative relationship between population trends and output per unit of labour, during the five-century period between the start of the thirteenth and the end of the seventeenth centuries.[1] Thus, an initial peak in the gross output of agriculture has been identified which coincides with the medieval demographic maximum of the opening decades of the fourteenth century. Not only was the cultivated area at full stretch at this time, but grain yields also appear to have reached a secular high under the stimulus of such labour-intensive techniques as manuring and marling, weeding, and the cultivation of fallow *inhoks* with legumes and rape. Their collective effect was to raise

I am grateful to Jenitha Orr and John Power for research assistance, to John Langdon and Mark Overton for supplying data, and to the participants of the Bellagio workshop for their helpful comments on an earlier version of this paper. Part of the research upon which this paper is based was undertaken whilst in the tenure of a Research Fellowship of the Economic and Social Research Council of the United Kingdom.

1 H. Van der Wee,'Introduction – the agricultural development of the Low Countries as revealed by the tithe and rent statistics, 1250–1800', pp. 1–23 in *idem* and E. Van Cauwenberghe, eds., *Productivity of land and agricultural innovation in the Low Countries (1250–1800)*, Leuven, 1978; E. Le Roy Ladurie, 'The end of the middle ages: the work of Guy Bois and Hugues Neveux', pp. 71–92 in *idem* and J. Goy, *Tithe and agrarian history from the fourteenth to the nineteenth centuries: an essay in comparative history*, Cambridge, 1982.

supplies of soil nitrogen, which, according to R. Shiel, was the single greatest constraint upon yields at this time.[2]

In the Low Countries H. Van der Wee has argued that adoption of these labour-intensive techniques was promoted by the subdivision of holdings, so that on average the smaller the size of holding, the higher the productivity of land, although the attendant low labour productivity has led B. H. Slicher van Bath to describe this as 'scarcely controlled poverty'.[3] With respect to yields, H. Neveux has demonstrated for the Cambrésis region of northern France that the distinctive feature of this period was not that high yields became universal, but that the range of yields moved significantly upwards to 10–21 hectolitres per hectare.[4] Certainly, yields per unit of seed (yield ratios) obtained at this time by Thierry d'Hireçon on his estates in Artois were impressive by any standard of pre-industrial agriculture.[5] Such high yields were, however, very much the product of an abundance of cheap labour and as, with the late medieval demographic recession, labour became progressively scarcer and dearer, so yields fell.

In France the fall in yields was both immediate and pronounced, although offset, it is believed, by a rise in labour productivity. Land fell out of cultivation and – notwithstanding a retreat from poorer soils and an enhanced ratio of grassland to arable – even that which remained under the plough became less productive as husbandry declined in intensity.[6] By the mid fifteenth century yields in the Cambrésis had fallen to 4–18 hectolitres per hectare.[7] Although there was some recovery in the late fifteenth and early sixteenth centuries, again under the stimulus of population growth, Neveux maintains that yields did not

---

2 R. Shiel, above, p. 51. *

3 Van der Wee, 'Introduction', p. 4; B. H. Slicher van Bath, 'The rise of intensive husbandry in the Low Countries', pp. 130–53 in J. S. Bromley and E. H. Kossmann, eds., *Britain and the Netherlands: papers delivered to the Oxford–Netherlands historical conference 1959*, London, 1960.

4 H. Neveux, *Les Grains du Cambrésis, fin du XIVe–début du XVIIe siécles. Vie et déclin d'une structure économique*, Paris, 1980, cited in Le Roy Ladurie, 'The end of the middle ages', pp. 83–5. For a comparable upward shift in maximum yields within English agriculture during the seventeenth century see P. Glennie, below, pp. 271–4. A yield of 10–21 hectolitres per hectare is equivalent to $11\frac{1}{7}$–24 bushels per acre.

5 J. M. Richard, 'Thierry d'Hireçon, agriculteur artésien', *Bibliothèque de l'Ecole des Chartes*, LIII, 1892, pp. 383–416; B. H. Slicher van Bath, *The agrarian history of western Europe AD 500–1850*, trans. O. Ordish, London, 1963, pp. 175–6.

6 Shiel, above, pp. 65–6.

7 Equivalent to $4\frac{1}{2}$–21 bushels per acre.

---

* Note: All cross-references in this chapter are supplied in the Bibliography at the end of this chapter.

regain their early-fourteenth-century level until the second half of the eighteenth century, and it was only in the nineteenth century that they rose significantly higher.[8] In the Low Countries the story was rather different. First, the decline in yields was postponed until the second half of the fifteenth century and was relatively muted. Second, based upon a range of new husbandry techniques, the recovery of the sixteenth century soon matched the productivity achievement of the earlier demographic peak, while during the course of the following century crop yields were pushed progressively higher, constituting – according to certain definitions – a veritable agricultural revolution.[9]

This equation of rising population with an increased intensity of production and thus higher yields at the price of lower labour productivity, and vice versa during periods of population decline, contrasts sharply with English accounts of the same period which have tended to stress the adverse effects of population growth for both land and labour productivity, especially under feudal socio-property relations.[10] M. M. Postan, for instance, sees population growth as having promoted a Ricardian extension of cultivation on to inferior soils during the thirteenth century, thereby depressing mean yields per acre; a view echoed by R. B. Outhwaite for the sixteenth century.[11] Concomitantly, the conversion of grassland to arable reduced supplies of pasturage, with adverse consequences for stocking densities and hence the manure

8 Le Roy Ladurie, 'The end of the middle ages', pp. 81–3.
9 Van der Wee, 'Introduction', pp. 2 and 9–10.
10 On the relationship between population density and agricultural intensity see E. Boserup, *The conditions of agricultural growth: the economics of agrarian change under population pressure*, London, 1965. On the adverse consequences of feudal socio-property relations for agricultural productivity see R. Brenner, 'Agrarian class structure and economic development in pre-industrial Europe', *Past and Present*, LXX, 1976, pp. 30–75, reprinted as pp. 10–63 in Aston and Philpin, *The Brenner debate: agrarian class structure and economic development in pre-industrial Europe*, 1985.
11 M. M. Postan, 'Medieval agrarian society in its prime: England', pp. 548–632 in *idem*, ed., *The Cambridge economic history of Europe*, I, *The agrarian life of the middle ages*, Cambridge, 2nd edn., 1966, pp. 556–9; R. B. Outhwaite, 'Progress and backwardness in English agriculture, 1500–1650', *EcHR*, XXXIX, 1986, pp. 1–18. Outhwaite postulates the following scenario: 'farmers, faced with a compelling need to grow grains in a time of expanding population, extended their cultivation onto marginal lands; they also extended grain cultivation at the expense of grazing land, in some places rotations became more intensive, with consequent reductions in fallowing; livestock holdings diminished, particularly among the lesser cultivators. Wherever these developments occurred they tended to have depressing influences on arable productivity' (pp. 5–6).

supplies which were a major source of soil nitrogen.[12] J. Z. Titow and D. L. Farmer are alike in attributing low grain yields in the late thirteenth and early fourteenth centuries on the estates of the Bishops of Winchester and Abbots of Westminster to this kind of ecological imbalance.[13] The peak in gross agricultural product output at this time through the expansion of the agricultural sector as a whole thus masks a deterioration in the per unit product of land, a development which exacerbated the inherent Malthusian tendency for the marginal productivity of labour in agriculture to fall and, consequently, for the growth of food supply to lag behind the growth of population.[14]

To compound matters Outhwaite believes that, far from promoting higher yields, the subdivision of holdings which was such a feature of the thirteenth century and, to a lesser extent, of the sixteenth, may actually have had the opposite effect, since '[the smallholder's] poverty, his limited acreage, and his family consumption requirements may have militated against the most effective means of raising his yields – decreasing his arable acreage, purchasing more livestock and increasing his dunging'.[15] Labour productivity in peasant agriculture consequently suffered, and accordingly Postan believes that it was the larger cultivators, and especially the demesne lords, with advantages of land and capital, who fared best.[16]

For subscribers to this pessimistic scenario the effects of population decline in the later middle ages were thus more beneficial than adverse. Lowered population levels allowed the concentration of cultivation on to the better soils and the abandonment of marginal land, to the

12 M. M. Postan, 'Village livestock in the thirteenth century', *EcHR*, XV, 1962, pp. 219–49, reprinted as pp. 214–48 in *idem, Essays on medieval agriculture and general problems of the medieval economy*, Cambridge, 1973. Shiel, above, pp. 67–8.

13 J. Z. Titow, *Winchester yields: a study in medieval agricultural productivity*, Cambridge, 1972, p. 30; D. L. Farmer, 'Grain yields on Westminster Abbey manors, 1271–1410', *Canadian Journal of History*, XVIII, 1983, p. 342.

14 J. D. Chambers, *Population, economy and society in pre-industrial England*, Oxford, 1972, pp. 24–5.

15 Outhwaite, 'Progress and backwardness', pp. 15–16.

16 'The higher quality of the lord's land, his superior command over capital, equipment, pastures and folds were bound to tell, and his yields were bound to be higher': Postan, 'Medieval agrarian society', p. 602. Yet H. Neveux argues that in the Cambrésis in the sixteenth century the emergence of substantial, commercialised farms retarded the growth of agricultural productivity: Le Roy Ladurie, 'The end of the middle ages', pp. 90–1. See also R. C. Allen, below, pp. 253–4, who questions whether stocking densities on small holdings were necessarily lower than those on demesnes.

benefit of mean yields. At the same time, with a better ratio of land to labour and a shift away from the more intensive techniques of production, labour productivity should have risen.[17] Moreover, both trends should have been reinforced by a swing back towards pastoralism as the demand for grain abated and rising per capita incomes promoted higher per capita consumption of meat, dairy produce, and other livestock products. Better ratios of grassland to arable and livestock to crops would have redressed the ecological imbalance within agriculture and released increased supplies of manure to the soil so that yields should eventually have risen to reach a higher mean level than either earlier or later.[18] Within the peasant sector declining levels of feudal rent should further have reinforced these trends.[19]

Whereas continental historians thus regard gains in productivity per unit area as only possible at the expense of productivity per unit labour, English historians argue that simultaneous increases in both were attainable once declining population created conditions of relative land abundance. The ultimate challenge, therefore, was to raise land and labour productivity together in conjunction with a general expansion of agricultural output and growth of population. Only when this had been achieved would the productivity constraints within agriculture cease to impede the progress of the economy at large. It is the resolution of this fundamental dilemma which constituted the so-called agricultural revolution. At its core in England's case lay, on the one hand, structural and tenurial changes in the units of production – notably the size and layout of farms and terms on which they were held – which transformed the productivity of labour, and, on the other, an ecological transformation of the methods of production, which yielded significant gains in the productivity of land.[20]

---

17 A. R. Bridbury, *Economic growth: England in the later middle ages*, London, 1962, pp. 52–3, claims that land and labour productivity both rose after 1350 but offers no direct evidence.

18 On the time taken to rebuild supplies of soil nitrogen see Shiel, above, pp. 60– 3. High grain yields under conditions of grassland abundance are reported for the late fifteenth century from the estates of Tavistock Abbey in Devon: H. P. R. Finberg, *Tavistock Abbey: a study in the social and economic history of Devon*, Cambridge, 1951, pp. 86–128.

19 R. H. Hilton, *The decline of serfdom in medieval England*, London and Basingstoke, 2nd edn., 1983.

20 Brenner, 'Agrarian class structure'; D. B. Grigg, 'Breaking out: England in the eighteenth and nineteenth centuries', pp. 163–89 in *idem, Population growth and agrarian change: an historical perspective*, Cambridge, 1980; J. R. Walton, 'Agriculture 1730–1900', pp. 239–66 in R. A. Dodgshon and R. A. Butlin, eds., *An historical geography of England and Wales*, London, 1978; M. Overton, 'Estimating crop yields

The key to the latter, it has long been believed, lay in an enhanced cycling of nutrients facilitated by the incorporation of improved fodder crops into new types of rotation, which allowed higher stocking densities, heavier dunging rates, higher arable yields, more fodder crops, more livestock, and so on in a progressively ascending spiral of progress.[21] Such a line of reasoning naturally reinforces the arguments of those who claim, conversely, that it was a deficiency of livestock which had hitherto, at times of population pressure, jeopardised arable productivity. Fortunately, the medieval data are of a quality which allow equations of this sort to be put to the test. These data relate exclusively to the demesne sector, which obviously combined land, labour, and capital in very different proportions from the peasant sector, and on the evidence of the Hundred Rolls of 1279 probably accounted for between a quarter and a third of the arable area.[22] It is therefore less representative of agriculture at large than the tithe data so widely employed by continental historians but capable of providing a more direct insight into productivity and its determinants. Nor are its lessons without relevance for the peasant sector.

II Productivity in medieval England: data and methods

Traditionally, medieval seignorial agriculture has been investigated via case studies of individual well-documented manors or estates.[23] Nevertheless, there are very few manors, and still fewer estates, for which there is a sufficiently long run of accounts to be able to chart trends in production and productivity over a period of more than just a few decades. The well preserved archive of the estates of the Bishops

---

from probate inventories: an example from East Anglia, 1585–1735', *JEH*, XXXIX, 1979, pp. 363–78; E. A. Wrigley, 'Urban growth and agricultural change: England and the continent in the early modern period', *Journal of Interdisciplinary History*, XV, 1985, pp. 683–728; Allen, below, pp. 236–54; Shiel, above, pp. 67–77; Overton, below, pp. 284–322.

21 E. Kerridge, *The agricultural revolution*, London, 1967; J. D. Chambers and G. E. Mingay, *The agricultural revolution 1750–1880*, London, 1966, pp. 54–62. See E. A. Wrigley, below, pp. 321–39, for the role of draught animals in the growth of labour productivity.

22 E. A. Kosminsky, *Studies in the agrarian history of England in the thirteenth century*, Oxford, 1956, pp. 87–95.

23 Examples include F. J. Davenport, *The economic development of a Norfolk manor, 1086–1565*, Cambridge, 1906; R. A. L. Smith, *Canterbury Cathedral Priory*, Cambridge, 1943; Finberg, *Tavistock Abbey*; J. A. Raftis, *The estates of Ramsey Abbey*, Toronto, 1957; P. D. A. Harvey, *A medieval Oxfordshire village: Cuxham 1240–1400*, Oxford, 1965.

of Winchester, with its almost continuous series of Pipe Rolls documenting agricultural production over the period 1208–1453 is quite alone in this respect.[24] Its evidence thus tends to loom disproportionately large in all discussions of medieval productivity change, although as an index of general trends its utility is circumscribed by its exceptional status as the possession of one of the wealthiest and most powerful ecclesiastical magnates in the land, together with the fact that the bulk of its constituent manors were concentrated in Hampshire and adjacent counties in southern England on land which, for the most part, was of below average quality and productivity (Figure 4.1).[25] Other well preserved archives similarly relate to the properties of large ecclesiastical institutions, with all the problems of representativeness which this implies, but there is additionally a great mass of miscellaneous documentary material for a whole range of other classes of estate, lay as well as ecclesiastical, which is much more fragmentary in its temporal coverage.[26] The latter is capable of adding very considerably to knowledge and understanding, but requires a type of approach akin to that developed by early modernists in conjunction with probate inventories.[27]

The approach adopted in this paper has therefore been to draw upon the full range of extant documentation and reconstruct trends in demesne husbandry for a cross-section of estates by means of a sample of accounts (a methodology analogous to that employed in this volume by R. C. Allen, P. Glennie and M. Overton in analyses of probate inventories).[28] This has been undertaken at two scales, that of the country as a whole and that of an individual county, Norfolk. For the former, a sample of 1,904 different accounts has been assembled representing some 873 separate demesnes, 41 per cent of them in lay ownership and 59 per cent in ecclesiastical. These are drawn from all

24 Titow, *Winchester yields*; D. L. Farmer, 'Grain yields on the Winchester manors in the later middle ages', *EcHR*, XXX, 1977, pp. 555–66.
25 K. Biddick, above, p. 97.
26 These sources are surveyed in J. L. Langdon, *Horses, oxen and technological innovation: the use of draught animals in English farming from 1066–1500*, Cambridge, 1986, pp. 82–5; B. M. S. Campbell, 'Towards an agricultural geography of medieval England', *AHR*, XXXVI, 1988, pp. 88–9. For the range of grange accounts extant for one particularly well-documented part of England, see B. M. S. Campbell, 'Agricultural productivity in medieval England: some evidence from Norfolk', *JEH*, XLIII, 1983, pp. 381–2.
27 M. Overton, below, pp. 300–3; P. Glennie, below, pp. 265 and 272–4; Allen, below, p. 247.
28 Below, p. 247, pp. 265, 272–4 and 300–3.

parts of the country, but with a bias towards the better documented and more densely populated counties of the south and east. Within this sample the vast majority of demesnes are represented by just one or two accounts.[29] In contrast, the sample assembled for Norfolk is altogether more comprehensive and solid.

Norfolk is one of the best documented counties in the country and in the middle ages was further distinguished by a high density of population and relatively intensive systems of husbandry.[30] Its data set comprises information extracted from all known extant grange accounts for the county, namely 1,900 accounts representing some 216 different demesnes (effectively a 10 per cent sample of all demesnes in the county). All classes of landlord are represented, from the mightiest magnates down to humble lords of a single manor, but with an inevitable bias towards the former and especially the estates of the greater ecclesiastical landlords, which account for 69 per cent of surviving records and 48 per cent of recorded demesnes. Because of its comprehensive nature this data set can be disaggregated to provide detailed information on individual demesnes, estates, and farming regions. The estate of the Prior of Norwich is, however, alone in retaining reasonably complete records from the whole of the period in question, although even its best documented demesnes cannot match those of the Bishopric of Winchester in their consistency of coverage.[31]

On the basis of this sample information, trends in the mean cereal acreage, the mean number of livestock, and the mean ratio of livestock to cereal acres per demesne can be charted over the 200-year period 1250–1449. The relevant statistics are summarised in Table 6.1

29 This sample was largely assembled by John Langdon of the University of Alberta in conjunction with his major study of the technology of haulage and traction in the middle ages and I am most grateful to him for making it available to me.

30 The Norfolk account rolls used in this study are drawn from the following public and private archives: Public Record Office; Norfolk Record Office (NRO); North Yorkshire Record Office; Nottinghamshire Record Office; West Suffolk Record Office; Bodleian Library, Oxford; British Library; Cambridge University Library; Canterbury Cathedral Library; Chicago University Library; Harvard Law Library; John Rylands Library, Manchester; Lambeth Palace Library; Nottingham University Library; Eton College; Christ's College, Cambridge; King's College, Cambridge; Magdalen College, Oxford; St George's Chapel, Windsor; Elveden Hall, Suffolk; Holkham Hall, Norfolk; Raynham Hall, Norfolk; Pomeroy and Sons, Wymondham. I am grateful to the relevant authorities for granting me access to these materials. For a full discussion of Norfolk agriculture based on a comprehensive analysis of these accounts, see my forthcoming book, *The geography of seignorial agriculture in medieval England*, in preparation for Cambridge University Press.

31 For example, C. Thornton, below, pp. 183–4.

and are weighted to take account of inconsistencies in spatial coverage. Thus, the Norfolk figures are the product of four regional sub-totals and the national figures of six (the weighted total for Norfolk being one of them).[32] These sub-totals are the mean of the individual manorial means which are in turn the mean of the annual means for those years for which relevant data are available.[33] The final aggregate figure for England has been derived by weighting each regional sub-total according to its respective shares of lay wealth in 1334 and population in 1377.[34] Other inconsistencies in the structure of the data are, however, less easily corrected. For instance, the diffusion of annual accounting as an administrative device means that small estates and manors are initially underrepresented with the result that the results for 1250–99 are likely to be inflated.[35] The selective impact of leasing has a similar effect upon the results for 1375–1425 and 1400–49, rendering those demesnes which remained in hand and for which production information is available less and less representative of the demesne sector at large.[36] This is further compounded by small sample size. The results for the first and last time periods thus need to be treated with

32 The six regional groupings are as follows: the north (Berwickshire, Northumberland, Durham, Yorkshire, Cumberland, Westmorland, Lancashire, Cheshire, Shropshire, Staffordshire, Derbyshire, Nottinghamshire), the south-west (Herefordshire, Worcestershire, Gloucestershire, Monmouthshire, Wiltshire, Dorset, Somerset, Devon, Cornwall), the south-east (Hampshire, the Isle of Wight, Surrey, Sussex, Kent), the midlands (Leicestershire, Rutland, Northamptonshire, Warwickshire, Bedfordshire, Buckinghamshire, Oxfordshire, Berkshire), the eastern counties (Lincolnshire, Huntingdonshire, Cambridgeshire, Suffolk, Essex, Hertfordshire, Middlesex, and Norfolk).

33 Glennie, however, would advocate the calculation of individual annual means as an intermediate step, below, p. 265.

34 These regional weightings are as follows: the north × 0.213, the south-west × 0.209, the south-east × 0.120, the midlands × 0.164, the eastern counties × 0.214, Norfolk × 0.081.

35 F. B. Stitt, 'The medieval minister's account', *Society of Local Archivists Bulletin*, XI, 1953, pp. 2–8; P. D. A. Harvey, 'Agricultural treatises and manorial accounting in medieval England', *AHR*, XX, 1972, pp. 170–82; P. D. A. Harvey, 'Introduction, Part II, accounts and other manorial records', pp. 12–71 of *idem*, ed., *Manorial records of Cuxham, Oxfordshire circa 1200–1359*, Oxfordshire Record Society, L, 1976.

36 On the farming of demesnes see F. R. H. Du Boulay, 'Who were farming the English demesnes at the end of the middle ages?', *EcHR*, XVII, 1965, pp. 443–55; B. Harvey, 'The leasing of the Abbot of Westminster's demesnes in the later middle ages', *EcHR*, XXII, 1969, pp. 17–27; R. A. Lomas, 'The priory of Durham and its demesnes in the fourteenth and fifteenth centuries', *EcHR*, XXXI, 1978, pp. 339–53; J. N. Hare, 'The demesnes lessees of fifteenth-century Wiltshire', *AHR*, XXIX, 1981, pp. 1–15; M. Mate, 'The farming out of manors: a new look at the evidence from Canterbury Cathedral Priory', *Journal of Medieval History*, IX, 1983, pp. 331–44.

Table 6.1 *England and Norfolk: demesne production trends, 1250–1449 (weighted 50-year staggered means)*

Years	Mean cereal acreage		Mean livestock units[a]		Livestock units per 100 cereal acres	
	England	*Norfolk*	*England*	*Norfolk*	*England*	*Norfolk*
1250–1299	176.7	149.2	64.2	45.6	41.9	30.5
1275–1324	176.7	140.8	67.7	46.5	44.1	33.0
1300–1349	155.7	126.6	64.8	45.9	47.9	36.3
1325–1374	134.7	115.3	63.8	47.2	55.8	41.0
1350–1399	124.9	110.6	75.0	49.3	62.8	44.6
1375–1424	123.9	120.1	78.6	43.3	69.9	36.1
1400–1449	117.4	140.7	89.3	43.5	78.6	30.9

Note
[a] (Horses × 1.0) + (oxen, cows, and bulls × 1.2) + (immature cattle × 0.8) + (sheep × 0.1) + (swine × 0.1).

Source See notes 29 and 30.

circumspection and especially so in the case of Norfolk, whose more comprehensive documentation renders it highly sensitive to such structural shifts in the composition of the data.

III The changing ratio of livestock to crops

As the figures summarised in Table 6.1 and graphed in Figure 6.1 indicate, the period 1250–1449 witnessed significant changes in the ratio of livestock to crops (identified by so many authors as one of the keys to arable productivity).[37] On the arable side the mean cereal acreage declined from a high point at the opening of the fourteenth century to a low point towards its close. This decline amounted to some 20 per cent in Norfolk – notwithstanding the county's natural bias towards arable husbandry – and 30 per cent within the country as a whole, and approached 40 per cent in the counties of the south west. Such reductions were achieved partly by the transfer of land via leasing to the non-demesne sector, partly by an increase in the frequency and duration of fallows, and partly by the conversion of arable to pasture.

37 Below, p. 155.

In much of the country it is also plain that this contraction in demesne cultivation had already begun well before the demographic hiatus of the mid fourteenth century. In Norfolk the mean cereal acreage shrank by an estimated 10 per cent during the decades prior to the Black Death and this was matched by a reduction of approximately 12 per cent within the country as a whole. An important contributory factor was the slump in grain prices of the 1330s which precipitated an acute agricultural depression for commercial cereal producers.[38] This is the first major set-back they had experienced in more than half a century. For most of the second half of the thirteenth century and the opening decade or so of the fourteenth century, rising grain prices and depressed real wages had encouraged demesne managers to bring as much land as possible under cultivation, hence the high mean cereal acreages of Norfolk and England at the start of the period under consideration. In fact, given the method by which these results have been derived, it is reassuring that the trends obtained for Norfolk and England should be so similar, especially for the central part of the period for which the data are structurally most consistent. In this context, it should be noted that Norfolk demesnes exhibited a mean sown acreage which was consistently below the national average (except in the very final period when, as already observed, the samples are least representative), as is consistent with the county's fragmented manorial structure and the consequent predominance within it of small demesnes.[39] Moreover, the credibility of these results is further reinforced by their correspondence to the specific experience of individual estates, such as that of the Prior of Holy Trinity Cathedral, Norwich (Figure 6.1).

The Prior of Norwich's estate comprised sixteen manors, three of them in the north-west of Norfolk, four in the centre, two in the east, and seven around Norwich.[40] As grain prices rose during the second

38 M. Prestwich, 'Currency and the economy of early fourteenth century England', pp. 45–58 in N. J. Mayhew, ed., *Edwardian monetary affairs, 1279–1344*, BAR, British series, XXXVI, Oxford, 1977. See also the observations of M. Mate in 'The agrarian economy of south-east England before the Black Death: depressed or buoyant?', pp. 78–109 in B. M. S. Campbell, ed., *Before the Black Death: studies in the 'crisis' of the early fourteenth century*, Manchester, 1991.

39 B. M. S. Campbell, 'The complexity of manorial structure in medieval Norfolk: a case study', *Norfolk Archaeology*, XXXIX, 1986, pp. 228–32.

40 NRO, DCN 40/13, 60/4, 60/10, 60/13, 60/14, 60/15, 60/18, 60/20, 60/23, 60/26, 60/28, 60/29, 60/33, 60/35, 60/37, 61/35–6, 62/1, 62/2; L'Estrange IB 1/4, 3/4 and 4/4; NNAS 20 D1–3; Raynham Hall, Norfolk, Townshend Manuscripts; Bodleian Library, Oxford, MS Rolls, Norfolk 20–45. A full handlist of the Norwich Cathedral Priory archive is available at the Norfolk Record Office.

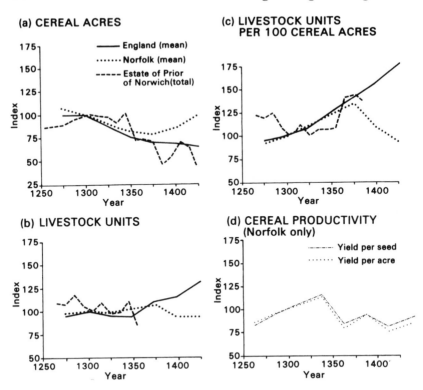

Figure 6.1 *England and Norfolk, 1250–1450: cereal acreages, livestock units, livestock units per 100 cereal acres, and cereal productivity*

half of the thirteenth century, successive Priors pursued a policy of expansion on their demesnes: additional land was purchased, further land was expropriated from their tenants, and fallows were reduced so that an enlarged proportion of the arable was brought under cultivation. By these means approximately 350 acres were added to the sown acreage between 1260 and 1310, amounting to an expansion of roughly 15 per cent. These developments were especially marked on the demesnes closest to Norwich, and most conspicuously of all on the demesne at Newton, to which approximately 150 acres were added between 1260 and 1340. Across the estate as a whole, however, the peak in cultivation came – as probably in the country as a whole – in the opening decade of the fourteenth century, by which time the Prior had almost 3,000 acres under cultivation.

During the 1310s and '20s cultivation fluctuated at around the c.1300 level, expanding or contracting according to the state of the grain market but not rising significantly higher, until in the 1330s there was an abrupt cut-back in the total sown acreage by 9.5 per cent, mainly because a decision was taken to lease the demesnes at Thornham, Hindringham, and Hindolveston (although on many of the other demesnes cultivation was maintained at more-or-less its existing level, and at *Heythe* near Norwich a wholly new demesne farm of some thirty sown acres was created). This was an unprecedented step, but by the mid 1340s, with a revival in grain prices, all three demesnes were back in hand and the sown acreage on the estate briefly returned to the level of some forty years earlier. Nevertheless, this recovery was short-lived, and from the 1350s cultivation on this estate underwent a long secular decline. Thereafter two or three of the demesnes were always at farm, with the result that during the 1350s, 1360s and 1370s the total acreage under cultivation was never more than approximately 75 per cent its previous maximum level. Then, in the late 1370s, a further price fall precipitated a renewed spate of leasings which reduced the acreage under the Prior's direct control to just 45 per cent of its *c.*1300 level. After a brief recovery in the 1390s and 1400s, the Prior finally abandoned direct management on all his demesnes in the 1420s and early 1430s. From this time on, demesnes which remained in hand became a relative rarity within the county, most of them the home farms of religious houses or minor gentry families.

These trends in cereal acreage had obvious implications for the numbers of livestock, since they were the product in part of the conversion of pasture to arable and vice versa. Counting livestock is, however, a much more complicated exercise than counting sown acres since some method has to be found of equating the different ages and categories of farm animal – horses, oxen, cows and other cattle, sheep, and swine. Historical opinion is divided as to how this should be done. Medieval historians such as Titow and Farmer have omitted swine from their calculations and employed weightings of 1.0 for horses, oxen, and cattle and 0.25 for sheep.[41] Apart from the fact that such weightings are obviously very crude, the omission of swine is unjustifiable, and a weighting of 0.25 is arguably too high for sheep. In contrast, early modern historians, notably J. A. Yelling in his analysis of seventeenth-century probate inventories, have employed weightings derived from

---

41 Titow, *Winchester yields*; Farmer, 'Grain yields on the Winchester manors'; *idem*, 'Grain yields on Westminster Abbey manors'.

those utilised by T. R. Coppock in his agricultural atlas of 1964 and based upon modern animal feed requirements.[42] A version of these is employed here and shown in Table 6.1. These weightings give lower absolute results than those obtained by Titow's method and – when the results for individual farms are mapped – a more coherent spatial pattern, although their relative trend remains much the same.

In both England and Norfolk the mean number of livestock units per demesne remained essentially static throughout the period 1250–1350, with the number of livestock on Norfolk demesnes well below the national average, partly because demesnes were themselves smaller, but also because of a natural bias towards arable production. After 1350 there was a brief and very marginal increase in livestock numbers in Norfolk, and a much more substantial and sustained increase in their numbers in the country as a whole. By the end of the fourteenth century demesnes carried on average 16 per cent more livestock than they had done at the beginning of the century, a trend which is if anything understated since flocks were increasingly accounted for separately and herds farmed out. This is no doubt one reason why livestock numbers appear to have fallen back to late-thirteenth-century levels in Norfolk, although this trend is also attributable to a decline in Norfolk's traditionally intensive, arable-based livestock husbandry. Certainly, for reasons of both accounting and economics, livestock numbers registered little absolute increase on the estates of the Prior of Norwich, in contrast to the country at large where demesne flocks and herds grew steadily in size until well into the fifteenth century (Figure 6.1(b)). Underpinning the latter development was a sustained rise in the absolute and relative importance of sheep, from roughly a fifth to a third of the total, a more modest increase in the importance of dairy cattle, and, concomitantly with the contraction in the arable sector, a decline in the relative importance of draught animals. The net result was a transformation in the livestock profile of many demesnes between the end of the thirteenth and the beginning of the fifteenth centuries.

Significantly, neither in Norfolk, nor in the country at large, did

---

42 J. A. Yelling, 'Probate inventories and the geography of livestock farming: a study of east Worcestershire, 1540–1750', *Transactions of the Institute of British Geographers*, LI, 1970, p. 115; R. C. Allen, *The 'capital intensive farmer' and the English agricultural revolution: a reassessment*, Discussion Paper 87–11, Department of Economics, University of British Columbia, 1987, pp. 27–33; *idem*, below, pp. 245–6; T. R. Coppock, *An agricultural atlas of England and Wales*, London, 1964, p. 213. For a variant on these weightings see G. Clark, below, p. 213.

the timing of the rise in livestock numbers synchronise with the contraction in cultivation. Demesnes may have been cultivating less land between 1300 and 1350, but the resources thus released do not seem to have been transferred to the pastoral sector. The explanation may be that the land was simply being cultivated less intensively or, more probably, that much of it was being leased out to tenants and thus transferred to the hard-pressed peasant sector. Only after 1350 did the withdrawal of land from cultivation coincide with a rise in the average number of livestock per demesne. As in later periods, this swing from corn to horn was most pronounced, neither in the traditionally arable east, nor in the traditionally pastoral north and west, but in an intermediate group of counties in the midlands and the south east which possessed comparative advantages for both arable and pastoral husbandry.[43] Within these counties the balance struck between these two sectors was determined by the prevailing terms of trade and when, as in the later fourteenth century, these shifted in favour of pastoral products, a substantial increase in livestock numbers was the result. Moreover, since at this time it was sheep numbers that expanded most dynamically, it was in the various downland counties of the south and east which possessed particular advantages for sheep farming that the rise in livestock units was most marked, averaging 50 per cent or more in Hampshire and the Isle of Wight, Surrey, Sussex and Kent.[44]

Given the contraction in mean cereal acreage which took place during the first half of the fourteenth century, and the expansion in mean livestock numbers which took place during the second half, it follows that mean stocking densities (livestock units per 100 cereal acres) must have improved steadily throughout the century. Table 6.1 and Figure 6.1(c) demonstrate that this was indeed the case. Stocking densities rose by almost a third c.1275–1350 and by a further 40 per cent c.1350–1425. Over the period as a whole stocking densities rose by an estimated 88 per cent and in real terms, given the problems of under-recording, the increase must have been even greater.[45] This trend was, however, far from universal.

The rise in stocking densities was least pronounced in the counties

---

43 A. Kussmaul, 'Agrarian change in seventeenth-century England: the economic historian as paleontologist', *JEH*, XLV, 1985, pp. 1–30.
44 Compared with other livestock the attraction of sheep lay in their lower unit costs due to their amenability to extensive forms of management.
45 The equivalent increase using Titow and Farmer's weightings of horses and cattle × 1.0 and sheep × 0.25 is 91 per cent.

north of the Trent, where the coverage of the sample is most sparse and no clear trend emerges in either the mean cereal acreage or mean livestock numbers. Here, stocking densities appear to have been much the same at the end of the period as they had been at the beginning. Much the same applies in Norfolk. In this county, a modest reduction in the mean cereal acreage in the middle decades of the fourteenth century, coupled with a small but real increase in livestock numbers after 1350, resulted in stocking densities which were 23 per cent higher in the period 1350–99 than they had been 1300–49 (a trend which is echoed on the estates of the Prior of Norwich where the equivalent increase was approximately 29 per cent). Nevertheless, this improvement was not maintained, and after 1375 stocking densities, at least on demesnes, gradually reverted to their original low level. Norfolk's comparative advantage lay mostly in intensive, arable-based pastoralism, and except in certain specific districts was ill-equipped to convert to the extensive, grass-based pastoralism which economic trends were increasingly favouring.[46] Elsewhere in the eastern counties the rise in stocking densities was more sustained, amounting to some 40 per cent over the fourteenth century as a whole, but was still significantly below the national average. By contrast, it was in the counties of central and southern England that the improvement in stocking densities was most pronounced, for it was here that cereal acreages contracted, and livestock numbers expanded, most markedly. The gain in potential nitrogen supply should therefore have been considerable with all that this implies for grain yields.

IV The productivity response

Other things being equal, the general contraction in arable cultivation and associated improvement in stocking densities which took place during the fourteenth century should have had beneficial consequences for arable productivity, especially in central and southern England

---

46 The exceptions were the Fens and Broadland (where there had always been much permanent pasture); the light, sandy soils of the west of the county (where there was a significant expansion of sheep farming); and the heavy clay soils of central and south-eastern Norfolk (where there was much conversion of arable to permanent grass, although probably more at the initiative of tenants than of landlords). The greatest changes occurred, however, in the fifteenth rather than the fourteenth century. For the distinctive features of pastoral husbandry in Norfolk see B. M. S. Campbell and J. P. Power, 'Mapping the agricultural geography of medieval England', *Journal of Historical Geography*, XV, 1989, pp. 28–37.

where these developments were most pronounced. If Titow is right in supposing that arable fields were suffering from a 'chronic state of under manuring' at the end of the thirteenth century, the opposite should have been the case by the close of the fourteenth century: more grassland and more livestock should together have enhanced the supply of mineral nitrogen to crops and resulted in better harvests.[47] Moreover, grain yields should further have benefited from increased sowings of legumes, which accounted for 7.0 per cent of the sown area at the beginning of this period and 17.5 per cent at the end.[48] Legumes – peas, beans and vetches – fixed nitrogen from the atmosphere and their incorporation within rotations thereby enhanced rather than depleted soil fertility. When fed to livestock they led to a significant improvement in the nitrogen content of manure and in their role as a fodder crop their increased cultivation further reinforced the trend towards higher stocking densities, especially in those regions and localities which were otherwise deficient in pasturage. Climatic changes apart, therefore, ecological circumstances would appear to have been broadly conducive to a significant improvement in yields over this period.[49] To what extent this was actually the case nevertheless remains very much to be seen. We are still, unfortunately, a long way from having a national series of yield data by which such relationships might be tested, although in the long term, given the temporal and spatial range of extant manorial accounts, construction of such a series ought to be feasible.[50] In the meanwhile it is necessary to make do with the long series of Winchester yields calculated by Titow and Farmer, which mostly relate to Hampshire and adjoining counties in southern England; the somewhat shorter series of Westminster yields calculated by Farmer, which relate to a wider scatter of demesnes with concentrations near London, in Essex and Hertfordshire, and on the Gloucestershire/Warwickshire border; and the series of yields for Norfolk which is presented here for the first time (Table 6.2).[51]

---

47 Titow, *Winchester yields*, p. 30; Shiel, above, pp. 70–2.

48 B. M. S. Campbell, 'The diffusion of vetches in medieval England', *EcHR*, XLI, 1988, p. 204.

49 H. H. Lamb, *Climate, history and the modern world*, London, 1982; Shiel, above, pp. 65–9.

50 Yield figures from a variety of published sources are collected together in B. H. Slicher van Bath, 'The yields of different crops, mainly cereals in relation to the seed *c.*810–1820', *Acta Historiae Neerlandica*, II, Leiden, 1967, pp. 78–97.

51 Titow, *Winchester yields*, disaggregates the yields by manor and year, but Farmer, unfortunately, publishes only mean figures for the Winchester and Westminster estates as a whole: Farmer, 'Grain yields on the Winchester manors'; *idem*, 'Grain

Table 6.2 *Mean gross yields per seed on the estates of the Bishops of Winchester and Abbots of Westminster, and in Norfolk, 1225–1453*

Years	Wheat	Barley	Oats
A. *Winchester*[a]			
1225–1249	4.09	4.69	2.68
1250–1274	3.87	4.03	2.52
1275–1299	3.75	3.25	2.18
1300–1324	3.90	3.57	2.21
1325–1349	3.96	3.74	2.25
1350–1380	3.66	3.53	2.43
1381–1410	3.88	4.13	2.93
1411–1453	3.66	3.64	3.03
B. *Westminster*[b]			
1271–1299	3.27	3.63	2.37
1300–1324	2.86	3.82	2.14
1325–1349	2.98	4.38	2.54
1350–1380	2.84	3.99	2.57
1381–1410	3.25	4.13	2.75
C. *Norfolk*[c]			
1250–1274	3.83	3.17	2.37
1275–1299	4.57	3.06	2.40
1300–1324	4.78	3.24	2.62
1325–1349	4.96	3.36	2.78
1350–1374	3.93	3.09	2.38
1375–1399	4.11	3.58	2.80
1400–1424	4.18	3.20	2.86
1425–1449	3.77	3.21	2.94

Source
[a] J. Z. Titow, *Winchester yields: a study in medieval agricultural productivity*,
Cambridge, 1972; D. L. Farmer,'Grain yields on the Winchester manors in the later
middle ages', *EcHR*, XXX, 1977, pp. 555–66.
[b] D. L. Farmer,'Grain yields on Westminster Abbey manors, 1271–1410', *Canadian
Journal of History*, XVIII, 1983, pp. 331–47.
[c] See note 30.

yields on Westminster Abbey manors'. For case studies of the Winchester demesne
of Rimpton, Somerset, and Westminster demesne of Kinsbourne, Hertfordshire,
see Thornton, below, pp. 183–210, and D. V. Stern, 'A Hertfordshire manor of
Westminster Abbey: an examination of demesne profits, corn yields, and weather
evidence', unpublished University of London Ph.D. thesis, 1978. Disaggregations
of the Norfolk data will be given in my forthcoming book, *The geography of seignorial
agriculture*.

The yield series for Winchester and Westminster have the merit that they derive from specific groups of demesnes, although in practice not all individual demesnes are consistently well recorded and represented. Such inconsistencies of coverage particularly affect the Westminster series due to the wide geographical scatter of demesnes – each with potentially divergent productivity trajectories – from which it is composed. By contrast, the Winchester series is more geographically concentrated, as well as longer and more completely documented. Geographically, the Norfolk series is most sharply focused of all, since it is constructed solely from accounts relating to that county. All three series incorporate yield ratios entered as marginal notes by the medieval auditors along with those calculated from information of seed sown and grain harvested given in consecutive accounts.[52]

For Norfolk, information of varying degrees of completeness is available for 121 different demesnes, representing a total of 1,085 individual harvests and a variety of different crops (i.e. an average of roughly nine harvests per demesne and five demesnes per year over a 200-year period). The Norfolk yield data are therefore substantial in volume, if fragmented in nature, and, if inferior in quality to those available for the Winchester estate, are nevertheless superior to those estimated from probate inventories where individual farms are never represented by more than a single harvest.[53] Spatially, most parts of the county and its constituent farming regions are covered, although this coverage is far from even. The biggest gaps occur in the central and western parts of the county, both of them areas of medium-to-poor soils. Conversely, information is fullest for the immediate environs of Norwich, as well as more generally in the north-west and extreme south of the county, partly because of the survival of particular estate archives. To try and minimise the impact of these variations in the spatial coverage of the data, and especially the fact that this does not remain consistent over time, each aggregate yield figure is the weighted product of four regional sub-means. Chronologically, there are no yield statistics for any date earlier than 1264–65, and there is a pronounced diminution in the quantity of surviving data after 1430. Between these two extremes there is a reasonably consistent coverage:

52 For the calculation of yields from consecutive accounts see Titow, *Winchester yields*, pp. 5–9. The yields entered by medieval auditors as marginal notes are discussed in J. S. Drew, 'Manorial accounts of St Swithun's Priory, Winchester', *English Historical Review*, LXII, 1947, reprinted as pp. 12–30 in E. M. Carus-Wilson, ed., *Essays in Economic History*, II, London, 1962, p. 22. See also Campbell, 'Agricultural productivity', p. 382.

53 Glennie, below, pp. 279–80.

the period from 1290–1340 is especially well recorded, with the 1300s standing out as by far the single best represented decade.

Given the very different documentary and arithmetic basis of the yield series for Norfolk as compared with those for the Winchester and Westminster estates, it is reassuring to note a quite high degree of correspondence between them. This is most marked in the case of barley, correlation coefficients producing results of 0.6164, 0.7222 and 0.9141, respectively, for Norfolk against Westminster, Winchester against Westminster, and Norfolk against Winchester over the period 1275–1399. Equivalent correlations for wheat yield results of 0.0860, −0.1303, and 0.6875 respectively, indicate a fair degree of correspondence between Norfolk and Winchester only, whilst in the case of oats there is no correspondence whatsoever, except that the lowest yields all tended to occur towards the beginning of the period, and the highest at the end. It should be noted that the correlations are consistently strongest between the two geographically most focused series, notably Norfolk and Winchester, which is heartening given that they are constructed from such contrasting assemblages of data and are calculated so differently.

In all three series gross yield ratios fluctuated between fairly narrow limits which never exceeded five-fold.[54] Certain of these fluctuations were shared in common – the upturn in the yield of all crops in the second quarter of the fourteenth century, the downturn in yield in the third quarter, and the recovery of the final quarter – which implies the influence of some over-arching factor such as climate.[55] But although the yields of barley and especially oats generally fared rather better after 1350 than before, wheat, the crop most responsive to nitrogen supplies, if anything fared worse. Nor is there much sign of an overall improvement in yields on a scale commensurate with the contemporary rise in stocking densities. The experience of Norfolk is a case in point. The abundance or otherwise of its harvests seems to bear little or no relation to the relative trend in livestock numbers. Impressive wheat yields were obtained in the first half of the fourteenth century in the face of stocking densities which were both absolutely and relatively low, and when stocking densities finally registered a modest improvement in the third quarter of the fourteenth century

54 Yet the thirteenth-century author of the *Husbandry* expected yield ratios of fourfold for oats, fivefold for wheat, and eightfold for barley: D. Oschinsky, *Walter of Henley and other treatises on estate management and accounting*, Oxford, 1971, p. 419.

55 Lamb, *Climate*; H. E. Hallam, 'The climate of eastern England 1250–1350', *AHR*, XXXII, 1984, pp. 124–32; Thornton, below, p. 194.

the yields of wheat, rye, barley and oats all fell (that of wheat, it would appear, irredeemably).

The post-1350 rise in stocking densities was more marked on the Westminster manors, and on the Winchester manors the improvement was dramatic, stocking densities more than doubling on the most favoured manors.[56] Yet on neither estate was any dramatic increase in mean yields forthcoming. Yields of barley and oats were generally rather better than they had been, but wheat yields, at least on the Winchester manors, tended to sag. This is not to deny that stocking densities had an influence upon yields, for at a local scale they patently did. Farmer has pointed out that after 1350 those Winchester manors which secured the best grain yields were those which raised their stocking densities most, and on the downland manors which operated a sheep-corn system of husbandry M. Stephenson has demonstrated a close correlation between sheep numbers and the yield of oats.[57] Nevertheless, at a general level the beneficial effects of high stocking densities were less dramatic than some historians have supposed. Manure may have become more abundant, but labour was becoming scarcer and dearer and farming systems were themselves changing, with the result that crops did not necessarily benefit from the potential increase in nitrogen supplies. Nor are the gross yield ratios of individual crops necessarily the most sensitive measure of productivity changes.

According to the seeding rate, the same yield ratio can be translated into very different yields per acre, and yet it was the latter in which medieval cultivators were most interested.[58] The yield of a particular crop was also to some extent dependent on the scale on which it was grown and the position which it occupied in rotations. For instance, Norfolk's superior wheat yields were a direct function both of the limited scale on which that crop was grown and the privileged position which it occupied in rotations, whereas its inferior barley yields reflected the reverse. A change in the scale on which a crop was grown could thus alter its mean rate of output independently of any real change in yields. Related to this is the fact that the various crops can hardly be regarded as equal since they possessed very different monetary and nutritional values. Wheat was consistently the most valuable crop

56 Farmer, 'Grain yields on Westminster Abbey manors', 1983, p. 342.
57 D. L. Farmer, 'Crop yields, prices and wages in medieval England', *Studies in Medieval and Renaissance History*, VI, 1983, p. 136; M. J. Stephenson, 'The productivity of medieval sheep on the great estates, 1100–1500', unpublished University of Cambridge Ph.D. thesis, 1987, pp. 176–87.
58 Campbell, 'Arable productivity'.

and throughout the period under consideration worth per bushel more than twice the value of oats, the least valuable crop.[59] One strategy which farmers might employ to raise the productivity of their land was therefore the substitution of higher for lower value crops.[60] Much the same applied to the frequency with which the land was sown, with, at constant yields, the higher the frequency of cropping the greater the productivity.[61] It might even be worth accepting lower yields per acre if these could be offset against a greatly increased frequency of cropping. Finally, there is also the question of the precise proportion of the harvest that was required to service the production system, in the form of seed corn, fodder for the livestock, and payments in cash and kind to the farm workers. Hence, as E. A. Wrigley has persuasively argued, historical discussion should focus on the net rather than the gross yield.[62]

V Aggregate cereal productivity

As P. Solar and M. Goossens demonstrate in their contribution to this volume, more satisfactory and comprehensive indicators of land productivity are required than the yield of any one crop.[63] In the case of arable productivity such measures should ideally take account of the proportion of the total sown acreage accounted for by each crop, the net yield of each crop after allowance for tithes, seed corn, and other on-the-farm deductions, the respective value of each crop, and the proportion of the total arable area that was sown each year.[64] Fortunately, virtually all the information required for the calculation of

59 Their different values in part reflected their different weights. In the early nineteenth century wheat weighed *c*.56–60 lbs. per bushel, rye *c*.53–55 lbs., barley *c*.49–50 lbs., and oats *c*.38 lbs. J. C. Loudon, *An encyclopaedia of agriculture*, London, 6th edn., 1866, p. xxiii; J. S. Bayldon, *The art of valuing rents and tillages*, London, 1827, p. 188.

60 P. Solar and M. Goossens, below, p. 372.

61 Glennie, below, p. 279.

62 E. A. Wrigley, 'Some reflections on corn yields and prices in pre-industrial economies', pp. 92–130 in *idem*, *People, cities and wealth: the transformation of traditional society*, Oxford, 1987.

63 Solar and Goossens, below, p. 372.

64 On the relationship between yields, cultivated area, and total output see M. Overton, 'Agricultural revolution? Development of the agrarian economy in early modern England', pp. 118–39 in A. R. H. Baker and D. Gregory, eds., *Explorations in historical geography: interpretative essays*, Cambridge, 1984, pp. 125–7. For productivity comparisons based on monetary value see G. Clark, below, pp. 214–9; Solar and Goossens, below, pp. 376–7, and P. O'Brien and G. Toniolo, below, pp. 390–6.

such weighted aggregate net yields is contained within manorial accounts. Most of these record the acreage sown with each crop, along with information relating to seeding rates, yields, and the price of grain. It is only the amount of land left unsown each year that presents a problem.

On some demesnes the fallowed area was actually recorded, but this was not always done consistently and in Norfolk it generally speaking was not done at all until after 1350. Even when the documents record fallow it is in the very specific sense of land subject to summer ploughing and due for cultivation the following year: arable land lying unsown as part of a convertible husbandry system (*friscus*) is not included. Of course, when, as at Rimpton, the arable was subject to a fixed and regular rotation of crops the proportion left unsown may be readily estimated, but outside the bounds of the regular commonfield system and in a county such as Norfolk this was rarely the case.[65] Estimates of the respective areas sown and unsown therefore require the painstaking reconstruction of crop rotations, an exercise which is itself only possible when there is a sufficient run of consecutive accounts naming the individual fields and plots being sown. Unfortunately, these conditions are rarely satisfied: there are, for instance, only 12 such cases out of the 216 Norfolk demesnes for which accounts are extant. It is for this reason that weighted aggregate yields are most conveniently calculated per sown acre rather than per arable acre, and, since recorded yields of legumes are prone to distortion due to the occasional practice of feeding them to livestock green and unthreshed, they may be further restricted to cereal crops alone.

Estimates for England and Norfolk of the percentage of the total cereal acreage accounted for by the principal grain crops – wheat, rye, maslin, barley, oats and dredge – are summarised in Table 6.3. These reveal a pattern of cropping which for 200 years remained remarkably stable in Norfolk but which changed significantly within the country as a whole. Nationally, wheat remained the pre-eminent cereal crop throughout the period 1250–1449, its share of the total cereal acreage varying within narrow limits and reaching a peak of almost 40 per cent during the first half of the fourteenth century. By comparison, the other winter grains – rye and maslin (a wheat–rye mixture) – were of relatively minor significance, and a significance which tended to diminish after 1350. As a result the winter sown grains, which had gradually expanded in importance during the period 1250–1349,

65 Thornton, below, pp. 185–6.

Table 6.3 *England and Norfolk: percentage of total cereal acreage under different crops, 1250–1449 (weighted 50-year staggered means)*

Years	Wheat	Rye	Maslin	Barley	Oats	Dredge
England						
1250–1299	34.3	5.9	1.0	15.0	40.7	2.6
1275–1324	36.2	6.1	1.4	16.2	35.6	3.5
1300–1349	39.2	5.8	2.6	16.7	30.3	4.7
1325–1374	38.7	4.7	2.1	18.4	27.9	7.0
1350–1399	36.0	4.0	1.1	21.9	28.2	7.5
1375–1424	36.7	2.2	0.7	24.4	25.2	7.8
1400–1449	38.2	1.6	0.4	27.4	23.7	6.9
Norfolk						
1250–1299	16.8	10.8	0.6	51.3	20.1	0.4
1275–1324	16.0	12.1	0.8	52.3	18.5	0.3
1300–1349	14.9	13.8	1.2	53.7	16.0	0.4
1325–1374	17.3	11.2	1.0	53.8	16.0	0.7
1350–1399	17.2	6.5	1.0	58.3	16.5	0.5
1375–1424	14.8	5.2	1.1	61.5	17.3	0.0
1400–1449	16.8	5.4	0.7	59.0	18.1	0.0

Source See notes 29 and 30.

occupied a steadily contracting share of the cereal acreage in the period 1350–1449. Overall, however, it was the spring grains – barley, oats and dredge (a barley–oats mixture) – which always had the edge, and it was within the spring sector that the greatest changes occurred.

Initially oats was by far the most important spring crop, rivalling even wheat in its share of the cereal acreage, but over time that share was progressively reduced as barley rose gradually to prominence. In the mid thirteenth century oats accounted for more than two-and-a-half times the area occupied by barley, yet by the opening of the fifteenth century it was barley which occupied the larger area. The rise of barley was paralleled by a growth in the relative importance of dredge, so that by the close of the period under consideration they together accounted for fully a third of the total cereal acreage. These developments were, of course, partly related to the fact that land was being withdrawn from cultivation, so it is no surprise to find that rye and oats – the crops most closely associated with the cultivation of poorer soils – should have declined in relative importance. But the rise of barley and dredge represent more than this, for their gains were absolute as well as relative. In effect, higher-value crops were being substituted for lower-value crops, since barley commanded a price significantly higher than oats. In Norfolk, by contrast, barley had always been the pre-eminent crop and all that happened was that this pre-eminence became more pronounced after 1350, so that by the close of the fourteenth century no less than 60 per cent of the county's cereal acreage was devoted to barley, a proportion unequalled anywhere else in the country. Unusually, this expansion seems to have been mainly at the expense of rye – a winter grain whose share of the total cereal acreage was halved during the second half of the fourteenth century – as barley rose to prominence as the leading crop on the light sandy soils in the south-west of the county.[66] By contrast, the respective shares of wheat and oats remained little changed, at just under a fifth of the total cereal acreage.

Associated with these changes in the relative importance of different crops were changes in their relative value (see Table 6.4). Over the entire period 1250–1449 the value per bushel of wheat, rye, barley and oats stood in the ratio 1.00, 0.71, 0.66, and 0.40 respectively. Thus, the winter grains were more valuable than the spring grains, with wheat the most valuable of the former and barley the most valuable of the latter. On the whole, the gap in relative value between the winter and spring grains tended to narrow before 1350, under the stimuli of expanding population and declining per capita incomes which encouraged the dietary substitution of lower- for higher-value grains, and to widen thereafter for more-or-less the opposite reasons.[67] The post-1350 decline in the relative value of individual cereal crops eroded the productivity of the arable sector in monetary terms and provided cultivators with a major incentive to modify their enterprise in favour of the more valuable crops. Equivalent ratios calculated for Norfolk from the unpublished price data collected by Lord Beveridge reveal similar, if more pronounced, trends.[68] Thus, the post-1350 decline in relative values was in excess of 20 per cent for oats and 25 per cent for barley as compared with 12 and 14 per cent respectively for the country as a whole, a differential deterioration which significantly reduced the

66 M. Bailey, *A marginal economy? East Anglian Breckland in the later middle ages*, Cambridge, 1989, pp. 282–4.
67 C. C. Dyer, *Standards of living in the later middle ages: social change in England, c.1200–1520*, Cambridge, 1989.
68 Lord Beveridge made extensive unpublished tabulations of regional price data which are now housed in the library of the London School of Economics and Political Science. Those for Norfolk – Box G9 – draw heavily upon the records of Norwich Cathedral Priory.

IV

Table 6.4 *England and Norfolk: trends in grain prices relative to wheat,*
1250–1449

Years	Wheat	Rye	Maslin	Barley	Oats	Dredge
England[a]						
1250–1299	1.00	0.79	0.89	0.68	0.38	0.53
1275–1324	1.00	0.75	0.87	0.70	0.41	0.55
1300–1349	1.00	0.77	0.88	0.71	0.40	0.55
1325–1374	1.00	0.68	0.84	0.68	0.42	0.55
1350–1399	1.00	0.66	0.83	0.61	0.39	0.50
1375–1424	1.00	0.64	0.82	0.65	0.41	0.53
1400–1449	1.00	0.68	0.84	0.61	0.37	0.49
Norfolk[b]						
1250–1299	1.00	0.65	0.82	0.72	0.40	0.56
1275–1324	1.00	0.72	0.86	0.77	0.44	0.60
1300–1349	1.00	0.67	0.83	0.74	0.49	0.61
1325–1374	1.00	0.61	0.80	0.65	0.46	0.55
1350–1399	1.00	0.68	0.84	0.55	0.36	0.45
1375–1424	1.00	0.71	0.85	0.56	0.43	0.49
1400–1449	1.00	0.58	0.79	0.53	0.38	0.45

Source
[a] Calculated from J. E. Thorold Rogers, *A history of agriculture and prices in England*,
I, Oxford, 1884.
[b] Calculated from unpublished Beveridge price data (Box G9) held in the library
of the London School of Economics and Political Science. I am grateful to the
London School of Economics for permission to use this information.

value of the grain harvest in the county and exacerbated the agricultural
depression of the closing decades of the fourteenth century.

The combined effect of these changes in the composition of the
cereal acreage and the relative value of the various grains, as Table 6.5
demonstrates, was to alter the relative value of the cereal acreage.
Converted into wheat equivalents on the basis of relative prices, the
cereal acreage registered a 5 per cent gain in value in Norfolk over the
period 1250–1349 (where it was already worth more than the national
average) and an 8 per cent gain within the country as a whole.
Thereafter, however, the value of the cereal acreage declined. The
substitution of higher- for lower-valued crops meant that nationally
this decline was only of the order of 5 or 6 per cent, but in Norfolk
the decline, was catastrophic and amounted to no less than 20 per
cent. Only by devoting a much larger share of its arable to wheat could
Norfolk have countered this decline, and yet such a change was not

Table 6.5 *England and Norfolk: changing relative value of the cereal acreage,*
1250–1449

	1250–1299	1275–1324	1300–1349	1325–1374	1350–1399	1375–1424	1400–1449
England	66.8	69.9	72.4	71.7	67.7	69.0	68.5
Norfolk	69.5	74.0	73.0	67.6	60.7	61.4	58.7

Note
Each figure is calculated according to the formula $\sum(a_i \cdot p_i)$ where a_i is the
proportion of the cropped acreage under crop i (Table 6.3) and p_i is the price of
crop i relative to wheat (Table 6.4).

Source Tables 6.3 and 6.4.

readily reconciled with rotational schemes whose successful operation
relied upon a heavy spring emphasis.[69] The only other alternative was
to offset the decline in the relative value of its produce by significantly
increasing its per unit output (such as was to occur under somewhat
less extreme circumstances in the second half of the seventeenth
century), but as the yield statistics summarised in Table 6.2 illustrate,
this does not appear to have happened.[70]

By combining information on the relative value and area of the
individual grain crops with weighted estimates of their yields it is possible
to derive an estimate of the weighted aggregate net yield per seed and
per acre, measured in wheat equivalents.[71] The results are summarised
in Table 6.6 and graphed in Figure 6.1(d). They are net in the sense
that tithe and seed corn have both been deducted, although no
allowance has been made for fodder, food liveries, or other on-the-
farm deductions which collectively could be at least as considerable.

69 Wheat eventually became the leading crop of east Norfolk, but probably not
   until the sixteenth century: M. Overton and B. M. S. Campbell, 'Five centuries
   of farming: agricultural change in medieval and early modern Norfolk, *c.*1250–
   *c.*1750', unpublished paper presented to the annual conference of the Economic
   History Society, Liverpool, 1990.
70 E. L. Jones, 'Agriculture and economic growth in England, 1660–1750: agricultural
   change', *JEH*, XXV, 1965, pp. 1–18, reprinted as pp. 67–81 in *idem, Agriculture
   and the industrial revolution*, Oxford, 1974.
71 The yields per acre are calculated by multiplying weighted mean yields per seed
   (Table 6.2) by weighted mean seeding rates computed for all demesnes with
   seeding information (the weights are by geographical location but *not* harvest year).
   The resultant yields are thus more widely representative of conditions within the
   county than if they had been derived solely from the rather limited population
   of demesnes and accounts with direct information of per-acre yields.

Table 6.6 *Norfolk: weighted aggregate net cereal yields, 1250–1449 (wheat bushel equivalents, net of tithe and seed)*

Years	n	Yield per seed	Yield per acre
1250–1274	19	1.46	5.69
1275–1299	36	1.68	6.47
1300–1324	42	1.85	6.95
1325–1349	56	2.05	7.68
1350–1374	45	1.48	5.32
1375–1399	39	1.64	6.30
1400–1424	25	1.44	5.08
1425–1449	10	1.59	5.58

Note
Figures are calculated according to the formula $Y = \sum (y_i \cdot p_i/p_w \cdot a_i/\Sigma a)$ where Y is weighted yield, y_i is the yield of crop i as yield per seed or in bushels per acre, p_i is the price of the crop per bushel, p_w is the price of wheat per bushel, a_i is the acreage under crop i.
n is the number of demesnes with yield information.

Source Tables 6.2 and 6.4.

On the evidence of five well-documented demesnes of varying levels of productivity, seed corn accounted for 51–88 per cent of total deductions in the case of wheat, 37–65 per cent in the case of rye, 48–63 per cent in the case of barley, and 28–48 per cent in the case of oats. In each case additional grain was set aside to meet other essential, recurrent commitments, notably food liveries for the farm workers and fodder for the livestock. As these figures indicate, the extent to which this was the case varied between crops and it will be noted that the proportion was smallest in the case of wheat, the most valuable crop, and greatest in the case of oats, the least valuable. The true net yield which was free for disposal after the immediate requirements of husbandry had been met was thus even smaller than the estimates of aggregate yield imply. On the intensively cultivated and high-yielding demesne at Hemsby, for instance, over the period 1261–1335 the net disposable surplus amounted to 78 per cent of the wheat harvest, 69 per cent of the rye, 49 per cent of the barley (the chief crop), and none of the oats, the whole of whose produce was consumed on the demesne as seed, fodder, and liveries.[72] On less productive demesnes these proportions were lower: respectively 25 per cent, 0 per cent, 29 per cent, and 0 per

72 NRO DCN 60/15/1–16.

cent on the low-yielding demesne at Thorpe Abbotts over the period 1336–79.[73]

To set these Norfolk estimates of aggregate yield in context an equivalent figure has been calculated for the Winchester manors over the period 1209–1349. This is based upon the yield information contained in Appendices B and L of Titow's *Winchester Yields*; details of the percentage cropped for eight randomly selected years, and data on prices derived from the Winchester Pipe Rolls and published by Farmer.[74] The result is a mean weighted aggregate net yield per acre of 5.13 bushels, a figure some 19 per cent lower than the mean figure for Norfolk over the period 1250–1349. Norfolk thus enjoyed a considerable productivity advantage over the Winchester manors, an advantage, moreover, which would have been even greater had it been possible to take the frequency of fallowing into account. For, whereas on most of the Winchester manors between a third and a half of the arable lay fallow each year, in much of Norfolk this proportion was considerably lower and in those parts of the county where cultivation was most intensive, much of the arable was under a continuous succession of crops. On the most productive and intensively cropped of these demesnes, such as Hemsby, Martham, Flegg and Ormesby, the weighted aggregate net yield per arable acre attained approximately 6–9 bushels. In contrast, at Brightwell and Harwell, the most productive demesnes on the entire Winchester estate, adherence to a two-course rotation of crops restricted the net yield per arable acre to approximately 4.2–5.0 bushels. On the estate as a whole the equivalent of 2 to 4 bushels of wheat were produced per arable acre per year after allowance for seed corn and tithes. In Norfolk the range of yields was much wider: the highest yielding Norfolk demesnes were twice as productive as their Winchester counterparts and at a crude estimate, arable land

---

73 NRO WAL 478/274x6. Compare the equivalent proportions calculated by Thornton for Rimpton, below, p. 193.

74 The yield data are drawn from Titow, *Winchester yields*, and from the unpublished researches of E. A. Wrigley, to whom I am grateful for supplying information. The years for which crop data have been obtained are 1265, 1274, 1284, 1286, 1296, 1302, 1321 and 1345. The data for five of these years was extracted from Table 6.VI of J. Z. Titow, 'Land and population on the Bishop of Winchester's estates 1209–1350', unpublished University of Cambridge Ph.D. thesis, 1962. A transcript of the data for 1286 was kindly supplied by John Langdon and the data for 1274 and 1296 was extracted from the relevant Pipe Rolls in the Hampshire Record Office, 159302 and 159315. The price data is drawn from D. L. Farmer, 'Some grain price movements in thirteenth-century England', *EcHR*, X, 1957–8, pp. 207–20.

in Norfolk was on average 50 per cent more productive than that on the Winchester manors.[75]

Arable productivity thus attained an impressive level in Norfolk, notwithstanding stocking densities which were well below the national average and significantly lower than those prevailing on the Winchester manors. On the evidence of Table 6.6 cereal productivity appears to have risen progressively from the mid 1260s to reach a peak in the first half of the fourteenth century, when it was boosted in the 1330s by a fortuitous run of good harvests. This trend was in part buoyed up by a steady improvement in relative prices, so that during the period 1325–49 the value of a bushel of Norfolk malted barley reached 95 per cent the value of a bushel of wheat, but it was also underpinned by a progressive increase in the intensity of husbandry. By the opening of the fourteenth century cultivation methods in the more fertile and densely-populated parts of the county had reached an extraordinary pitch of intensity and required lavish inputs of labour in the preparation of the seed bed and weeding and harvesting of the crop.[76] These methods were sustained by high grain prices, low wages, and an abundance of labour, but as labour became progressively scarcer and dearer following the demographic collapse of the mid fourteenth century, and then as prices fell from the late 1370s, so husbandry methods became correspondingly less intensive.

On the Prior of Norwich's demesne at Martham in east Norfolk the number of man-days per sown acre worked by the permanent staff of farm servants was reduced from 10.42 in the period 1300–24 to 8.21 in the period 1400–24, a reduction of 21 per cent.[77] Over the same period the employment of casual labour was curtailed even more drastically so that total labour inputs per acre were probably reduced by a third or more.[78] The net result at Martham was a significant reduction in arable productivity, for by 1400–24 the weighted aggregate

75 See Thornton, below, pp. 191–2, for a detailed comparison of arable productivity at Martham and Rimpton, which reveals the former to have been almost exactly twice the latter.

76 B. M. S. Campbell, 'Agricultural progress in medieval England: some evidence from eastern Norfolk', *EcHR*, XXXVI, 1983, pp. 26–46.

77 Labour inputs per sown acre at Rimpton, as calculated by Thornton, were in fact consistently higher: below, Table 7.7, pp. 204–7. This discrepancy narrows when labour inputs are calculated per *arable* acre, and shifts in Martham's favour when casual labour is taken into account. There is also the question of the relative efficiencies of the customary labour relied upon by Rimpton and hired labour which predominated at Martham.

78 Campbell, 'Agricultural progress', pp. 38–9.

net yield per cereal acre was some 40 per cent lower than it had been in 1300–24. Over the same period the reduction in productivity within the county as a whole was some 27 per cent. In both cases the general deterioration in relative grain prices, especially those of barley, the crop in which Norfolk specialised, accounted for a large part of the decline, but a genuine reduction in yields, particularly of wheat, also played its part. As will be seen from Table 6.6, aggregate productivity fluctuated considerably over the period 1350–1449, no doubt reflecting the impact of weather conditions on the quality of the harvest, but with lowered labour inputs it never regained the high level of the early fourteenth century. Two additional developments further reinforced the decline in arable productivity. First, as the intensity of husbandry was lowered, so the frequency of fallowing increased, with the result that a reduced proportion of the arable was under crops in any one year. Second, as part of the general improvement in working conditions, farm workers were given an increasingly generous allowance of food, thus raising production costs.[79] In effect, the net yield shrank.

VI Productivity trends at the intensive and extensive margins of cultivation

The discrepancy in the scale of the productivity decline between Martham and Norfolk serves as a reminder that aggregate trends invariably subsume a considerable diversity of experience. This is exemplified by five demesnes of Norwich Cathedral Priory, each of which possesses a good run of accounts for both the early fourteenth and the early fifteenth centuries.[80] As will be seen from Table 6.7, four of these five demesnes registered a decline in aggregate productivity in excess of the county average, and at Martham and Hindolveston this decline was in excess of 40 per cent. On both these demesnes the net yield per acre of wheat, barley, and legumes was substantially lower in 1400–24 than it had been in 1300–24 and only oats fared as well or better. Wheat had always occupied the most privileged position on these two demesnes, occupying the first course in rotations and thus

---

79 C. C. Dyer, 'Changes in nutrition and the standard of living in England, 1200–1500', pp. 35–44 in R. W. Fogel, ed., *Long-term changes in nutrition and the standard of living*, Section B7, the proceedings of the Ninth International Economic History Congress, Bern, 1986.
80 NRO DCN 40/13; DCN 60/18/15–24 & 53–62; DCN 60/23/11–20; NNAS 5905–15 20 D2 & 5916–17 20 D3; DCN 60/29/15–20 & 40–46; DCN 60/33/14–24 & 31; L'Estrange IB 1/4 & 3/4; DCN 60/35/14–22 & 43–52.

Table 6.7 *Productivity on five Norfolk demesnes of the Prior of Norwich, 1300–24 and 1400–24*

	Hindolveston	Martham	Plumstead	Sedgeford	Taverham	Mean
Wheat – net yield per acre (bushels)						
1300–24	16.5 (14)	16.5 (16)	13.1 (11)	13.3 (16)		14.8
1400–24	10.7 (8)	9.2 (11)	8.7 (6)	11.6 (16)	7.91 (7)	10.1
% change	−35.2	−44.2	−33.6	−12.4		−32.2
Rye – net yield per acre (bushels)						
1300–24	8.5 (8)		8.8 (8)	5.1 (16)	5.9 (14)	6.6
1400–24			7.6 (4)	4.3 (14)	6.4 (9)	6.1
% change			−13.1	−15.8	+8.7	−7.3
Barley – net yield per acre (bushels)						
1300–24	13.8 (14)	13.0 (16)	9.5 (11)	11.7 (16)	6.9 (14)	11.0
1400–24	8.3 (8)	11.4 (11)	10.5 (7)	9.7 (17)	12.1 (9)	10.4
% change	−39.6	−12.5	+10.8	−17.4	+75.9	−5.1
Oats – net yield per acre (bushels)						
1300–24	6.9 (14)	13.0 (16)	8.5 (11)	6.3 (16)	4.6 (13)	7.8
1400–24	7.0 (8)	16.4 (8)	9.4 (5)	5.5 (17)	7.9 (9)	9.2
% change	+1.9	+25.9	+10.8	−12.1	+70.9	+17.7
Legumes – net yield per acre (bushels)						
1300–24	5.5 (14)	7.5 (15)	6.9 (11)	3.7 (16)	3.4 (13)	5.4
1400–24	4.7 (8)	4.0 (9)	5.3 (5)	3.7 (17)	1.5 (7)	3.8
% change	−14.8	−46.3	−22.8	0.0	−54.7	−28.0
Weighted aggregate net yield per acre[a]						
1300–24	9.064	10.191	7.312	7.214	4.450	7.646
1400–24	4.701	5.989	5.049	5.382	5.142	5.253
% change	−48.1	−41.2	−31.0	−25.4	+15.6	−31.3
Mean sown acreage						
1300–24	165.3	194.3	218.5	410.8	132.1	224.2
1400–24	132.3	177.2	198.7	293.1	83.0	176.9
% change	−20.0	−8.8	−9.1	−28.7	−37.2	−21.1

Notes
[a] See Table 6.6.
Figures for each manor following the productivity measure are the number of recorded harvests.

Source See note 80.

receiving the maximum benefit from ploughings and manurings. When the latter were reduced as husbandry became less intensive its harvest was consequently disproportionately affected. What, however, was wheat's loss was oats' gain. The latter had always been penalised by being placed at the end of a long and demanding sequence of cropping, hence it actually benefited from the lowered intensity of husbandry. Significantly, this pattern is repeated to some degree across all five demesnes, with wheat exhibiting the greatest absolute decline in yield and oats the greatest relative improvement.

Nevertheless, it will be noted that at Sedgeford the overall yield decline was a relatively modest 11.5 per cent across all five main crops, and at Taverham there was actually a 15.6 per cent gain, with rye and especially barley and oats performing significantly better in the later than in the earlier period. Significantly, it was on these two demesnes that the contraction in cultivation was greatest and it was at Taverham, the least productive of the five, that there was most scope for an improvement in yields. Nor was the experience of Taverham unique. On Ely Cathedral's demesne at Brandon on the Norfolk–Suffolk border a 50 per cent reduction in the area under cultivation between 1340 and 1390 was accompanied by a 45 per cent improvement in aggregate cereal productivity, as part of which the yields of rye, barley and oats all increased substantially.[81] Brandon, like Taverham, was located on poor sandy soils and obtained yields in the first half of the fourteenth century which were both absolutely and relatively low. Under these circumstances genuine productivity benefits do appear to have accrued from a withdrawal of tillage to the better soils and a lengthening in the duration of fallows.

What the contrasting experience of these various demesnes appears to be demonstrating is the divergence of the productivity response at the intensive and extensive margins of cultivation. In this respect, Martham, Hindolveston, Plumstead and Sedgeford all represent versions of the former, since on all four demesnes individual crop yields and aggregate productivity were both at a peak when labour inputs and sown acreages were at a maximum in the first half of the fourteenth century. Thereafter, as the population declined and wage rates rose, so labour inputs were reduced and productivity suffered. In fact, so great was the reduction in output per acre that on occasion, as at Martham, there was little if any concomitant gain in labour productivity. On this demesne the weighted aggregate net yield per 1,000 man days worked by the *famuli* declined by 20 per cent from 0.5127 bushels in 1300–24 to 0.4116 bushels in 1400–24 (at constant prices the equivalent figure is 0.5292 bushels), although this fails to take account of the substantial decline in the employment of casual labour between these two periods.[82] The normal expectation, however, is that with a reversion to more

81 Chicago University Library, Bacon Roll 643–59; Public Record Office SC 6/1304/22–36; Elveden Hall, Suffolk, Iveagh Collection 148, Phillipps 26523.
82 Thornton, below, p. 209.

extensive methods of production, labour productivity should have improved. The predominantly positive relationship between physical productivity and population trends exhibited by these four demesnes is much the same as that envisaged by Le Roy Ladurie for northern France and Van der Wee for the Low Countries over the same period, both of which, like much of Norfolk, were areas of relatively intensive arable husbandry.[83] Yet as the experience of Taverham and Brandon demonstrate, this was by no means the universal response.

Taverham and Brandon were situated at the extensive margin of cultivation, on light soils which were incapable of sustaining intensive methods of production. As wage rates rose and, in due course, prices fell, cultivation was substantially curtailed on both demesnes. In Ricardian fashion, cropping became increasingly concentrated on to the better land, with corresponding benefits for individual crop yields, and associated with this went an improvement in the ratio of high- to low-value crops which constituted a source of aggregate productivity growth. The performance of these two demesnes conforms much more closely to the expectations of those English historians who have stressed the productivity benefits of a reduction in the intensity of arable husbandry and a contraction in the area under cultivation. At Taverham and Brandon it was, indeed, as Postan, Titow, Farmer, and Outhwaite have argued, when cultivation was at its fullest stretch in the early fourteenth century that mean yields were lowest, although this does not mean that soils were necessarily becoming exhausted.[84]

Nevertheless, although Norfolk contained a variety of productivity responses, in aggregate the relationship between yields and population trends was more positive than negative. The county was one of the most intensively cultivated in the country and, accordingly, it was the experience of the intensive margin of cultivation which prevailed. Except possibly on the lightest and poorest soils, output per acre was highest when labour inputs were greatest and not when livestock were most numerous. The net result, as Neveux found in the Cambrésis region of France, was that the range of yields narrowed as population declined and labour inputs were reduced.[85] There may have been gains at the

83 Van der Wee, 'Introduction'; Le Roy Ladurie, 'The end of the middle ages'.
84 Postan, 'Medieval agrarian society'; J. Z. Titow, *English rural society 1200–1350*, London, 1969, pp. 52–4; Farmer, 'Grain yields on Westminster Abbey manors', 1983; Outhwaite, 'progress and backwardness'. Compare also productivity trends on the Westminster demesne at Kinsbourne, Herts.; Stern, 'A Hertfordshire manor'.
85 Le Roy Ladurie, 'The end of the middle ages', p. 85.

lower end of the yield spectrum but, at least in Norfolk, these were more than offset by losses at the upper. How representative Norfolk is of the country at large is, however, a moot point and one deserving of further investigation. By the early fourteenth century England had evolved a variety of different types of agricultural system of differing degrees of intensity, each of which will have responded to the demographic and economic changes of the fourteenth century in its own unique way.[86] Norfolk was certainly unusual in the relatively small scale on which cultivation contracted and stocking densities increased in the period 1350–1449 and its productivity history may consequently yet prove to have been more the exception than the rule.

VII The duration of Norfolk's late medieval productivity decline

If the high yields sustained in early-fourteenth-century Norfolk subsequently declined, as methods of husbanding soil nitrogen became less careful, when did productivity begin to recover? In the Low Countries the sixteenth century appears to have been the key period, although it was not until the seventeenth century that the medieval productivity peak was exceeded. The sixteenth century was also a time of recovery in northern France, although the early fourteenth century continued to set the standard for productivity until the latter part of the eighteenth century. For Norfolk a partial answer is provided by comparing medieval gross yields per acre calculated from manorial accounts with a series of yield estimates for the period 1584–1739 made by M. Overton from valuations of standing crops contained in probate inventories.[87] To facilitate comparison, the latter have been calculated for farms with a minimum sown acreage of twenty acres and aggregated to produce county means using the same system of regional weighting as that employed with the accounts. Weighted aggregate gross yields per cereal acre have also been calculated using information on crop proportions and prices contained in the inventories and the results indexed, taking 1250–74 as the base period, to produce an

---

86 Campbell and Power, 'Mapping'; B. M. S. Campbell, 'People and land in the middle ages, 1066–1500', pp. 69–121 in R. A. Dodgshon and R. A. Butlin, eds., *An historical geography of England and Wales*, London, 2nd edn., 1990, pp. 89–92.

87 See M. Overton, below, pp. 298–305. Gross yields are employed in the comparison because of the absence of reliable information on seeding rates for the early modern period. Tithes are assumed to have comprised 10 per cent of yield throughout.

overall index of cereal productivity.[88] Also included are a series of
yield estimates for the late eighteenth and early nineteenth centuries
assembled from various sources.

Apart from the major gaps in the resultant time series – most
notably 1450–1584 but also 1600–27, 1641–59, and 1740–69 – several
problems, mostly unresolvable, attend its interpretation. In the first
place the estimates themselves are based upon different sources of
evidence and have been calculated in different ways: the medieval
yields by measurement, the early modern by estimation, and those for
the late eighteenth and early nineteenth centuries by observation.
Methods of estimating absolute yields from probate inventories are
themselves a matter of debate and the results subject to margins of
error of the order ± 2 bushels an acre.[89] In the case of the lesser crops
– rye and oats – this error is likely to be one of overestimation, due to
problems of small sample size, likely price undervaluation by the
appraisers, and distortions arising from the inclusion of straw in the
valuations. Additional, largely unresolvable, problems arise from
the employment of customary as opposed to statute measures of area
and volume and from differences in the sizes of farm being compared.[90] Caution must therefore be exercised in making comparisons.
Nevertheless, given available data sources, this yield series is the best
obtainable and the first to present statistics for the same unit area over
such a long span of time.[91]

On the evidence of Table 6.8, neither the high wheat and barley
yields nor the high aggregate productivity of the first half of the
fourteenth century were significantly bettered until the early eighteenth
century. When yields and aggregate productivity rose over the period

88 As P. O'Brien and G. Toniolo observe: 'how much produce a medieval peasant
   obtained from a 50-hectare plot of land compared with his modern successor
   cultivating the same plot is a question that can only be tackled by valuing the mix
   of crops harvested at prices prevailing in medieval and modern times' (below,
   p. 390).
89 Glennie, below, pp. 256–71.
90 Several contributors to this volume note, however, little correlation between
   yields and farm size: Overton, below, pp. 309–11; Allen, below, pp. 246–9.
91 It improves upon M. Whitney, 'The yield of wheat in England over seven centuries',
   Science, CVIII, 1923, pp. 320–4; M. K. Bennett, 'British wheat yield per acre for
   seven centuries', *Economic History* (a supplement of *The Economic Journal*), III, 1935,
   pp. 12–29, reprinted as pp. 54–72 in W. E. Minchinton, ed., *Essays in agrarian
   history*, I, Newton Abbot, 1968; and G. Stanhill, 'Trends and deviations in the yield
   of the English wheat crop during the last 750 years', *Agro-Ecosystems*, III, 1976,
   pp. 1–10. The Norfolk series is further discussed in M. Overton and B. M. S.
   Campbell, 'Five centuries of farming'.

Table 6.8 *Norfolk: gross cereal yields per acre, 1250–1854*

Years	Wheat (bushels)	Rye (bushels)	Barley (bushels)	Oats (bushels)	WACY[a]	Index[b]
1250–1274	13.2	8.8	15.7	13.5	9.3	100
1275–1299	14.9	10.3	15.8	13.8	10.3	111
1300–1324	14.9	10.0	16.1	13.3	11.0	118
1325–1349	15.6	10.5	17.2	15.0	11.9	127
1350–1374	11.4	8.9	15.3	11.9	8.6	92
1375–1399	12.9	10.1	17.3	14.0	9.7	104
1400–1424	12.7	9.9	14.9	13.9	8.0	86
1425–1449	10.7	12.0	15.4	14.5	8.9	96
1584–1599	11.7	11.9	11.7	15.4	8.2	85
1628–1640	17.3	11.6	11.9	18.4	9.4	98
1660–1679	12.8	14.1	13.9	13.1	8.2	85
1680–1709	14.7	9.0	15.3	20.0	8.5	89
1710–1739	16.9	14.4	22.0	26.4	12.9	134
1760s[c]	25.5	25.0	30.9	38.3		
1790s[d]	24.0		32.0			
c.1800[e]	20.0					
c.1800[f]	24.0		36.0	40.0		
c.1836[g]	23.3		32.0	36.3	20.7	216
1854[h]	30.0		38.0	46.0	25.5	266

Notes
Unlike those for Norfolk and Suffolk in Overton, below, p. 302, inventory yields are for farms with 20 or more cropped acres, and are not weighted by harvest year. Inventory averages conceal wide fluctuations as well as being subject to error.
[a] Weighted aggregate cereal yield, see Table 6.6.
[b] Index of weighted aggregate gross yield per cereal acre. 1250–74 = 100.

Source
1250–1449, from manorial accounts (see note 30); 1584–1739 from probate inventories (see Overton, below, pp. 298–305).
[c] Calculated from A. Young, *The farmer's tour through the east of England*, 4 vols., London, 1771, IV, pp. 230–45.
[d] N. Kent, *General view of the agriculture of the county of Norfolk with observations for the means of its improvement*, London, 1796, pp. 56 and 59.
[e] W. Marshall, *The review and abstract of the county reports to the Board of Agriculture, III, Eastern Department*, York, 1818, p. 349.
[f] A. Young, *General view of the agriculture of the county of Norfolk*, London, 1804, p. 303.
[g] R. J. P. Kain, *An atlas and index of the tithe files of mid-nineteenth-century England and Wales*, Cambridge, 1986, p. 72.
[h] *Reports by the poor law inspectors on agricultural statistics (England)*, BPP, LIII, 1st series Cd.1928, London, 1854–5.

1584–1640 they were therefore recovering to an essentially medieval level of productivity and, as Glennie has suggested for Hertfordshire, may have done so via the employment of medieval-type methods of land management.[92] Moreover, the economic incentives for an intensification of husbandry techniques were much the same: high prices and a cheap and abundant labour supply. Thereafter, as prices sagged and wages rose, cereal productivity – in late medieval fashion – fell (a development reinforced by worsening climatic conditions).[93] Yields and cereal productivity remained below the best medieval standards for the remainder of the seventeenth century, but from the opening of the new century they began to rise again and to do so more vigorously than ever before. By the 1720s and '30s mean yields of Norfolk's two principal crops were back on a par with the record set almost exactly four centuries earlier, while the harvests obtained on some individual farms began to better the medieval best. The spectrum of yields was once more moving upwards and evidently continued to do so for the remainder of the eighteenth century, since by that century's close mean wheat and barley yields were respectively 40 and 70 per cent higher.[94] The steepness of this rise in productivity was unprecedented and, for the first time, the rise in yields ante-dated rising prices and falling wages. As such it reflected the adoption of new types of husbandry system which harnessed and cycled larger quantities of nitrogen.[95]

Chronologically, the experience of Norfolk thus falls midway between that of the Low Countries, where the medieval productivity peak was exceeded in the seventeenth century, and northern France, where it was not exceeded until the later eighteenth century. As has been noted, all three of these areas lay at the intensive margin of cultivation where labour inputs were patently a major determinant of the rate at which land yielded so that, contrary to much English writing on the subject, the correlation between land productivity and population

92 'The higher crop yields of the later seventeenth century cannot be seen as indicating a decisive break between medieval and modern agriculture, but rather continuity in the techniques by which land productivity could be raised': P. Glennie, 'Continuity and change in Hertfordshire agriculture, 1550–1700: II – trends in crop yields and their determinants', *AHR*, XXXVI, 1988 pp. 155–6.

93 M. Overton, 'Weather and agricultural change in England, 1660–1739', *Agricultural History*, LXIII, 1989, pp. 77–88.

94 This contrasts with R. C. Allen's chronology for Oxfordshire, based on a much smaller sample of inventories, which places the bulk of the yield increases firmly in the seventeenth century: below, pp. 247–8.

95 Shiel, above, pp. 68–79, 74–5; Overton, below, pp. 319–22.

levels was essentially positive.[96] Elsewhere the story may have been very different, although C. Thornton's meticulous analysis of Rimpton in Somerset, where husbandry was at an altogether lower pitch of intensity, reveals some striking Norfolk parallels.[97] Nevertheless, Norfolk is not England, and much work remains to be done before it can be established how representative or otherwise it is of the country at large. Of the complexity of the productivity equation, however, it leaves no doubt. Strategies for raising productivity included substituting higher-yielding for lower-yielding and higher-value for lower-value crops, reducing fallows and cultivating the land more frequently, and adopting more efficient seeding techniques which increased the net as a proportion of the gross yield. These were all ways in which an increased return could be obtained from the land irrespective of any improvement in yield levels *per se*. Having an adequate supply of fertiliser to keep the land in good condition of course helped, but livestock manure was not the only source of fertiliser, and large numbers of livestock were no guarantee that arable fields would be adequately manured.[98] Throughout the medieval period and probably much of the early modern, keeping land in good heart required labour as much as livestock – to supervise herds; pen flocks in movable folds; gather and spread manure; dig marl; cart night soil, sea sand, and any other extraneous sources of fertiliser that might be available; plough and harrow the land; eliminate weeds, and harvest with care – and it was consequently when labour was cheapest and most abundant that the most intensive arable farming systems attained their peak of productivity. Under medieval technological and economic conditions, however, high output per unit area was bought at the expense of low output per worker and it was to require a structural and technological transformation of agriculture before both were able to expand together.

96 See above, pp. 146–8.
97 Thornton, below, pp. 193–5.
98 Biddick, below, p. 115.

BIBLIOGRAPHY
CHAPTER IV

All cross-references are to chapters within Bruce M. S. Campbell and Mark Overton, eds., *Land, Labour and Livestock: Historical Studies in European Agricultural Productivity*, Manchester and New York, 1991:

Robert C. Allen, 'The two English agricultural revolutions, 1450–1850', pp. 236–54.

Kathleen Biddick (with Catrien C.J.H. Bijleveld), 'Agrarian productivity on the estates of the bishopric of Winchester in the early thirteenth century: a managerial perspective', pp. 95–123.

Gregory Clark, 'Labour productivity in English agriculture, 1300–1860', pp. 211–35.

Paul Glennie, 'Measuring crop yields in early modern England', pp. 255–83.

Patrick O'Brien and Gianni Toniolo, 'The poverty of Italy and the backwardness of its agriculture before 1914', pp. 385–409.

Mark Overton, "The determinants of crop yields in early modern England', pp. 284–322.

Robert S. Shiel, 'Improving soil productivity in the pre-fertiliser era', pp. 51–77.

Peter Solar and Martine Goossens, 'Agricultural productivity in Belgium and Ireland in the early nineteenth century', pp. 364–84.

Christopher Thornton, 'The determinants of land productivity on the bishop of Winchester's demesne of Rimpton, 1208 to 1403', pp. 183–210.

E.A. Wrigley, 'Energy availability and agricultural productivity', pp. 323–339.

V

A NEW PERSPECTIVE ON MEDIEVAL AND EARLY MODERN AGRICULTURE: SIX CENTURIES OF NORFOLK FARMING c.1250-c.1850*

I

INTRODUCTION

Since the late nineteenth century, ideas about the development of English agriculture from the sixteenth century onwards have been dominated by notions of an agricultural revolution. This was originally conceived as a phenomenon of the century after 1750, when English agriculture was transformed by rapid technological change made possible by the replacement of outmoded agrarian institutions. Subsequent contributions have challenged both the nature and the timing of this revolution, so that now there are also claims that an agricultural revolution took place between 1560 and 1673, as well as between 1650 and 1750. These revisions have encouraged a more gradualist interpretation of developments after 1750, which has been reinforced by recent estimates of agricultural output demonstrating that growth was more rapid in the first half of the eighteenth century than in the second. While there is no consensus over the timing and pace of an agricultural revolution, there is a fairly general agreement that English agriculture underwent a fundamental technological transformation between the mid-sixteenth and the mid-eighteenth century, brought about by the introduction of new fodder crops,

*Earlier versions of this paper were presented to seminars at The Queen's University of Belfast, Trinity College, Dublin, University of Alberta, Edmonton, University of British Columbia, Vancouver, University of Washington, Seattle, and the Centre of East Anglian Studies at the University of East Anglia, Norwich, as well as to the annual conference of the Economic History Society, Liverpool, 1990. We are grateful for the opportunities these presented to discuss both our evidence and ideas. The research from which this paper springs began in the early 1970s, when we were both postgraduate students in Cambridge. We have since both received personal research fellowships from the Economic and Social Research Council which greatly facilitated the lengthy tasks of data collection and analysis. Our debts to other scholars are too numerous to mention, but specific thanks are due to the staff of the Norfolk Record Office, to Jenitha Orr and Meemee Wong for research assistance, and to Anne Rook for drawing the diagrams.

V

which had a decisive impact on "productivity" in terms of grain yields per acre.[1]

The most significant consequence of this productivity improvement, especially in the century after 1750, is taken to have been the ability of British agriculture — albeit aided by increased food imports — to feed an ever-growing population. By 1850 an estimated 6.5 million extra mouths were being fed from home production compared with 1750.[2] Industrialization would have been impossible without this population growth, and without industrialization the economy would probably have remained relatively static, with economic growth the exception rather than the rule. But the transformation was more complex than this, for industrialization, by definition, entailed a progressive reduction in the proportion of the population employed in agriculture: an essential precondition for structural economic change was therefore a significant rise in the productivity of labour employed in agriculture.[3]

Thus the twin achievements of eighteenth- and nineteenth-century agriculture are seen as the ability to match population growth with rising agricultural production, and structural economic change with major gains in agricultural labour productivity. This appears all the more remarkable when set against the perceived experience of earlier centuries. Although one historian claims that the growing population of the sixteenth and early seventeenth centuries elicited a corresponding revolution in agricultural production, most others regard the cessation of population growth by the mid-seventeenth century as indicative of a failure of agricultural output to keep up with expanding demand. The verdict on thirteenth- and early fourteenth-century agriculture is even more unfavourable. Not only did agriculture fail to

[1] An example is in one of the most recent contributions: Gregory Clark, "Yields per Acre in English Agriculture, 1250-1860: Evidence from Labour Inputs", *Econ. Hist. Rev.*, 2nd ser., xliv (1991), p. 459, who argues that "the agricultural revolution thus pre-dates the industrial revolution", on the basis of the trend in wheat yields per acre.

[2] J. D. Chambers and G. E. Mingay, *The Agricultural Revolution, 1750-1880* (London, 1966), pp. 3-4; G. E. Mingay, "Dr Kerridge's 'Agricultural Revolution': A Comment", *Agric. Hist.*, xliii (1969), p. 497; R. B. Outhwaite, "Rural England, 1500-1750", *Histoire Sociale / Social History*, ii (1968), pp. 85-97.

[3] N. F. R. Crafts, "Income Elasticities of Demand and the Release of Labour by Agriculture during the British Industrial Revolution", *Jl. European Econ. Hist.*, ix (1980), p. 167; E. A. Wrigley, *Continuity, Chance and Change: The Character of the Industrial Revolution in England* (Cambridge, 1988), pp. 10-11.

meet the challenge of population growth, but attempts to expand the area under production in conditions of technological inertia are believed to have driven down the productivities of both land and labour, thus negating economic growth and precipitating a Malthusian crisis of major proportions. When plague struck in 1348-9 it therefore struck a population that was probably already in decline.[4]

According to this interpretation medieval agriculture failed because it destroyed the fragile ecological equilibrium on which the sustained production of crops and animals ultimately rested. Nor was this the first example of such a phenomenon. Archaeologists have speculated that attempts to raise agricultural production during the Romano-British period may likewise have led to a progressive loss of soil nitrogen, resulting in ecological stress and productivity decline on the lighter and poorer soils.[5] A double dilemma therefore confronted pre-industrial agriculture: how to raise both land and labour productivity under conditions of population growth; and how to raise agricultural output without jeopardizing the fertility of the soils on which it depended.

This article explores these themes over a period of six centuries for the county of Norfolk. More specifically it is concerned with three issues: the nature and extent of technological change in farming from the thirteenth to the nineteenth century; the provenance, character and timing of the agricultural revolution; and the relationship between population growth and agricultural productivity. In exploring these issues it makes two further contributions. First, it bridges the gaps that have developed in historical writing between the largely independent accounts of medieval and early modern agriculture and, to a lesser extent, between the literature on the early modern period and that on the eighteenth and nineteenth centuries. Secondly, the construction of these bridges breaks new methodological ground, through quantitative

[4] Richard M. Smith, "Demographic Developments in Rural England, 1300-48: A Survey", in Bruce M. S. Campbell (ed.), *Before the Black Death: Studies in the "Crisis" of the Early Fourteenth Century* (Manchester, 1991), pp. 25-78.

[5] S. Applebaum, "Roman Britain", in H. P. R. Finberg (ed.), *The Agrarian History of England and Wales*, i, *A.D. 43-1042* (Cambridge, 1972), pp. 246-7; Martin K. Jones, "Agricultural Productivity in the Pre-Documentary Past", in Bruce M. S. Campbell and Mark Overton (eds.), *Land, Labour and Livestock: Historical Studies in European Agricultural Productivity* (Manchester, 1991), pp. 86-93; Eric Klingelhöfer, *Settlement and Land Use in Micheldever Hundred, Hampshire, 700-1100* (*Trans. Amer. Philos. Soc.*, lxxxi pt. 3, Philadelphia, 1991), pp. 50-4, 73.

V

comparisons of agricultural statistics derived from manorial accounts, probate inventories and nineteenth-century agricultural surveys.

This reconstruction of farm enterprises for a single geographical area over such a long period of time gives a new perspective to ideas both of continuity and discontinuity in English agriculture. The major discontinuity in Norfolk's crop production came after 1740, during the era of the traditional agricultural revolution, when the proportions of land under various crops changed dramatically and crop yields rose to unprecedented heights. While there was a remarkable continuity in the mix of crops during the preceding five hundred years, there were more subtle discontinuities in the geography of crop (and livestock) production, as farmers increasingly adapted their husbandry systems to the demands of the market.

There was also considerable discontinuity in the pace of technological advance. The transformation of the eighteenth and nineteenth centuries had an even longer genesis than has been thought, since almost all the technological innovations that brought it about can be found as far back as the thirteenth century. But a thirteenth-century agricultural revolution did not materialize, and it was in the seventeenth century that developments in the livestock sector, especially the doubling of stocking densities, led to the integration of crop and livestock husbandry, paving the way for the breakthrough in crop yields during the eighteenth century. In contrast to the emphasis on arable farming found in writing on the subject, the livestock sector emerges as the more dynamic over the whole period of this study, since advances in livestock productivity far outweighed those for crops.

The eighteenth century also marks another break with a long-established pattern. Although crop yields fluctuated within the same broad limits between 1250 and 1700, this fluctuating pattern challenges the common assumption that, in pre-industrial England, when population grew, crop yields would fall. In the late thirteenth and early fourteenth centuries, and again in the late sixteenth and early seventeenth centuries, yields did not fall as population grew: on the contrary, they rose. Conversely, yields fell as the population fell in the late fourteenth and early fifteenth centuries and, again, in the late seventeenth century. Thereafter the relationship changed subtly: yields began to grow in the early eighteenth century, while population numbers remained static;

by the early nineteenth century, encouraged by renewed population growth, they had risen to unprecedented levels. This observation fuels the debate over the relationship between population growth and agricultural change in pre-industrial societies, directing attention to both the determinants of crop yields, and to the relationships between crop yields, agricultural productivity and agricultural output.

These findings are discussed in the concluding sections of the paper (VIII, IX and X). They emerge from the cumulative analysis of information on crop proportions, crop yields, livestock proportions and livestock densities, assembled in Sections IV, V, VI and VII, which is preceded by a brief discussion of accounts and inventories in Section III. To help set these results in a wider context, Section II of the paper presents a brief review of the historiography of English agriculture from the Middle Ages to the nineteenth century.

II

THE HISTORIOGRAPHY OF AGRICULTURAL CHANGE

The literature on medieval agriculture, as represented by the influential writings of M. M. Postan (deriving from those of Wilhelm Abel on the Continent), J. Z. Titow, David Grigg and Robert Brenner, is dominated by a concept of agrarian crisis.[6] This verdict derives from the fusion of two schools of thought: on the one hand, the emphasis of the English classical economists on the diminishing returns to labour and capital applied to land, and, on the other, the emphasis of Marxist historians on the exploitative nature of the socio-property relations embodied in

---

[6] Wilhelm Abel, *Agrarkrisen und Agrarkonjunktur in Mitteleuropa vom 13. bis zum 19. Jahrhundert*, 3rd edn. (Berlin, 1935); trans. Olive Ordish, as *Agricultural Fluctuations in Europe from the Thirteenth to the Twentieth Centuries* (London, 1980); Wilhelm Abel, *Die Wüstungen des ausgehenden Mittelalters*, 2nd edn. (Stuttgart, 1955); M. M. Postan, "Medieval Agrarian Society in Its Prime: England", in M. M. Postan (ed.), *The Cambridge Economic History of Europe*, i, *The Agrarian Life of the Middle Ages*, 2nd edn. (Cambridge, 1966), pp. 549-632; J. Z. Titow, *English Rural Society, 1200-1350* (London, 1969); D. L. Farmer, "Crop Yields, Prices and Wages in Medieval England", *Studies in Medieval and Renaissance Hist.*, vi (1983), pp. 117-55; David Grigg, *Population Growth and Agrarian Change: An Historical Perspective* (Cambridge, 1980), pp. 64-82; Robert Brenner, "Agrarian Class Structure and Economic Development in Pre-Industrial Europe", *Past and Present*, no. 70 (Feb. 1976), pp. 30-75, repr. in T. H. Aston and C. H. E. Philpin (eds.), *The Brenner Debate: Agrarian Class Structure and Economic Development in Pre-Industrial Europe* (Cambridge, 1985), pp. 10-63 (subsequent references are to this version).

V

feudalism.[7] Hence the assessment of seigneurial agriculture by Edward Miller and John Hatcher that "even highly organized and superficially efficient estates were failing in one quite basic requirement of good husbandry: the keeping of the land in good heart"; and Brenner's even more pessimistic assessment of peasant agriculture, asserting that "the surplus-extraction relations of serfdom tended to lead to the exhaustion of peasant production *per se*; in particular, the inability to invest in animals for ploughing and as a source of manure led to deterioration of the soil, which in turn led to the extension of cultivation to land formerly reserved for the support of animals. This meant the cultivation of worse soils and at the same time fewer animals — and thus in the end a vicious cycle of the destruction of the peasants' means of support. The crisis of productivity led to demographic crisis, pushing the population over the edge of subsistence".[8] Recent research has led to some qualification of these views, revealing medieval agriculture to have been more varied, dynamic and

[7] Yujiro Hayami and Vernon W. Ruttan, *Agricultural Development: An International Perspective* (Baltimore and London, 1971), pp. 28-34; M. M. Postan and John Hatcher, "Population and Class Relations in Feudal Society", *Past and Present*, no. 78 (Feb. 1978), pp. 24-37, repr. in Aston and Philpin (eds.), *Brenner Debate*, pp. 64-78 (subsequent references are to this version); David Grigg, *The Dynamics of Agricultural Change* (London, 1982), pp. 50-9; Mark Overton and Bruce M. S. Campbell, "Productivity Change in European Agricultural Development", in Campbell and Overton (eds.), *Land, Labour and Livestock*, pp. 29-35; Maurice Dobb, *Studies in the Development of Capitalism* (London, 1946); William Lazonick, "Karl Marx and Enclosures in England", *Rev. Radical Polit. Economics*, vi (1974), pp. 1-59; R. H. Hilton, "Introduction", in R. H. Hilton (ed.), *The Transition from Feudalism to Capitalism* (London, 1976), pp. 9-30; Brenner, "Agrarian Class Structure"; Robert Brenner, "The Agrarian Roots of European Capitalism", *Past and Present*, no. 97 (Nov. 1982), pp. 16-113, repr. in Aston and Philpin (eds.), *Brenner Debate*, pp. 213-327 (subsequent references are to this version); Michael Dunford and Diane Perrons, *The Arena of Capital* (London and Basingstoke, 1983), pp. 90-123; John E. Martin, *Feudalism to Capitalism: Peasant and Landlord in English Agrarian Development* (Atlantic Highlands, N.J., 1983); R. J. Holton, "Marxist Theories of Social Change and the Transition from Feudalism to Capitalism", *Theory and Society*, x (1981), pp. 833-67; R. J. Holton, *The Transition from Feudalism to Capitalism* (London, 1985). For the historiography of medieval soil exhaustion, see Nils Hybel, *Crisis or Change: The Concept of Crisis in the Light of Agrarian Structural Reorganization in Late Medieval England*, trans. James Manley (Aarhus, 1989).

[8] Edward Miller and John Hatcher, *Medieval England: Rural Society and Economic Change, 1086-1348* (London, 1978), p. 217; Brenner, "Agrarian Class Structure", p. 33. On the ecological shortcomings of medieval agriculture Brenner and Postan are united: "We might therefore expect that at times and in regions in which the animal population was reduced to the barest minimum the land was bound to suffer. Apparently it suffered in many parts of medieval England": Postan, "Medieval Agrarian Society", pp. 556-7; although in other crucial respects their interpretations of this period are fundamentally different: Aston and Philpin (eds.), *Brenner Debate*.

adaptable than has hitherto been appreciated.[9] Nevertheless stress continues to be laid on its technological backwardness and ecological excesses, and the possibility that agriculture's inadequacies contributed to a Malthusian positive check remains a matter of considerable debate.[10]

This predominantly negative assessment of thirteenth- and fourteenth-century agriculture finds some echo in the interpretation of the sixteenth century advanced by R. B. Outhwaite.[11] Using "productivity" as his yardstick of progress, he suggests that population pressure may well have prompted a Ricardian extension of cultivation onto "marginal" lands, with deleterious consequences for the efficiency of the agricultural sector. A similarly pessimistic picture is presented by both D. M. Palliser and Roger Schofield, who suggest that on this occasion a Malthusian crisis was only averted through the operation of preventive checks in the form of controls upon nuptiality and hence fertility.[12] Eric Kerridge, on the other hand, believes that agriculture experienced

---

[9] For a categorical statement of medieval agriculture's technological backwardness and inertia, see G. E. Fussell, "Social Change but Static Technology: Rural England in the Fourteenth Century", *History Studies*, i (1968), pp. 23-32. Recent revisions to this view include P. F. Brandon, "Demesne Arable Farming in Coastal Sussex during the Later Middle Ages", *Agric. Hist. Rev.*, xix (1971), pp. 113-34; Bruce M. S. Campbell, "Agricultural Progress in Medieval England: Some Evidence from Eastern Norfolk", *Econ. Hist. Rev.*, 2nd ser., xxxvi (1983), pp. 26-46; Mavis Mate, "Medieval Agrarian Practices: The Determining Factors?", *Agric. Hist. Rev.*, xxxiii (1985), pp. 22-31; Mark Bailey, *A Marginal Economy? East Anglian Breckland in the Later Middle Ages* (Cambridge, 1989); Kathleen Biddick, *The Other Economy: Pastoral Husbandry on a Medieval Estate* (Berkeley and Los Angeles, 1989); Christopher Thornton, "The Determinants of Land Productivity on the Bishop of Winchester's Demesne of Rimpton, 1208 to 1403", in Campbell and Overton (eds.), *Land, Labour and Livestock*, pp. 183-210. The most positive verdict on medieval agriculture to date is that given by H. E. Hallam in his *Rural England, 1066-1348* (London, 1981).

[10] For example, Christopher Dyer, *Standards of Living in the Later Middle Ages: Social Change in England, c.1200-1520* (Cambridge, 1989), pp. 40-1, 127-31. See also Bruce M. S. Campbell, "Ecology versus Economics in Late Thirteenth- and Early Fourteenth-Century English Agriculture", in Del Sweeney (ed.), *Agriculture in the Middle Ages: Reality and Image* (forthcoming, 1994). For an evaluation of the evidence bearing upon the operation of the Malthusian positive check in this period, see Smith, "Demographic Developments in Rural England", pp. 52-61.

[11] R. B. Outhwaite, "Progress and Backwardness in English Agriculture, 1500-1650", *Econ. Hist. Rev.*, 2nd ser., xxxix (1986), pp. 1-18.

[12] D. M. Palliser, "Tawney's Century: Brave New World or Malthusian Trap?", *Econ. Hist. Rev.*, 2nd ser., xxxv (1982), pp. 339-53; Roger Schofield, "The Impact of Scarcity and Plenty on Population Change in England, 1541-1871", *Jl. Interdisciplinary Hist.*, xiv (1983), pp. 265-91, repr. in Robert I. Rotberg and Theodore K. Rabb (eds.), *Hunger and History: The Impact of Changing Food Production and Consumption Patterns on Society* (Cambridge, 1985), pp. 67-94.

V

little difficulty in feeding a growing population. He characterizes the period 1560-1673 as a time of marked technological progress and productivity growth. For him "the agricultural revolution took place in England in the sixteenth and seventeenth centuries and not in the eighteenth and nineteenth".[13]

There is a similar lack of consensus over the fortunes of agriculture during the hundred years after 1650. Joan Thirsk, for instance, in one of the most careful recent assessments, characterizes the late seventeenth century as a period of "agricultural depression". While recognizing that sluggish prices stimulated ingenuity and diversification, she believes that dramatic increases in agricultural production did not come until the "agricultural revolution" which took place after 1750.[14] Other interpretations of the period are much more optimistic. For example, E. L. Jones and A. H. John both argue for a sustained rise in agricultural output after 1650 as the consequence of crop innovations and a rise in land productivity.[15] In Jones's view, between 1650 and

[13] Eric Kerridge, *The Agricultural Revolution* (London, 1967), pp. 13, 328. Kerridge's arguments are accepted by Brenner, who likewise believes that early modern England witnessed an "agricultural revolution": Brenner, "Agrarian Roots of European Capitalism", p. 308.

[14] Joan Thirsk, "Seventeenth-Century Agriculture and Social Change", in Joan Thirsk (ed.), *Land, Church and People: Essays Presented to Professor H. P. R. Finberg* (*Agric. Hist. Rev.*, xviii, supp., 1970), pp. 148-77, repr. in Joan Thirsk, *The Rural Economy of England* (London, 1984), pp. 183-216; Joan Thirsk (ed.), *The Agrarian History of England and Wales*, v, *1640-1750* (Cambridge, 1985), ii, *Agrarian Change*, pp. xix-xxxi; Joan Thirsk, *England's Agricultural Regions and Agrarian History* (Basingstoke, 1987); Joan Thirsk (ed.), *The Agrarian History of England and Wales*, iv, *1500-1640* (Cambridge, 1967).

[15] E. L. Jones's writing on this subject is mostly contained in his *Agriculture and the Industrial Revolution* (Oxford, 1974), but see also E. L. Jones, "English and European Agricultural Development", in R. M. Hartwell (ed.), *The Industrial Revolution* (Oxford, 1970), pp. 42-76; E. L. Jones, "Agriculture, 1700-80", in Roderick Floud and Donald McCloskey (eds.), *The Economic History of Britain since 1700*, 2 vols. (Cambridge, 1981), i, pp. 66-86. A. H. John's contributions include "The Course of Agricultural Change, 1660-1760", in L. S. Pressnell (ed.), *Studies in the Industrial Revolution Presented to T. S. Ashton* (London, 1960), pp. 125-55, repr. in W. E. Minchinton (ed.), *Essays in Agrarian History*, 2 vols. (Newton Abbot, 1967), i, pp. 223-53; A. H. John, "Agricultural Productivity and Economic Growth in England, 1700-1760", *Jl. Econ. Hist.*, xxv (1965), pp. 19-34, repr. in E. L. Jones (ed.), *Agriculture and Economic Growth in England, 1650-1815* (London, 1967), pp. 172-93; A. H. John, "Aspects of Economic Growth in the First Half of the Eighteenth Century", *Economica*, new ser., no. 28 (1961), pp. 176-90, repr. in both W. E. Minchinton (ed.), *The Growth of English Overseas Trade in the Sixteenth and Seventeenth Centuries* (London, 1969), pp. 165-83, and E. M. Carus-Wilson (ed.), *Essays in Economic History*, ii (London, 1962), pp. 360-73.

1750, "English agriculture underwent a transformation in its techniques out of all proportion to the rather limited widening of its market".[16] A recent review considers there is a "widespread historiographic impression that England had an agricultural revolution *circa* 1650 to 1750"; a verdict which has found support in the work of Robert C. Allen.[17]

These views have influenced opinion about the succeeding hundred years, the era of the traditional agricultural revolution.[18] The latter is now seen as a much more gradual phenomenon with, it is acknowledged, long antecedents. The retreat from the belief in a revolution during these centuries has recently become more pronounced, so that G. E. Mingay considers "in many ways the hundred years that ended in 1850 may be seen as a base, or rather a preparation, a limited but essential preparation, for the greater changes yet to come", and although the achievements of the hundred years after 1750 were remarkable, "it could hardly be said that they amounted to an agricultural revolution".[19] In this case the verdict on the period 1750-1850 is as much influenced by comparisons with subsequent agricultural developments as with those that had gone before.

A different perspective is provided by the estimates of N. F. R. Crafts and others of the rate of growth of agricultural output during this key period.[20] These indicate that growth rates accelerated during the first half of the eighteenth century, slackened somewhat during the following half-century, but rose

[16] Jones, *Agriculture and the Industrial Revolution*, p. 67.

[17] Immanuel Wallerstein, *The Modern World-System*, ii, *Mercantilism and the Consolidation of the European World-Economy* (London, 1980), p. 263; Robert C. Allen, "The Two English Agricultural Revolutions, 1459-1850", in Campbell and Overton (eds.), *Land, Labour and Livestock*, pp. 236-54; J. Yelling, "Agriculture, 1500-1730", in R. A. Dodgshon and R. A. Butlin (eds.), *An Historical Geography of England and Wales*, 2nd edn. (London, 1990), pp. 181-98.

[18] For the use of the term "agricultural revolution", see Mark Overton, "Agricultural Revolution? Development of the Agrarian Economy in Early Modern England", in Alan R. H. Baker and Derek Gregory (eds.), *Explorations in Historical Geography: Interpretative Essays* (Cambridge, 1984), pp. 118-39; Mark Overton, "Agricultural Revolution? England, 1540-1850", in Anne Digby and Charles Feinstein (eds.), *New Directions in Economic and Social History* (London and Basingstoke, 1989), pp. 9-21; J. V. Beckett, *The Agricultural Revolution* (Oxford, 1990).

[19] G. E. Mingay (ed.), *The Agrarian History of England and Wales*, vi, *1750-1850* (Cambridge, 1989), pp. 953, 971.

[20] N. F. R. Crafts, "British Economic Growth, 1700-1831: A Review of the Evidence", *Econ. Hist. Rev.*, 2nd ser., xxxvi (1983), pp. 83-4; R. V. Jackson, "Growth and Deceleration in English Agriculture, 1660-1790", *Econ. Hist. Rev.*, 2nd ser., xxxviii (1985), pp. 333-51.

V

dramatically in the first half of the nineteenth century, reaching a rate of over 1 per cent per annum. Unfortunately these calculations are not based on the direct evidence of physical output, but are derived from demand equations using evidence from prices and wages, together with assumptions about demand elasticities. New evidence of growth rates based on contemporary estimates of the output of agricultural products show a different trend: growth is more rapid in the fifty years after 1750 than the fifty years before and culminated in a rate of growth in the first half of the nineteenth century of just over 0.8 per cent per annum. More significantly, this new evidence suggests that by 1700 agricultural output, land productivity *and* labour productivity were all rising together, and that from the mid-century, perhaps for the first time in English history, they were rising in conjunction with population growth.[21]

The most marked dichotomy in the historiography of this six-hundred-year period is between interpretations of the medieval and early modern periods. Between them lie the fifteenth and early sixteenth centuries; a murky, ill-documented and under-researched period notable for three main developments. First, a swing from arable to pasture and retreat from marginal land as the infamous sheep ate up men.[22] Secondly, structural change in the size and layout of the fields and farms which formed the units of production.[23] Thirdly, tenurial change, associated with the break-up of demesnes and growth of leasehold and copyhold at

[21] The estimates are in Mark Overton, "Land and Labour Productivity in English Agriculture, 1650-1850", in Peter Mathias and John A. Davis (eds.), *The Nature of Industrialization*, v, *Agriculture and Industrialization* (Oxford, forthcoming), which also reviews other estimates of output and productivity.

[22] For evidence of this land-use shift, see Bruce M. S. Campbell, "People and Land in the Middle Ages, 1066-1500", in Dodgshon and Butlin (eds.), *Historical Geography of England and Wales*, pp. 105-11; Bruce M. S. Campbell, "Land, Labour, Livestock and Productivity Trends in English Seignorial Agriculture, 1208-1450", in Campbell and Overton (eds.), *Land, Labour and Livestock*, pp. 153-9. Settlement retreat is discussed in Maurice Beresford and John G. Hurst (eds.), *Deserted Medieval Villages* (London, 1971), pp. 3-75; A. R. H. Baker, "Changes in the Later Middle Ages", in H. C. Darby (ed.), *A New Historical Geography of England* (Cambridge, 1973), pp. 207-17.

[23] Dyer, *Standards of Living in the Later Middle Ages*, pp. 141-3. For case-studies of structural change, see Bruce M. S. Campbell, "The Extent and Layout of Commonfields in Eastern Norfolk", *Norfolk Archaeology*, xxxviii (1981), pp. 5-32; Marjorie Keniston McIntosh, *Autonomy and Community: The Royal Manor of Havering, 1200-1500* (Cambridge, 1986), pp. 116-26.

the expense of the old servile tenures.[24] Brenner and other Marxist historians interpret these developments as the rise of capitalist production relations, which they regard as a necessary prerequisite for the emergence of the new technology of the "agricultural revolution".[25] But they are not alone in attributing significant productivity gains to the dismantling of feudal institutions.[26]

A further documentary discontinuity separates those who would attribute these revolutionary changes to the seventeenth and early eighteenth centuries from those who date them to the late eighteenth and early nineteenth centuries. Once more, the intervening years witnessed important institutional and structural changes — with further tenurial restructuring, renewed interest by landlords in estate management, and the spread of enclosure — which had further important consequences for land and labour productivity and the nature of farm enterprises.[27] For those who would plump for an "agricultural revolution" after 1750 these developments provide some of the essential preconditions.

Differences of interpretation are, of course, the very grist to the mill of history, but it is important to distinguish between those which derive from alternative interpretations of the evid-

---

[24] J. Ambrose Raftis, *Tenure and Mobility: Studies in the Social History of the Medieval English Village* (Toronto, 1964); R. H. Hilton, *The Decline of Serfdom in Medieval England* (Studies in Econ. Hist., London, 1969); Margaret Spufford, *A Cambridgeshire Community: Chippenham from Settlement to Enclosure* (Dept. of English Local Hist., Occasional Paper, no. 20, Leicester, 1965), pp. 31-8; McIntosh, *Autonomy and Community*, pp. 116-26.

[25] Brenner, "Agrarian Roots of European Capitalism"; Martin, *Feudalism to Capitalism*; Dunford and Perrons, *Arena of Capital*, pp. 102-20.

[26] G. D. Snooks, *Economic Growth during the Last Millenium: A Quantitative Perspective for the British Industrial Revolution* (Australian National Univ., Working Papers in Econ. Hist., no. 140, Canberra, 1990), pp. 30-3.

[27] These are discussed in Chambers and Mingay, *Agricultural Revolution*; M. E. Turner, *English Parliamentary Enclosure: Its Historical Geography and Economic History* (Folkestone, 1980); J. R. Wordie, "Rent Movements and the English Tenant Farmer, 1700-1839", in Paul Uselding (ed.), *Research in Economic History: An Annual Compilation of Research*, vi (Greenwich, Conn., 1981), pp. 193-43; J. R. Wordie, "The Chronology of English Enclosure, 1500-1914", *Econ. Hist. Rev.*, 2nd ser., xxxvi (1983), pp. 483-505; J. R. Wordie, *Estate Management in Eighteenth-Century England* (London, 1982); G. E. Mingay, "The Size of Farms in the Eighteenth Century", *Econ. Hist. Rev.*, 2nd ser., xiv (1962), pp. 469-88; G. E. Mingay, *Enclosure and the Small Farmer in the Age of the Industrial Revolution* (London, 1968); G. E. Mingay, *English Landed Society in the Eighteenth Century* (London, 1963); J. V. Beckett, "Landownership and Estate Management", in Mingay (ed.), *Agrarian History of England and Wales*, vi, pp. 545-640.

V

ence and those which arise from the way in which that evidence has been assembled. Broad temporal, spatial and sectoral comparisons require data that have been systematically gathered and consistently analysed. If the criteria for comparison are quantitative, it is important that, when possible, they are measured, and measured according to a common methodology.[28] This is especially difficult when comparing periods with dissimilar historical sources, yet it is only recently that quantitative measures of agricultural production have been produced from single sources.[29] If a broader and internally more consistent picture of the evolution of English agriculture is to emerge, it is therefore essential that the construction of these measures is taken further and the traditional periodization of the past is transcended. As a step in that direction, this article presents a comparison of evidence from medieval account rolls, early modern probate inventories and nineteenth-century agricultural statistics, in order to cast new light on medieval and early modern farming.

[28] This is a recurring criticism by reviewers of the Cambridge *Agrarian Histories of England and Wales*, for example, Bruce M. S. Campbell, "Laying Foundations: The Agrarian History of England and Wales, 1042-1350", *Agric. Hist. Rev.*, xxxvii (1989), pp. 190-1; Kathleen A. Biddick, "Malthus in a Straitjacket? Analyzing Agrarian Change in Medieval England", *Jl. Interdisciplinary Hist.*, xx (1990), pp. 624-7; Mark Overton, "Depression or Revolution? English Agriculture, 1640-1750", *Jl. Brit. Studies*, xxv (1986), p. 350; H. J. Habakkuk, "The Agrarian History of England and Wales: Regional Farming Systems and Agrarian Change, 1640-1750", *Econ. Hist. Rev.*, 2nd ser., xl (1987), p. 285; E. A. Wrigley, "Early Modern Agriculture: A New Harvest Gathered In", *Agric. Hist. Rev.*, xxxv (1987), p. 69.
[29] For example, Bruce M. S. Campbell, "Towards an Agricultural Geography of Medieval England", *Agric. Hist. Rev.*, xxxvi (1988), pp. 24-39; Bruce M. S. Campbell and John P. Power, "Mapping the Agricultural Geography of Medieval England", *Jl. Hist. Geography*, xv (1989), pp. 24-39; J. A. Yelling, "Changes in Crop Production in East Worcestershire, 1540-1867", *Agric. Hist. Rev.*, xxi (1973), pp. 18-34; Mark Overton, "The Determinants of Crop Yields in Early Modern England", in Campbell and Overton (eds.), *Land, Labour and Livestock*, pp. 284-322; Paul Glennie, "Continuity and Change in Hertfordshire Agriculture, 1550-1700: I, Patterns of Agricultural Production", *Agric. Hist. Rev.*, xxxvi (1988), pp. 55-75; M. E. Turner, "Arable in England and Wales: Estimates from the 1801 Crop Return", *Jl. Hist. Geography*, vii (1981), pp. 291-302; Mark Overton, "Agriculture", in John Langton and R. J. Morris (eds.), *An Atlas of Industrializing Britain, 1780-1914* (London, 1986), pp. 34-53. The "Feeding the City" project at the Centre for Metropolitan History, Institute of Historical Research, London, has assembled a systematic database of agricultural and land-use information for ten counties around London in the period 1270-1339.

III
DEMESNE ACCOUNTS AND PROBATE INVENTORIES

Accounts furnish a plethora of detailed information about the demesne-farming activities of manorial lords and are most abundant for the period $c.1270$-$c.1400$. They follow a fairly standardized format and each normally records the activities of an entire farming year, from Michaelmas to Michaelmas, specifying the crops sown and harvested, together with livestock numbers at the start and end of the year. Accounts survive for all classes of estate, although large estates are better represented than small, and ecclesiastical better than lay.[30]

Inventories likewise survive in considerable numbers and are the principal source of information about farming practice between the mid-sixteenth and mid-eighteenth centuries.[31] They were drawn up as part of the probate procedure following the death of a farmer, and record the crops — both in the barn and in the field — and livestock on the farm. Each provides a snapshot view of a farm at a specific point in time and therefore provides less comprehensive information than do accounts. Indeed only those made during the months immediately preceding the harvest — in June and July — record all field crops. Moreover inventories do not follow a standard format, so the number that may be used to compile a particular statistic depends on the way in which the information is presented, with the result that different groups of inventories have to be used to measure different things. Each farm is usually recorded only once and some demographic bias can be expected in the data towards the farms of the

[30] For a discussion of manorial accounts, see P. D. A. Harvey, "Agricultural Treatises and Manorial Accounting in Medieval England", *Agric. Hist. Rev.*, xx (1972), pp. 170-82, and, especially, *Manorial Records of Cuxham, Oxfordshire, circa 1200-1359*, ed. P. D. A. Harvey (Oxfordshire Rec. Soc., 1, and Roy. Comm. Hist. MSS., Jt. pubn., 23, Oxford, 1976), "Introduction".

[31] Mark Overton, *A Bibliography of British Probate Inventories* (Dept. of Geography, Univ. of Newcastle, Newcastle upon Tyne, 1983); Mark Overton, "English Probate Inventories and the Measurement of Agricultural Change", *A. A. G. Bijdragen*, xxiii (Wageningen, 1980), pp. 205-15; Mark Overton, "Probate Inventories and the Reconstruction of Agrarian Landscapes", in Michael Reed (ed.), *Discovering Past Landscapes* (London, 1984), pp. 167-94; Mark Overton, "Computer Analysis of an Inconsistent Data Source: The Case of Probate Inventories", *Jl. Hist. Geography*, iii (1977), pp. 317-26; Mark Overton, "Computer Standardization of Probate Inventories", in J.-P. Genet (ed.), *Standardisation et échange des bases de données historiques* (Paris, 1988), pp. 145-51; Mark Overton, "Computer Analysis of Probate Inventories: From Portable Micro to Mainframe", in Peter Denley and Deian Hopkin (eds.), *History and Computing* (Manchester, 1987), pp. 96-104.

V

old and infirm. Unlike the accounts, however, inventories relate to a very wide range of farm sizes, from the smallest to some of the largest, but with those of substantial yeomen predominating.

On the whole inventories are less reliable than the accounts, so the evaluation of their agricultural content gains much from a juxtaposition with medieval and nineteenth-century sources. National agricultural statistics were inaugurated in 1867, but local statistics survive for earlier dates and, while these are neither geographically comprehensive nor consistent, they cover many areas of the country. They include the 1801 crop return, the tithe files of c.1836 and county statistics for the 1830s and 1850s.[32]

The extent to which direct comparison is possible between these three principal groups of sources depends in part upon their respective patterns of survival. Manorial accounts provide representative coverage of only certain parts of central, southern and eastern England; probate inventories are also patchy in their coverage, as are the tithe files and crop returns.[33] A full reconstruction of agricultural trends over the six-hundred-year period, from the advent of manorial accounts in the mid-thirteenth century to the advent of official agricultural statistics in the latter part of the nineteenth century, will therefore only ever be possible for certain regions and counties.

One of those counties is Norfolk, long celebrated as one of the country's premier arable counties and the county most

[32] D. B. Grigg, "The Changing Agricultural Geography of England: A Commentary on the Sources Available for the Reconstruction of the Agricultural Geography of England, 1770-1850", *Trans. Inst. Brit. Geographers*, xli (1967), pp. 73-96; W. E. Minchinton, "Agricultural Returns and the Government during the Napoleonic Wars", *Agric. Hist. Rev.*, i (1953), pp. 29-43, repr. in Minchinton (ed.), *Essays in Agrarian History*, ii, pp. 103-20; Turner, "Arable in England and Wales"; M. Turner, "Agricultural Productivity in England in the Eighteenth Century: Evidence from Crop Yields", *Econ. Hist. Rev.*, 2nd ser., xxxv (1982), pp. 489-510; R. J. P. Kain and H. C. Prince, *The Tithe Surveys of England and Wales* (Cambridge, 1985); Roger J. P. Kain, *An Atlas and Index of the Tithe Files of Mid-Nineteenth-Century England and Wales* (Cambridge, 1986); Phillip Dodd, "The Agricultural Statistics for 1854: An Assessment of Their Value", *Agric. Hist. Rev.*, xxxv (1987), pp. 159-70.

[33] There is no national listing of accounts, although a summary register of manorial records may be consulted at the National Register of Archives, Quality Court, Chancery Lane, London. A handlist of grange accounts for ten counties around London — Essex, Middlesex, Hertfordshire, Bedfordshire, Buckinghamshire, Northamptonshire, Oxfordshire, Berkshire, Surrey and Kent — is being compiled by the "Feeding the City" project. For the spatial limitations to probate inventories as a source of yields, see Paul Glennie, "Measuring Crop Yields in Early Modern England", in Campbell and Overton (eds.), *Land, Labour and Livestock*, pp. 277-9; Turner, "Arable in England and Wales"; Kain, *Atlas and Index of the Tithe Files*.

closely associated with the genesis of the agricultural revolution. Norfolk is well served by extant accounts, inventories and tithe files. For the period between c.1250 and c.1450 there are approximately two thousand accounts representing in excess of two hundred different demesnes belonging to a wide range of different landlords, both lay and ecclesiastical.[34] Some three thousand farm inventories survive for the period 1584 to 1739.[35] Very few 1801 crop returns are extant for Norfolk, but the tithe files of the mid-1830s provide land-use and crop information for about two-thirds of tithe districts within the county. This series of sources is rounded off by a detailed set of agricultural statistics produced in 1854, based upon data from almost all the farms in the county.[36]

There are a number of methodological problems in deriving comparable measures from these sources.[37] The most important stem from the fact that accounts and inventories deal with units of different sizes, as shown in Table 1. Peasant farms are missing from the medieval material, whereas some of the very largest farms are missing from the early modern. This means that comparisons of absolute figures — crop acreages or livestock numbers — would be misleading, since they would reflect differences

[34] No attempt is made to list here all these accounts, which are drawn from the following archives: Public Record Office, London (hereafter P.R.O.); Norfolk Record Office, Norwich; North Yorkshire Record Office, Northallerton; Nottinghamshire Record Office, Nottingham; West Suffolk Record Office, Bury St Edmunds; Bodleian Library, Oxford; British Library, London (hereafter Brit. Lib.); Cambridge University Library; Canterbury Cathedral Library; Chicago University Library; Harvard Law Library, Cambridge, Mass.; John Rylands Library, Manchester; Lambeth Palace Library, London; Nottingham University Library; Eton College; Christ's College, Cambridge; King's College, Cambridge; Magdalen College, Oxford; St George's Chapel, Windsor; Elveden Hall, Suffolk; Holkham Hall, Norfolk; Raynham Hall, Norfolk; Pomeroy and Sons, Wymondham. We are grateful to the authorities concerned for access to these materials. A handlist of the individual accounts is available on request.

[35] The inventories used in this study are from the Norwich Consistory Court and are housed in the Norfolk Record Office. All available inventories were consulted with the exception of those for the period 1600-28. The numbers of inventories that can be used to calculate a particular measure varies because of the form in which information is presented. See Overton, "Measurement of Agricultural Change", p. 211.

[36] Turner, "Arable in England and Wales", p. 294; Kain, Atlas and Index of the Tithe Files, pp. 67-83; Reports of Poor Law Inspectors on Agricultural Statistics (England), 1854, Parliamentary Papers, 1854-5 (C. 1928), liii.

[37] For a fuller discussion of the methodological difficulties of combining information from accounts and inventories, see Mark Overton and Bruce M. S. Campbell, "Norfolk Livestock Farming, 1250-1740: A Comparative Study of Manorial Accounts and Probate Inventories", Jl. Hist. Geography, xviii (1992), pp. 377-96.

TABLE 1
NORFOLK: FREQUENCY DISTRIBUTIONS OF TOTAL SOWN ACREAGE[+]
OF DEMESNES AND FARMS REPRESENTED BY ACCOUNTS AND
INVENTORIES[*]

Sown acreage	1250-1349 N	%	1350-1449 N	%	1584-1640 N	%	1660-1739 N	%	1854 %
20–< 50	11	8.8	9	8.5	54	74.0	56	49.6	—
50–<100	29	23.2	32	30.2	12	16.4	43	38.1	—
100–<150	30	24.0	34	32.1	4	5.5	7	6.2	—
150–<200	26	20.8	16	15.1	3	4.1	1	0.9	—
200–<250	15	12.0	8	7.6	0	0.0	4	3.5	—
250–<300	4	3.2	1	0.9	0	0.0	1	0.9	—
300–<350	3	2.4	4	3.8	0	0.0	0	0.0	—
350–<400	5	4.0	2	1.9	0	0.0	0	0.0	—
400+	2	1.6	0	0.0	0	0.0	1	0.9	—
All	125	100.0	106	100.0	73	100.0	113	100.0	—
Mean all farms (acres)	152.5		132.7		27.0		41.4		49.1
Mean farms >20 acres	152.5		132.7		48.5		68.4		—

[*]Sources: 1250-1449, from manorial accounts: for location, see n. 34; 1584-1739, from probate inventories made June–July: for location, see n. 35.

[+] Cereals, together with peas, beans, vetches, buckwheat, turnips and clover. The sown acreage excludes pasture, meadow and fallow.

in farm sizes much more than differences in farming practice. Instead, comparisons must be based on relative measures, in the form of ratios and proportions. Since these may be calculated in a variety of ways, care must be taken to ensure an absolutely consistent methodology. To control for differences in farming patterns between large and small farmers, inventories have only been used for farms of at least twenty sown acres, equivalent to the smallest medieval demesne for which accounts are available. Since the spatial coverage of the data is irregular, aggregate county means are regionally weighted.[38] It is these aggregate means that provide the basis for comparison with the tithe files and the 1854 statistics, neither of which provides data at the level of individual farms. The former refer to "tithe districts", which are roughly equivalent to a parish and, although the latter are aggregations of returns from individual farms, the data are only available for nineteen poor-law unions.

[38] The county means are derived from four regional sub-means.

TABLE 2

NORFOLK: CROP COMBINATIONS 1250-1854*

	1250-1349	1350-1449	1584-1640	1660-1739	c. 1836	1854
% Grain acreage						
Wheat	18.8	17.5	28.7	19.8	48.4	49.0
Rye	13.1	6.9	16.4	11.4	—	1.0
Maslin	0.9	0.9	0.6	1.5	—	—
Barley	48.0	56.3	44.0	54.4	45.9	42.0
Oats	18.6	17.5	10.3	12.9	5.8	8.0
Dredge	0.6	1.0	0.0	0.0	—	—
% Sown acreage						
Grain	86.5	86.8	86.9	83.4	48.8	52.1
Legumes	13.5	13.2	9.0	13.7	26.9	24.4
Fodder[a]	13.5	13.2	12.7	16.6	51.2	46.5
Turnips[b]	0.0	0.0	0.1	7.2	24.3	22.1
Buckwheat	0.0	0.0	1.0	1.6	—	—
Clover	0.0	0.0	0.0	2.3	25.0[c]	21.4
Hemp, flax and hops	0.0	0.0	0.27	0.05	—	0.03
% Legume acreage						
Vetches	3.1	9.7	22.1	9.9	—	1.7
Clover	0.0	0.0	0.0	13.1	92.9	87.7
Bare fallow as % arable acreage	—	—	—	—	2.1	1.3
Grass[d] as % grass and arable	—	—	—	—	—	24.5

*Sources: 1250-1449, from manorial accounts: for location, see n. 34; 1584-1739, from probate inventories made in June–July with 20 or more sown acres: for location, see n. 35; c. 1836, Roger J. P. Kain, *An Atlas and Index of the Tithe Files of Mid-Nineteenth Century England and Wales* (Cambridge, 1986), p. 72; 1854, *Reports of Poor Law Inspectors on Agricultural Statistics (England), 1854*, Parliamentary Papers, 1854-5 (C. 1928), liii.

[a]Legumes, roots and buckwheat (excludes potatoes and carrots).

[b]Mean turnip acreage from August–December inventories as per cent of mean sown acreage June and July inventories.

[c]"Seeds".

[d]Meadow, permanent and rough pasture (excluding clover).

IV

CROP PROPORTIONS

The least problematic comparisons can be made between the proportions of the sown or grain acreage devoted to different crops. (See Table 2.) All four sources can be used for these indices, but only the accounts and inventories provide evidence of the proportion of farms on which the crops were grown. (See Table 3.) At an aggregate level, Tables 2 and 3 reveal that patterns of cropping in Norfolk were remarkably stable during the five

V

TABLE 3
NORFOLK: PERCENTAGES OF FARMS GROWING PARTICULAR CROPS
1250-1739*

	1250-1349	1350-1449	1584-1640	1660-1739
Wheat	96.8	88.8	87.5	89.9
Rye	79.8	54.2	64.6	60.3
Maslin	23.2	20.6	11.8	12.0
Barley	100.0	100.0	91.9	94.1
Oats	100.0	98.1	54.7	63.4
Dredge	12.8	16.8	0.0	0.0
Legumes	96.8	99.1	75.5	79.1
Vetches	5.2	26.0	50.9	44.1
Clover	0.0	0.0	0.0	15.9
Buckwheat	0.0	0.0	14.4	12.6
Turnips	0.0	0.0	0.2	44.7
Hemp, flax and hops	0.0	0.0	4.4	2.5

*Sources: 1250-1449, from manorial accounts: for location, see n. 34; 1584-1739, from probate inventories made in June and July with 20 or more sown acres, except turnips from June–December inventories: for location, see n. 35.

hundred years prior to 1740, in contrast to the far-reaching changes that evidently took place afterwards. Some new crops were introduced and some established crops rose or declined in relative importance but, on the whole, farmers in early modern Norfolk grew the same crops, in much the same proportions, as their medieval forebears. Nevertheless there were changes in both the geography of cereal cropping, and in the rotations of which these crops were a part.

Throughout this long period and, indeed, until well into the nineteenth century, Norfolk's dominant crop was barley. This was already the case in the mid-thirteenth century, when barley was still very much a minor crop in much of the rest of the country.[39] Throughout the Middle Ages Norfolk barley was traded up and down the east coast and across the North Sea.[40]

[39] On fifteen demesnes of St Benet's abbey in eastern Norfolk barley accounted for 64 per cent of the cereal acreage in 1238-46: Norfolk R.O., Diocesan Est/1 and 2/1; Church Comm. 101426 3/13. Within Norfolk as a whole, barley accounted for 51 per cent of the cereal acreage in 1250-99, as compared with a national average of 15 per cent. For the data on which the national mean is based, see Campbell and Power, "Mapping the Agricultural Geography of Medieval England", p. 25.

[40] For Norfolk's medieval grain trade, see E. M. Carus-Wilson, "The Medieval Trade of the Ports of the Wash", *Medieval Archaeology*, vi-vii (1962-3), p. 185; Vanessa Parker, *The Making of King's Lynn* (London, 1971), pp. 1-18; A. Saul, "Great Yarmouth in the Fourteenth Century: A Study in Trade, Politics and Society" (Univ. of Oxford D.Phil. thesis, 1975), pp. 226, 368-71, 374; Dorothy M. Owen (ed.), *The Making of King's Lynn* (Recs. Social and Econ. Hist., new ser., ix, London, 1984), pp. 42-8; R. H. Britnell, *Growth and Decline in Colchester, 1300-1525* (Cambridge,

(cont. on p. 56)

TABLE 4
NORFOLK: THE PRICES OF RYE, BARLEY AND OATS RELATIVE TO WHEAT*

	Wheat	Rye	Barley	Oats
1250-1299	1.00	0.65	0.72	0.40
1300-1349	1.00	0.67	0.74	0.49
1350-1399	1.00	0.68	0.55	0.36
1400-1499	1.00	0.58	0.53	0.38
1584-1640	1.00	0.73	0.59	0.37
1660-1735	1.00	0.61	0.53	0.35
c. 1836	1.00	0.62	0.57	0.40

*Sources: Medieval ratios calculated from London School of Economics, Beveridge Price Data, box G9. Early modern ratios calculated from prices given in probate inventories: for location, see n. 35.

This specialism persisted throughout the sixteenth, seventeenth and early eighteenth centuries, despite a general expansion of barley production in many other parts of the country and a corresponding decline in its price relative to other grains (Table 4).[41] By the 1730s over 80 per cent of all barley exported from England came from East Anglian ports.[42] For at least six hundred years barley was the preferred crop of most Norfolk farmers; its share of the county's grain area never fell below 40 per cent, and for significant periods exceeded 50 per cent. The concentration on barley was facilitated by intensive rotational systems, which relied upon half-year rather than full-year fallows and accordingly gave priority to spring-sown crops (virtually all the barley being spring- rather than winter-sown).[43] Indeed in

(n. 40 cont.)

1986), pp. 246-7; R. H. Britnell, "The Pastons and Their Norfolk", Agric. Hist. Rev., xxxvi (1988), pp. 137-9; Campbell, "Ecology versus Economics". For Norfolk's contribution to London's grain supplies, see F. J. Fisher, "The Development of the London Food Market, 1540-1640", Econ. Hist. Rev., v (1935), pp. 46-64, repr. in E. M. Carus-Wilson (ed.), Essays in Economic History (London, 1954), pp. 135-51; N. J. Williams, The Maritime Trade of the East Anglian Ports, 1550-1590 (Oxford, 1988); Bruce M. S. Campbell et al., A Medieval Capital and Its Grain Supply: Agrarian Production and Distribution in the London Region, c.1300 (Hist. Geog. Research ser., no. 30, n. pl., 1993), pp. 47, 69-70, 181.

[41] Nationally, barley rose from an estimated 15 per cent to 27 per cent of the demesne cereal acreage between 1250-99 and 1400-49: the trend was especially pronounced in the eastern, midland and northern counties.

[42] David Ormrod, English Grain Exports and the Structure of Agrarian Capitalism, 1700-1760 (Univ. of Hull, Occasional Papers in Econ. and Social Hist., no. 12, Hull, 1985), p. 38.

[43] These rotations are discussed in Bruce M. S. Campbell, "The Regional Uniqueness of English Field Systems? Some Evidence from Eastern Norfolk", Agric. Hist. Rev., xxix (1981), pp. 16-28; Bruce M. S. Campbell, "Arable Productivity in

(cont. on p. 57)

V

the Middle Ages there were even some farms on which a state of barley monoculture effectively prevailed, in so far as its share of the grain area exceeded 70 or even 80 per cent of the total.[44] Intriguingly, barley attained its greatest pre-eminence during the demographic lulls of 1350-1499 and 1660-1735, when (as Table 4 shows) the price of barley relative to wheat was at its lowest level.

Wheat, the principal winter cereal, was the most highly priced crop of all and the leading commercial crop of much of the rest of south, central and eastern England, but it was of lesser importance in Norfolk.[45] Although consistently grown on nine out of ten Norfolk farms, its share of the grain area remained below a fifth of the total during 1250-1449 and 1660-1739. For a time, between 1584 and 1640, wheat expanded to occupy over a quarter of the grain acreage, but this gain was not sustained. By the nineteenth century, however, it occupied nearly half the cereal acreage and had supplanted barley as the county's leading cereal, suggesting a dramatic transformation from the early eighteenth century onwards.

Rye, the other principal winter-sown cereal, was grown on significantly fewer farms and was only dominant on Norfolk's lightest and least fertile soils, which were not suitable for wheat.[46] Over time its fortunes waxed and waned according to the extent to which these lighter soils were drawn into cultivation in response to the demand for land, and to the absolute and relative prices of grain. Prior to 1350 rye was commonly used as a cheap grain

(n. 43 cont.)
Medieval English Agriculture" (unpubd. paper presented to the UC-Caltech conference on "Pre-Industrial Developments in Peasant Economies: The Transition to Economic Growth", Huntington Library, San Marino, May 1987), pp. 31-6, 53-7.

[44] Demesnes devoting 70 per cent or more of their cereal acreage to barley included Ashby, Aylmerton, Burgh in Flegg, Costessey, Feltwell, Gimingham, Hanworth, Heigham by Norwich, Hemsby, Horning, Hoveton, Intwood, Keswick, Little Hautbois, Ludham, Martham, North Elmham, North Walsham, Ormesby, Reedham, Ringstead, Scottow and Sloley, while at Calthorpe, Flegg, Horsham, Thwaite and Tunstead this proportion exceeded 80 per cent. Four and a half centuries later the area immediately to the north of Aylsham and North Walsham was still sowing the county's largest acreages of barley: Kain, *Atlas and Index of the Tithe Files*, p. 76.

[45] Wheat accounted for an estimated 37 per cent of the national demesne cereal acreage in the period 1250-1349, as compared with only 18 per cent in Norfolk. It was especially prominent as a cereal in the two-field country of the north-east, the west midlands and south-west.

[46] Demesnes devoting 40 per cent or more of their cereal acreage to rye included East Wretham, Hargham, Hilgay, West Harling and West Tofts; all on the Breck edge. This compared with a county average of 13 per cent in the period 1250-1349 and 7 per cent in the period 1350-1449, and a national average of 6 per cent and 4 per cent respectively.

livery for farm servants, but thereafter its cultivation contracted as wage rates rose and dietary standards improved.[47] Changes in demand influenced its price relative to wheat, so that by the fifteenth century its relative share of the cereal acreage had contracted. By 1584-1640, however, with arable husbandry again in the ascendant and living standards once more declining, it had staged a comeback, only to lose ground again after 1660 as demographic pressure eased and dietary standards improved. Throughout these centuries there was a consistent background demand for rye-straw, which was especially valued for thatching because of its length. Significantly, by the mid-nineteenth century, with the improvement of much light land, a wider choice of crop breeds, and improved rural housing standards and diets, rye had contracted to only 1 per cent of the grain acreage.[48]

The fluctuating fortunes of rye — a bread grain — contrast with the dwindling importance of oats, which in Norfolk was primarily a fodder crop. There was a pronounced drop in the proportion of farms cultivating oats between the Middle Ages and early modern period, which was coupled with a contraction in its share of the total grain acreage. This trend is the more remarkable given a two- to threefold increase in the ratio of farm horses to sown acres over the same period. (See below, Table 6.) Evidently it was necessary to devote no more than one cereal acre in every five or six to the production of fodder, in order to satisfy the requirements of horse haulage and traction. Indeed the more oats were augmented with legumes, "horsemeat" (a legume-oats mixture), hay and grass, the smaller the share of the grain acreage it was necessary to devote to oats. Improved yields had the same effect, so that a two-and-a-half-fold increase in the ratio of workhorses to cereal acres between the Middle Ages and the mid-nineteenth century was matched by a trebling of oat yields. Over the same period the proportion of the grain acreage under oats contracted from 18 to 8 per cent of the total: the bare minimum necessary to service the needs of traction.

From as early as the mid-thirteenth century Norfolk was exceptional in the importance it attached to legumes as a source

[47] Christopher Dyer, "Changes in Diet in the Late Middle Ages: The Case of Harvest Workers", *Agric. Hist. Rev.*, xxxvi (1988), pp. 28-32.
[48] The decline in the consumption of rye bread is discussed in Sir William Ashley, "The Place of Rye in the History of English Food", *Econ. Jl.*, xxxi (1921), pp. 285-308, and in his *The Bread of Our Forefathers* (Oxford, 1928).

V

of human and animal food.[49] At this time several of the demesnes belonging to St Benet's abbey in eastern Norfolk were already devoting an eighth or more of their sown acreage to peas and beans.[50] By the early fourteenth century, when the intensive arable husbandry of this locality was at its most developed, this proportion had risen to a fifth or even a quarter on some demesnes.[51] Overall, legumes — principally peas, but also vetches and beans — occupied a remarkably consistent 13 per cent of the county's cropped acreage throughout the period 1250-1449. Subsequently their importance diminished somewhat, so that, by the late sixteenth and early seventeenth centuries, they occupied 9 per cent of the cropped area and were grown on three out of four farms. By 1660-1739, however, they had recovered to medieval levels of cultivation, partly due to the advent and gradual diffusion of clover.

Norfolk farmers pioneered the cultivation of clover in England and much has been made of the crop's revolutionary effects.[52] Nevertheless a comparison of inventories with the tithe files suggests that the principal benefits did not come until after 1740. Between 1660 and 1739 no more than 15 per cent of large farms grew clover and it accounted for only an eighth of the legume acreage, whereas by the 1830s clover comprised a quarter of the sown acreage and around 90 per cent of all legumes cultivated. In other words, beans, vetches and, above all, peas, long retained their medieval pre-eminence. Of these old-established crops, it is interesting to observe that vetches, introduced to Norfolk in the late thirteenth century, continued their diffusion — mainly

---

[49] Nationally, legumes accounted for an estimated 6 per cent of the demesne sown acreage in the period 1250-99, the proportion being lowest in the northern, midland and south-western counties.

[50] Norfolk R.O., Diocesan Est/1 and 2/1; Church Comm. 101426 3/13.

[51] During 1250-1349 demesnes on which legumes accounted for at least a fifth of the sown acreage included Alderford, Crownthorpe, Forncett, Guton in Brandiston, Hanworth, Hudeston, Hunstanton, Popinho, Scratby, Seething, Thornham and Tivetshall; at Bunwell, Flegg, Fordham, Lessingham, Loddon, Osmundiston, Sloley and Wiggenhall this proportion rose to a quarter.

[52] R. M. Garnier, "The Introduction of Forage Crops into Great Britain", *Jl. Roy. Agric. Soc. England*, 3rd ser., vii (1896), pp. 82-97; G. E. Fussell, "The Low Countries' Influence on English Farming", *Eng. Hist. Rev.*, lxxiv (1959), pp. 611-22; G. E. Fussell, "New Crops in Norfolk", *Amateur Historian*, iv (1958), pp. 1-8; G. E. Fussell, "'Norfolk Improvers': Their Farms and Methods", *Norfolk Archaeology*, xxxiii (1964), pp. 332-44; G. E. Fussell, "Adventures with Clover", *Agriculture*, lii (1955), pp. 342-5; Naomi Riches, *The Agricultural Revolution in Norfolk* (Chapel Hill, 1937).

at the expense of peas — so that by the late sixteenth century the proportion of farms growing them had doubled.[53] In addition to vetches and clover, other new crops made their appearance. The first known reference to buckwheat in Norfolk occurs in 1480 at North Walsham, and by the late sixteenth century around 14 per cent of farmers were growing it, mostly in eastern Norfolk. It remained a specialism peculiar to this area, where it was probably used as a green manure in preparation for a wheat crop.[54] Turnips, in contrast, appeared in the 1580s in market gardens, moved to the fields on one or two farms by the 1630s, but spread rapidly to most parts of the county from the 1660s onwards. By the 1710s they were grown by over half of Norfolk's farmers, albeit still, for the most part, on a comparatively small scale.[55] Although some farmers were already cultivating quite large acreages at this time, within the county as a whole the crop only constituted about 7 per cent of the total sown acreage. On many farms, judging by the periods of the year at which turnips are mentioned in inventories, they were probably sown in August after the harvest as a catch crop for their green tops rather than for their roots.[56] As with clover, a comparison of the inventory data with the nineteenth-century cropping statistics makes it clear that turnips still had much ground left to conquer in the early eighteenth century. By the 1830s, however,

---

[53] Bruce M. S. Campbell, "The Diffusion of Vetches in Medieval England", *Econ. Hist. Rev.*, 2nd ser., xli (1988), pp. 193-208.

[54] In 1480 buckwheat is mentioned as part of the tithe received at North Walsham: Norfolk R.O., Diocesan Est/12. J[ohn] W[orlidge], *Systema Agriculturae*, 4th edn. (London, 1697), p. 41, describes its use as a green manure. He also considered (with several other contemporary writers) that the crop was grown on poor soils as a food for poultry. In Norfolk, however, it was largely confined to the fertile soils of the east and was grown by some of the most progressive farmers in the county, who were also introducing turnips and clover. Moreover the size of their poultry flocks (measured by value) does not seem to have differed from those of farmers not cultivating buckwheat with equivalent-sized holdings.

[55] Mark Overton, "The Diffusion of Agricultural Innovations in Early Modern England: Turnips and Clover in Norfolk and Suffolk, 1580-1740", *Trans. Inst. Brit. Geographers*, new ser., x (1985), pp. 205-21.

[56] As an integral part of the Norfolk four-course rotation turnips were supposed to be sown in March, whereas it is in the autumn that most are mentioned in inventories. Calculation of the proportion of the cropped acreage under turnips is complicated by the fact that they may not have been sown until other crops had been harvested. The figures from inventories in Table 1 are therefore derived by expressing the mean turnip acreage from inventories made from August to December as a percentage of the mean cropped acreage from June and July inventories for the same year.

V

the turnip acreage had risen to occupy nearly a quarter of the arable area.

On this evidence, therefore, patterns of cropping in Norfolk exhibited remarkable continuity up to the early eighteenth century but considerable change thereafter. Indeed the magnitude of the changes that occurred during the hundred years after 1740 were out of all proportion to those which had occurred during the preceding five hundred years. This stability in cropping is at odds with the view that the period from 1640-1750 witnessed a widespread diversification of arable husbandry through the cultivation of industrial crops, such as hops, hemp, flax, coleseed and dye plants.[57] These crops could be found on Norfolk farms, but systematic analysis of inventories indicates that fewer than 5 per cent of farmers represented in inventories (with more than twenty sown acres) were growing them. Nor were these industrial crops new to Norfolk agriculture in the seventeenth century. The commercial production of flax, hemp, coleseed, dye plants and teasels is documented as early as the late thirteenth and early fourteenth centuries, when the payment of tithes in flax and hemp suggests that these crops may have assumed particular prominence on peasant smallholdings.[58] They also continued, by and large, to be grown in the same parts of the county.

Nevertheless continuity in crops and crop proportions does not necessarily imply a continuity in methods of production. Husbandry techniques — the methods of ground preparation, fertilization, weeding, harvesting and rotational systems — are a subject on which the accounts cast much light and the inventories little. On the basis of the medieval evidence it would certainly be a mistake to regard any of these techniques as fixed or constant, for many were contingent upon the cost of labour and the price of grain.[59] In response to these influences, more intensive methods were adopted before 1310 but subsequently abandoned in the later fourteenth century. These changes in the intensity of cultivation took the form of modifications to both the length and nature of cropping sequences and to the frequency and duration of

---

[57] This is the argument of Joan Thirsk, in her editorial introduction to *Agrarian History of England and Wales*, v, *1640-1750*, i, *Regional Farming Systems*, pp. xxiv-xxvi.

[58] Campbell, ''Agricultural Progress in Medieval England'', p. 41.

[59] *Ibid.*, pp. 38-40.

fallows and, as such, were facilitated by the inherent flexibility of the county's field systems.[60]

Medieval rotations and fallowing practices may be reconstructed in graphic detail whenever consecutive accounts survive giving the names of field divisions within which the individual crops were sown. Reconstructions of cropping plans on a dozen demesnes scattered through the county confirm the extreme diversity of rotational and fallowing practices. There were demesnes on which convertible husbandry prevailed, with three or four years of crops followed by an equal or longer period during which the land lay unsown; demesnes on which land might be fallowed once every third, fourth or fifth year; and demesnes on which fallowing took place so infrequently as to constitute virtually continuous cropping.[61] Contrasting rotational systems sometimes co-existed on soils of different quality on the same demesne and the precise nature of cropping sequences usually varied a good deal from field to field and from year to year. The flexibility of rotations was, in fact, one reason why Norfolk subsequently proved so receptive to the introduction of new crops. At Hunstanton, for example, a crop-book of 1705-11 records 312 different cropping sequences on 493 separate plots of ground.[62] These too exemplify a variable and flexible system and reveal the incorporation of clover and ley grasses into an essentially medieval scheme of cropping. A more radical departure from medieval traditions can be found in the rotations recorded on three farms in west Norfolk between 1739 and 1751. These are some of the earliest examples of a Norfolk four-course rotation, in which wheat was succeeded by turnips, barley and

[60] M. R. Postgate, "Field Systems of East Anglia", in Alan R. H. Baker and Robin A. Butlin (eds.), *Studies of Field Systems in the British Isles* (Cambridge, 1973), pp. 303-5; J. Williamson, "Peasant Holdings in Medieval Norfolk: A Detailed Investigation into the Holdings of the Peasantry in Three Norfolk Villages in the Thirteenth Century" (Univ. of Reading Ph.D. thesis, 1976), pp. 272-306; Campbell, "Regional Uniqueness of English Field Systems?"; H. E. Hallam, "Farming Techniques: Eastern England", in H. E. Hallam (ed.), *Agrarian History of England and Wales*, ii, *1042-1350* (Cambridge, 1988), pp. 272-81; R. H. Britnell, "Eastern England", in Edward Miller (ed.), *Agrarian History of England and Wales*, iii, *1348-1500* (Cambridge, 1991), pp. 194-210.

[61] Rotations have been reconstructed for demesnes at Ashill, Bircham, Felbrigg, Keswick, Langham, Little Ellingham, Ormesby, Martham, Reedham, Sedgeford, Taverham, Thornage and Thorpe Abbotts in Norfolk, as well as Brandon, Redgrave and Rickinghall in north Suffolk.

[62] Norfolk R.O., L'Estrange Coll., BH/4.

V

clover.[63] Thereafter this sequence of cropping spread to the rest of the county, although strict adherence to the Norfolk four-course was rare. Clover leys often lasted several years; other crops such as oats and legumes were inserted into the rotation; and fallows were not entirely abandoned.[64] In direct contrast to medieval practice, however, it was a firm principle of these new rotations that the same land never bore grain crops in consecutive years.

Aside from the direct evidence of rotations, fundamental changes in both the nature of rotations and methods of husbandry can be inferred from shifts in the relative importance of winter and spring corn in particular regions of the county. (See Map.)[65] In the Middle Ages, winter corn dominated the south and west, whereas spring crops, with a particular emphasis on barley, occupied over 75 per cent of the cereal acreage on the fertile soils of eastern Norfolk. By the late sixteenth century, however, this pattern had been reversed. Winter corn (almost exclusively wheat) now dominated the cereal acreage in the east, while spring-sown crops gained steadily in relative importance on the light and relatively infertile soils of south-western Norfolk, as the cultivation of spring-sown barley expanded at the expense of winter-sown rye.[66] By the early seventeenth century, in direct

[63] "Management of Three Farms in the County of Norfolk", *Gentleman's Magazine*, xxii (1752), p. 501.

[64] Endless examples of rotations are given in William Marshall, *The Rural Economy of Norfolk*, 2 vols. (London, 1787); Arthur Young, *The Farmer's Tour through the East of England*, 4 vols. (London, 1771); Arthur Young, *General View of the Agriculture of the County of Norfolk* (London, 1804); Nathaniel Kent, *General View of the Agriculture of the County of Norfolk* (London, 1796). The four-course rotation was rare on the Coke estates of west Norfolk in the 1790s, but spread rapidly in the first two decades of the nineteenth century: R. A. C. Parker, *Coke of Norfolk: A Financial and Agricultural Study, 1707-1842* (Oxford, 1975), pp. 157-8.

[65] Discussion of the changing geography of crop and livestock production is based on systematic mapping of a wide range of variables from accounts and inventories. We hope to publish more of these maps in the future, but maps of livestock farming are to be found in Overton and Campbell, "Norfolk Livestock Farming", pp. 384, 390. Some early modern maps (calculated on a different basis) may be found in Mark Overton, *Agricultural Regions in Early Modern England: An Example from East Anglia* (Dept. of Geography, Univ. of Newcastle upon Tyne, Seminar Paper, no. 42, Newcastle upon Tyne, 1983). For the nineteenth century, see the maps in Kain, *Atlas and Index of the Tithe Files*; Susanna Wade Martins, *A Great Estate at Work: The Holkham Estate and Its Inhabitants in the Nineteenth Century* (Cambridge, 1980), pp. 20-4.

[66] Western and south-western demesnes on which barley registered a significant gain in its share of the cereal acreage included Ashill, Brandon, East Lexham, Feltwell, Great Cressingham and Heacham. See also Bailey, *Marginal Economy*, p. 237.

contrast to the situation three centuries earlier, it was west Norfolk that had become the stronghold of spring-cropping and commercial barley production. Specialization in wheat by east Norfolk farmers was paralleled by a switch to pastoral husbandry on the heavy clay soils of central and south-eastern Norfolk. Direct evidence of the precise timing of the conversion of arable to pasture remains elusive but, by the time that inventories become available in the 1580s, it is plain that the change-over had in many cases already taken place.[67] The effect of subsequent price trends, especially after 1660, was merely to confirm this development, as is evident in the growing predominance of farms within these localities with livestock but either few, or no, crops. This parallels similar developments in many other parts of the country and in Norfolk, at least, is apparently without medieval precedent.[68] Further shifts in the geography of crop production took place between the eighteenth and nineteenth centuries. The differences between east and west became much less marked, as a greater proportion of wheat was grown in the west and a greater proportion of barley once more in the east.[69] Indeed the highest concentrations of barley production were to be found in the 1830s exactly where they had been in the Middle Ages.

Since these spatial changes were associated with land of different qualities, other things being equal, they should have produced corresponding changes in crop yields. Heavy land which had yielded indifferently in the Middle Ages was taken out of cultivation; a greater proportion of the county's very best soils were

[67] Joan Thirsk, "The Farming Regions of England", in Thirsk (ed.), *Agrarian History of England and Wales*, iv, pp. 46-9; K. Skipper, "Wood-Pasture and Sheep-Corn: The Early Modern Regions of Norfolk Reconsidered" (Univ. of East Anglia M.A. thesis, 1989).

[68] Unless there were significant numbers of peasant producers who specialized almost exclusively in livestock. For examples of the emergence of specialist pastoral-farming regions during the fifteenth century, see Christopher Dyer, *Warwickshire Farming, 1349-c.1520: Preparations for Agricultural Revolution* (Dugdale Soc., Occasional Papers, no. 27, Oxford, 1981); Andrew Watkins, "Cattle Grazing in the Forest of Arden in the Later Middle Ages", *Agric. Hist. Rev.*, xxxvii (1989), pp. 12-25; H. S. A. Fox, "The Chronology of Enclosure and Economic Development in Medieval Devon", *Econ. Hist. Rev.*, 2nd ser., xxviii (1975), pp. 181-202. See also Harold Fox, "Peasant Farmers, Patterns of Settlement and *Pays*: Transformations in the Landscapes of Devon and Cornwall during the Later Middle Ages", in P. Higham (ed.), *Landscape and Townscape in the South-West* (Exeter, 1990), p. 64.

[69] Clare Sewell Read, "Recent Improvements in Norfolk Farming", *Jl. Roy. Agric. Soc. England*, xix (1858), p. 275.

V

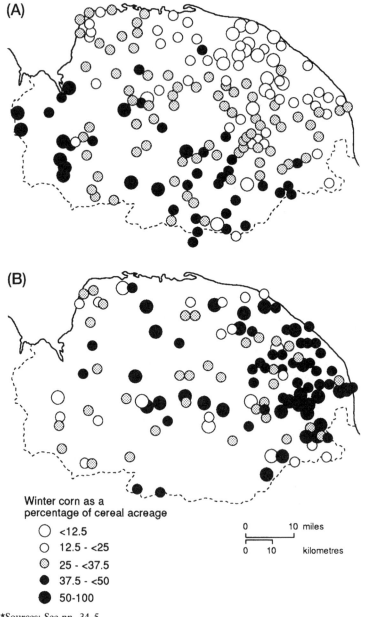

MAP
WINTER-SOWN CEREALS AS A PERCENTAGE OF ALL CEREALS IN
NORFOLK
(A) 1250-1449 AND (B) 1584-1739*

(A)

(B)

Winter corn as a
percentage of cereal acreage

○ <12.5
○ 12.5 - <25
◉ 25 - <37.5
● 37.5 - <50
● 50-100

0   10 miles
0   10   kilometres

*Sources: See nn. 34-5.

devoted to wheat, and a greater proportion of its poor soils to barley.

V
CROP YIELDS

Crop yields per acre seem universally accepted by historians as the key index of agricultural progress and are often equated with "productivity". The word "productivity" has been described as "one of the most used, abused and misused words in our vocabulary", but it can be simply defined as the ratio of outputs to inputs.[70] In practice productivity indices vary, depending on the combinations of outputs and inputs that are considered and the units in which they are measured. The most important inputs, and therefore the most important productivities, are usually taken to be land and labour. Thus two of the most common measures of the agricultural productivity of a region are the output of agricultural products divided by the amount of land in agricultural production and by the number of workers employed in agriculture.[71] As yet, there are virtually no direct measures of labour productivity for English agriculture before the nineteenth century, although indirect measures, derived from estimates of the proportion of the work-force in agriculture and from wage rates, have been produced.[72] Fortunately the situation concerning land productivity is less bleak.

[70] V. H. Beynon and A. M. Houston, *Productivity: The Concept, Its Measurement and a Literature Review* (Nat. Econ. Development Office, London, 1969), p. 1. For further discussion of the issue of agricultural productivity in a historical context, see Overton and Campbell, "Productivity Change in Agricultural Development", pp. 7-17; Overton, "Land and Labour Productivity".

[71] Many economists favour a productivity measure, such as total-factor productivity, which embraces all of the separate factor productivities and relates output to a weighted combination of inputs. Difficulties in obtaining data for calculating total-factor productivity can be considerable, and it is impossible to derive a measure of total-factor productivity in English agriculture based on physical measures of inputs and outputs before the eighteenth century.

[72] E. A. Wrigley, "Urban Growth and Agricultural Change: England and the Continent in the Early Modern Period", *Jl. Interdisciplinary Hist.*, xv (1985), pp. 683-728, repr. in both Robert I. Rotberg and Theodore K. Rabb (eds.), *Population and Economy: From the Traditional to the Modern World* (Cambridge, 1986), pp. 123-68, and in E. A. Wrigley, *People, Cities and Wealth: The Transformation of Traditional Society* (Oxford, 1987), pp. 157-93; Mark Overton, "The Critical Century? The Agrarian History of England and Wales, 1750-1850", *Agric. Hist. Rev.*, xxxviii (1990), pp. 185-9; Gregory Clark, "Labour Productivity in English Agriculture, 1300-1860", in Campbell and Overton (eds.), *Land, Labour and Livestock*, pp. 211-35; Overton, "Land and Labour Productivity". Partial measures of labour

(cont. on p. 67)

Crop yields per sown acre can be directly calculated from manorial accounts and can be estimated indirectly from probate inventories. Before discussing the evidence from Norfolk, it is important to stress that yields per sown acre are only a partial measure of productivity: changes in yields per acre cannot be equated directly with changes in farm output or with changes in agricultural productivity as a whole.[73] Thus an increase in land productivity could arise at the cost of a decline in one or more of the other factor productivities, particularly the productivity of labour. Yield per sown acre is a restricted index of land productivity and is not the same as total agricultural output divided by the agricultural area. Obviously crop yields per acre take no account of livestock output, and cereal yields exclude the output of such farm products as fruit and vegetables, industrial crops, timber and turf. Yields per sown acre also fail to take account of the frequency with which the land is cropped. For example, high grain yields per acre on one farm might be associated with a long period of fallow, so that total grain output per acre of arable could be lower than for a comparable farm with lower yields but a shorter fallow.[74] It is also preferable to measure yields net of on-the-farm inputs such as seed and fodder, to get an indication of the grain available for consumption.[75] While this is possible for the Middle Ages, since accounts report the quantities of grain both sown and fed to livestock, it is not possible for the early modern period, when inventories are silent on both counts.[76]

Manorial accounts have long been used to produce crop yields per acre, but it is only comparatively recently that yields have been estimated from inventories.[77] Yields are not recorded dir-

---

(n. 72 cont.)

productivity are calculated from manorial accounts by Campbell for Martham ("Agricultural Progress in Medieval England", pp. 38-9) and Thornton for Rimpton ("Determinants of Land Productivity", pp. 204-7).

[73] For a discussion of this issue, see Overton and Campbell, "Productivity Change in Agricultural Development", pp. 7-17.

[74] As exemplified by the comparison of cereal productivity on the demesnes of Martham (Norfolk), Cuxham (Oxfordshire) and Rimpton (Somerset), in Thornton, "Determinants of Land Productivity", p. 192.

[75] B. H. Slicher van Bath, *The Agrarian History of Western Europe, A.D. 500-1850*, trans. Olive Ordish (London, 1963), pp. 18-23, 172-4, 177; E. A. Wrigley, "Some Reflections on Corn Yields and Prices in Pre-industrial Economies", in Wrigley, *People, Cities and Wealth*, pp. 92-130.

[76] Campbell, "Land, Labour, Livestock and Productivity Trends", pp. 170-2.

[77] Lord Beveridge, "The Yield and Price of Corn in the Middle Ages", *Econ. Hist.*, ii (1927), repr. in Carus-Wilson (ed.), *Essays in Economic History*, i, pp. 13-25; M. K.

(cont. on p. 68)

ectly in inventories, but can be inferred by comparing valuations of standing grain and harvested grain. The resulting estimates reflect the inventory appraisers' forecasts of yields and depend on assumptions about the precise ways in which they valued standing crops. Since the methodology is not straightforward, it has generated some debate, and the estimates shown in Table 5 and illustrated in the Graph are based on a refinement of Allen's modifications of the original method.[78] No attempt has been made to correct for distortions arising from the use of outsize customary acres and bushels. The scale of this distortion is likely to have diminished over time, as statute measures gained in currency, and by the eighteenth and nineteenth centuries (when the earliest reports on customary measures become available) the problem was no longer an important one in Norfolk.[79] Other potential

(n. 77 cont.)
Bennett, "British Wheat Yield per Acre for Seven Centuries", *Econ. Hist.*, iii (1935), pp. 12-29, repr. in Minchinton (ed.), *Essays in Agrarian History*, i, pp. 55-72; J. Z. Titow, *Winchester Yields: A Study in Medieval Agricultural Productivity* (Cambridge, 1972).

[78] Mark Overton, "Estimating Crop Yields from Probate Inventories: An Example from East Anglia, 1585-1735", *Jl. Econ. Hist.*, xxxix (1979), pp. 363-78; Mark Overton, "Agricultural Productivity in Eighteenth-Century England: Some Further Speculations", *Econ. Hist. Rev.*, 2nd ser., xxxvii (1984), p. 250, n. 37; Paul Glennie, "Continuity and Change in Hertfordshire Agriculture, 1550-1700: II, Trends in Crop Yields and Their Determinants", *Agric. Hist. Rev.*, xxxvi (1988), pp. 145-61. Robert C. Allen, "Inferring Yields from Probate Inventories", *Jl. Econ. Hist.*, xlviii (1988), pp. 117-25; Mark Overton, "Re-Estimating Crop Yields from Probate Inventories", *Jl. Econ. Hist.*, l (1990), pp. 931-5; Overton, "Determinants of Crop Yields", pp. 298-305; Glennie, "Measuring Crop Yields", pp. 255-83.

[79] During the Middle Ages statute perches are recorded at Hunstanton (Estfeld): Norfolk R.O., L'Estrange Coll. BG/2; Ketteringham: P.R.O., C134 F2(14); Marham: P.R.O., C134 F1(14); Quidenham: P.R.O., C133 F118(13); Saham: P.R.O., C134 F15(3); and Wymondham: P.R.O., C134 F2(16). Whereas non-statute perches were in use at Broome — 18½ ft.: P.R.O., C133 F114(7); Hudeston — 18½ ft.: P.R.O., C133 F118(8); Hunstanton (Westfeld) — 15½ ft.: Norfolk R.O., L'Estrange Coll. BG/2; Martham — 18½ ft.: Brit. Lib., Stowe MS. 936, fo. 37; Osmundiston — 16 ft.: Elveden Hall, Suffolk, Cornwallis (Bateman) MSS., box 47/2; Sedgeford — 17½ ft.: Williamson, "Peasant Holdings in Medieval Norfolk", p. 258; and Sheringham — 21½ ft.: P.R.O., C134 F8(20). On price evidence Lord Beveridge believed that Norwich cathedral priory changed from heaped to razed measures between 1344 and 1353: London School of Economics, Beveridge Price Data, box G9. The early modern and eighteenth-century evidence is largely negative since the standard authorities fail to mention Norfolk examples of non-statute acres, perches and bushels, although as late as 1800 such customary measures still prevailed in certain parts of the country: see Giles V. Harrison, "Agricultural Weights and Measures", in Thirsk (ed.), *Agrarian History of England and Wales*, v, ii, pp. 815-25; *A Return from Each Country in England and Wales, of The Different Measures ... under Which Wheat, Barley, Oats and Flour Are Sold*, Parliamentary Papers, 1854 (1761), lxv; Ronald Edward Zupko, *A Dictionary of English Weights and Measures: From Anglo-Saxon Times to the Nineteenth Century* (Madison, 1968).

V

sources of error are the magnitude of the allowance that should be made for the deduction of tithes, and differences in the farm sizes from which the estimates are derived. For the purpose of estimating gross yields there is no alternative but to assume that tithes represented a constant 10 per cent of the grain harvest, a degree of consistency which is unlikely to have applied in practice.[80] As far as the influence of farm size is concerned, medievalists tend to favour the view that yields recorded for seigneurial demesnes were superior to those obtained on peasant holdings in the same locality.[81] By the sixteenth and seventeenth centuries, however, no significant relationship is apparent between farm size and yields.[82]

Yields of individual cereal crops are given in Table 5 and shown in the Graph. As will be seen, there is a gap of 130 years between the 1450s, when the data from accounts effectively end, and the 1580s, when the inventory data begin. A gap of a further hundred years — broken only by the highly selective yield evidence assembled by Kent, Marshall and Young — occurs between the 1730s, when the inventory data peter out, and c.1836, when yield estimates are available from the tithe files.[83] For the mid-nineteenth century the report accompanying the agricultural statistics of 1854 includes some yield estimates, and shortly thereafter the results of several comprehensive surveys of yields are avail-

[80] Emmanuel Le Roy Ladurie and Joseph Goy, *Tithe and Agrarian History from the Fourteenth to the Nineteenth Centuries: An Essay in Comparative History*, trans. Susan Burke (Cambridge, 1982), pp. 24-60.

[81] Postan, "Medieval Agrarian Society", p. 602; Titow, *English Rural Society*, pp. 80-1; Dyer, *Standards of Living in the Later Middle Ages*, pp. 127-31. For a dissentient view, see Campbell, "Agricultural Progress in Medieval England", pp. 39-41.

[82] Overton, "Determinants of Crop Yields", p. 309-11, using evidence from Norfolk, Suffolk and Lincolnshire; Allen, "Two English Agricultural Revolutions", pp. 246-9, for Oxfordshire.

[83] Accounts for a handful of manors do continue into the second half of the fifteenth century but are too few and unrepresentative to provide the basis for a reliable county estimate. Kain and Prince, *Tithe Surveys*; Kain, *Atlas and Index of the Tithe Files*: the only exception is the estimate produced by Arthur Young for a handful of farms in Norfolk: Arthur Young, *Farmer's Tour through the East of England*, iv, pp. 230-7. Robert C. Allen and Cormac Ó Gráda, "On the Road Again with Arthur Young: English, Irish and French Agriculture during the Industrial Revolution", *Jl. Econ. Hist.*, xlviii (1988), pp. 97-104, consider Young's yields to be representative although they do not compare them with either inventory or tithe evidence, or any other contemporary material. Cf. Eric Kerridge, "Arthur Young and William Marshall", *History Studies*, 1 (1968), pp. 43-65; G. E. Mingay, *Arthur Young and His Times* (London, 1975), pp. 15-16.

TABLE 5

NORFOLK: GROSS YIELDS 1250-1854*

(bushels per acre)

	Wheat	Rye	Barley	Oats	W.A.C.Y.[a]	Index[b]
1250-1274	13.2	8.8	15.7	13.5	9.3	100
1275-1299	14.9	10.3	15.8	13.8	10.3	111
1300-1324	14.9	10.0	16.1	13.3	11.0	118
1325-1349	15.6	10.5	17.2	15.0	11.9	127
1350-1374	11.4	8.9	15.3	11.9	8.6	92
1375-1399	12.9	10.1	17.3	14.0	9.7	104
1400-1424	12.7	9.9	14.9	13.9	8.0	86
1425-1449	10.7	12.0	15.4	14.5	8.9	96
1584-1599	11.7	11.9	11.7	15.4	8.2	85
1628-1640	17.3	11.6	11.9	18.4	9.4	98
1660-1679	12.8	14.1	13.9	13.1	8.2	85
1680-1709	14.7	9.0	15.3	20.0	8.5	89
1710-1739	16.9	14.4	22.0	26.4	12.9	134
1760s[c]	25.5	25.0	30.9	38.3	—	—
1790s[d]	24.0	—	—	—	—	—
c. 1800[e]	20.0	—	—	—	—	—
c. 1800[f]	24.0	—	36.0	40.0	—	—
1836[g]	23.3	—	32.0	36.3	20.7	216
1854[h]	30.0	—	38.0	46.0	25.5	266

*Sources: 1250-1449, from manorial accounts: for location, see n. 34; 1584-1739, from probate inventories made June–August with 20 or more sown acres, not weighted by harvest year: for location, see n. 35.

[a] Weighted Aggregate Cereal Yield. See n. 86.

[b] Index of W.A.C.Y. 1250-74 = 100.

[c] Calculated from Arthur Young, *The Farmer's Tour through the East of England*, 4 vols. (London, 1771), iv, pp. 230-7.

[d] Nathaniel Kent, *General View of the Agriculture of the County of Norfolk* (London, 1796), pp. 56, 59.

[e] William Marshall, *The Review and Abstract of the County Reports to the Board of Agriculture*, iii, *Eastern Department* (York, 1818), p. 349.

[f] Arthur Young, *General View of the Agriculture of the County of Norfolk* (London, 1804), pp. 251, 303, 306-8.

[g] Kain, *Atlas and Index of the Tithe Files*, p. 72.

[h] *Reports of Poor Law Inspectors on Agricultural Statistics (England), 1854*.

able.[84] Unfortunately differences in the relative values and extent of cultivation of the leading cereals limit the utility of individual yield figures as a measure of productivity change. As Patrick K. O'Brien and Gianni Toniolo have recently commented, "how much produce did a medieval peasant obtain from a 50-hectare

[84] *Reports of Poor Law Inspectors on Agricultural Statistics (England), 1854*, p. 39; P. G. Craigie, "Statistics of Agricultural Production", *Jl. Roy. Statistical Soc.*, xlvi (1883), pp. 1-47.

V

GRAPH
CEREAL YIELDS IN NORFOLK 1250-1854*

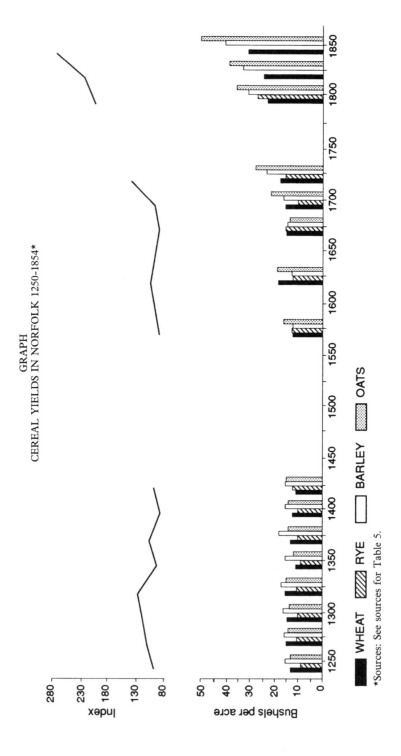

WHEAT ▨ RYE □ BARLEY ▦ OATS

*Sources: See sources for Table 5.

plot of land compared with his modern successor cultivating the same plot is a question which can only be tackled by valuing the mix of crops harvested at prices prevailing in medieval and modern times".[85] Therefore Table 5 and the Graph also include an index of aggregate cereal yields, calculated by multiplying the yield figure for each crop by its price relative to wheat, and by the proportion of the cereal acreage it occupied.[86] This represents a single integrated measure of the mean volume of output per cereal acre over time.

How credible are the trends thus revealed? Wheat and barley were the two most widely grown and recorded crops, so their yields are the most securely documented. In the medieval period barley yields were consistently higher than wheat yields, although between 1584 and 1640 this relationship was reversed. This inversion reflects the fact that more of the wheat crop was being grown on the better soils of the east, and more of the barley on the poorer soils of the west and south-west. After 1660, with the resurgence of barley cultivation, the medieval relationship between wheat and barley yields was re-established and was still apparent in the 1830s. Throughout this long period the accounts, inventories and tithe files agree that wheat and barley gave the best yields on the county's most fertile and intensively cultivated soils, in the Fens and in eastern and northern Norfolk, and the worst yields on the light and infertile sands of the west and south-west.[87] In fact a wide yield differential existed between these two areas until well into the nineteenth century.[88] The only major

[85] Patrick K. O'Brien and Gianni Toniolo, "The Poverty of Italy and the Backwardness of Its Agriculture before 1914", in Campbell and Overton (eds.), *Land, Labour and Livestock*, p. 390.

[86] Symbolically, $Y = \Sigma \, (y_i \cdot p_i/p_w \cdot a_i/\Sigma a)$, where Y is weighted yield, y_i is the yield of crop i in bushels per acre, p_i is the price of the crop per bushel, p_w is the price of wheat per bushel, a_i is the acreage under crop i. For the derivation of this index, see Campbell, "Land, Labour, Livestock and Productivity Trends", pp. 165-74.

[87] The accounts also show that yields were least variable where they were at their highest and most variable where they were relatively low.

[88] In the period 1250-1349 weighted aggregate net cereal yields per acre ranged from a maximum of 12.12 bushels at Hemsby and 11.09 bushels at Martham, on the rich loam soils of the Flegg district of east Norfolk, to 4.46 at Gateley and 4.01 bushels at Wymondham, both on heavy soils in mid-Norfolk, and 3.31 bushels at Brandon and 3.32 bushels at East Wretham, on the light sandy soils of Breckland. At this date, therefore, there was a differential of three-and-a-half-fold between the highest- and lowest-yielding demesnes. The differential in cereal output per *arable* acre was, of course, even greater. For 1584-1640 wheat yields ranged from 4 to 24 bushels per acre, barley from 3 to 23. For 1660-1739 the corresponding figures were 3 to 32, and 6 to 36.

V

modification to this continuity in the geography of crop yields occurred on the heavy clay soils of south-eastern and central Norfolk: whereas in the Middle Ages these had yielded indifferently, by the 1830s their yields were well above average for the county.[89] This trend is already apparent from the inventory data and is testimony to the evolution of improved techniques for managing heavy land.

Compared with wheat and barley, the yield estimates for rye and oats — both minor crops — are more susceptible to error. Apart from the obvious problem of small sample sizes, there is the additional possibility that these crops were undervalued by inventory appraisers, since they were often produced for on-the-farm consumption and were not widely marketed. This may lead to some inflation of the yield estimates, as may the fact that no allowance has been made for the value of straw.[90] Hence, perhaps, the fact that in the sixteenth and seventeenth centuries oats and rye appear to have fared somewhat better relative to wheat and barley than they had done in the Middle Ages. On the other hand, the superior oat yields of the late seventeenth century are consistent with the crop's subsequent status as Norfolk's highest yielding cereal, which suggests that the apparent improvement in yields may indeed have been genuine. As such it can probably be related to husbandry changes which enhanced the status of oats within rotations and reduced the acreage on which they were grown.[91]

There are good reasons, therefore, for accepting as largely plausible the long-term trend of yields summarized in Table 5. The level, as opposed to the trend, of yields in the sixteenth and seventeenth centuries is most open to question, but it seems unlikely that the margin of error is more than 2 bushels per acre.[92] On this assumption, and in the light of existing literature

[89] For low yields on the heavy soils of south-east Norfolk in the Middle Ages, see Bruce M. S. Campbell, "Arable Productivity in Medieval England: Some Evidence from Norfolk", *Jl. Econ. Hist.*, xliii (1983), pp. 379-404.

[90] Glennie, "Measuring Crop Yields", pp. 265-6.

[91] During the Middle Ages oats were commonly sown at the runt end of rotations and therefore thickly. On many manors their yields improved after 1350 as rotations were shortened and fallows increased in frequency.

[92] The trend in wheat yields estimated from labour inputs "shows that there is little disagreement between the probate and labour input methods": Clark, "Yields per Acre in English Agriculture", p. 457.

on the course of crop productivity, three features stand out as of particular significance.

First, the Norfolk evidence reverses the prevailing assumptions about trends in medieval yields. There is no sign of a downward productivity trend as population pressure mounted within this most populous and intensively cultivated of medieval counties during the critical period between 1250 and 1349. On the contrary, yields tended to be higher before the Black Death, when arable husbandry was at fullest stretch and intensive methods were encouraged by high prices and low wages, rather than after, when the opposite conditions caused land to be withdrawn from cultivation and fallowing frequencies to rise.[93] Likewise yields rose between the periods 1584-99 and 1628-40 — when population was rising, grain prices were high and wage rates depressed — but then fell away between the periods 1628-40 and 1660-79, when population pressure slackened, prices stagnated and wages rose.

Secondly, contrary to the claims of Kerridge, Jones and, more recently, Allen and Yelling, in Norfolk at least, the breakthrough in grain productivity came in the eighteenth century and not in the seventeenth.[94] Wheat and barley yields remained at medieval levels until the first decades of the eighteenth century. Over the preceding five centuries wheat, rye, barley and oat yields were at their maxima during the first half of the fourteenth century. Thereafter, when yields peaked again in the 1630s, they were returning to an essentially medieval level and may well have been obtained by employing basically medieval methods of production.[95] Subsequently this ceiling was possibly breached by rye in the 1660s and oats in the 1680s, but not by barley and wheat (the two leading crops) until after 1710. It was only after 1710 that the mean yields of all four crops simultaneously bettered the earlier standard of productivity.[96] The weighted index of cereal

[93] Campbell, "Land, Labour, Livestock and Productivity Trends", pp. 144-9.

[94] Kerridge makes the extravagant claim that: "Inferior practices in the seventeenth century gave increases twice as great as the medieval standard of excellence, and the best, increases four times as great as the best medieval ones. At the end of the eighteenth century, yields were hardly more than in the early seventeenth. That is the measure of the advance that had been made by then": Kerridge, *Agricultural Revolution*, p. 329. See also Jones, "Agriculture and Economic Growth"; Allen, "Two English Agricultural Revolutions"; Yelling, "Agriculture, 1500-1730", pp. 193-5.

[95] Glennie, "Continuity and Change in Hertfordshire Agriculture: II", pp. 155-6.

[96] Much the same holds true of Hampshire, where yields estimated from inventories may be compared with those obtained on 24 demesnes of the bishops of Winchester:

(cont. on p. 75)

V

yields in the Graph lends dramatic emphasis to the fact that the turning-point came in the early eighteenth century: the index remains within the range 85-127 from 1250 until 1709 and only subsequently exhibits a decisive break with the past, rising marginally but decisively to 134, in 1710-39.

Thirdly, this yield rise, once initiated, evidently continued more or less unabated until the opening of the nineteenth century, when, according to the evidence assembled by Kent, Marshall and Young, wheat, barley and oat yields were 50-60 per cent higher than they had been in the 1730s. This steep rate of increase is without historical precedent; it also marks a break with the past in anticipating the renewed rise in population and associated changes in prices and wages.[97] Thereafter, for the next thirty or so years of the new century, the rate of increase slackened until a further upsurge in wheat yields — whose progress had hitherto lagged behind that of barley and oats — took place between the 1830s and the 1850s.[98] These trends seem to vindicate the view of an "agricultural revolution" (defined rather narrowly in terms of grain yields per acre) as an eighteenth-century phenomenon and also the arguments for a "second agricultural revolution" in the second quarter of the nineteenth century, since by the 1850s output per cereal acre was roughly twice what it had been in the 1730s and 1330s.[99]

At first sight, this Norfolk chronology of the growth in yields — and also, by implication, output — conflicts with estimates of agricultural output and productivity for England as a whole produced by Crafts and R. V. Jackson. The latter both consider that output and productivity were growing faster between 1700 and 1760 than they were between 1760 and 1800. Clark's recent estimates also suggest that the rate of growth in wheat yields was faster in the first half of the eighteenth century than it was in the second. Reconciling these various estimates is difficult, not only because they are calculated using different methods from different evidence but also, more importantly, because they measure

(n. 96 cont.)
Glennie, "Measuring Crop Yields", pp. 271-6; Titow, *Winchester Yields*; Overton and Campbell, "Productivity Change in European Agricultural Development", pp. 39-41.

[97] E. A. Wrigley and R. S. Schofield, *The Population History of England, 1541-1871: A Reconstruction* (Cambridge, 1989), pp. 402-12.

[98] Vindicating the opinion of Read, "Recent Improvements", pp. 274-5.

[99] F. M. L. Thompson, "The Second Agricultural Revolution, 1815-1880", *Econ. Hist. Rev.*, 2nd ser., xxi (1968), pp. 62-77.

different things. Cereal yield per sown acre is not the same as output, and is only a partial component of both land productivity and total factor productivity. In any case trends in Norfolk may have differed from those in other parts of England.[100]

VI
LIVESTOCK PROPORTIONS

Livestock occupy a subordinate position in most accounts of English agricultural development, despite their considerable contribution to the supply of food and industrial raw materials and their crucial role in the maintenance of arable husbandry through the provision of haulage, traction and manure. Yet livestock farming had greater potential for commercial development than did arable farming. Livestock farmers could respond more readily to the demands of distant markets because the costs of transporting their products were lower relative to those of arable farmers. Live animals could be walked to market; butter, cheese and wool were high in value relative to their bulk and hence better able to withstand the costs of overland carriage. Notwithstanding Norfolk's reputation as an arable producer, it is its livestock sector that emerges as consistently the more dynamic and, in certain respects, the more progressive branch of farming.[101]

The problems of comparing trends in livestock are much greater than those associated with crops and their yields, since stocking patterns varied considerably with farm size and category of farmer.[102] This is especially true of sheep. In the mid-nineteenth century the agricultural statistics — our most reliable source — demonstrate that sheep accounted for 33 per cent of

[100] For further discussion of estimates of output and productivity, see Overton, "Land and Labour Productivity"; for evidence of yields in other parts of England, see Overton and Campbell, "Productivity Change in Agricultural Development", pp. 38-41.

[101] Livestock are considered in Overton and Campbell, "Norfolk Livestock Farming".

[102] M. M. Postan, "Village Livestock in the Thirteenth Century", *Econ. Hist. Rev.*, 2nd ser., xv (1962), pp. 219-49, repr. in M. M. Postan, *Essays on Medieval Agriculture and General Problems of the Medieval Economy* (Cambridge, 1973), pp. 214-48; Kathleen Biddick, "Medieval English Peasants and Market Involvement", *Jl. Econ. Hist.*, xlv (1985), pp. 823-31; Robert C. Allen, *The "Capital Intensive Farmer" and the English Agricultural Revolution: A Reassessment* (Dept. of Economics, Univ. of British Columbia, Discussion Paper, no. 8711, Vancouver, 1987).

Norfolk livestock (Table 6).[103] In the Middle Ages, during the periods 1250-1349 and 1350-1449, the corresponding proportions were smaller, at 21 and 32 per cent respectively. These figures are almost certainly an understatement, both for the demesne sector and for agriculture as a whole. In the first place, they relate exclusively to demesne flocks, the largest of which were often managed on an inter-manorial basis and — increasingly during the fourteenth century — accounted for separately.[104] More seriously, it seems probable that at this time sheep were much more a peasant than a demesne animal. This is implicit in institutional arrangements which allowed lords to rely upon their tenants' sheep to dung their demesne lands.[105] It is also strongly suggested by Norfolk's massive contribution to the 1341-2 wool tax, which amounted to over an eighth of that collected from the country as a whole and two-and-a-half times that contributed by any other county.[106] This is a far greater contribution than might have been expected on the evidence of Norfolk's demesne flocks alone.

Whereas before 1350 seigneurial foldcourse owners had been more interested in their grain harvest than their wool clip and were content to exploit their tenants' animals for manuring the arable, from the mid-1370s this pattern began to change. As grain prices fell and labour costs rose, many landlords leased out their demesnes but retained their flocks in hand and exploited and extended their foldcourse rights, in order to expand their own sheep numbers at the expense of those of their tenants.[107] The attraction lay in sheep farming's lower costs of production and its capacity to produce meat, milk and wool at a time of uncertain

[103] Total livestock units are calculated as follows: (horses x 1.0) + (oxen x 1.2) + (adult cattle [cows + bulls] x 1.2) + (immature cattle x 0.8) + (sheep x 0.1) + (swine x 0.1). The weightings are based on feed requirements: for their derivation, see Campbell, "Land, Labour, Livestock and Productivity Trends", pp. 156-7.

[104] Norwich cathedral priory adopted central sheep accounting in 1392, after which sheep are rarely recorded in the accounts of individual manors: Norfolk R.O., L'Estrange Coll. IB 3/4. For other examples of central sheep accounting, see F. M. Page, "'Bidentes Hoylandie': A Medieval Sheep Farm", Econ. Hist., i (1929), pp. 603-5; R. A. L. Smith, "The Estates of Pershore Abbey" (Univ. of London M.A. thesis, 1939), pp. 215-16; R. H. Hilton, "Winchcombe Abbey and the Manor of Sherbourne", Univ. Birmingham Hist. Jl., ii (1949-50), pp. 50-2.

[105] Williamson, "Peasant Holdings in Medieval Norfolk", pp. 272-301; Campbell, "Regional Uniqueness of English Field Systems?", pp. 17-25; Postgate, "Field Systems of East Anglia"; Mark Bailey, "Sand into Gold: The Foldcourse System in West Suffolk, 1200-1600", Agric. Hist. Rev., xxxviii (1990), pp. 40-57.

[106] M. Ormrod, "The Crown and the English Economy, 1290-1348", in Campbell (ed.), Before the Black Death, pp. 178-9.

[107] Bailey, "Sand into Gold", pp. 43-51.

markets.[108] This trend is apparent in the greatly expanded importance of sheep as a demesne animal after 1350 and a corresponding
expansion in the mean size of demesne flocks. For instance, sheep
numbers increased fourfold on the estates of the prior of Norwich
between 1300 and 1500.[109] By the first half of the sixteenth
century the county's greatest flockmasters were managing flocks
of a thousand or more animals and the latent conflict of interests
between foldcourse owners and their tenants was a mounting
source of rural tension.[110] Such was the scale of this seigneurial
expropriation of folding rights that by the close of the sixteenth
century comparatively few sheep remained in the hands of tenant
farmers. Instead, the majority of recorded sheep were concentrated in the hands of a few substantial flockmasters, mostly
scattered through the west and south-west of the county.[111]

By the sixteenth and seventeenth centuries, therefore, the ownership pattern of the thirteenth century had been inverted. Sheep
were now disproportionately a landlord animal, as is apparent in
the highly skewed distribution of flock sizes recorded in the
inventories.[112] In fact many of the largest flocks of all would have
been owned by flockmasters whose inventories would not have
been presented to the Consistory Court at Norwich, but are more
likely to have had their probate dealt with by the Prerogative
Court at Canterbury. Unfortunately none of these inventories are
available for the period before 1660 and, for consistency, none
of those that survive after 1660 have been included in the statistics
presented here. As a result sheep are seriously underestimated in
the livestock statistics for 1584-1640 and 1660-1739 summarized
in Table 6.[113] Between 60 and 70 per cent of accounts record

---

[108] Mavis Mate, "Pastoral Farming in South-East England in the Fifteenth
Century", *Econ. Hist. Rev.*, 2nd ser., xl (1987), pp. 523-36.

[109] Norfolk R.O., L'Estrange Coll. IB 4/4; DCN 62, 64.

[110] K. J. Allison, "Flock Management in the Sixteenth and Seventeenth Centuries",
Econ. Hist. Rev., 2nd ser., xi (1958), pp. 98-112; Diarmaid MacCulloch, "Kett's
Rebellion in Context", *Past and Present*, no. 84 (Aug. 1979), pp. 51-3.

[111] Some of the county's greatest flockmasters managed as many as 15,000 animals:
Allison, "Flock Management", pp. 99-101; A. Simpson, *The Wealth of the Gentry,
1540-1660: East Anglian Studies* (Cambridge, 1963), pp. 179-216.

[112] In the period covered by the inventories used here 70 per cent of farmers had
no sheep recorded. Of those who did, the mean flock size was 86 animals, the median
30, the minimum 2, and the maximum 1,737.

[113] B. A. Holderness, "East Anglia and the Fens: Norfolk, Suffolk, Cambridgeshire,
Ely, Huntingdonshire, Essex and the Lincolnshire Fens", in Thirsk (ed.), *Agrarian
History of England and Wales*, v, i, p. 228, also points to the underenumeration of
sheep in inventories.

TABLE 6
NORFOLK: LIVESTOCK STATISTICS 1250-1854*

	1250-1349	1350-1449	1584-1640	1660-1739	1854
% Livestock units[a]					
Cattle (excl. oxen)	45.9	43.8	[52.9][b]	[58.3]	40.3
Cattle	58.5	48.8	[53.4]	[58.3]	40.3
Horses	17.0	15.0	[36.2]	[27.2]	22.6
Oxen	12.7	5.0	[0.5]	[0.0]	0.0
Sheep	21.1	32.6	[4.9]	[10.9]	33.2
Swine	3.4	3.8	[5.5]	[3.8]	3.9
Livestock ratios[c]					
Immature : adult cattle[d]	0.82	0.52	0.84	1.79	—
Immature : adult cattle[e]	0.72	0.47	0.78	1.63	—
Sheep : cattle[e]	4.59	7.87	[0.74]	[5.47]	8.42
Oxen : horses[e]	0.66	0.37	0.05	0.00	0.00
Beasts per 100 cereal acres					
Livestock[d]	35.0	40.7	[76.9]	[76.7]	—
Livestock[e]	32.1	36.2	[50.9]	[69.7]	60.7
Cattle (excl. oxen)[e]	14.7	16.3	41.4	37.2	23.9
Cattle[e]	18.7	18.2	41.4	37.2	23.9
Horses[e]	5.4	5.3	16.8	12.5	13.7
Oxen[e]	4.1	2.2	0.0	0.0	0.0
Sheep[e]	68.7	113.7	[17.6]	[205.2]	201.4
Swine[e]	10.9	13.6	22.3	18.0	23.9
Draught beasts per 100 sown acres[e]	8.1	6.3	14.4	10.6	10.7

*Sources: 1250-1449, from manorial accounts: for location, see n. 34; 1584-1739, from probate inventories made June-July with 20 or more sown acres: for location, see n. 35; 1854, *Reports of Poor Law Inspectors on Agricultural Statistics (England)*, 1854.

[a]See n. 103.

[b]Figures in square brackets involve sheep numbers which are subject to error.

[c]All farms with a minimum cattle herd size of 10.

[d]Means of ratios calculated for each farm or demesne.

[e]Aggregate mean: mean number of first animal type for the whole county divided by the mean number of the second animal type or by the mean crop acreage for the county.

sheep in the Middle Ages, but a mere 30 per cent of farm inventories include them. In Lincolnshire and Kent, where the Norfolk institution of the foldcourse did not exist, the proportion of inventories mentioning sheep is around 70 per cent.[114] It is certainly difficult to believe that the stocking density of sheep in 1584-1640 was inferior to that of 1350-1449, and it seems plausible to suppose that their share of livestock units throughout the early modern period was in the range 20-30 per cent, rather than the 5-11 per cent actually recorded for the farms with extant inventories. If this was indeed the case, it follows that the relative importance of all other categories of livestock is overstated, although not their stocking densities.

Data for other classes of livestock are more reliable. Allowing for the underestimation of sheep, swine, for instance, stand out as comprising a consistent 3-5 per cent of total livestock units throughout the period 1250-1854. Draught animals — horses and oxen — also comprised a fairly consistent 20-30 per cent of livestock units, although the number of horses in the early modern period may be slightly exaggerated by the inclusion of horses used for non-agricultural purposes. Horses were replacing oxen for draught as early as the late twelfth century and this process made steady progress throughout the Middle Ages, the first two-horse and one-man teams appearing on light-land demesnes towards the end of the fourteenth century.[115] A few oxen remained in Norfolk right down to the nineteenth century, but they had been virtually eliminated by the 1630s. The final stronghold of draught-oxen in Norfolk was the Fens but, after drainage in the seventeenth century, the Fens were to be an area of horse-power as well as horse-breeding.

Given Norfolk's naturally strong land-use bias towards arable, it was a remarkable achievement that non-working animals formed such a comparatively large proportion of livestock units from so early a date. This testifies to the intensity and effectiveness of the mixed-farming system that was already firmly in place in the thirteenth century and upon which subsequent centuries were to improve. This system gave priority to the more

[114] C. W. Chalklin, *Seventeenth Century Kent* (London, 1965), p. 100; Joan Thirsk, *English Peasant Farming: The Agrarian History of Lincolnshire from Tudor to Recent Times* (London 1957), pp. 34, 72, 87, 106.
[115] Campbell, "Towards an Agricultural Geography", pp. 91-4; John Langdon, *Horses, Oxen and Technological Innovation: The Use of Draught Animals in English Farming from 1066-1500* (Cambridge, 1986), pp. 50-1.

V

productive classes of livestock — horses rather than oxen for draught, cattle rather than sheep, adults rather than immatures — and sustained them on a mixture of temporary and permanent pasturage, managed grassland, hay and fodder crops of various types.[116] Notwithstanding the county's reputation for sheep farming, the distinctive institutions with which sheep farming was associated and the fact that there were certain types of land on which sheep alone would thrive, it was cattle that — with the possible exception of the fifteenth and early sixteenth centuries — constituted the core of Norfolk's intensive pastoral regime over this six-hundred-year period.

Cattle accounted for 40 per cent of livestock units in the mid-nineteenth century and, allowing for the underenumeration of sheep, accounted for a similar proportion throughout the Middle Ages. It is improbable that they accounted for less between 1584 and 1739, and after 1660 may well have accounted for significantly more. Throughout the Middle Ages, and until well into the seventeenth century, the low ratio of immature cattle to adults indicates that herds were geared towards dairying, with the breeding of replacement oxen and milking cattle a secondary consideration.[117] This made sound economic sense in a husbandry system that aimed at maximizing output per unit area of land, since cattle-based dairying is more productive of human food per unit area than most other forms of pastoral activity.[118] During the Middle Ages cattle assumed greatest prominence where integrated mixed-farming systems were most fully developed, notably on the fertile soils of central and eastern Norfolk, within ready access of the Norwich market and the textile-producing villages to the north.

By the early modern period cattle husbandry had undergone a spatial reorganization.[119] First, as noted earlier, increasing numbers of farmers on the heavy clay soils of south-central and south-

[116] Bruce M. S. Campbell, "Intensive Pastoral Husbandry in Medieval England: A Norfolk Perspective", in Edwin B. Dewindt (ed.), *The Salt of Common Life: Individuality and Choice in the Medieval Town, Countryside and Church. Essays Presented to J. Ambrose Raftis on the Occasion of His 70th Birthday* (Michigan, 1994).

[117] Bruce M. S. Campbell, "Commercial Dairy Production on Medieval English Demesnes: The Case of Norfolk", in Annie Grant (ed.), *Animals and Their Products in Trade and Exchange (Anthropozoologica*, xvi, numéro spécial, 4, Paris, 1992), pp. 107-18.

[118] I. G. Simmons, *The Ecology of Natural Resources* (London, 1974), pp. 201-6.

[119] Maps illustrating this reorganization are in Overton and Campbell, "Norfolk Livestock Farming", pp. 384, 390.

eastern Norfolk abandoned the unrewarding task of trying to cultivate their stiff and intractable soils and turned almost exclusively to pastoral husbandry.[120] Secondly, a proportion of these farmers, no doubt with an eye to the changing demands of the Norwich and, possibly, the metropolitan markets, concentrated their efforts not on dairying but on meat production. Many of the animals in question were not bred in the county but were brought in from outside, and there are enough references to Scottish, northern and Welsh steers to demonstrate that Norfolk graziers — especially in the Waveney valley — had become part of an inter-regional livestock trade that entailed the movement of stock over considerable distances. A century later, Kent reckoned that one-half of Norfolk cattle were driven from Scotland, a quarter from Wales and Ireland, while the remaining quarter were home-bred.[121] Henceforth, until the ploughing-up campaign of the Napoleonic Wars, southern and central Norfolk was to be a predominantly pastoral farming region which satisfied its grain requirements by drawing upon the surrounding arable districts. Thirdly, the mixed farmers on the fertile soils of the east of the county also began to fatten bullocks as an important adjunct to cereal farming.[122]

The emergence of bullock-fattening as an independent specialism in its own right shows up in the presence of herds with a demographic structure strongly biased towards immatures, especially after 1660 when the ratio of immature to adult cattle doubled. (See Table 6.) This, in turn, implies a higher turnover of animals, as they were finished more rapidly, generating a demand for young stock from breeding areas. Fattening was essentially a supply response to the significant changes in market demand from the late seventeenth century, and it was with the object of increasing fodder supplies that many Norfolk farmers adopted the cultivation of ley grasses, expanded their barley

[120] Shin-Ichi Yonekawa, "Champion and Woodland Norfolk: The Development of Regional Differences", *Jl. European Econ. Hist.*, vi (1977), pp. 163-76; Thirsk (ed.), *Agrarian History of England and Wales*, iv, pp. 46-7.

[121] Kent, *General View*, p. 101. For an example of this trade, see D. M. Woodward, "Cattle Droving in the Seventeenth Century: A Yorkshire Example", in W. H. Chaloner and Barrie M. Ratcliffe (eds.), *Trade and Transport: Essays in Economic History in Honour of T. S. Willan* (Manchester, 1977), pp. 35-57.

[122] Kent, *General View*, p. 33; Marshall, *Rural Economy of Norfolk*, i, p. 125; Holderness, "East Anglia and the Fens", pp. 234-6; Wade Martins, *Great Estate at Work*, p. 24.

V

acreage and experimented with new crops.[123] This revitalized mixed-farming systems and promoted a significant increase in cattle numbers on arable farms. Nowhere were these developments more pronounced than in eastern Norfolk, which regained its fourteenth-century prominence as an important cattle producer, albeit with bullock-fattening rather than dairying its principal goal.

VII
STOCKING DENSITIES

More striking than any of these changes in the composition and ownership of flocks and herds was an apparent doubling in the stocking densities of virtually all classes of livestock between the Middle Ages and the early modern period. This is significant because it implies dramatic increases in both the output and the productivity of the livestock sector. The ratio of draught animals — horses and oxen — to sown acres also more than doubled and was of considerable significance, since it represented a gain in the amount of working capital per cultivated acre and presumably led to increases in labour productivity.[124] The magnitude of the differences in stocking densities is so great that it raises questions about the reliability of the comparison between accounts and inventories. This is a complicated problem, since the underenumeration of sheep, the inclusion of non-agricultural horses, the development of farms exclusively devoted to livestock and the introduction of new crops into the sown acreage, all need to be taken into account when interpreting changes in stocking densities. How these densities are measured is also important. Stocking densities can be expressed as a ratio of livestock units to either the cereal acreage or the sown acreage, with average ratios for the county being calculated either as the mean of farm densities or from the aggregate totals of acres and animals. These issues are considered elsewhere, with the conclusion that the

[123] Mark Overton, "An Agricultural Revolution, 1650-1750", in Mark Overton et al., *Agricultural History: Papers Presented to the Economic History Society Conference* (Canterbury, 1983), pp. 9-13; Overton, *Agricultural Regions in Early Modern England*; Overton, "Diffusion of Agricultural Innovations"; Overton, "Determinants of Crop Yields". See Thirsk, "Seventeenth-Century Agriculture and Social Change", for other responses to low cereal prices.

[124] E. A. Wrigley, "Energy Availability and Agricultural Productivity", in Campbell and Overton (eds.), *Land, Labour and Livestock*, pp. 323-39.

aggregate ratio of livestock units to cereal acres is the most robust measure.[125]

The most serious problem, given that the average size of farm represented by accounts is significantly larger than that recorded by inventories, is that stocking densities varied with farm size. Nevertheless the evidence from inventories shows that stocking densities only varied inversely with farm size up to a maximum of about fifty acres. Above this size no particular relationship is apparent. Yet, on farms of more than fifty acres, mean stocking densities roughly doubled between 1259-1450 and 1660-1740, from 35.9 to 62.5. Moreover for farms over twenty acres (employed in Table 6) the greatest rise in stocking densities took place between the late sixteenth century and the mid-seventeenth century (a comparison between inventories), rather than between the Middle Ages and the late sixteenth century (a comparison between accounts and inventories).[126] Thus the dramatic differences in stocking densities are not easily dismissed as merely the result of distortions arising from the different sources employed in the comparison.

The strength of the inverse relationship between stocking density and sown area revealed by the inventory data raises intriguing questions about the nature of the equivalent relationship in the Middle Ages.[127] At present it is widely believed, on little direct evidence, that in the thirteenth and fourteenth centuries stocking densities on peasants' holdings were inferior to those on demesnes, on the grounds that lords had greater command over capital and enjoyed privileged access to pastoral resources.[128] Moreover royal purveyancing and high levels of feudal rent, including customary dues such as heriot and obituary, struck directly at the peasants' ability to build up flocks and herds.[129] If

[125] Overton and Campbell, "Norfolk Livestock Farming".

[126] Means of total livestock units per 100 cereal acres were 37.6 for 1425-49, 38.3 for 1584-99, and 62.4 for 1628-40: Overton and Campbell, "Norfolk Livestock Farming". Between 1584 and 1739, 22 inventoried farms with at least fifty cropped acres have been identified in parishes for which there are also documented demesnes. A comparison of these two closely comparable sets of farms reveals 6 with stocking densities at or below the medieval average and 16 with densities above. Overall, stocking densities on the inventoried farms were 80 per cent higher than on the corresponding demesnes. This disparity is already apparent before 1640 and becomes more pronounced thereafter.

[127] Allen, "Two English Agricultural Revolutions", p. 253, raises the same point.

[128] Postan, "Medieval Agrarian Society", p. 554; Postan, "Village Livestock in the Thirteenth Century".

[129] J. R. Maddicott, The English Peasantry and the Demands of the Crown, 1294-1341 (Past and Present Supplement, i, Oxford, 1975), repr. in T. H. Aston (ed.), Landlords,

(cont. on p. 85)

V

this was indeed the case, then one of the most striking differences between medieval agriculture and that of later centuries was the comparatively undeveloped scale of the peasants' pastoral sector. The transformation of their relative poverty in livestock during the fourteenth century, into the wealth that is so apparent at the close of the late sixteenth century, also implies a major process of capital accumulation within the peasant sector during the intervening period.[130] Such a process would certainly accord with the views of those who argue that it was the decline of feudal socio-property relations that provided the scope for capital accumulation and the fuller development of productive forces, but it remains to be demonstrated that this was in fact the case. Certainly a fuller investigation of medieval peasant livestock needs to be placed high on any future research agenda.

While livestock densities provide some impression of manure potential and of the relative importance of the cereal and pastoral sectors (on the assumption that legumes and other fodder crops were essentially pastoral products) it provides no true measure of whether changes in stocking densities were the consequence of a genuine improvement in the ratio of livestock to the total area of farmland (as opposed to the cereal or sown acreage) or merely of a relative shift in the ratio of cereal to pastoral land use. To establish this would require information on the areas under ley grasses, fallows and the various forms of permanent pasture, which neither accounts nor inventories provide. To calculate stocking densities in terms of the total farm area — the ideal — is therefore out of the question.[131]

There can be no doubt that the cereal and sown acreages varied as a proportion of the total farmed area. In the 1830s, after

(n. 129 cont.)
Peasants and Politics in Medieval England (Cambridge, 1987), pp. 285-359; A. R. H. Baker, "Evidence in the Nonarum Inquisitiones of Contracting Arable Lands in England during the Early Fourteenth Century", Econ. Hist. Rev., 2nd ser., xix (1966), pp. 518-32.
[130] Sidney Pollard and David W. Crossley, The Wealth of Britain, 1085-1966 (London, 1968), p. 65; R. H. Hilton, "A Crisis of Feudalism", Past and Present, no. 80 (Aug. 1978), pp. 15-16, repr. in Aston and Philpin (eds.), Brenner Debate, p. 133; Dyer, Warwickshire Farming, pp. 30-2; Dyer, Standards of Living in the Later Middle Ages, pp. 144-5; McIntosh, Autonomy and Community, pp. 226-7.
[131] For other ways of calculating the balance between crops and stock, see J. A. Yelling, "Probate Inventories and the Geography of Livestock Farming: A Study of East Worcestershire, 1540-1750", Trans. Inst. Brit. Geographers, li (1970), pp. 111-26.

centuries of reclamation, the cereal and sown acreages accounted for an estimated 38 and 77 per cent of the total land area respectively, with the remainder made up of fallows (2 per cent), grassland (21 per cent), commons (11 per cent) and woodland (4 per cent).[132] Prior to the widespread adoption of the Norfolk four-course rotation (which reduced the grain acreage to half the arable acreage), the grain acreage probably accounted for a larger proportion of a smaller arable area in both the medieval and early modern periods. At its medieval peak, *c.*1300, the cereal acreage may have matched or even exceeded that of the 1830s. Certainly, on the evidence of both manorial accounts and inquisitions *post mortem* (which record land use on the estates of lay tenants-in-chief of the crown), fallows and grassland held in severalty were both at a minimum *c.*1300 and the average ratio of arable to grassland (measured by area) was 5.0 to 1.0 (or 3.7 to 1.0 if measured by value).[133] The corresponding ratio in 1836 was 5.9 to 1.0, or 3.9 to 1.0 if commons are included.[134]

After 1350 the arable and cereal acreages contracted and the areas of temporary and permanent pasture expanded, which, other things being equal, should have produced an improvement in stocking densities.[135] Such a trend is indeed recorded by the accounts, but the gain was a modest 13 per cent and was not sustained after 1375, which implies that it may be understated (due to the under-recording of sheep) and that the peasant sector was the principal beneficiary through the leasing of demesne herds, herbage and rights of pasturage, of which there is considerable evidence.[136] After 1450 there are signs that the arable acreage continued to decline and the proportion of pasture to increase, for the ensuing hundred years was the peak period of settlement contraction and abandonment in the county.[137] It was this period

---

[132] Kain, *Atlas and Index of the Tithe Files*, p. 72.

[133] For a detailed presentation of the inquisitions *post mortem* data, see Bruce M. S. Campbell, "Medieval Land Use and Land Values", in Peter Wade-Martins (ed.), *An Historical Atlas of Norfolk* (Norwich, 1993), pp. 48-9.

[134] Calculated from Kain, *Atlas and Index of the Tithe Files*, p. 72.

[135] Campbell, "Land, Labour, Livestock and Productivity Trends".

[136] For the farm of demesne dairies and their herds, see Campbell, "Commercial Dairy Production on Medieval English Demesnes".

[137] K. J. Allison, "The Lost Villages of Norfolk", *Norfolk Archaeology*, xxxi (1957), pp. 116-62; P. Wade-Martins, "The Development of the Landscape and Human Settlement in West Norfolk from 350-1650 A.D., with Particular Reference to the Launditch Hundred" (Univ. of Leicester Ph.D. thesis, 1971); David Dymond, *The Norfolk Landscape* (London, 1985), pp. 135-46.

V

which saw the beginnings of piecemeal enclosure and important changes in the foldcourse as an institution. It is probable that increasing proportions of the county's heavy land were laid down to grass, in the face of high wage rates and low grain prices.[138] By 1600 it seems likely that there was a higher ratio of grassland to arable than in 1300, partly because there were now significant numbers of specialist pasture farms with little or no arable at all, but also because mixed farms maintained higher grassland ratios. The trend towards a higher ratio of livestock to cereal acres that is apparent before 1640 becomes even more pronounced after 1660. On this occasion, however, rising livestock numbers appear to have been accompanied by a significant growth in both the arable and cereal acreages. The mean sown acreage recorded in inventories increased from fifty-five acres in the first half of the seventeenth century to eighty-five acres by the second half. It could be that the sample of inventories is biased in the latter period towards larger farmers, that average farm size was increasing, that the arable acreage was extending at the expense of pasture, or that all three of these factors were responsible for the increasing acreages. Of these possibilities, the extension of arable at the expense of pasture is most likely, since there is no reason to suppose any significant change in the types of farm represented by inventories during the course of the late seventeenth century and, while farm size could have been increasing, it is unlikely to have risen by over 50 per cent. Yet as arable was encroaching on pasture, livestock densities were simultaneously increasing, which can only imply a growing reliance upon fodder crops as part of an arable rotation. As fodder cropping grew in significance, so arable and pastoral husbandry became more closely integrated and mixed-farming systems rose in intensity, a development reinforced by a higher turnover of animals as greater emphasis was placed upon the rearing and fattening of younger beasts. At the same time, it seems almost certain, although our data reveal little direct evidence of it, that livestock productivity, as manifest by higher carcass weights and greater milk and wool yields, also rose significantly.[139] By 1700 Norfolk's cereal acreage was probably

[138] Campbell, "Extent and Layout"; D. P. Dymond, "The Parish of Walsham-le-Willows: Two Elizabethan Surveys and Their Medieval Background", *Proc. Suffolk Inst. Archaeology*, xxxiii (1974), pp. 195-211.
[139] Annie Grant, "Animal Resources", pp. 149-87, in Grenville Astill and Annie Grant (eds.), *The Countryside of Medieval England* (Oxford, 1988); P. L. Armitage, "A Preliminary Description of British Cattle from the Late Twelfth to the Early

(cont. on p. 88)

much the same as in 1300, but there were perhaps twice as many livestock and those livestock were undoubtedly more productive. Thereafter, especially with the revival of grain prices after 1740, stocking densities fell back somewhat, but by 1854 they remained well above those of the Middle Ages; a tribute to the boost provided to pastoral as well as to arable productivity by wider adoption of the Norfolk four-course rotation.[140]

VIII
TECHNOLOGICAL EVOLUTION AND AGRICULTURAL REVOLUTION

Taken together, this new evidence of crop proportions, crop yields, livestock proportions and stocking densities demands several important revisions to existing ideas of the nature and course of agrarian change between the thirteenth and the nineteenth centuries. Before reviewing these, however, it is necessary to reiterate that the data from accounts and inventories give only a limited picture of the fortunes of farm enterprises on only certain categories of farm. Some new pieces are added to the puzzle and the guesses about some of the others are better informed, but limitations of the historical record make it impossible for the complete picture to be reconstructed. Peasant farming in the Middle Ages and the activities of the great gentlemen flockmasters of the sixteenth and seventeenth centuries remain serious lacunae. Information is also lacking on the actual volume of crop and livestock output, the size of the cultivated area, and the relative importance of arable and pasture. Nor is material available on the changing magnitude of farming inputs, which makes it impossible to calculate fluctuations in the profitability of farming, or to measure agricultural productivity other than in terms of crop yields per acre.

The evidence from manorial accounts and probate inventories suggests that agricultural technology was far from static during this long period. Medieval and early modern farmers exhibited

(n. 139 cont.)

Sixteenth Century", *The Ark*, vii (1980), pp. 405-13; Clark, "Labour Productivity in English Agriculture", pp. 214-19.

[140] In east Worcestershire, the only area for which broadly comparable data are available, stocking densities fell continuously from the mid-sixteenth to the mid-eighteenth centuries as farmers increasingly specialized in wheat. This response indicates the development of an extensive farming system in contrast to the development of intensive systems in Norfolk. Yelling, "Probate Inventories and the Geography of Livestock Farming".

V

considerable ingenuity, adaptability and innovation in their husbandry practices. Indeed they had to, if yields were not to fall. Reserves of soil nitrogen had been continually depleted for millennia and, in a sense, farmers had to run in order to stand still by finding new ways of replacing the nitrogen taken out by crops. Legumes were particularly important in this respect, because they are able to convert atmospheric nitrogen into soil nitrogen which can be taken up by subsequent cereal crops. Contrary to the impression given by some historians, animal (or human) manure did not add new nitrogen to the soil: it was merely a means of recycling nitrogen that had been removed by harvested crops.[141]

Although there are abundant examples of the careful use of manures in the Middle Ages (including the application of night-soil from Norwich), there was no overall correlation between crop yields and stocking densities.[142] This is because crop and livestock production varied in the extent to which they were integrated and therefore in the rate at which nitrogen was recycled and restored to the soils from which it had been removed. Historians are right to have diagnosed medieval agriculture as characterized by relatively low stocking densities compared with later periods, but they have misarticulated the relationship between the arable and pastoral sectors and, in particular, the extent to which the productivity of the former was a function of the size of the latter.[143] High stocking densities, and hence a high manure potential, were no guarantee of high yields if arable and pastoral husbandry were managed as largely separate enterprises.[144] It is an obvious point, but growing crops could not benefit from manure which remained locked within the pastoral sector or was applied in such a way as to be dissipated through

[141] Robert S. Shiel, "Improving Soil Fertility in the Pre-Fertiliser Era", in Campbell and Overton (eds.), *Land, Labour and Livestock*, pp. 51-77.

[142] For the medieval use of "urban manure" — possibly night-soils — see Campbell, "Agricultural Progress in Medieval England", p. 34. See also Young, *Farmer's Tour through the East of England*, ii, p. 66, on the same in the eighteenth century.

[143] Biddick, *Other Economy*, p. 65.

[144] Kathleen Biddick, "Agrarian Productivity on the Estates of the Bishopric of Winchester in the Early Thirteenth Century: A Managerial Perspective", in Campbell and Overton (eds.), *Land, Labour and Livestock*, p. 115. A correlation of the weighted aggregate net yield per acre against the number of livestock units per 100 cereal acres for Norfolk, for the period 1250-1449, gives a correlation coefficient of +0.037. Indeed at Felbrigg, between 1401 and 1420, a correlation of the weighted aggregate yield per seed and per acre against the number of livestock units per 100 cereal acres, using five-year means, gives correlation coefficients of -0.71 and -0.57 respectively: Norfolk R.O., WKC 2/130-1/398x6. Yet see Titow, *Winchester Yields*, pp. 30-1.

leaching and oxidization. Where manure supplies were scarce, much could be gained by minimizing waste and ensuring their systematic and well-timed application to the soil. In these respects, some farmers with low stocking densities were much more assiduous than those with high ones, as is implicit in the fact that significantly higher stocking densities in the late sixteenth and early seventeenth centuries failed to elicit yields per acre that were superior to those of the Middle Ages.

It is in fact Norfolk's stocking densities rather than its crop yields that, on the evidence presented here, most distinguishes early modern from medieval agriculture. Whereas the best medieval yields were not significantly bettered until well into the eighteenth century, seventeenth-century stocking densities were roughly twice those of the fourteenth century.[145] In this sense, at least, Kerridge is correct in identifying a "revolution" in early modern farming. A switch of emphasis towards livestock farming was already under way in the late fourteenth century and continued through the fifteenth into the early sixteenth century. Unfortunately the latter stages of this movement cannot be documented until inventories become available in the late sixteenth century, when particularly significant gains appear to have been registered by the smallholdings of the peasantry. At first, increased livestock were accommodated on land withdrawn from arable cultivation and converted to pasture, with some heavy-land farmers abandoning cultivation altogether. But fodder cropping and an expansion of temporary pasturage must also have played an increasing part, for stocking densities continued to rise on mixed farms until well into the seventeenth century, as pasture reverted once again to arable. Thus more livestock may well have been supported by a reduced acreage of pasture. This suggests that the output of forage and fodder per acre must have risen above medieval levels although this cannot be demonstrated explicitly from the evidence.

One way in which fodder and forage supplies could have been increased was by blurring the distinction between permanent pasture and permanent arable, through wider adoption of the ley

---

[145] The chronology of crop yields in Norfolk accords reasonably well with that established, by Guy Bois, Joseph Goy, Emmanuel Le Roy Ladurie, Hugues Neveux, Herman van der Wee and others, for parts of northern France and the Low Countries from tithe and other related data: Campbell, "Land, Labour, Livestock and Productivity Trends", pp. 178-82.

V

husbandry which had been practised in some parts of Norfolk since at least the fourteenth century.[146] At the same time, the productivity of ley husbandry could have been upgraded by the substitution of sown for self-seeded grasses.[147] Kerridge argues strongly for this development but inventories are problematic in their treatment of meadow and pasture because only those crops grown with the "industry and manurance of man" were meant to be included.[148] Thus they excluded natural grass or pasture, but might have included sown grass leys since these involved expenditure of capital and labour. As the seventeenth century advanced, inventory appraisers increasingly recorded sown grass, which points to the progressive expansion and improvement of ley husbandry. These methods undoubtedly helped to further the development of integrated mixed-farming systems and to restore yields to something approaching their early fourteenth-century peak, but it was not until after 1700 that yields were raised to significantly higher levels.

It seems probable that after 1650, unlike the period after 1350, the arable acreage did not fall. Contrary to the assumption of both Jones and John, the terms of trade moved only slightly in favour of livestock at the expense of crops, and this could have been more than offset by government inducements to maintain arable cultivation, together with the development of both new markets and new ways of marketing grain.[149] As a result the arable acreage may actually have expanded. Such a development would have squeezed supplies of permanent pasture yet further, thus providing farmers with a greater incentive to devote an

---

[146] Convertible husbandry systems, with three or four years of crops followed by three or four years when the land reverted to grass, were in operation on the de Clare demesne at Great Bircham between 1341 and 1349, and on the de Felbrigg demesne at Felbrigg between 1400 and 1408: P.R.O., SC 6/930/17-23; Norfolk R.O., WKC 2/130/398x6. Eric Stone drew attention to the probable existence of such a system in "The Estates of Norwich Cathedral Priory, 1100-1300" (Univ. of Oxford D.Phil. thesis, 1956), p. 347.

[147] Carolina Lane, "The Development of Pastures and Meadows during the Sixteenth and Seventeenth Centuries", Agric. Hist. Rev., xxviii (1980), pp. 18-30.

[148] Overton, "Reconstruction of Agrarian Landscapes", pp. 169-70.

[149] Jones, Agriculture and the Industrial Revolution, p. 72; John, "Agricultural Productivity and Economic Growth", pp. 19-25; M. W. Flinn, "Agricultural Productivity and Economic Growth: A Comment", Jl. Econ. Hist., xxvi (1966), pp. 93-8; Overton, "Agricultural Revolution, 1650-1750", pp. 6-7; Patrick O'Brien, "Agriculture and the Home Market for English Industry, 1660-1820", Eng. Hist. Rev., c (1985), pp. 773-800; but see also the comments of Glennie, "Continuity and Change in Hertfordshire Agriculture: II", pp. 157-8.

increased proportion of their sown acreage to fodder production. They did this through the widespread adoption of clover and especially turnips. These crops prompted the further integration of livestock and crops since they were grown as part of an arable rotation, and, whether by accident or design, the increased cultivation of clover added new supplies of nitrogen to the soil.[150] Significantly it is from this date that a clear correlation emerges between stocking densities and crop yields on individual farms, indicative of the wider diffusion of genuinely integrated mixed-farming systems.[151]

The focus of livestock husbandry was also changing. Norfolk had long been precocious in its high ratio of non-draught to draught animals, a development facilitated by its equally precocious preference for horses for draught work. Within the non-draught sector, cattle assumed prominence and, from at least the mid-thirteenth century, herds exhibited a strong demographic bias towards mature females, indicative of a specialist interest in dairying. From the mid-seventeenth century, however, this bias began to tilt in the opposite direction, as immature cattle were increasingly favoured over adults and meat production took precedence over dairying. This marks an important new departure. Stock had for long been bought in from breeders in Scotland, Wales and the north of England, to be fattened over the summer on pasture farms in the marshes and river valleys. But after 1660 this practice spread to a second group of farms in the arable areas of eastern Norfolk, where bullocks were fattened on turnips and clover and probably also on barley.[152]

By 1700 east Norfolk farmers were moving towards the system of farming that was to have dramatic effects for the whole county a century later. Although they had some of the best land, they strove to maintain and increase soil fertility and were uniquely receptive to new technology. East Norfolk farmers were the first to grow buckwheat and, from the mid-seventeenth century, were the first to grow clover. Turnips were also grown here at an early

---

[150] The role of legumes in fixing nitrogen from the air was not properly understood until the late nineteenth century (Shiel, "Improving Soil Fertility", p. 54), but seventeenth-century farmers were well aware that clover was the "mother of corn": Walter Blith, *The English Improver Improved* (London, 1652), pp. 184-5; Worlidge, *Systema Agriculturae*, p. 26.

[151] Overton, "Determinants of Crop Yields", p. 312; Allen, "Two English Agricultural Revolutions", p. 253.

[152] Holderness, "East Anglia and the Fens", pp. 234-6.

V

date. These farmers continued to obtain the highest cereal yields, as their forebears had done in the Middle Ages. Indeed these east Norfolk farmers had been in the vanguard of progressive farming since at least the thirteenth century, when a similarly intensive and integrated mixed-farming system had developed. At that time, however, partly because of the environmental limitations of the technology involved and partly for institutional and economic reasons, it failed to develop or spread to much of the rest of the county.[153]

The story was very different in the eighteenth century. The evidence from inventories vindicates the view of both Kent and Marshall that the traditional "agricultural revolution" started in east Norfolk.[154] Here, by the 1730s, a few farmers were achieving yields which were unprecedented by the standards of the previous five centuries.[155] These pushed up mean yields for the county as a whole which, for the first time, broke away from medieval levels. Furthermore, this occurred without the stimulus of falling wages, rising prices and vigorously expanding demand. Indeed trends in agricultural wages convey a strong impression that labour productivity was also rising. By the mid-eighteenth century rising exports demonstrate that English agriculture was clearly producing a surplus, and a significant proportion of that surplus was being exported from Norfolk.[156]

Between 1740 and 1800, under the stimulus of renewed population growth and rising demand, the new husbandry of the east spread to much of the rest of the county, where clover, and more especially turnips, could help reclaim light land for cereal production, in conjunction with other improvements such as the addition

---

[153] As M. M. Postan has observed: "The real problem of medieval technology is not why new technological knowledge was not forthcoming, but why the methods, or even the implements, known to medieval men were not employed, or not employed earlier or more widely than they in fact were": M. M. Postan, *The Medieval Economy and Society* (London, 1972), p. 42. For a discussion of the constraints upon agricultural progress at this time, see Campbell, "People and Land", pp. 81-100; Campbell, "Ecology versus Economics".

[154] Marshall, *Rural Economy of Norfolk*, i, p. 125; Kent, *General View*, p. 33.

[155] A good example is provided by a farm at Billockby. In 1728 it grew wheat, barley and oats, together with buckwheat, clover and turnips, and was fattening Scottish cattle. Wheat yields — at 26 bushels per acre — and barley yields — at 33 bushels — were just at the medieval maxima for this part of the county. Norfolk R.O., INV 78/30.

[156] Ormrod, *English Grain Exports*; Nathaniel Kent, "Exported Produce of Norfolk", *Annals of Agriculture*, xxii (1794), pp. 34-41.

of massive quantities of marl and lime to the soil.[157] As a result, by the 1830s, high grain yields could be found in many parts of the county and the cultivation of turnips and clover had become so widespread that they constituted a quarter each of the total sown acreage. More significant than the rise in yields, however, was the extension of the arable acreage which these crops permitted, for this probably made a proportionately greater contribution to the rise in total grain output.[158] As a contemporary commentator observed: "we sow on these improved farms five times as many acres of wheat, twice as many of barley; of the former we grow three times as much on an acre, of the latter twice as much as formerly".[159] Associated with these developments was a greatly expanded volume of fodder: while cattle were the beneficiary of this in much of the east of the county, sheep remained the dominant animal in the west.[160] In fact it was the growth in fodder supplies that enabled the expansion in arable acreage to take place without much sacrifice in stocking densities, which implies that absolute numbers of cattle and especially sheep were also increasing. These gains in pastoral production reinforced the powerful upward trend in agricultural output as a whole. If the existence of such a trend in physical output is considered to represent the essence of an "agricultural revolution", there are certainly grounds for reinstating the late eighteenth and early nineteenth centuries as the principal revolutionary era.

By the 1830s the full potential of legume-based intensive husbandry seems to have been reached. Indeed if the comparison between the contemporary estimates around 1800 and the evidence of the tithe commissioners is valid, then yields had risen little over the first three decades of the nineteenth century. Between the 1830s and 1850s, however, yields of wheat jumped again. It is possible that by this time nitrogen was no longer the "limiting factor" in crop growth, so further applications of nitro-

---

[157] Hugh C. Prince, "The Changing Rural Landscape, 1750-1850", pp. 7-83, in Mingay (ed.), *Agrarian History of England and Wales*, vi, p.46; Hugh C. Prince, "The Origins of Pits and Depressions in Norfolk", *Geography*, xlix (1964), pp. 15-32; Marshall, *Rural Economy of Norfolk*, i, p. 259, ii, p. 364; Parker, *Coke of Norfolk*, p. 156.

[158] For England as a whole it has been estimated that between 1750 and 1800 the cultivated area grew by 0.42 per cent per annum, total agricultural output by 0.44-0.81 per cent, and total land productivity by 0.12-0.38 per cent: Overton, "Land and Labour Productivity".

[159] "Management of Three Farms in the County of Norfolk", p. 502.

[160] Wade Martins, *Great Estate at Work*, p. 24.

gen may have had little effect on yields. The element most likely to have been deficient was phosphorous, and this mid-nineteenth-century rise in yields coincides with the importation of large quantities of phosphate fertilizer from overseas, dubbed by F. M. L. Thompson a "second agricultural revolution". There is much contemporary Norfolk evidence of the intensive application of imported phosphate fertilizers and also of imported feed-stuffs such as cattle-cake.[161] Thereafter yields rose little until the second half of the twentieth century, when artificial fertilizers, pesticides and herbicides were to revolutionize the physical output of farming once again.[162]

This long-term perspective demonstrates that most of the components of the technological package embodied in the Norfolk four-course rotation — the use of legumes, a reduction of fallows, manure-intensive husbandry, and the integration and mutual development of arable and pastoral husbandry — had been in place since the Middle Ages. Turnips were added as a fodder crop from at least the 1630s, and clover was being sown for fodder in the 1660s. It was the wider cultivation of the latter which from the mid-eighteenth century greatly enhanced the supply of nitrogen to the soil.[163] In the following century, nitrogen — in the form of feedstuffs and fertilizers — together with other plant nutrients, were imported from abroad, and in the twentieth century the chemical industry has produced vast quantities of nitrogen from the air using energy from fossil fuels.[164]

IX
POPULATION GROWTH AND AGRICULTURAL CHANGE

The evidence of changes in yields reverses the commonly accepted view of the relationship between the direction of population change and the trend of crop yields. Until the early eighteenth

---

[161] Thompson, "Second Agricultural Revolution"; Wade Martins, *Great Estate at Work*, p. 16; N. Bacon, *Report on the Agriculture of Norfolk* (London, 1844), p. 111; Read, "Recent Improvements", pp. 276-80, 287-8; Parker, *Coke of Norfolk*, pp. 158-61; B. Almack, "On the Agriculture of Norfolk", *Jl. Roy. Agric. Soc. England*, v (1842), pp. 307-57.

[162] F. R. Harper, "Crop Production in England and Wales, 1950-1980", *Jl. Roy. Agric. Soc. England*, cxlii (1981), pp. 42-54.

[163] G. P. H. Chorley, "The Agricultural Revolution in Northern Europe, 1750-1880: Nitrogen, Legumes and Crop Productivity", *Econ. Hist. Rev.*, 2nd ser., xxxiv (1981), pp. 71-93.

[164] Shiel, "Improving Soil Fertility", pp. 58-61, 67.

century the trends in yields suggest a Boserupian rather than a Malthusian response to the stimulus of population increase, in so far as population growth, accompanied by falling real wages and rising grain prices, was associated with rising not falling yields.[165] Conversely, yields fell when, after 1350, and again after 1650, population growth eased, wage rates rose and grain prices fell.[166] The decline in yields was greater in the fourteenth century, as was the decline in population, than it was after 1650.[167]

Historians have tended to follow Ricardo in arguing that extending the arable acreage involves the cultivation of land of poorer quality, which will in turn give poorer yields per acre and lower mean yields overall. Although neither accounts nor inventories can reveal the process directly, it is clear that mean yields tended to be at a maximum when the arable acreage was also at a maximum — as in the early fourteenth and early seventeenth centuries — rather than vice versa. In the short-term, provided the extension to the arable acreage involves ploughing out permanent pasture, cereal crops cultivated on the new arable will benefit from the reserves of nitrogen stored in the pasture land. This nitrogen boost can give yields on the new arable that are potentially twice those on old-established arable but, after twenty years or so, yields will fall back as the nitrogen is used up.[168] Thus, as Christopher Thornton has shown for the Winchester demesne of Rimpton in Somerset, some of the yield increases in the thirteenth century could have been due to this short-term

[165] Grigg, *Dynamics of Agricultural Change*, pp. 21-43; Postan and Hatcher, "Population and Class Relations", pp. 69-70; Ester Boserup, *The Conditions of Agricultural Growth: The Economics of Agrarian Change under Population Pressure* (London, 1965); Ester Boserup, *Population and Technology* (Oxford, 1981); E. A. Wrigley, "Malthus's Model of a Pre-Industrial Economy", in Michael Turner (ed.), *Malthus and His Time* (New York, 1986), pp. 3-18; E. A. Wrigley, "The Classical Economists and the Industrial Revolution", in Wrigley, *People, Cities and Wealth*, pp. 21-45.

[166] E. H. Phelps Brown and Sheila V. Hopkins, "Seven Centuries of Building Wages", *Economica*, new ser., no. 22 (1955), pp. 195-206; E. H. Phelps Brown and Sheila V. Hopkins, "Seven Centuries of the Prices of Consumables Compared with Builders' Wage-Rates", *Economica*, new ser., no. 23 (1956), pp. 296-314, both repr. in Carus-Wilson (ed.), *Essays in Economic History*, ii, pp. 168-96, and in Henry Phelps Brown and Sheila V. Hopkins, *A Perspective on Wages and Prices* (London, 1981), pp. 1-59.

[167] John Hatcher, *Plague, Population and the English Economy, 1348-1530* (London and Basingstoke, 1977); Wrigley and Schofield, *Population History of England*, pp. 207-15.

[168] Shiel, "Improving Soil Fertility", pp. 72-3; Overton, "Determinants of Crop Yields", pp. 293-4.

V

bonus. Once arable land reverts to pasture it takes about a hundred years for the reserves of soil nitrogen to regenerate. By the late sixteenth century, therefore, a re-extension of the arable acreage could again have led to short-term yield increases.[169]

Even in the longer-term, when reserves of nitrogen in former pasture land have been depleted, the Ricardian assumption only holds in the absence of technological change and if all other inputs per acre (including the rotational system and the frequency with which land is sown) remain constant. It has been demonstrated that considerable technological progress was achieved in the Middle Ages, and there is abundant evidence for the Middle Ages that other inputs were increased considerably. Such a process of intensification is directly observable before 1315 in medieval accounts, which record reductions in fallow, the substitution of higher- for lower-value crops, high seeding rates, intensive manuring and the lavish use of labour to prepare the soil and weed and harvest the crop.[170] Inventories do not contain such information, but it would seem likely that similar processes were at work in the late sixteenth and early seventeenth centuries, given that yields, cultivated acreage and wage trends were moving in the same directions as they had done before 1315. This evidence accords with Boserup's argument that yields will rise under conditions of population pressure, through an intensification of production which can serve to drive down labour productivity.[171]

Although in Norfolk mean yields rose in response to pressure of population in both the thirteenth and sixteenth centuries, the evidence of prices suggests that nationally agricultural output was failing to keep pace with growing demand.[172] Compared with the increase in demand (population almost doubled between 1541 and 1656 from around 2.7 million to 5.3 million and the magnitude of the increase was roughly the same during the century before 1300), the rise in yields was comparatively modest.

This indicates the danger of taking yields per sown acre as the sole guide to agricultural productivity. The overall productivity of agriculture, taking all factor inputs into account, may not have been rising, and indeed was probably falling during these periods,

[169] Thornton, "Determinants of Land Productivity", pp. 196-8, employs this argument in his study of Rimpton.

[170] Campbell, "Agricultural Progress in Medieval England", pp. 26-46.

[171] Boserup, *Population and Technology*.

[172] Pollard and Crossley, *Wealth of Britain*, p. 95.

since the improved returns to land may have been offset by falling returns to labour and capital, especially if higher yields were achieved through the intensification of labour inputs. If total agricultural productivity (calculated as the ratio of total outputs to total inputs) was indeed falling, then the agricultural sector would have been responsible for driving down living standards in such a way as to induce Malthusian-like demographic responses. Likewise, although yields dropped in subsequent periods, if the contraction in output was proportionately less than the reduction in inputs, overall agricultural productivity could well have been rising, as labour and capital were deployed with greater efficiency. This is more likely to have happened during the drop in yields from 1650 to 1700 than it was from 1350 to 1450 since, on the evidence of stocking densities, livestock output was probably significantly higher in the late seventeenth than it had been in the late fourteenth century. Under these circumstances, higher per capita output and incomes in agriculture would have relaxed the pressures for Malthusian preventive curbs to fertility, paving the way in due course for renewed population growth.

The adjectives "Malthusian" and "Boserupian" tend to be used rather loosely by historians, the former to mean that limitations of agricultural supply impose a constraint on population growth, and the latter to mean that population pressure stimulates a rise in agricultural output through rising yields. The two views are frequently held as mutually exclusive interpretations of the relationship between population growth and agrarian change, and strictly speaking they are, since Boserup's prime assumption is that population growth is independent of food supply. But this is not to say that a Malthusian check to population growth is incompatible with rising yields under conditions of population pressure, for the experience of Norfolk appears to demonstrate just that.[173]

This discussion of the relationship between productivity and population growth has suggested that land and labour productivity were inversely related before the eighteenth century, since increases in grain yields were likely to have been at the expense of the productivity of labour, and vice versa. Yet from the eight-

[173] This argument is developed in an unpublished paper, Mark Overton and Bruce M. S. Campbell, "Population Change and Agricultural Productivity in England, 1250-1850".

V

eenth century both land and labour productivity were rising together.[174] While technological change explains some part of the eventual rise in crop yields, it does not, by and large, explain improvements in labour productivity. With the exception of an increase in the draught power available from livestock, there is no evidence of technical innovations which would have materially added to the efficiency of farm labour until the end of the eighteenth century.[175]

X

INSTITUTIONS AND MARKETS

In the absence of substantial food imports, it is of course rising labour productivity, rather than the productivity of land alone, that is a necessary pre-condition for an expansion in the proportion of the nation's workforce employed in the industrial and tertiary sectors of the economy.[176] On the basis of changes in the estimated proportion of the population resident in towns, E. A. Wrigley has inferred that labour productivity in English agriculture must have doubled between the early seventeenth and the early nineteenth centuries.[177] Clark, on the other hand, working from changes in real wage rates, considers the rise in agricultural labour productivity to have begun earlier and amounted to a quadrupling between *c.*1300 and *c.*1850.[178] Clearly much remains to be learnt about the timing and scale of this transformation. Placing the kinds of indices employed by Wrigley and Clark on a firmer empirical footing will help, but this needs to be coupled

[174] Overton, "Land and Labour Productivity".

[175] Wrigley, "Energy Availability", pp. 323-39. For the contribution of improved material technology to the productivity of agricultural labour after 1750, see E. J. T. Collins, "Labour Supply and Demand in European Agriculture, 1800-1880", in E. L. Jones and S. J. Woolf (eds.), *Agrarian Change and Economic Development: The Historical Problems* (London, 1969), pp. 61-94; E. J. T. Collins, "The Age of Machinery", in G. E. Mingay (ed.), *The Victorian Countryside*, 2 vols. (London, 1981), i, pp. 200-13; George Grantham, "The Growth of Labour Productivity in the Production of Wheat in the *cinq grosses fermes* of France, 1750-1929", in Campbell and Overton (eds.), *Land, Labour and Livestock*, pp. 340-63.

[176] Nicholas F. R. Crafts, "British Industrialization in Its International Context", *Jl. Interdisciplinary Hist.*, xix (1989), pp. 415-28; N. F. R. Crafts, "The New Economic History and the Industrial Revolution", in Peter Mathias and John A. Davis (eds.), *The Nature of Industrialization*, i, *The First Industrial Revolutions* (Oxford, 1989), pp. 25-43; Wrigley, *Continuity, Chance and Change*, pp. 10-11.

[177] Wrigley, "Urban Growth and Agricultural Change", p. 138; Overton, "Critical Century?", pp. 185-6.

[178] Clark, "Labour Productivity in English Agriculture", pp. 219-21.

with more explicit investigation of the employment of labour within agriculture using manorial accounts, farm accounts and the like.[179]

Nevertheless, although agricultural labour productivity was rising from at least the sixteenth century, it was not until the eighteenth century that this was matched by rising land productivity and expanding total output. Nor was it until the end of that century that the strong positive relationship between the rate of growth in population and the rate of growth in food prices, which had existed from the Middle Ages, was finally broken.[180] That it was, reflects the marriage of an effective technology to an appropriate farm structure, which together were capable of responding to rising demand by raising the productivity of land without sacrificing the productivity of labour. To understand how this marriage came about shifts attention from the forces of production to the relations of production. It was institutions and markets which provided the crucial link between land and labour productivity and, hence, the overall productivity of the agricultural sector.

Such key institutional and structural developments as the substitution of waged for servile labour, break-up and leasing-out of demesnes, engrossment of holdings, establishment of more competitive terms of tenure and transformation of property rights exercised a powerful indirect influence upon the course of agricultural productivity growth.[181] Thus the rise in labour productivity has been ascribed to a more efficient, motivated, better-fed and harder-working labour force, to the substitution of first animal and then mechanical power for human labour, to the elimination of peasant smallholdings and creation of a system of large capitalist farms, and to the replacement of open-field agriculture by farming in enclosed fields under private property rights.[182]

---

[179] For a pioneering attempt to measure labour productivity on an individual demesne, see Thornton, "Determinants of Land Productivity", pp. 201-7.

[180] Overton, "Land and Labour Productivity"; Overton and Campbell, "Productivity Change in European Agricultural Development", pp. 44-5; Wrigley and Schofield, *Population History of England*, pp. 402-12.

[181] See above, nn. 6, 27. See also Douglass C. North and Robert Paul Thomas, *The Rise of the Western World: A New Economic History* (Cambridge, 1973).

[182] Gregory Clark, "Productivity Growth without Technical Change in European Agriculture before 1850", *Jl. Econ. Hist.*, xlvii (1987), pp. 419-32; Clark, "Labour Productivity in English Agriculture"; Wrigley, "Energy Availability"; Patrick K. O'Brien and Caglar Keyder, *Economic Growth in Britain and France, 1780-1914: Two*

(cont. on p. 101)

Likewise gains in land productivity have been assumed to depend on these changes in property rights, together with a growth in the size of farms.[183] But the relationships between these structural changes and trends in productivity are far from resolved and demand more research. Judicious application of the comparative approach may also help in establishing the relative importance of the different variables.[184]

These institutional changes were in turn linked to changing market opportunities. Markets were the essential mediator in a commercialized economy between the supply of and demand for agricultural products, yet developments in their nature and operation remain insufficiently understood. Over time, changes occurred in the efficiency with which the market operated (thereby raising or lowering transactions costs), in the size and composition of demand, and in the degree to which farmers participated in the market both to obtain farm inputs and to dispose of their produce.[185] Many of these developments are

---

(*n. 182 cont.*)
Paths to the Twentieth Century (London, 1978); Robert C. Allen, "The Growth of Labor Productivity in Early Modern English Agriculture", *Explorations in Econ. Hist.*, xxv (1988), pp. 117-46; Allen, "Two English Agricultural Revolutions", pp. 236-54; Brenner, "Agrarian Roots of European Capitalism"; Dunford and Perrons, *Arena of Capital*, pp. 120-3.

[183] Ernle, *English Farming*, pp. 207-23; Michael Turner, "English Open Fields and Enclosures: Retardation or Productivity Improvements", *Jl. Econ. Hist.*, xlvi (1986), pp. 669-92; Allen and Ó Gráda, "On the Road Again"; J. P. Cooper, "In Search of Agrarian Capitalism", *Past and Present*, no. 80 (Aug. 1978), pp. 20-65, repr. in Aston and Philpin (eds.), *Brenner Debate*, pp. 138-91.

[184] See, for instance, Peter Solar and Martine Goossens, "Agricultural Productivity in Belgium and Ireland in the Early Nineteenth Century", in Campbell and Overton (eds.), *Land, Labour and Livestock*, pp. 364-84; Allen and Ó Gráda, "On the Road Again". For a pioneering attempt at a critical evaluation of the sources of labour productivity growth in French wheat production 1750-1929, see Grantham, "Growth of Labour Productivity".

[185] R. H. Britnell, *The Commercialisation of English Society, 1000-1500* (Cambridge, 1993). A recent review of market development is to be found in J. A. Chartres, "City and Towns: Farmers and Economic Change in the Eighteenth Century", *Hist. Research*, lxiv (1991), pp. 138-55. The relationship between marketing and agricultural development has attracted more attention in France than Britain: Abbott Payson Usher, *The History of the Grain Trade in France, 1400-1710* (Cambridge, Mass., 1913); George Grantham, "Jean Meuvret and the Subsistence Problem in Early Modern France", *Jl. Econ. Hist.*, xlix (1989), pp. 184-200; D. R. Weir, "Markets and Mortality in France, 1600-1789", in J. Walter and R. S. Schofield (eds.), *Famine, Disease and Social Order in Early Modern Society* (Cambridge, 1989). For an early but flawed analysis of the development of the corn market in England, see N. S. B. Gras, *The Evolution of the English Corn Market from the Twelfth to the Eighteenth Century* (Cambridge, Mass., 1910); a critique is by E. Kneisel, "The Evolution of the English Corn Market", *Jl. Econ. Hist.*, xiv (1954), pp. 46-52.

amenable to closer investigation. For instance, manorial accounts represent a particularly rich and detailed source for exploring the level of commercial involvement of the demesne sector at a relatively early date, and information on the payment of money rents and patterns of wealth recorded in surviving tax schedules can be used to make inferences about the corresponding commercial involvement of the peasantry.[186] Once commercialized, farmers were exposed to changes in the size and composition of demand, as populations expanded and contracted, living standards rose and fell, dietary preferences changed, and new configurations emerged in the social and geographical distribution of wealth. In this context, more systematic investigation of the social history of diet will do much to help make sense of changes in the composition of agricultural output.

Certainly, on the evidence of the changes in husbandry practice documented here, the market was structuring agricultural production in Norfolk from at least the thirteenth century. From the end of that century light-soil farmers in south-west Norfolk, with potentially lucrative trading contacts via the River Ouse and the port of King's Lynn, discovered that their best comparative advantage lay in commercial barley production and expanded its cultivation accordingly.[187] As barley became more generally cultivated, its price fell both absolutely and relatively to the point at which, in the fifteenth century, farmers on the better soils of east Norfolk were encouraged to shift from barley to wheat, a trend reinforced during the sixteenth century, as demand for bread-wheat grew from Norwich and London. At the same time a more clearly defined and buoyant demand for meat and dairy produce, especially from Norwich, coupled with more favourable terms of trade for pastoral produce, encouraged the emergence of specialist livestock farms on the heavy soils of the centre and south-east of the county.[188] Subsequently, in the late seventeenth and early eighteenth centuries, increasing demand for quality

[186] Bruce M. S. Campbell, "How Commercialised Was the Seigniorial Sector of English Agriculture, circa 1300? Some Evidence from the Hinterland of London", in R. H. Britnell and Bruce M. S. Campbell (eds.), *A Commercialising Society? England, 1000-1300* (Manchester, forthcoming); E. A. Kosminsky, *Studies in the Agrarian History of England in the Thirteenth Century*, ed. R. H. Hilton, trans. R. Kisch (Oxford, 1956), pp. 152-96; Biddick, "Medieval English Peasants and Market Involvement".
[187] Bailey, *Marginal Economy*, pp. 153-6; P.R.O., E101/574/25.
[188] J. L. Bolton, *The Medieval English Economy, 1150-1500* (London, 1980), pp. 254, 346, 349; Dyer, *Standards of Living in the Later Middle Ages*, pp. 199-202.

V

malt from brewers and distillers in London and the Low Counties, a government policy of subsidizing the export of malt, new methods of marketing grain, and the growing practice of using barley to fatten bullocks, induced a further expansion of barley production at a county level — the crop for which Norfolk possessed a particular comparative advantage.[189]

Integral to these developments were the changing provisioning requirements of cities such as Norwich and London. Much has been written about the stimulus provided by the presence of major cities to agricultural progress, but to date — notwithstanding the lead long ago provided by J. H. von Thünen — there has been little attempt to map the provisioning zones of individual cities in a specific way.[190] The matter is an important one for, as urban hinterlands expanded and contracted, so farmers altered the crops and livestock they produced and the intensity of their production. Processes of this kind partly underlay the changing patterns of production observed in Norfolk.

Although estimates of medieval urban populations are currently undergoing some revision — a population of c.25,000 has been suggested for Norwich c.1330, and between 80,000 and 100,000 for London c.1300 — it is beyond dispute that England was more urbanized in the seventeenth century than it had been in the thirteenth.[191] London was probably twice as large c.1600 than it had been c.1300 and its food-supply hinterland was correspond-

[189] Mark Overton, "Agricultural Change in Norfolk and Suffolk, 1580-1740" (Univ. of Cambridge Ph.D. thesis, 1981), pp. 257-9; Ormrod, *English Grain Exports*; J. A. Chartres, "The Marketing of Agricultural Produce", in Thirsk (ed.), *Agrarian History of England and Wales*, v, ii, pp. 406-502, repr. in J. A. Chartres (ed.), *Agricultural Markets and Trade, 1500-1750* (Cambridge, 1990), pp. 157-253; See Riches, *Agricultural Revolution*, p. 24, for Norfolk's market advantages.

[190] Notably E. A. Wrigley, "A Simple Model of London's Importance in Changing English Society and Economy, 1650-1750", *Past and Present*, no. 37 (July 1967), pp. 44-70, repr. in Wrigley, *People, Cities and Wealth*, pp. 133-56; Wrigley, "Urban Growth and Agricultural Change"; John Langton and Göran Hoppe, *Town and Country in the Development of Early Modern Western Europe* (Hist. Geography Research ser., no. 11, Norwich, 1983); George Grantham, "Agricultural Productivity and Urban Provisioning Zones before the Industrial Revolution", *Jl. Econ. Hist.* (forthcoming). On the work of J. H. von Thünen, see Peter Hall (ed.), *Von Thünen's Isolated State: An English Edition of "Der isolierte Staat"*, trans. Carla M. Wartenberg (Oxford, 1966); Michael Chisholm, *Rural Settlement and Land-Use: An Essay on Location* (London, 1962), pp. 20-32.

[191] Elizabeth Rutledge, "Immigration and Population Growth in Early Fourteenth-Century Norwich: Evidence from the Tithing Roll", *Urban History Yearbook, 1988*, pp. 15-30; Derek Keene, *Cheapside before the Great Fire* (London, 1985).

ingly wider, although its precise extent has yet to be charted.[192] This hinterland expanded dramatically in subsequent centuries as the metropolis grew inexorably larger, providing a major spatial and temporal dynamic to the process of agrarian change. Metropolitan growth also benefited the many smaller market centres within its hinterland which serviced the trade it generated. Within Norfolk and Suffolk, for instance, John Patten estimates that the urban population grew by 50 per cent between 1603 and the 1670s, in contrast to a rural population increase of only 11 per cent.[193] The commercial opportunities offered by these expanding urban populations transformed the economics of agricultural production in Norfolk.

Norfolk is not England, still less Britain, and much useful work remains to be done reconstructing developments in the rest of the country. Nevertheless, although the particular course of agricultural development outlined here may be unique to that county, it is likely that the general influences on that development operated on a national scale. In the Middle Ages Norfolk was already responding to the influence of concentrated urban demand, although within the country as a whole such market penetration remained partial.[194] Subsequently further market expansion, encouraged by the increase in urbanization, promoted wider and more intense regional specialization.[195] What in the Middle Ages

[192] Derek Keene, "Medieval London and Its Region", *London Jl.*, xiv (1989), pp. 99-111; James G. Galloway and Margaret Murphy, "Feeding the City: London and Its Agrarian Hinterland", *London Jl.*, xvi (1991), pp. 3-14; Bruce M. S. Campbell, James A. Galloway and Margaret Murphy, "Rural Land-Use in the Metropolitan Hinterland, 1270-1339: The Evidence of *Inquisitiones Post Mortem*", *Agric. Hist. Rev.*, xl (1992), pp. 1-22; Fisher, "London Food Market"; Wrigley, "Simple Model of London's Importance".

[193] John Patten, "Population Distribution in Norfolk and Suffolk during the Sixteenth and Seventeenth Centuries", *Trans. Inst. Brit. Geographers*, lxv (1975), p. 62.

[194] Campbell, "People and Land", pp. 81-92; Campbell, "Ecology versus Economics".

[195] For market development, see Alan Everitt, "The Marketing of Agricultural Produce, 1500-1640", in Thirsk (ed.), *Agrarian History of England and Wales*, iv, pp. 496-522, repr. in Chartres (ed.), *Agricultural Markets and Trade*, pp. 15-141; Chartres, "Marketing of Agricultural Produce"; Eric Kerridge, "Early Modern English Markets", in B. L. Anderson and A. J. H. Latham (eds.), *The Market in History* (Beckenham, 1986), pp. 121-53; Ann Kussmaul, *A General View of the Rural Economy of England, 1538-1840* (Cambridge, 1990), pp. 103-25. Examples of market-related agricultural specialization include: Yelling, "Changes in Crop Production in East Worcestershire"; John Broad, "Alternate Husbandry and Permanent Pasture in the Midlands, 1650-1800", *Agric. Hist. Rev.*, xxviii (1980), pp. 77-89; Peter Edwards, "The Development of Dairy Farming on the North Shropshire Plain in the

(cont. on p. 105)

V

had been a feature of only certain parts of the country had by the seventeenth century become much more general. As different regions became increasingly drawn into this burgeoning market nexus, so more farmers intensified, innovated, and thereby secured higher yields. The pattern has yet to be mapped out in detail, but already it is clear that this process emerges in Hertfordshire and also, possibly, in Oxfordshire — both better placed to take advantage of the London market — before it does in Norfolk.[196] Each of these counties responded in its own way to the demands of the market: none the less a particular combination of circumstances enabled Norfolk to be conspicuously successful and to give its name to the most productive system of nineteenth-century farming in England.

A time perspective of six centuries within a single geographical area inevitably places existing interpretations of agrarian change in a new light. In particular, the evidence presented here offers no support for those verdicts on medieval agriculture that emphasize its technological inertia and ecological shortcomings. On the contrary, land productivity on medieval demesnes set a standard that was not to be exceeded for four centuries. Nor can any evidence be found to substantiate some of the more extravagant claims for the progress of cereal productivity over the sixteenth and seventeenth centuries. In fact it is livestock rather than crops that emerges as the more dynamic sector in early modern Norfolk agriculture. Taking the six centuries as a whole, and notwithstanding the revisionism of recent decades, it is the period after 1740 that clearly emerges as having undergone the most rapid and profound transformation of technology and productivity. Although many areas of uncertainty remain, these conclusions vindicate the comparative approach adopted in this paper and invite wider application of that approach elsewhere.

The Queen's University of Belfast   *Bruce M. S. Campbell*
University of Newcastle upon Tyne   *Mark Overton*

(n. 195 cont.)
Seventeenth Century", *Midland Hist.*, iv (1978), pp. 175-89; Glennie, "Continuity and Change in Hertfordshire Agriculture: I"; see also Overton and Campbell, "Productivity Change in European Agricultural Development", pp. 41-2.
[196] Overton and Campbell, "Productivity Change in European Agricultural Development", pp. 40-1.

Norfolk livestock farming 1250–1740: a comparative study of manorial accounts and probate inventories

Mark Overton and Bruce M. S. Campbell

Livestock farming occupies a subordinate position in most accounts of agricultural development in pre-industrial England. Although medieval and early modern diets were dominated by the consumption of grain in one form or another they were not exclusively vetegarian: meat, and especially milk, butter, cheese, and eggs were all consumed in significant quantities. Animals also provided many essential raw materials: wool for manufacture into textiles, hides for leather, skins for parchment and vellum, and tallow for lighting. Above all, in this technologically organic and animate world it was animals that drew the plough, hauled the cart, and provided manure: arable farming at its most arable was in fact mixed farming.

Not only is the pastoral sector usually treated as of lesser importance than the arable, in some accounts it is also treated as subsidiary and dependent. According to such interpretations crops and animals competed with each other for land, so that an inverse relationship existed between the size of the arable and pastoral sectors: each could only expand at the expense of the other.[1] Thus as the demand for grain grew under pressure of population the pastoral sector was

"Reprinted from *Journal of Historical Geography*, 18, pp. 377–396, © (1992), with permission from Elsevier".

VI

bound to contract, with adverse consequences for the availability of manure and energy and, hence, for the productivity of both land and labour. Such notions also posit a direct relationship between the number of livestock and the area of grassland, with the supply of grassland seen as a simple function of environmental conditions. Yet neither view is borne out by the historical evidence. The absence of a simple and direct relationship between the supply of grassland and number of livestock is already apparent in the second half of the thirteenth century.[2] Even in the eighteenth century, when the evidence of marriage seasonality supposedly reveals a spatial dichotomy between an "arable" east and a "pastoral" west, it is based merely on the location of livestock rearing: many of the most developed and intensive fattening and dairying regimes remained firmly rooted in the supposedly "arable" east.[3]

Far from being passive, the pastoral sector possessed a considerable dynamic of its own. Gregory Clark has recently estimated that the share of livestock products in English agricultural output rose from approximately a quarter to a half between 1300 and 1850, and that livestock productivity (measured as the output of livestock products per acre) rose six-fold over the same period in comparison with a two-fold rise in crop output per acre.[4] These estimates provide support for the view that livestock farming was the leading sector of technological change and productivity growth within English agriculture. Even productivity growth in the arable sector ultimately derived from developments in the livestock sector; from the spread of fodder crops, which contributed to rising land productivity, and from the more intensive use of draught animals, which contributed to rising labour productivity.

Clark's figures, while highlighting the importance of changes in the livestock sector, are for two benchmark years five and a half centuries apart. Quantifying the more continuous development of livestock husbandry from the middle ages to the nineteenth century is a more difficult undertaking and this paper is the first to present such a comparison, albeit for the single county of Norfolk. This involves combining two sources, manorial accounts and probate inventories, which have hitherto been studied separately.

Norfolk is normally considered to be an arable county *par excellence*. The Domesday Survey of 1086 shows that land-use in parts of the county was already strongly biased in favour of arable, and some two centuries later the *Inquisitiones Post Mortem* demonstrate that this trend had intensified following the demographic and economic upswing of the twelfth and thirteenth centuries.[5] Thereafter, as population declined during the late fourteenth and fifteenth centuries, the county experienced widespread settlement contraction and abandonment and the conversion of much arable to grass. Nevertheless, the resultant swing from corn to horn was less marked than in many other parts of the country.[6] After 1541 Norfolk shows up on Ann Kussmaul's marriage-seasonality index as predominantly "arable", and by 1836 the tithe files indicate that the ratio of arable to grassland stood at four to one.[7] Nevertheless, to label Norfolk as "arable" on the basis of its land-use and marriage patterns is to misrepresent the very significant contribution which livestock made to the agricultural output of the county and to under-rate the crucial contribution which livestock made to the development of integrated mixed-farming systems in the thirteenth century and again in the eighteenth century.

Manorial accounts and probate inventories

Systematic analysis of long-term trends in agricultural production and productivity between the medieval and early modern periods is still in its infancy.[8] Manorial accounts and probate inventories—two familiar and extensively used sources—nevertheless possess considerable potential for making comparisons between these two periods.[9] Norfolk, with over 2,000 extant grange accounts and more than 3,000 inventories, is well served by both.

Manorial accounts (see Table 1) follow a fairly standardized format and record livestock by type, age, and sex at both the start and end of the farming year (usually at Michaelmas), together with net gains and losses during the year. They also provide accurate details of the acreages sown with crops, but *not* of the total arable area, the total area of grass, or of total farm acreages. Accounts only relate to demesne farms, although opinion varies as to the scale and nature of the principal differences between the demesne and non-demesne sectors. The earliest extant Norfolk accounts date from 1238 but they survive in their largest numbers from 1275 to 1375 and deteriorate quite significantly thereafter.[10] Although a wide range of demesnes is represented, the record is biased towards ecclesiastical estates. The spatial coverage of accounts is good and especially so for the east of the county.

Probate inventories, like manorial accounts, record livestock numbers at a single point in time, dependent on the date of the farmer's death. They likewise record the acreage sown with crops but not the areas of fallow or pasture, nor of most meadow. Inventories are less easy to deal with than accounts because they do not follow a standard format.[11] Descriptions of both crops and livestock vary considerably in the level of detail given, and quantities are sometimes omitted or combined for several items. Thus the number of inventories which can be used to calculate a particular agricultural statistic depends on the way in which the information is presented, with the result that different groups of inventories have to be used to measure different things. Although any individual

TABLE 1
Manorial accounts and probate inventories

	Accounts	Inventories
Period	12 months	Snapshot
Same farms	Sometimes	Rarely
Land value	No	No
Crop acreages	Yes	Yes
Seed	Yes	No
Fallows	Sometimes	Rare
Rotations	Sometimes	No
Yields	Direct	Indirect
Meadow	Indirect	Problematic
Grass leys	None	Problematic
Pasture	Indirect	Rare
Livestock numbers	Yes	Yes
Livestock output	Yes	No
Disposal prices	Yes	Valuations
Equipment	Purchases and repairs	Yes
Buildings	Indirect	Indirect
Labour	Yes	No

inventory may be subject to a disturbingly wide variety of errors of omission (animals taken as a heriot are just one example of unrecorded goods), averages from a collection are less likely to be misleading. Inventories survive for farms of a wide range of sizes (although the very largest and smallest are both under-represented) and for most parts of Norfolk, although coverage in the north-west is poor. No inventories are extant from the period of the Civil War and Commonwealth and few contain usable information after 1740. Nor have those dating from 1600–27 been used in this study.[12]

The comparison of spatial and temporal trends from accounts and inventories poses many problems. Specific difficulties will be considered in the context of particular measures of agricultural change discussed below, but three general problems need to be mentioned before that discussion can get underway. The first is peculiar to the inventories and concerns the period of the year at which they were compiled. Unlike the accounts, which record crops sown over the year and the stock of animals at Michaelmas, inventories simply record the crops and stock on a farm when the farmer died. Livestock statistics taken from inventories made in September and October could be used for comparison with those given by the accounts, but if this strategy were adopted it would be impossible to use the same farms to calculate livestock densities per cereal or per cropped acre. Only inventories made in June and July record all the field crops on a farm grown during the year (with the exception of turnips) and, since the calculation of livestock densities must be calculated using the same set of farms for a particular period, livestock statistics have, perforce, also been taken from June and July inventories. Fortunately, as Table 2 demonstrates, the 2–4 month discrepancy between the figures taken from the inventories and accounts does not appear to pose a serious problem of comparability.

The second methodological problem is more serious and concerns the absence of key information from either or both sources. Manorial accounts record the numbers of livestock but not their values; probate inventories record both. Therefore comparative measures have to be derived from information on quantities. Although accounts record livestock products, inventories do not, so direct comparisons cannot be made of livestock output or productivity.[13] Finally, neither source records total farm areas so livestock densities can only be calculated in terms of the cereal or the sown acreage. These restrictions to the

TABLE 2
Norfolk: monthly livestock statistics

Months	1584–1640				1660–1740			
	Horses*	Cattle*	Imm.:Ad.†	LUs‡	Horses*	Cattle*	Imm.:Ad.†	LUs‡
December January	4·8	12·5	0·83	18·5	5·5	16·4	0·83	24·2
February March	4·7	12·0	0·82	18·7	6·1	18·0	1·01	26·7
April May	4·5	10·9	0·92	17·0	6·6	20·3	1·06	31·3
June July	4·7	13·0	1·00	18·6	5·8	17·5	1·16	24·7
August September	5·1	14·3	1·02	20·9	5·6	16·0	0·90	23·5
October November	5·6	14·2	0·85	22·8	5·6	18·0	1·08	27·1
All	4·9	12·8	0·91	19·4	5·9	17·7	1·01	26·2

* Mean herd sizes; † Ratio of immature to adult cattle. ‡Total livestock units (see Table 5). All inventories for all months.

TABLE 3

Norfolk: total sown acreage* of demesnes and farms represented by accounts and inventories†

Sown acreage	1250–1349 N	1250–1349 %	1350–1449 N	1350–1449 %	1584–1640 N	1584–1640 %	1660–1739 N	1660–1739 %	1854
< 50	11	8·8	9	8·5	54	74·0	56	42·1	
50– < 100	29	23·2	32	30·2	12	16·4	43	32·3	
100– < 150	30	24·0	34	32·1	4	5·5	7	5·3	
150– < 200	26	20·8	16	15·1	3	4·1	1	0·8	
200– < 250	15	12·0	8	7·6	0	0·0	4	3·0	
250– < 300	4	3·2	1	0·9	0	0·0	1	0·8	
300– < 350	3	2·4	4	3·8	0	0·0	0	0·0	
350– < 400	5	4·0	2	1·9	0	0·0	0	0·0	
400 +	2	1·6	0	0·0	0	0·0	1	0·8	
All	125	100·0	106	100·0	73	100·0	113	100·0	
Mean all farms	152·5 acres		132·7 acres		27·0 acres		41·4 acres		49·1 acres
Mean > 20 acres	152·5 acres		132·7 acres		48·5 acres		68·4 acres		

* Cereals plus peas, beans, vetches, buckwheat, turnips, and clover. The sown acreage excludes pasture, meadow and fallow. † June and July inventories for all farms with recorded crops.

range of comparative measures available necessitates a rather oblique view of the development of livestock husbandry.

The third and most serious problem in comparing accounts and inventories is demonstrated in Table 3 which shows that farm sizes (indicated by total sown acreages) are larger for farms represented by accounts than for those represented by inventories.[14] Although significant changes undoubtedly occurred in the structure and tenure of farms over the period in question, there can be no doubt that accounts and inventories describe fundamentally different samples from their respective farm populations. To compensate for this discrepancy most of the comparisons that follow will be made using inventory farms with more than 20 cropped acres (corresponding in size to the smallest recorded demesne). Even so inventories still omit the smallest farms in the county. Calculations based on manorial surveys suggest a mean farm size of some 15 acres in the early seventeenth century, which compares with a mean cropped acreage (excluding grass and fallow) of 27 acres from inventory farms.[15] In the fourteenth century there was undoubtedly a more polarized farm structure and the great mass of highly fragmented peasant holdings probably meant that mean farm size was much smaller.[16]

As might be expected, the average number of livestock per farm is also smaller for the farms recorded by inventories, although as Table 4 indicates (using cattle herds) the differences are not so great as for the cropped acreage, possibly reflecting the increased stocking densities discussed below. On the other hand, Table 4 also shows that herd sizes for inventory farms with more than 20 cropped acres are more closely comparable with those of demesnes. But given that accounts and inventories refer to farms of different sizes, comparisons of mean herd sizes probably reveals more about differences between the sources than about differences in farming practice. Moreover, the range of farm sizes represented by inventories can change over time, and can also vary considerably between collections of inventories for the same period in different areas of the country. Unfortunately historians working with inventories have tended to use

TABLE 4

Norfolk: size of cattle herds (oxen omitted)

| Size | Farms >20 sown acres* | | | | | | | | All farms* | | | | | 1854 |
| | 1250–1349 | | 1350–1449 | | 1584–1640 | | 1660–1740 | | 1584–1640 | | 1660–1740 | | |
	N	%	N	%	N	%	N	%	N	%	N	%	
<10	26	24·1	11	12·5	19	38·0	14	17·5	109	54·2	112	42·4	
10–<20	24	22·2	20	22·7	17	34·0	21	26·3	56	27·9	69	26·1	
20–<30	25	23·1	26	29·5	4	8·0	18	22·5	14	7·0	41	15·5	
30–<40	17	15·7	21	23·9	6	12·0	13	16·3	12	6·0	14	5·3	
40–<50	11	10·2	6	6·8	2	4·0	8	10·0	4	2·0	13	4·9	
50+	5	4·6	4	4·5	2	4·0	6	7·5	6	3·0	15	5·7	
All	108	100·0	88	100·0	50	100·0	80	100·0	201	100·0	264	100·0	
Mean	22·2		25·1		17·1		25·1		13·4		18·2		6·1

* June and July inventories.

herd size as their indicator of change in livestock husbandry which casts doubt upon their conclusions and makes comparison impossible between the results presented here and other published studies.[17] Changes in livestock husbandry based on accounts and inventories should therefore be measured in relative rather than absolute terms.

Trends in relative distributions of livestock

Comparisons of relative livestock distributions reveal a remarkably coherent story. Linking inventories with accounts charts the final demise of the ox as a draught animal in Norfolk (Figure 1 and Table 5). Horses were replacing oxen for draught as early as the late twelfth century and this trend continued throughout the middle ages, with the first two-horse and one-man teams appearing on light-land demesnes towards the end of the fourteenth century.[18] A few oxen remained in Norfolk right down to the nineteenth century, but as a draught animal they had been virtually eliminated by the 1630s. Figure 1 shows that—with the exception of an eccentric farmer in the east—oxen lingered longest on the heaviest soils, particularly in south-east Norfolk and the Fens, where their employment complemented a pastoral regime geared towards cattle.[19] It was only after the Fenland had been drained in the mid-seventeenth century that it became an area of horse-power as well as horse-breeding.

Draught animals also emerge as having comprised a remarkably consistent fifth to a third of total livestock units (Table 5). Given Norfolk's naturally strong land-use bias towards arable it was a remarkable achievement that non-working animals formed such a comparatively large proportion of livestock units from so early a date. Cattle assumed particular prominence, although they may have been superseded by sheep during the fifteenth and early sixteenth centuries. Throughout the middle ages and until well into the seventeenth century the low ratio of immature cattle to adult cattle [Table 5 and Figures 2(a) and 2(b)] indicates that herds were geared towards dairying.[20] This made sound economic sense in a husbandry system that aimed at maximizing output per unit area of land since cattle-based dairying is more productive of human food per unit area

TABLE 5

Norfolk: trends in pastoral production

Years	Oxen per 100 horses	Horses & oxen as % livestock units	Horses & oxen per 100 sown acres	Cattle* per 100 cereal acres	Immature cattle per 100 adults†	Sheep per 100 cattle*	Sheep per 100 cereal acres	Swine per 100 cereal acres	Fodder crops‡ as % of total
1250–1274	77	32·4	8·5	11·7	72	475	55·6	13·1	12·3
1275–1299	88	34·4	9·6	14·0	74	339	47·5	8·0	14·6
1300–1324	86	27·1	8·6	15·2	77	545	82·6	10·3	12·9
1325–1349	47	24·4	8·1	17·3	63	507	87·5	12·7	13·4
1350–1374	43	19·7	7·9	22·4	59	489	109·7	15·7	13·0
1375–1399	39	19·2	7·3	20·7	45	529	109·6	15·7	12·6
1400–1424	23	22·0	5·3	10·3	37	[882]	[91·1]	9·8	12·0
1425–1449	36	16·6	5·9	13·2	45	[1249]	[164·9]	16·8	10·5
1584–1599	5	34·4	12·1	28·6	67	[70]	[10·2]	22·7	12·8
1628–1640	2	35·1	14·8	48·2	74	[65]	[19·3]	20·9	11·9
1660–1679	0	25·6	14·0	37·0	104	[671]	[258·4]	20·7	17·6
1680–1709	0	18·9	9·4	30·2	215	[686]	[211·4]	18·6	16·7
1710–1740	0	25·4	10·4	45·9	160	[166]	[85·8]	17·8	17·4
1854		22·6	10·7	23·9		842	201·0	23·9	46·5

* Oxen excluded; † Immature cattle are calves, and heifers, bullocks and steers under two years. Adult cattle are cows, bulls, and heifers, bullocks and steers over two years. Oxen are excluded. Calculations for a minimum herd size of 10 with an imposed maximum ratio of 400; ‡ Peas, beans, vetches, clover and turnips; June and July inventories for farms with > 20 cropped acres. Figures in square brackets are unlikely to be representative. All ratios and percentages are calculated at an aggregate level.

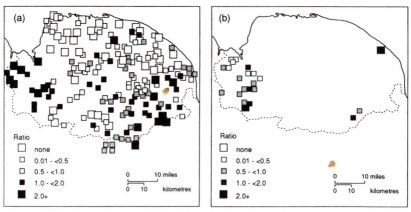

Figure 1. Norfolk: ratio of oxen to horses (a) 1250–1449 (b) 1584–1640. 818 farms without oxen are omitted from map (b).

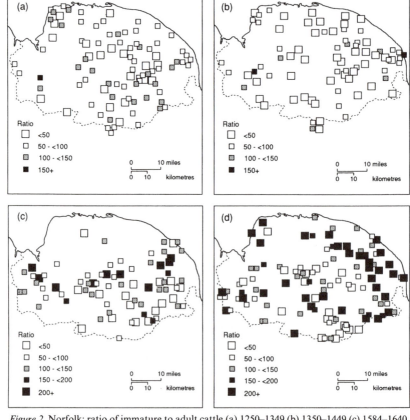

Figure 2. Norfolk: ratio of immature to adult cattle (a) 1250–1349 (b) 1350–1449 (c) 1584–1640 (d) 1660–1740.

than most other forms of pastoral activity. From the early fourteenth century many landlords also found it more profitable to lease out their herds and dairy houses rather than manage them directly. In this way many peasant farmers gained access to a valuable source of capital, since it was the norm for the lessees to retain all or most of the calves as well as the milk produced by the cows. Under these circumstances the true ratio of immature to adult cattle is often under-stated in the accounts.

During the middle ages cattle assumed greatest prominence where integrated mixed-farming systems were most fully developed, notably on the fertile soils of central and eastern Norfolk within ready access of the markets afforded by Norwich and the textile-producing villages around Worstead and North Walsham. By the early modern period, however, a change was taking place in both the geography and nature of cattle husbandry. Although farms on the heavy soils of central and south-eastern Norfolk began to concentrate on dairying (indicated on Figures 2(c) and 2(d) by a low ratio of immatures to adults), within the county at large there was a general move away from dairying towards the fattening of younger cattle, as revealed by the increasing ratio of immature to adult animals in Table 5.

Two groups of farmers were involved in the move towards fattening. The first, in the marshes of the Waveney valley and in the Fens, specialized almost exclusively in fattening beasts, many of which were brought from outside the county. By the mid-seventeenth century there are enough inventory references to Scottish, Northern, and Welsh steers to demonstrate that Norfolk graziers were becoming part of an inter-regional livestock trade which entailed the movement of stock over considerable distances. Just over a century later, Nathaniel Kent reckoned that one half of Norfolk cattle were driven from Scotland, and a quarter from Wales and Ireland, with only the remaining quarter being home-bred.[21] The second group, in eastern Norfolk, were mixed farmers, who practised fattening as an important adjunct to cereal production. Thus, after the mid-seventeenth century, eastern Norfolk regained its fourteenth-century prominence as an important cattle producer, but with bullock fattening rather than dairying its principal goal.[22]

The switch from dairying to fattening was due in part to market developments; both in supplying stores to fatten, and in the emergence of a larger and more differentiated demand for animal products. This encouraged further specialization in livestock production, and fattening was more appropriate than dairying in eastern Norfolk since cattle were increasingly integrated with arable farming and fed on crops (including cereals) grown in arable rotations. In contrast, Suffolk farmers continued to specialize in the production of dairy products.

Cattle thus constituted the core of Norfolk's intensive pastoral regime, notwithstanding the county's reputation for sheep farming, the distinctive institutions—notably the foldcourse—with which sheep farming was associated, and the fact that there were certain types of land on which sheep alone would thrive. Sheep present the most difficulties with both accounts and inventories because of major shifts in their pattern of ownership coupled with changes in their management and documentation. During the thirteenth and early fourteenth centuries sheep were undoubtedly present in large numbers within the county as the 1341–42 wool tax illustrates. They were a predominantly peasant animal and many landlords merely contented themselves with asserting their superior right to fold their tenants' sheep on their demesne lands. During the fifteenth and sixteenth centuries, however, many foldcourse owners progressively expropriated the fold rights of their tenants, thus transforming the sheep from a peasant animal to the landlord animal which it had so patently become by the close of the sixteenth century.[23]

Thus both demesne accounts and inventories are unrepresentative of those farmers who specialized in sheep, the former omitting peasant animals and the latter the large flockmasters whose probate might have been handled by the Prerogative Court. Between 60% and 70% of accounts record sheep in the middle ages, but a mere 30% of farm inventories include them. In Lincolnshire and Kent, where the Norfolk institution of the foldcourse did not exist, the proportion of inventories mentioning sheep is around 70%.[24] Moreover, the presence of the inventory of a large flockmaster can distort mean figures considerably, as is evident from columns 6 and 7 in Table 5. The only reliable figure for sheep in that table is that for 1854. This provides further evidence that Norfolk inventories probably under-record sheep considerably, although the number of sheep in the county undoubtedly rose between the early eighteenth and the nineteenth centuries as sheep husbandry associated with new fodder crops developed on the light lands of northern and western Norfolk.[25]

Stocking densities

While changes in the character and geography of cattle husbandry can be charted with some confidence the calculation and interpretation of stocking densities is more problematic. Yet the most remarkable finding in the comparison of accounts and inventories is a near doubling in stocking densities, both for beasts of traction and for cattle and swine (Table 5). The increase in the density of beasts of traction suggests that labour productivity was rising,[26] and increased livestock densities imply a considerable increase in both the output and productivity of the livestock sector. Historians have traditionally looked to grain yields as the indicator of agricultural land productivity, yet grain output per cereal acre was no higher at the end of the seventeenth century than it had been at the beginning of the fourteenth: on the evidence of stocking densities the more dramatic productivity gains were to be found in the livestock sector.[27]

This evidence therefore needs some scrutiny, for stocking densities can be calculated in several ways and vary considerably with farm size. Table 6 shows the results of some alternative methods of calculation for farms of varying sizes. Equating the various livestock types is through a system of livestock units (given at the foot of Table 6) based on modern food requirements.[28] Since neither accounts nor inventories give total farmed areas, livestock densities can only be calculated in terms of sown acres or cereal acres. Of these the ratio using cereal acres is probably the more reliable as it is less susceptible to the fundamental changes in composition of the cropped acreage. From the mid-seventeenth century inventories document the introduction of both clover and turnips into Norfolk husbandry, which were probably replacing permanent pasture as a source of fodder and reducing the areas of fallow. This would have tended to deflate the density of livestock per *recorded* cropped acre as unrecorded permanent pasture and fallow were replaced by turnips and clover. By the 1730s only about 5% of the cropped area was under clover and 13% under turnips so the degree of distortion is not great. By 1854, however, the two crops together

TABLE 6
Norfolk stocking densities (alternative methods of calculation)

Years	N			Livestock units per 100 sown acres*			Livestock units per 100 sown acres†		
	A	B	C	A	B	C	A	B	C
1250–1274		31			26·4			24·1	
1275–1299		52			29·2			25·4	
1300–1324		55			31·7			29·2	
1325–1349		73			32·5			31·2	
1350–1374		63			41·1			37·9	
1375–1399		52			33·9			36·0	
1400–1424		31			22·9			23·0	
1425–1449		13			41·8			33·7	
1584–1599	24	22	46	139·8	47·4	103·6	113·7	36·2	54·1
1628–1640	30	22	52	161·5	73·1	134·2	129·0	47·0	72·8
1660–1679	16	15	30	133·8	77·3	113·4	109·6	74·9	82·9
1680–1709	20	23	43	182·1	57·5	101·6	171·1	51·6	50·1
1710–1740	19	26	45	159·1	55·3	108·7	148·8	53·2	67·9
1854								31·6	

Years	N			Livestock units per 100 cereal acres*			Livestock units per 100 cereal acres†		
	A	B	C	A	B	C	A	B	C
1250–1274		31			30·6			27·5	
1275–1299		52			32·1			29·8	
1300–1324		55			36·8			33·5	
1325–1349		73			37·6			36·1	
1350–1374		63			47·3			43·5	
1375–1399		52			39·0			41·2	
1400–1424		31			26·9			26·2	
1425–1449		13			47·9			37·6	
1584–1599	18	19	50	120·7	55·3	97·7	104·1	38·3	54·0
1628–1640	23	21	53	196·8	91·3	148·0	177·4	62·4	95·0
1660–1679	15	15	37	164·8	97·2	130·8	123·4	88·1	96·8
1680–1709	15	22	40	172·0	67·5	102·8	157·3	62·2	61·3
1710–1740	15	25	41	172·4	67·5	123·0	173·8	63·9	78·1
1854								60·7	

A Farms > 0 and < 20 cropped acres; B Farms > 20 cropped acres; C All farms, these may exceed the sum of A and B because the cropped acreage cannot be calculated for some farms; * Means of individual farm ratios (imposed maximum individual ratio of 300); † Mean total livestock units divided by mean total sown or cereal acres (aggregate ratio). Total livestock units = (horses × 1·0) + (oxen, cows, and bulls × 1·2) + (immature cattle × 0·8) + (sheep × 0·1) + (swine × 0·1). June and July inventories.

accounted for 50% of the cropped area, which explains why the livestock density for the cereal acreage in 1854 is more consistent with earlier figures than the density based on the cropped acreage.[29]

Stocking densities can be calculated either as the mean of ratios calculated for individual demesnes or farms ("farm means") or by dividing the mean number of livestock units for all farms by the mean of their cropped or cereal acreage ("aggregate means"). Both methods are employed in Table 6 although of the two the aggregate mean is probably the more representative indicator of stocking densities. Very small farms with only a few acres of arable crops can produce very high livestock densities and thus weight the farm mean disproportionately towards farms occupying a small acreage. While these very high densities had important implications for small farmers they were not representative of the majority of farmland in the county.

A more serious problem concerns the behaviour of stocking density with farm size. Table 6 gives stocking densities for farms in three size groups and shows that farms with less than 20 cropped acres had much the highest densities. For farms over 20 acres the greatest rise in stocking densities takes place between the late sixteenth century and the mid-seventeenth century (a comparison between inventories), rather than between the middle ages and the late sixteenth century (a comparison between accounts and inventories). This suggests the increase is not simply a product of differences between the two sources. Tables 7 and 8 explore the relationship between stocking densities and farm size further. Although the number of farms in directly comparable size categories becomes rather small it is clear that in the case of the inventories an inverse relationship between stocking densities and farm size existed up to about 50 acres, but thereafter there was no consistent relationship. Mean stocking densities for farms above 50 acres rose from 35·9 for the period 1250–1450 to 62·5 for the period 1660–1740, which further suggests that the rise is genuine.

There are other possible causes of error and distortion in the stocking-density figures, but taken together they would tend to increase the early modern figures rather than reduce them. Although crop acreages may be understated in inventories for various reasons, so too may livestock numbers. As has been noted, sheep are almost certainly under-represented—pushing mean stocking densities down—although this may be partially compensated by the inclusion of some non-agricultural horses. Whereas virtually all demesnes have crops, some inventories record farms with livestock but no crops [see Table 9 and Figures 3(c) and 3(d)]. Many of these pastoral farms are quite small but some are those

TABLE 7
Norfolk: stocking densities and farm size from manorial accounts
(mean livestock units per 100 cereal acres)

Cereal acres	1250–1349				1350–1449			
	No. of demesnes	Stocking density			No. of demesnes	Stocking density		
		Min	Mean	Max		Min	Mean	Max
< 50	13	20·0	46·6	81·5	15	6·7	45·7	125·9
50–< 100	37	8·3	36·6	102·5	32	5·7	46·5	155·2
100–< 150	33	7·0	33·0	70·6	34	7·6	41·6	142·3
150–< 200	19	5·1	36·4	77·5	10	20·6	39·5	65·2
200–< 250	7	14·4	27·0	34·3	6	15·2	37·2	52·1
250–< 300	5	19·1	39·1	63·4	6	17·3	42·6	50·9
300–< 350	5	14·1	26·2	34·8	1	28·4	28·4	28·4
350 +	3	25·3	32·8	38·7	0			
All	122	5·1	35·7	102·5	104	5·7	43·2	155·2

TABLE 8

Norfolk: stocking densities and farm size from probate inventories
(mean livestock units per 100 cereal acres)

Cereal acres	No. of farms	1584–1640 Stocking density				No. of farms	1660–1740 Stocking density			
		Min	Mean	Max	N > 300		Min	Mean	Max	N > 300
< 12·5	26	25·8	119·9	247·5	12	29	43·6	149·9	282·4	12
12·5 – < 25	31	25·8	93·0	287·1	0	27	17·8	110·7	253·1	1
25 – < 50	19	16·4	92·7	194·6	1	23	11·7	79·1	143·6	0
50 – < 75	6	5·7	29·8	72·9	0	14	5·6	71·3	212·0	0
75 – < 100	2	19·0	38·1	57·2	0	6	11·9	53·9	112·6	0
100 – < 150	4	27·3	57·7	75·7	0	3	19·2	35·8	65·1	0
150 – < 200	1		19·4			2	76·4	79·1	81·8	0
350 +	0					2	55·2	72·4	89·7	0
All	89	5·7	92·8	287·1	13	105	5·6	102·3	282·4	13

N > 300 is the number of farms exceeding the imposed maximum ratio of 300. June and July inventories from all farms.

of substantial graziers. Their exclusion inevitably leads to some understatement of overall stocking densities. Finally, individual farm ratios have been restricted to an imposed maximum of 300, a qualification which has a disproportionately greater impact on mean stocking densities calculated for the early modern period than those for the middle ages when such high stocking densities are never registered (Table 8).

The inverse relationship between stocking densities and farm size so clearly apparent in the case of the inventories raises intriguing questions about medieval stocking densities on sub-demesne farms. The usual assumption, originating from the work of M. M. Postan, suggests that these would have been *lower* than demesne densities, thus depressing overall medieval densities yet further relative to those for the early modern period.[30] If this was indeed the case it points to the fifteenth and sixteenth centuries as a period of major capital formation for peasant farmers through the build up of flocks and herds and raises fundamental questions as to why the early modern "norm" should have been inverted during

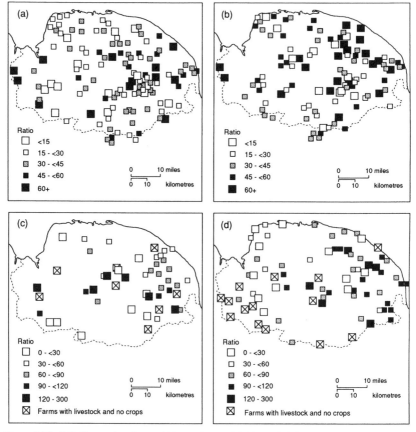

Figure 3. Norfolk: livestock units per 100 cereal acres (a) 1250–1349 (b) 1350–1449 (c) 1584–1640 (d) 1660–1740.

the thirteenth and fourteenth centuries. Alternatively, the assumption that seignorial demesnes commanded higher stocking densities than those prevailing on peasant farms in the same locality may itself be false.[31] It is certainly an issue that warrants closer investigation.

While mean stocking densities were rising, it would appear from the rather limited inventory sample that their geography exhibited a significant degree of continuity (Figure 3). Low densities were consistently found on the light and relatively poor soils of much of northern, north-western, and western Norfolk; and high stocking densities (as might be expected) were found in the Fens, in many parts of the Broadland, and on the good loam soils of east Norfolk. Figures 3(c) and 3(d) also show the larger farms specializing exclusively in livestock. These tended to be concentrated disproportionately in certain parts of the county—in the Fens, on the heavy soils of central Norfolk, and on the heavy soils of the south east—and in the last two locations may reflect a new development of the fifteenth and sixteenth centuries.

The doubling of stocking densities between the early fifteenth century and the period after 1660, or perhaps after 1628, has implications for the supply of fodder, although this issue must remain in some doubt since accounts and inventories omit most pasture and meadow. One possible explanation for higher stocking densities is the maintenance of a higher ratio between grassland and arable. This, after all, was the development which underpinned the improved stocking densities of much of the country during the century or so that followed the Black Death, when on the average Norfolk demesne there was 25 pence worth of several grassland to every 100 pence worth of arable.[32]

By the late sixteenth century, however, it is virtually certain that the arable acreage was expanding again, given the pressure of demand for food reflected in rising cereal prices, and pressure on the land reflected in rising rents and levels of reclamation.[33] Another possibility, therefore, is that by the sixteenth and seventeenth centuries grassland was simply more productive. Enclosure, of which there was a good deal in the east and south of the county, may have been one means by which the productivity of pastures was improved.[34] Better grassland management may have been another, with the periodic ploughing and seeding of pastures replacing the medieval practice of merely leaving land to tumble down to grass. But the most important development was the replacement

TABLE 9
Norfolk: evidence of "grassland" farming, 1584–1740

Years	All farms			Farms > 20 cropped acres	
	% Farms with livestock but no crops	% Farms with "summerlays"	% Farms with "grass"	% Farms with "summerlays"	% Farms with "grass"
1584–1599	10·2	0·0	9·8	0·0	7·5
1628–1640	9·3	0·0	22·7	0·0	26·3
1660–1679	8·1	0·0	22·0	0·0	30·8
1680–1709	12·3	3·5	36·8	15·4	43·3
1710–1740	9·1	7·4	24·0	6·2	21·3

June and July inventories.

of the rigid division of permanent pasture and permanent arable with ley farming or convertible husbandry, whereby temporary grass was rotated around the farm. This practice had been a feature of Norfolk husbandry since at least the fourteenth century, and forms the backbone of Eric Kerridge's sixteenth and early seventeenth-century "agricultural revolution".[35] Its significance has usually been seen in terms of cereal production, but the cultivation of grassland and the sowing of selected seed might well have contributed to increased yields of hay. C. Lane considers that "grass" on a farm in the sixteenth century usually consisted of natural grasses which were neither selected nor sown with the result that there was a predominance of permanent over temporary pastures.[36] In contrast, by the end of the seventeenth century selected grasses (not just clovers) were increasingly sown on land that had been cultivated. This encouraged a shift from permanent to temporary pastures which could have produced higher grass yields.

Inventories cannot be persuaded to provide grass yields, but from the mid-seventeenth century onwards they increasingly record "leys" and "summerleys". The fact that these were recorded suggests they were made "with the industry and manurance of man" and hence that labour had been expended in producing them.[37] It is highly probable (though inventories cannot reveal it directly) that these leys were part of an arable rotation, and therefore represent an upgraded and more widely practised version of convertible husbandry. Table 9 shows how leys and grass were increasingly recorded in Norfolk inventories, which echoes Paul Glennie's findings for Hertfordshire.[38]

Historians have probably undervalued the significance of grassland improvement in comparison with the more conspicuous innovation of new fodder crops. By the first decade of the eighteenth century roughly half of Norfolk farmers were growing turnips and a quarter clover, although the acreages were relatively small: just over a century later one half of the arable area was under the two crops. These crops were a more intensive form of fodder than grass and enabled the arable acreage to expand at the expense of pasture while maintaining if not increasing the quantity of fodder available to animals. The increased livestock densities of the late seventeenth and early eighteenth centuries were thereby sustained into the nineteenth century even though more grain was being produced from an expanding arable acreage.[39]

Another way of explaining the rise in stocking densities is to question why medieval stocking levels were not higher, especially since the technological means of increasing fodder supplies were available, and indeed practised, on some demesnes. In the middle ages commercial incentives were restricted by the more circumscribed nature of the market for pastoral products and the greater relative premium that attached to grain production. Royal taxation, arbitrary purveyancing, and oppressive levels of feudal rent all posed a further disincentive to the investment of scarce and expensive capital in flocks and herds.[40] A growth in demand, cheaper capital, the decline of feudalism as an institution, and the reduction in the demands of the crown relative to their peak in the first half of the fourteenth century, may all therefore have been necessary preconditions for the fuller development of the pastoral sector. Improved stocking densities from the late sixteenth century may thus have been dependent on a combination of commercial, financial, and institutional changes.

Implications and conclusions

The interaction between the arable and pastoral sectors as revealed by manorial accounts and probate inventories was more complex and dynamic than has often been appreciated. During the thirteenth and fourteenth centuries in Norfolk (particularly east Norfolk), and elsewhere in the more agriculturally developed parts of the country, livestock gained from the development of integrated mixed-farming systems. Thereafter, during the fifteenth and early sixteenth centuries, there was a reversion to more extensive methods and in Norfolk at least the arable and pastoral sectors became less closely integrated. It was at this time that significant capital accumulation appears to have taken place through the build-up of flocks and herds, particularly among the peasantry who may hitherto have been livestock deficient. This process of capital accumulation was to be of enduring benefit since the gain in stocking densities was to outlast the circumstances of labour shortage and land abundance which had brought it into being. During the sixteenth century improved stocking densities were maintained despite a re-expansion of arable cultivation and were raised still further during the seventeenth century, largely through the renewed development of integrated mixed-farming systems (pioneered once again by the farmers of east Norfolk). At the same time some farmers specialized almost exclusively in pastoral production, others switched from dairying to fattening, and sheep farming became confirmed as the preserve of specialist flockmasters. At a national scale all these developments culminated in the eighteenth century with the clearer crystallization of "pastoral" and "arable" regions by which there was a sharper spatial differentiation between regions which bred and reared young animals (the "pastoral") and those which fattened, milked, and worked them (the "arable").[41] Norfolk belonged emphatically to the latter. In fact, it was the demands of regions such as this that induced others to specialize in the rearing of replacement stock, ultimately resulting in the fuller articulation of pastoral production on national, regional and local lines.

While changing institutional structures allowed many of these developments to take place, they were also in large part a function of the progressive widening and deepening of market demand for pastoral products as social differentiation coupled with urban growth to create larger and increasingly concentrated markets. In satisfying such demand the pastoral sector possessed significantly greater commercial potential than the arable. Live animals could be walked to market, and butter, cheese, and wool were high in value relative to their bulk and hence better able than grain to withstand the costs of overland carriage. This meant that livestock were less dependent than crops upon proximity to markets or cheap water communications for their commercial development and ensured that pastoral production in relatively peripheral regions became increasingly geared towards the demands of the core.[42]

As individual farms and regions became more specialized a clearer differentiation emerged between breeding, fattening, and dairying as separate agricultural enterprises. Such developments are clearly evident in studies of livestock husbandry for other parts of the country, although exact quantitative comparisons are not possible because of varying methodologies employed with probate inventories. In east Worcestershire, for example, stocking densities fell progressively from the sixteenth century compared with the rise in Norfolk; north Shropshire saw the rise of intensive dairying as did Hertfordshire, in contrast to

VI

the decline of dairying and rise of fattening in Norfolk.[43] In the final analysis, the subtleties of regional and local specialization render national generalizations about a "pastoral" west and an "arable" east rather meaningless. Paradoxically, for much of the pre-industrial period it was in the supposedly arable east that pastoral husbandry assumed its most dynamic and developed forms, often in conjunction with equally developed mixed-farming systems.

Acknowledgements

We are grateful to the ESRC for supporting the earlier stages of the research upon which this paper is based, to Jenitha Orr and Meemee Wong for research assistance, and to Anne Rook for drawing the maps.

Notes

[1] M. M. Postan, Medieval agrarian society in its prime: England, in *idem* (Ed.), *The Cambridge economic history of Europe*, I, *The agrarian life of the middle ages* (Cambridge 2nd edn 1966) 553–6; R. B. Outhwaite, Progress and backwardness in English agriculture, 1500–1650 *Economic History Review* **39** (1986) 1–18

[2] Bruce M. S. Campbell and John Power, Mapping the agricultural geography of medieval England *Journal of Historical Geography* **15** (1989) 24–39; John P. Power and Bruce M. S. Campbell, Cluster analysis and the classification of medieval demesne-farming systems *Transactions of the Institute of British Geographers* new series **17** (1992) 227–45.

[3] Ann Kussmaul, *A general view of the rural economy of England 1538–1840* (Cambridge 1990)

[4] Gregory Clark, Labour productivity in English agriculture, 1300–1860, in Bruce M. S. Campbell and Mark Overton (Eds), *Land, labour and livestock: historical studies in European agricultural productivity* (Manchester 1991) 214–19

[5] H. C. Darby, *Domesday England* (Cambridge 1977) 131–3; Bruce M. S. Campbell, Medieval land-use and land-values, in Peter Wade-Martins (Ed.), *Norfolk historical atlas* (forthcoming)

[6] Bruce M. S. Campbell, Land, labour, livestock and productivity trends in English seignorial agriculture, 1208–1450, in Campbell and Overton, *Land, labour and livestock*, 153–9

[7] Kussmaul, *op. cit.*, 188; R. J. P. Kain, *An atlas and index of the tithe files of mid-nineteenth-century England and Wales* (Cambridge 1986) 72–4

[8] Mark Overton and Bruce M. S. Campbell, Productivity change in European agricultural development, in Campbell and Overton, *Land, labour and livestock*, 1–50

[9] Introductions to the sources may be found in P. D. A. Harvey (Ed.), *Manorial records of Cuxham, Oxfordshire circa 1200–1359* (Oxfordshire Records Society **50** 1976); Mark Overton, English probate inventories and the measurement of agricultural change *A. A. G. Bijdragen* **23** (1980) 205–15; *idem*, Probate inventories and the reconstruction of agrarian landscapes, in M. Reed (Ed.), *Discovering past landscapes* (London 1984) 167–94. A list of studies using inventories to study agricultural change is in Mark Overton, *A bibliography of British probate inventories* (Department of Geography University of Newcastle upon Tyne 1983)

[10] The Norfolk manorial accounts used in this study are drawn from the following public and private archives: Public Record Office, Norfolk Record Office, North Yorkshire Record Office, Nottinghamshire Record Office, West Suffolk Record Office, Bodleian Library Oxford, British Library, Cambridge University Library, Canterbury Cathedral Library, Chicago University Library, Harvard Law Library, John Rylands Library Manchester, Lambeth Palace Library, Nottingham University Library, Eton College, Christ's College Cambridge, King's College Cambridge, Magdalen College Oxford, St George's Chapel

Windsor, Elveden Hall Suffolk, Holkham Hall Norfolk, Raynham Hall Norfolk, Pomeroy and Sons Wymondham. We are grateful to the relevant authorities for granting access to these materials. A detailed handlist of these accounts is available upon request

[11] The methodological implications of this are developed in Mark Overton, Computer analysis of an inconsistent data source: the case of probate inventories *Journal of Historical Geography* **3** (1977) 317–26; *idem*, Computer analysis of probate inventories: from portable micro to mainframe, in D. Hopkin and P. Denley (Eds), *History and Computing* (Manchester 1987) 96–104; *idem* Computer standardization of probate inventories in J-P. Genet (Ed.), *Standardisation et échange des bases de données historiques* (Paris 1988) 145–51

[12] The inventories are preserved in the Norfolk Record Office and come from the Norwich Consistory Court

[13] J. A. Yelling, Probate inventories and the geography of livestock farming: a study of east Worcestershire, 1540–1750 *Transactions of the Institute of British Geographers* **51** (1970) 114–15 claims that inventories can be used to study livestock output. For the considerable potential of accounts in studying livestock demography and productivity see Kathleen Biddick, *The other economy: pastoral husbandry on a medieval estate* (Berkeley and Los Angeles 1989)

[14] In this and the following tables data for 1250–1449 are taken from manorial accounts and data for 1584–1740 from probate inventories. The 1854 data are from *Reports by the poor law inspectors on agricultural statistics (England)*, British Parliamentary Papers LIII 1st series 1928 (London 1854–55) 34–55

[15] J. Spratt, Agrarian conditions in Norfolk and Suffolk 1600–1650 (unpubl. M.A. thesis, University of London 1935) 127–8

[16] Bruce M. S. Campbell, The extent and layout of commonfields in eastern Norfolk *Norfolk Archaeology* **38** (1981) 21–3; J. Williamson, Peasant holdings in medieval Norfolk: a detailed investigation into the holdings of the peasantry in three Norfolk villages in the thirteenth century (unpubl. Ph.D. thesis, University of Reading 1976)

[17] For example: W. Harwood Long, Regional farming in seventeenth-century Yorkshire *Agricultural History Review* **8** (1960) 103–14 (who also appears to ignore seasonality problems); C. W. Chalklin, *Seventeenth-century Kent* (London 1965); and Joan Thirsk, *English peasant farming: the agrarian history of Lincolnshire from Tudor to recent times* (London 1957)

[18] John Langdon, *Horses, oxen and technological innovation: the use of draught animals in English farming from 1066–1500* (Cambridge 1986) 50–1; Bruce M. S. Campbell, Towards an agricultural geography of medieval England *Agricultural History Review* **36** (1988) 91–4

[19] Compare George Grantham, The growth of labour productivity in the production of wheat in the *Cinq Grosses Fermes* of France, 1750–1929, in Campbell and Overton, *Land, labour and livestock*, 350

[20] Bruce M. S. Campbell, Commercial dairy production on medieval English demesnes: the case of Norfolk, in Annie Grant (Ed.), *Animals and their products in trade and exchange, Archaeozoologica, Quatrième Numéro Spécial* (Paris 1992); *idem*, Intensive pastoral husbandry in medieval England: a Norfolk perspective, in E. B. Dewindt (Ed.), *Festschrift for Professor Ambrose Raftis* (Kalamazoo forthcoming)

[21] For an example of this trade see D. Woodward, Cattle droving in the seventeenth century: a Yorkshire example, in W. H. Chaloner and B. M. Ratcliffe (Eds), *Trade and transport: essays in economic history in honour of T. S. Willan* (Manchester 1977) 35–57; N. Kent, *General view of the agriculture of the county of Norfolk* (London 1796) 101

[22] *Ibid.*, 33; B. A. Holderness, East Anglia and the fens, in Joan Thirsk (Ed.). *The agrarian history of England and Wales VI 1640–1750: regional farming systems* (Cambridge 1984) 197–238; W. Marshall. *The rural economy of Norfolk* (2 vols London 1787) I, 125

[23] Mark Bailey, Sand into gold: the foldcourse system in West Suffolk, 1200–1600 *Agricultural History Review* **38** (1990) 43–51; K. J. Allison, Flock management in the sixteenth and seventeenth centuries *Economic History Review* **11** (1958) 98–112

[24] C. W. Chalklin, *Seventeenth–century Kent*, 100; Thirsk, *English peasant farming*, 34, 72, 87, 106

[25] S. Wade Martins, *A great estate at work: the Holkham estate and its inhabitants in the nineteenth century* (Cambridge 1980) 24

[26] E. A. Wrigley, Energy availability and agricultural productivity, in Campbell and Overton, *Land, labour and livestock*, 323–39; Clark, *op. cit.*, 230–1

[27] Campbell, Land, labour, livestock and productivity trends, 178–82; *idem* and Mark Overton,

VI

A new perspective on medieval and early modern agriculture: six centuries of Norfolk farming, c.1250–c.1850 *Past and Present* (forthcoming)

[28] These are the units adopted by Yelling, *op. cit.*, 115. For a discussion of some alternatives see Campbell, Land, labour, livestock and productivity trends, 156–7

[29] Mark Overton, The diffusion of agricultural innovations in early modern England: turnips and clover in Norfolk and Suffolk 1580–1740 *Transactions of the Institute of British Geographers* new series **10** (1985) 205–21; Mark Overton, The determinants of crop yields in early modern England, in Campbell and Overton, *Land, labour and livestock*, 284–322; Campbell and Overton, A new perspective on medieval and early modern agriculture

[30] Postan, *op. cit.*, 554; *idem*, Village livestock in the thirteenth century *Economic History Review* **15** (1962) 219–49, reprinted in *idem, Essays on medieval agriculture and general problems of the medieval economy* (Cambridge 1973) 214–48

[31] Robert C. Allen, The two English agricultural revolutions, 1450–1850, in Campbell and Overton, *Land, labour and livestock*, 253

[32] Campbell, Medieval land use and land values

[33] P. J. Bowden, Agricultural prices, farm profits and rents, in Joan Thirsk (Ed.). *The agrarian history of England and Wales* IV *1500–1640* (Cambridge 1967) 593–685; *idem*, Agricultural prices, wages, farm profits and rents, in Joan Thirsk (Ed.). *The agrarian history of England and Wales* VII *1640–1750: agrarian change* (Cambridge 1985) 593–695

[34] S. Yonekawa, Champion and woodland Norfolk: the development of regional differences *Journal of European Economic History* **6** (1977) 163–76; M. R. Postgate, Field systems of East Anglia, in Alan R. H. Baker and Robin A. Butlin (Eds), *Studies of Field Systems in the British Isles* (Cambridge 1973) 287–90; David Dymond, *The Norfolk Landscape* (London 1985) 142–5. J. A. Johnston, Seventeenth century agricultural practice in six Lincolnshire parishes *Lincolnshire History and Archaeology* **18** (1983) 10, gives an example of meadow land doubling in value following enclosure in the seventeenth century

[35] Bruce M. S. Campbell, Agricultural progress in medieval England: some evidence from eastern Norfolk *Economic History Review* **36** (1983) 43; Campbell and Overton, A new perspective on medieval and early modern agriculture; Eric Kerridge, *The agricultural revolution* (London 1967)

[36] C. Lane, The development of pastures and meadows during the sixteenth and seventeenth centuries *Agricultural History Review* **28** (1980) 18–30

[37] The normal rule was that crops grown without the "industry and manurance of man" should be excluded from inventories: R. S. Burn, *Ecclesiastical law* (6 vols, London 3rd edn 1775) IV, 240

[38] Paul Glennie, Continuity and change in Hertfordshire agriculture 1550–1700: I—patterns of agricultural production *Agricultural History Review* **36** (1988) 63–4

[39] Mark Overton, Land and labour productivity in English agriculture, 1650–1850, in Peter Mathias and J. A. Davis (Eds), *The nature of industrialization vol. 5: Agriculture and industrialization* (Blackwell, 1993)

[40] Gregory Clark, The cost of capital and medieval agricultural technique *Explorations in Economic History* **25** (1988) 265–94; J. R. Maddicott, *The English peasantry and the demands of the Crown, 1294–1341* Past and Present Supplement **1** (Oxford 1975), reprinted in T. H. Aston (Ed.), *Landlords, peasants and politics in medieval England* (Cambridge 1987) 285–359; R. Brenner, Agrarian class structure and economic development in pre-industrial Europe *Past and Present* **70** (1976) 30–75, reprinted in T. H. Aston and C. H. E. Philpin (Eds), *The Brenner debate: agrarian class structure and economic development in pre-industrial Europe* (Cambridge 1985) 10–63

[41] Kussmaul, *op. cit.*

[42] The distances involved might be very considerable, for example, Ian Blanchard, The continental European cattle trade, 1400–1600 *Economic History Review* **39** (1986) 427–60

[43] Yelling, *op. cit.*; *idem*, Livestock numbers and agricultural development, 1540–1750: a study of East Worcestershire, in T. R. Slater and P. J. Jarvis (Eds), *Field and forest: an historical geography of Warwickshire and Worcestershire* (Norwich, 1982) 281–99; P. Edwards, The development of dairy farming on the north Shropshire plain in the seventeenth century *Midland History* **4** (1978) 175–89; Glennie, *op. cit.*, 55–76; see also Overton and Campbell, Productivity change in European agricultural development, 41–2

VII

Commercial Dairy Production on Medieval English Demesnes: The Case of Norfolk

Part I

A general feature of medieval English agriculture as compared with that of virtually all later centuries was the relatively undeveloped character of its pastoral husbandry. As A. Grant has recently emphasized, '(documentary evidence) generally shows a very low productivity by modern standards' (Grant, 1988: 176). Thus, archaeozoological evidence indicates that animal size was small and there is little evidence of selective breeding (Grant, 1988: 176–7; Armitage, 1980). Thirteenth-century manorial accounts and agricultural treatises demonstrate that milk yields and fleece weights were both correspondingly low (Trow-Smith, 1957: 119–23; Biddick, 1989: 94–5, 109; Stephenson, 1988: 370–81; Oschinsky, 1971: 431). Pastoral farming remained heavily reliant upon forage rather than fodder, which depressed stocking densities and ensured that extensive, prevailed over intensive, forms of management. Stocking densities on medieval demesnes were generally consistently lower than those prevailing in the same localities in the seventeenth century and after (Overton and Campbell, 1992), and there is a widespread belief that stocking densities on medieval peasant holdings were lower still – the reverse of the situation pertaining in later centuries (Postan, 1962: 219–49; 1966: 553–5; Allen, 1991: 246, 253). In the absence of artificial grasses, clover, and turnips, and without water meadows, ley farming, and other forms of improved grassland, which collectively were to revolutionize livestock husbandry from the seventeenth century on (Kerridge, 1967; Overton, 1991), M.M. Postan believed that medieval stocking densities were largely a function of available supplies of temporary and permanent pasture (Postan, 1966: 554). As a result, and with certain notable exceptions, there was only limited integration of arable and pastoral husbandry within medieval agriculture.

Yet it was through the development of mixed-farming systems that the path to greater productivity ultimately lay (Overton and Campbell, 1991: 35, 42–4). By alternating land between arable and grass, growing more leguminous fodder crops, and maximising the manure that was returned to the soil, the circulation of nitrogen – the principal limitation to plant growth – was enhanced to the mutual benefit of both sectors (Shiel, 1991; Overton, 1991: 285–97). The perfection of such mixed-farming systems provided the key to the organic revolution which English agriculture underwent during the eighteenth and early nineteenth centuries. Although integrated mixed-farming systems certainly existed within medieval English agriculture, and examples may be cited of fodder cropping, stall-feeding, and convertible husbandry (Campbell, 1983; Mate, 1985; Brandon, 1971; Searle, 1974: 272–99), these were outnumbered by those in which arable and pastoral husbandry were conducted as more-or-less separate enterprises. K. Biddick believes that this was the case during the early thirteenth century on the estates of the bishops of Winchester in southern England (Biddick, 1991: 115–19). It shows up even more conspicuously in much of northern England, where lowland demesnes were frequently stocked with working animals only and the rearing of replacement stock was confined to specialist livestock farms located around the upland margins (Blanchard, 1967: 168–74; Campbell and Power, 1989: 36). It is therefore no surprise to find that at this date there was often little correlation between stocking densities and yields (Overton and Campbell, 1991: 35, 43).

Circa 1300, therefore, pastoral husbandry stood in a decidedly inferior position to arable husbandry. G. Clark has recently estimated that at this date the livestock sector accounted for approximately 25 per cent of agricultural production in the lowland counties of England, whereas by 1850 this proportion had grown to 50 per cent (Clark, 1991: 214–19). It follows that for much of the intervening period progress in pastoral husbandry was greater than that in arable. Moreover, it was within pastoral husbandry that the greatest productivity gains were made. Clark calculates that by 1850 stocking densities per cultivated acre were 25 per cent higher than *c.* 1300, fleece weights had increased by two-and-a-half fold, carcass weights of cattle and sheep had trebled, and milk yields had risen by fourfold. By contrast, grain yields merely doubled (Campbell, 1991: 179–81; Campbell and Overton, 1993). If pastoral husbandry was the most dynamic agricultural sector after 1300 why, at this date, did it remain so comparatively undeveloped?

In part the explanation lies in the imperative which high rural population densities, low income levels, and imperfect development of the market gave to cereal production. But the social and property relations embodied in feudalism also served as a deterrent to the fuller development of pastoral husbandry. Flocks and herds were valuable capital assets and as such attracted the asset stripping activities of feudal magnates. Estates which came into the custody of the Crown were usually stripped of all but their working animals before being returned to their owners (Biddick, 1991: 100–104). Lords, in their turn, via their exaction of feudal rent, deprived the peasantry of crucial investment capital which might otherwise have served to enhance the size of flocks and herds (Brenner, 1976: 33). Indeed, feudal dues such as heriot – the payment to the lord of a deceased tenant's best beast – struck directly at the pastoral sector. Outbreaks of murrain, rinderpest, and other livestock diseases were a further scourge which periodically decimated the flocks and herds painstakingly built up by lords and peasants (Kershaw, 1973: 106–11; Mate, 1991: 85–6, 92–3). The spread of such diseases was encouraged by the prevalence in much of the country of communal methods of flock and herd management, methods which obstructed the kind of selective breeding which in later centuries was so to enhance carcass weights, fleece weights, and milk yields. Medieval farmers, in fact, operated under a number of technological constraints, not the least of which were the limited range and relatively low productivity of available fodder crops (principally oats, inferior grains, peas, and vetches) and a reliance upon natural rather than artificial grass. Deficiencies in the supply of animal foodstuffs naturally circumscribed both the number of animals that could be supported and their size, weight, and quality (Postan, 1972: 59; Grant, 1988: 177).

Nevertheless, pastoral husbandry was not entirely backward and inert *c.* 1300 and research is beginning to reveal the developments which the pastoral sector underwent during the course of the twelfth and thirteenth centuries, in response to the expansion of population, foundation of markets, growth of cities, and general commercialization of the economy. J. Langdon has documented the wider adoption of the horse for draught work, and especially haulage (Langdon, 1984; 1986). This formed one component within the greater regional differentiation of pastoral husbandry systems and allowed the evolution of more intensive systems of husbandry (Campbell and Power, 1989; Campbell, forthcoming/1996). The greater speed and strength of the horse, for instance, promoted higher standards of soil preparation in conjunction with a reduction in the size and number of plough-teams. This released scarce pastoral resources to the support of other types of livestock, the more so as horses were in part fed on oats and other fodder crops (Campbell, 1988: 95–7). Where these developments occurred arable and pastoral husbandry became more closely integrated and livestock were released from an exclusive dependence upon temporary and permanent grassland, allowing the mutual expansion of arable and pastoral husbandry. As Biddick has observed of the estates of Peterborough Abbey over this period: 'The changing composition of livestock in the herding economy of the estate characterizes a pastoral sector of some dynamism and complexity and dispels any notion of linear relations between animal and cereal husbandry' (Biddick, 1989: 65). In densely populated and intensively cultivated east Norfolk B.M.S. Campbell has shown how the conflicting land-use demands of arable and pastoral husbandry were reconciled via the cultivation of fodder crops – oats, peas, and vetches – stall feeding of certain livestock, and employment of generally labour-intensive methods of management (Campbell, 1983). Similar methods have been documented in parts of Kent and coastal Sussex (Smith, 1943; Brandon, 1971), where E. Searle has also identified the appearance by the early fourteenth century of convertible husbandry (Searle, 1974: 272–99). By the late thirteenth century pastoral-farming systems therefore varied widely in their character, intensity, and productivity. Of these systems, by far the most productive per unit area of food, and intensive per unit of capital and labour, was cattle-based dairying (Simmons, 1974: 20–22 and 170–72).

Part II

Dairying is an inevitable adjunct of all forms of cattle rearing (Shaw, 1956: 354) but, as an object in itself, tended in this period to be restricted to the most populous and commercialized districts since it required a high economic rent to justify its high overhead costs arising from its relatively intensive use of labour and land and the capital requirements of byres, dairy houses, and cheese- and butter-making equipment, plus, of course, the herds themselves. Before 1350 the counties whose cattle husbandry was most strongly geared towards dairying were Middlesex, Kent, Essex, and Norfolk, closely followed by the neighbouring counties of Hertfordshire and Suffolk. After 1350 – with a relative swing from arable to pasture – these same six counties continued to stand out with a pastoral economy distinctive from that encountered in much of the rest of the country, and their emphasis upon herds dominated by female adults became even more pronounced. The composition of cattle herds in the Thames-valley counties of Surrey, Berkshire, Buckinghamshire, and Oxfordshire also appears to have trended in the same direction. The concentration of these dairying counties in East Anglia and the immediate environs of London – among the least grassy counties in medieval England – is highly significant and anticipated patterns of specialization which emerged even more strongly during the early modern period. In the Middle Ages this was the most populous and commercialized part of the country and the most exposed to the influence of major urban food markets. London, served by a dense network of subordinate trade centres and with a population in 1300 approaching 100,000 (Keene, 1984), can be assumed to have had an impact over a wide area and must have been the ultimate destination for a significant proportion of the butter and cheese produced in the surrounding counties, as well as for many of the surplus calves – suitably reared and fattened – which were an inevitable by-product of dairying (Murphy and Galloway, 1992). Norwich, with a population in the 1330s of approximately 25,000 (Rutledge,

1988), had a similar effect but on a smaller scale and is undoubtedly one reason for the highly developed state of dairying in Norfolk, a county more associated with intensive arable – than pastoral – farming systems.

Norfolk's excellent coverage by extant manorial accounts allows the characteristics of its pastoral husbandry to be reconstructed in considerable detail. Over the period 1250–1450 roughly 2,000 accounts are extant representing over 200 different demesnes and a variety of different estates – large and small, lay and ecclesiastical.[1] Each account records in detail the stock present on the demesne at the start and end of the farming year (Michaelmas – Michaelmas), gains and losses from birth, death, purchase and sale etc. during the year, and the income from sales of livestock and their products. On demesnes where dairying was a prominent enterprise the accounts sometimes contain a separate dairy account which records the cheeses and butters made, their method of disposal, and any income that was realized from cash sales.

Since the object of dairying was to maximize milking potential, herds geared towards that objective tended to be dominated by adult females with an accompanying bull. Often some younger animals will also have been present, but only as many as were necessary to maintain the population of dairy cows at full strength, so that overall a strong demographic imbalance in favour of adult females would have existed (herds geared towards rearing and fattening, by contrast, would have been imbalanced in the opposite direction). According to Walter of Henley an annual rate of reproduction of one calf per cow was the ideal, in order to keep the cows in milk. However, as Biddick points out, with a forty-week gestation period for calves and an interval of at least three to four weeks from calving to first heat, cows had only three mating opportunities per year to maintain yearly production of a calf (Biddick, 1989: 90). Subsequently, of course, a substantial proportion of the calves would have been sold off, along with such sterile and decrepit milkers as needed replacing. Unlike herds producing animals for meat and draught there would have been few intermediate sales or transfers. Given its intensive nature, dairying often became the paramount pastoral activity within a generally intensive pastoral economy. In Norfolk the oats-fed horse often partially or wholly replaced the grass-fed ox for draught, thereby releasing scarce grassland resources to the support of the dairy herd. Cattle herds geared towards dairying thus usually contained only a small proportion of oxen, and sometimes none at all.

---

[1] The accounts are scattered among 22 public and private archives. They are listed in Campbell, 2000: 453–6.

Table 1: Norfolk, 1250–1449: number of immature cattle per 100 adults (cows + bulls) (oxen, and herds below 10 in size, omitted).
Source: manorial accounts.

Immature cattle per 100 adults	Number of herds	% of herds
Less than 25	11	8.6
25 – 49.9	29	22.7
50 – 74.9	40	31.3
75 – 99.9	24	18.8
100 – 124.9	13	10.2
125 – 149.9	7	5.5
150+	4	3.1
TOTAL	128	100.0

In Norfolk demesne dairy herds generally contained between 5 and 25 cows, the number tending to be higher after 1350 than before. There appears to have been a natural upper limit of 35–40 cows per herd, with, on average, one bull to every 13.5 cows. As Table 1 shows, the demographic bias in favour of adult animals was often highly marked, a sure sign that dairying rather than rearing or fattening was the principal object of cattle husbandry. The typical demesne herd thus contained 10–40 animals – sometimes less, sometimes more – plus such oxen as were required for draught work. The herd maintained by the prior of Norwich on his demesne at Hemsby is a well-documented and good example.

Hemsby was one of the prior's largest and most valuable demesnes, being situated on the rich loam soils of Flegg with access to the alluvial grazings of Broadland. Between 1266 and 1335 the prior maintained a herd of 27 – 77 cattle on this demesne, the maximum being recorded in 1318 following two decades of steady expansion, and the minimum just three years later in 1321, following the devastating cattle plague (probably an outbreak of rinderpest) of 1319–20.[2] On average the herd comprised 46 cows and their followers plus up to 21 oxen maintained for draught work. The need to rear replacement work animals meant that the demographic bias in favour of mature females was less marked than on some other demesnes. Even so, adults outnumbered immatures by a ratio of 1.00 : 0.62. There were, in fact, rarely fewer than 20 cows on the demesne and when the herd was at full strength – in the mid 1290s and 1310s – there were almost twice this number, with, on average, only one bull to every 28.5 cows. The herd was managed by a full-time cowman, while dairy production was the

---

[2] Norfolk Record Office (hereafter NRO) DCN 60/15/1–16; NRO L'Estrange IB 4/4; Bodleian Library Oxford, MS Rolls, Norfolk, 47.

responsibility of a head dairymaid and assistant. An inventory of 1352 records the existence of a dairy equipped with one bench, five Eastland tables, one table with two trestles, one table for drying cheese, five cheese vats, two pressing-boards, one stoup (wooden bucket), one churn, nine dishes, nine plates, twelve saucers, two hanging tables, one press, one jug, and one broken tong (Yaxley, 1988: 14–15). There was also a stable which accommodated both the demesne's working horses and its cattle. The same inventory records similarly equipped dairies on the prior's manors of Great Plumstead and Newton (where there is also specific reference to a cowhouse), both, significantly, located within a few miles of Norwich (Yaxley, 1988: 5–7, 16–18). The accounts of these and other dairying demesnes record a regular annual outlay on salt, cheese cloths, and replacement items of equipment involved in the cheese and butter-making processes. At Costessey in 1278–79, for example, salt, stoups, a board, buckets, a press, plates, a bench, a churn, and sundry other items were all bought for the dairy at a total cost of 3s 8¾d.[3]

With the exception of Broadland and the fen-edge, Norfolk was one of medieval England's least grassy counties, and in the drier and more free-draining parts of west Norfolk grassland was both scarce and of poor quality. On the evidence of Inquisitions *Post Mortem* arable exceeded several grassland in value by a ratio of four to one, as compared with a ratio of two-and-a-half to one in the country as a whole (Campbell, 1990: 82). Nevertheless, on the evidence of the ratio of immature cattle to adults calculated for demesnes with a minimum herd size of ten (oxen omitted), there were few parts of the county in which dairying was not practised (Figure 1). It was as much a feature of the demesnes at Brandon, East Wretham, and West Harling in sandy Breckland, or of Sedgeford, Gnatingdon, and West Newton on the light sands of north-west Norfolk, as it was of districts where environmental conditions were better suited to grass growth. In fact, at Acle, Ludham, and Reedham in Broadland, and Wimbotsham and Hilgay on the fen-edge, the abundance of good grazing promoted an emphasis upon rearing as much as dairying, as reflected in immature to adult ratios well in excess of 100. Some bias towards rearing rather than dairying (anticipating a sub-regional specialism which was to become even more pronounced in the seventeenth century) is also apparent on certain of the demesnes situated on the heavy soils of southern and central Norfolk – Ditchingham, Earsham, Hempnall, Forncett, East Carleton, Attleborough, Hingham, Bradenham, and Sporle – where the prevalence of ox-ploughing with relatively large teams ensured a steady demand for replacement animals. Widespread as dairying was, however, it does seem to have been a particular

---

[3] Public Record Office (hereafter PRO) SC 6/933/13.

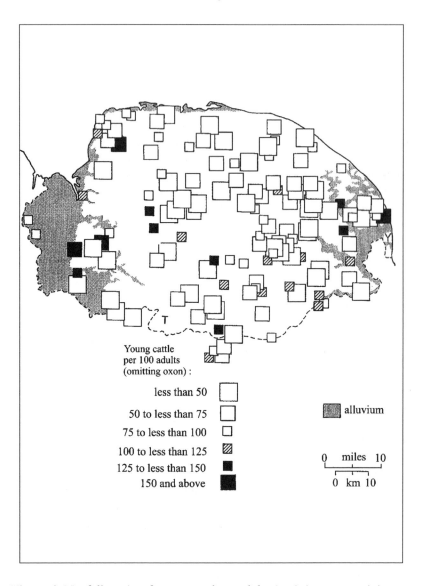

Figure 1: Norfolk: ratio of young cattle to adults (omitting oxen; minimum herd size of 10).

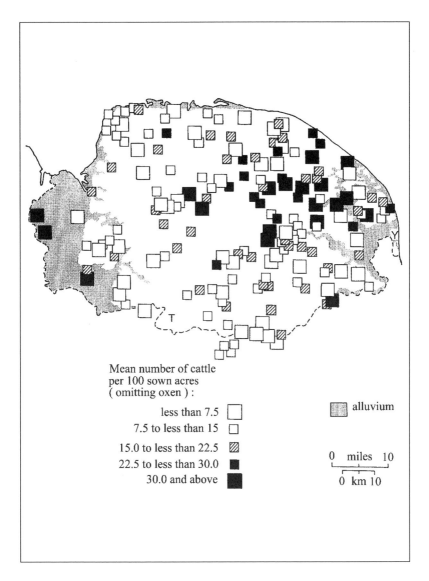

Figure 2: Norfolk: ratio of cattle (omitting oxen) to sown acres.

specialism of east-central and north-eastern Norfolk. On demesne after demesne in this area, as a comparison of Figures 1 and 2 shows, above-average stocking densities of cattle other than oxen were combined with ratios of immature cattle to adults which strongly favoured the latter. Notable examples include Gateley, Mileham, Gressenhall, Foxley, Hainford, Wroxham, Tunstead, Horning, Burgh-in-Flegg, and *Heythe*, but there was scarcely a demesne in this area on which dairying was not practised. In this respect, the intensive character of pastoral husbandry echoed the intensive character of arable husbandry as undertaken on the same farms. The latter was characterized by intensive rotations, heavy seeding rates, systematic manuring, high labour inputs, and the cultivation of fodder crops (notably oats and legumes) (Campbell, 1983). Dairying thus formed one component of an intensive mixed-farming system which employed high levels of input to obtain remarkably high levels of agricultural output per unit area. It represented, in effect, medieval agriculture at its technological and productive best.

One objective of demesne dairying was, of course, to satisfy the consumption requirements of the lord's household and his farm-workers, in whose diet cheese formed an important component, especially at harvest time. At Sedgeford in north-west Norfolk, for example, C. Dyer has shown that between 1256 and 1341 dairy produce accounted for a fifth of the value of all foodstuffs consumed by harvest workers (Dyer, 1988: 25). The bulk of the milk, cheese, and butter concerned would have been produced from the cows and ewes maintained on the manor. On the prior of Norwich's seven demesnes of Gnatingdon, Thornham, North Elmham, Taverham, Monks Granges, Plumstead, and Martham in 1326–27 manorial consumption accounted for 47.5 per cent of all cheeses produced, a proportion which rose to 76 per cent at Plumstead and 77 per cent at Monks Granges.[4] Yet there were other manors on which the market formed the main destination for the cheeses produced. Martham sold 66 per cent of its cheeses in 1326–27 and Thornham 96 per cent. In the heartland of cheese production, in east-central and north-eastern Norfolk, consumption in fact almost invariably took second place to sale and there is a clear implication that specialization in dairying was a response to market opportunities. Between 1307 and 1315 the Norwich Cathedral Priory manor at Attlebridge sold 58.5 per cent of its cheeses and 79 per cent of its butters; between 1305 and 1338 the sacristan of Norwich's manor at Bauburgh sold 62.5–89.9 per cent of its cheeses and 80 per cent of its butters; 1296–97 the queen's manor at Cawston sold 93 per cent of its cheeses and 94 per cent of its butters (the remainder being paid as tithe); during the 1270s the royal manor

---

[4] NRO DCN 62/1.

at Costessey sold 94 per cent of its cheeses and butters and during the same decade the earl of Norfolk's Broadland manor of Acle sold its entire output of cheese and butter.[5]

Norfolk's dense network of over 120 markets must have provided a ready outlet for this dairy produce, much of which may eventually have found its way onto the Norwich food market. Costessey, for example, for which a series of detailed though damaged dairy accounts survive from the 1270s, was actively engaged in the large-scale commercial production of butter and cheese and possibly traded with Norwich directly.[6] It was situated in the valley of the River Wensum, four miles north-west of the city, and maintained a herd of 25–30 milking cows. This was a well managed herd for on the three occasions when there are legible figures of the number of cows kept and calves born the calving rate was 100 per cent (although two out of three calves born were subsequently sold). Such a high fertility rate reflected both a favourable ratio of labour to animals – the herd was under the charge of a permanent cowman while the dairy was staffed by a permanent dairymaid – and the careful culling of aged and sterile females. This high fertility rate was matched by similarly favourable milk yields to judge from the quantities of cheese and butter produced and sold. One year the sale of cheese, butter, milk, and calves produced by the 25 cows kept on the demesne yielded an income of £6 8s 4d, another – this time from a herd of 26 cows – an income of £6 12s 0d. On both occasions this was equivalent to a gross income of just over 5 shillings per cow.

Auditors sometimes calculated the annual income per cow and appended a note to this effect on the account. At Plumstead, Martham, and North Elmham, for instance, it was calculated in 1326–27 that the lactage of each cow yielded an income of 2s 7d, 4s 7d, and an impressive 6s 0d respectively.[7] On other demesnes, and increasingly during the fourteenth century, the cows were farmed out to a lessee in return for an annual rent. The income that could be generated in this way was often considerable and it is clear that a single cow could be more profitable than several acres of good arable land. Sometimes cows were farmed for their milk only, with the lord retaining their issue. This was the arrangement at Burgh-in-Flegg in 1296–97 where the rental was 4s 0d per cow, and an identical rental prevailed at Hautbois in 1363 and Horning in 1372.[8] Similar rates sometimes applied when the lessee was entitled to both the lactage and the calves, as at Wroxham in 1342–43 (3s 4d per cow), Hainford

---

[5] NRO DCN 61/11–13 and 16–19; PRO SC 6/1090/4; PRO SC 6/933/13; PRO SC 6/929/1–7.

[6] PRO SC 6/933/13.

[7] NRO DCN 62/1.

[8] PRO SC 6/1090/4; NRO Diocesan Est/2, 2/15 and 17.

in 1363–64 (4s 0d per cow), and Haveringland in 1356–57 and 1376–77 (4s 0d per cow, although 3s 4d per cow in 1364–65).[9] Usually, however, lords were able to demand a higher rent when lessees retained both lactage and calves, since the latter were worth anything between 8d and 15d each. The farm of milk and calves was 4s 9d at Ludham in 1355, 5s 0d at Foxley in 1305–06, Gimingham in 1358–59 and 1391–92, and Tunstead in 1359–60, 5s 6d at Melton in 1332–33 but 6s 0d in 1366–67 and 1369–70, as also at Thurning in 1319–20 and Horning in 1372, and 6s 8d at Gateley in 1326–27 and Arminghall in 1347–48.[10] These are remarkably high rental levels, given that the lessees also had to make a livelihood as well as cover their expenses, and they testify to the potentially greater intensity and productivity of peasant as opposed to demesne husbandry. The arrangement seems to have been that the herd continued to be managed using the grassland resources of the demesne but that the lessee was responsible for calving, milking, and the manufacture of butter and cheese using the dairying equipment of the demesne, as well as for marketing these products. As an arrangement it must have operated to the benefit of both parties for it endured for many years on significant numbers of demesnes.

The intensive and profitable management of grassland which these rental rates imply is reflected in the high value placed upon grassland in the main area of commercial dairying. Inquisitions *Post Mortem* reveal a concentration of high meadow values in central and north-eastern Norfolk. Beeston, Billingford, Ingham, and Stratton all had meadowland assessed at 36d an acre, and at Knapton and Belaugh, respectively, assessments of 40d and 48d were returned.[11] Valuations of 24d an acre are also quite common in the area, as on the group of demesnes represented by Foxley, Foulsham, Kerdiston, Stinton, Cawston, Witchingham, Hockering, and Tuddenham in central Norfolk.[12] To some extent these high valuations – which compare with a mean of 18d within the country as a whole – must reflect the relative scarcity of meadow as a resource, for on all of them there was less than one acre of meadow to every 12 acres of arable and on several a ratio of one to 40 or worse, but this cannot be the entire explanation, for meadowland was in equally scarce supply in other

---

[9]NRO NRS 2848 12 F1; British Library Add. Roll 26060; British Library Add. Charter 15199–202.

[10] NRO Diocesan Est/10; PRO SC 6/935/19; PRO DL 29/288/4719 and 4734; PRO DL 29 288/4720; NRO DCN 60/25/1–3; NRO NRS 2796 12 E2; NRO Diocesan Est/2, 2/17; NRO DCN 62/1 and 7.

[11] PRO C133 File 47 (13); C134 File 48 (9); C133 File 29 (3); C132 File 42 (6); C132 File 37 (4); C133 File 1 (7).

[12] PRO C134 File 83; C133 File 34 (8); C134 File 72 (18); C134 File 21 (4); C133 File 7 (5); C133 File 51 (7); C133 File 34 (8); C133 File 102 (1).

parts of the county where valuations were lower. Such meadowland needed to have been highly productive to have sustained these high valuations, and this, in turn, was probably related to favourable environmental circumstances (strong loam soils and adequate ground-water levels), intensive and effective methods of grassland management, and the specialized and commercially successful dairying which prevailed in the area. In parts of Suffolk and Essex at this time meadow values were even higher, which may point to the presence of even more intensive and productive dairy-farming systems.

Table 2: England and Norfolk: trends in cattle (omitting oxen) per 100 sown acres, and immature cattle per 100 adults, 1250–1449.[a]

Years	Cattle per 100 sown acres		Immature cattle per 100 adults[b]	
	England	Norfolk	England	Norfolk
1250–1299	11.15	11.39	119	85
1275–1324	10.80	12.63	110	86
1300–1349	12.46	14.11	102	79
1325–1374	12.79	17.01	95	66
1350–1399	15.71	18.91	102	53
1375–1424	16.47	13.88	122	53
1400–1449	20.04	9.70	110	52

[a] Norfolk trends calculated from all extant accounts for all recorded demesnes. The figures are the means of the individual manorial means, weighted geographically to control for changes in the spatial coverage of the data.

National trends calculated from a sample of 1,904 accounts representing 792 different demesnes. Means for five sub-regions have been calculated from the individual manorial means. These have then been combined with the corresponding figures for Norfolk to produce a single national figure using weightings based on the respective regional shares of lay wealth in 1334 and population in 1377. (For further details see Campbell, 1991a: 151–3).

[b] based on demesnes with a minimum herd size of 10.

Part III

Over time, as will be seen from Table 2 and Figure 3A, cattle husbandry, as measured by the number of cattle other than oxen per 100 sown acres, gained steadily in relative importance throughout the period 1250–1399. In this, Norfolk's experience paralleled that of the country at large with the exception that, nationally, stocking densities of cattle continued to rise right down to the middle of the fifteenth century and, possibly, beyond, whereas in Norfolk they eventually reverted to their late thirteenth-century level. Until 1375 at both levels the rise in stocking densities of cattle was accompanied by a progressively

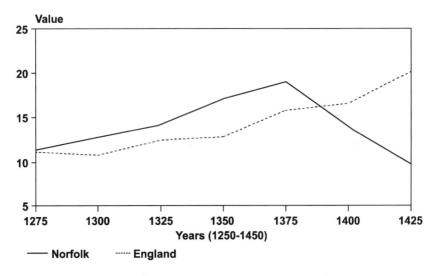

Figure 3A: cattle/100 sown acres (omitting oxen), 50 year means

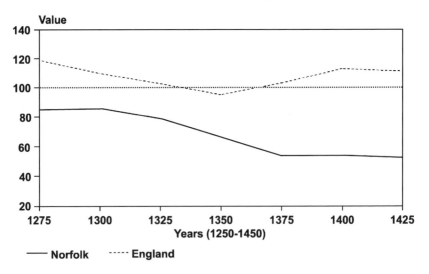

Figure 3B: Young cattle/100 adults (omitting oxen; minimum herd size of 10), 50 year means.

greater emphasis upon adult animals, as dairying gained relative to rearing (Figure 3B). This trend was especially pronounced in Norfolk, where dairying had always been the more important activity, and it persisted right down to the middle of the fifteenth century, by which time adult cattle exceeded the number of recorded immatures by almost two to one. As such it was reinforced by the gradual substitution of horses for oxen throughout Norfolk and the reduced premium which this consequently placed on the rearing of replacement animals. On the other hand, the proliferation of leasing arrangements after 1375, which excluded immature cattle from the stock enumerated on the demesne, means that this trend, along with the contemporary decline in stocking densities of cattle, is partially a figment of the method of recording. It certainly deviates from developments at a national level, where there was an abrupt return to the *status quo* of the late thirteenth century, with immatures outnumbering adults and a re-emphasis in many parts of the country upon oxen as draught animals.

On this evidence it would appear that commercial dairying in Norfolk attained its peak of development as a demesne activity during the third quarter of the fourteenth century, at a time when population decline, relative prices, and associated changes in demand were encouraging a swing from grain to livestock (Campbell, 1990: 105–11). That this trend was not sustained thereafter reflects several factors. First, the progressive withdrawal of demesne lords from direct management meant that dairying increasingly became a peasant rather than seigniorial activity, albeit employing working capital provided by lords. Second, continued population decline, rising living standards, and changes in relative prices reduced the market for dairy produce. By the early fifteenth century, for instance, dairy produce accounted for barely 10 per cent by value of the foodstuffs consumed by harvest workers at Sedgeford, as workers consumed less bread and cheese than in the thirteenth century and more ale and meat (Dyer, 1989: 157–60). Third, rising costs, especially of labour, and falling prices encouraged a shift to more extensive forms of livestock enterprise for which other parts of the country enjoyed a greater comparative advantage. By the close of the fourteenth century the intensive pastoral and arable husbandry in which Norfolk specialized, and of which dairying was one manifestation, had become too expensive to remain profitable. In the quest for a lower-cost alternative, lords increasingly turned to sheep farming. The incentive to do so lay less in high wool prices – for these stagnated throughout much of the fifteenth century (Lloyd, 1973) – than in the fact that sheep had lower labour and feeding costs than cattle and produced a variety of products – meat, milk, and wool – which provided a hedge against uncertain markets. This switch from cattle to sheep, which echoed trends in the country at large (Mate, 1987), is reflected in a ratio of sheep to cattle which was double in 1400–49 what it had been 1350–99. Not until the sixteenth century, when population growth and associated price and wage trends encouraged a return to more intensive forms of husbandry, would Norfolk again become a county in which cattle predominated over sheep (Thirsk, 1967: 40–49; Overton and Campbell, 1992).

Part IV

A. Grant, in a valuable recent survey of the animal resources of medieval England, doubted whether milk could have been very intensively exploited in the twelfth and thirteenth centuries (Grant, 1988: 156–7). Nevertheless, the example of Norfolk suggests otherwise. It also points to the importance of market demand, and the high levels of economic rent consequent upon it, as a stimulus to the development of more intensive and productive pastoral-farming systems. If, therefore, pastoral husbandry remained comparatively extensive and undeveloped in much of the rest of the country the explanation may lie in part with the inadequacy of market demand and depressing effect of low levels of economic rent (Campbell, forthcoming/1995). Although the leading urban centres were larger *c.* 1300 than has hitherto been appreciated, the proportion of the population resident in towns remained low, both by comparison with other European countries and with the situation prevailing in England from the late sixteenth century on (Smith, 1991: 50–51). A socially polarized distribution of wealth further restricted commercial demand for livestock products. Moreover, the commercial links between town and country remained imperfectly developed. Had purchasing power been greater *c.* 1300, a higher proportion of the population resident in towns, and the institutions and arteries of commerce more fully developed, the prospects for progress in pastoral husbandry along the lines outlined in this paper would have been considerably enhanced. It was arguably the resolution of these obstacles, as much as technological progress *per se*, that was to promote the fuller development of pastoral husbandry in later centuries.

* * *

I am grateful to John Langdon of the University of Alberta for data and to John Power, Jenitha Orr, and Gill Alexander of The Queen's University of Belfast for research assistance. Part of the research on which this paper is based was undertaken whilst in receipt of an Economic and Social Research Council Fellowship.

BIBLIOGRAPHY

Allen R.C. (1991): 'The two English agricultural revolutions, 1459–1850', in: B.M.S. Campbell and M. Overton eds, *Land, Labour and Livestock: Historical Studies in European Agricultural Productivity*, MUP, Manchester: 236–54.

Armitage P. (1980): 'A preliminary description of British cattle from the late twelfth to the early sixteenth century', *The Ark*, 7: 405–13.

Biddick K. (1989): *The Other Economy: Pastoral Husbandry on a Medieval Estate*, University of California Press, Berkeley, Los Angeles, and London.

Biddick K. (1991): 'Agrarian productivity on the estates of the bishopric of Winchester in the early thirteenth century: a managerial perspective', in: B.M.S. Campbell and M. Overton eds, *Land, Labour and Livestock: Historical Studies in European Agricultural Productivity*, MUP, Manchester: 95–123.

Blanchard I.S.W. (1967): 'Economic change in Derbyshire in the late Middle Ages, 1272–1540', unpublished Ph.D. thesis, University of London.

Brandon P.F. (1971): 'Demesne arable farming in coastal Sussex during the later Middle Ages', *Agricultural History Review*, 19: 113–34.

Brenner R. (1985): 'Agrarian class structure and economic development in pre-industrial Europe', in: T.H. Aston and C.H.E. Philpin eds, *The Brenner Debate: Agrarian Class Structure and Economic Development in Pre-industrial Europe*, CUP, Cambridge: 10–63.

Campbell B.M.S. (1983): 'Agricultural progress in medieval England: some evidence from eastern Norfolk', *Economic History Review*, 2nd series, 36: 379–404.

Campbell B.M.S. (1988): 'Towards an agricultural geography of medieval England', *Agricultural History Review*, 36: 87–98.

Campbell B.M.S. and Power J.P. (1989): 'Mapping the agricultural geography of medieval England', *Journal of Historical Geography*, 15: 24–39.

Campbell B.M.S. (1990): 'People and land in the Middle Ages, 1066–1500', in: R.A. Dodgshon and R.A. Butlin eds, *An Historical Geography of England and Wales*, Academic Press, London, 2nd edn: 69–121.

Campbell B.M.S. (1991): 'Land, labour, livestock, and productivity trends in English seignorial agriculture, 1208–1450', in: B.M.S. Campbell and M. Overton eds, *Land, Labour and Livestock: Historical Studies in European Agricultural Productivity*, MUP, Manchester: 144–82.

Campbell B.M.S. (forthcoming/1995): 'Ecology versus economics in late thirteenth- and early fourteenth-century English agriculture', in D. Sweeney, ed, *Agriculture in the Middle Ages: Technology, Practice, and Representation*, Philadelphia, University of Pennsylvania Press: 76–108.

Campbell B.M.S. (forthcoming/1996): 'The livestock of Chaucer's reeve: fact or fiction?', in E.B. Dewindt, ed, *The Salt of Common Life: Individuality and Choice in the Medieval Town, Countryside and Church. Essays Presented to J. Ambrose Raftis*, Kalamazoo, Medieval Institute, Western Michigan University: 271–305.

Campbell B.M.S. (2000): *English Seigniorial Agriculture 1250–1450*, CUP, Cambridge.

Campbell B.M.S. and Overton M. (1993): 'A new perspective on medieval and early modern agriculture: six centuries of Norfolk farming *c.* 1250–*c.* 1850', *Past and Present*, 138.

Clark G. (1991): 'Labour productivity in English agriculture, 1300–1860', in: B.M.S. Campbell and M. Overton eds, *Land, Labour and Livestock: Historical Studies in European Agricultural Productivity*, MUP, Manchester: 211–35.

Dyer C. (1988): 'Changes in diet in the late Middle Ages: the case of harvest workers', *Agricultural History Review*, 36: 21–37.

Dyer C. (1989): *Standards of Living in the Later Middle Ages: Social Change in England c.1200-1520*, CUP, Cambridge.

Grant A. (1988): 'Animal resources', in: A. Grant and G. Astill eds, *The Countryside of Medieval England*, Basil Blackwell, Oxford: 149–87.

Keene D. (1984): 'A new study of London before the Great Fire', *Urban History Yearbook*: 11–21.

Kerridge E. (1967): *The Agricultural Revolution*, George, Allen and Unwin, London.

Kershaw I. (1976): 'The great famine and agrarian crisis in England, 1315–1322', in: R.H. Hilton ed., *Peasants, Knights and Heretics: Studies in Medieval English Social History*, CUP, Cambridge: 85–132.

Langdon J. (1984): 'Horse hauling: a revolution in vehicle transport in twelfth- and thirteenth-century England?', *Past and Present*, 103: 37–66.

Langdon J. (1986): *Horses, Oxen and Technological Innovation: The Use of Draught Animals in English Farming from 1066–1500*, CUP, Cambridge.

Lloyd T.H. (1973): 'The movement of wool prices in medieval England', *Economic History Review*, Supplement 6, Cambridge.

Mate M. (1985): 'Medieval agrarian practices: the determining factors?', *Agricultural History Review*, 33: 22–31.

Mate M. (1987): 'Pastoral farming in south-east England in the fifteenth century', *Economic History Review*, 2nd series, 40: 523–36.

Mate M. (1991): 'The agrarian economy of south-east England before the Black Death: depressed or buoyant?', in: B.M.S. Campbell ed., *Before the Black Death: Studies in the 'Crisis' of the Early Fourteenth Century*, MUP, Manchester: 79–109.

Murphy M. and Galloway J. (1992): 'Marketing animals and animal products in London's hinterland *circa* 1300', *Anthropozoologica*, 16: 93–100.

Oschinsky D. (1971): *Walter of Henley and Other Treatises on Estate Management and Accounting*, OUP, Oxford.

Overton M. and Campbell B.M.S. (1991): 'Productivity change in European agricultural development', in: B.M.S. Campbell and M. Overton eds, *Land, Labour and Livestock: Historical Studies in European Agricultural Productivity*, MUP, Manchester: 1–50.

Overton M. and Campbell B.M.S. (1992): 'Norfolk livestock farming 1250–1740: a comparative study of manorial accounts and probate inventories', *Journal of Historical Geography*, 18: 377–96.

Overton M. (1991): 'The determinants of crop yields in Early Modern England', in: B.M.S. Campbell and M. Overton eds, *Land, Labour and Livestock: Historical Studies in European Agricultural Productivity*, MUP, Manchester: 284–322.

Postan M.M. (1962): 'Village livestock in the thirteenth century', *Economic History Review*, 2nd series, 15: 219–49.

Postan M.M. (1966): 'Medieval agrarian society in its prime, 7: England', in: M.M. Postan ed., *The Cambridge Economic History of Europe, I, The Agrarian Life of the Middle Ages*, CUP, Cambridge, 2nd edn: 548–632.

Postan M.M. (1972): *The Medieval Economy and Society: An Economic History of Britain in the Middle Ages*, Weidenfeld and Nicolson, London.

Rutledge E. (1988): 'Immigration and population growth in early-fourteenth-century Norwich: evidence from the tithing roll', *Urban History Yearbook*: 15–30.

Searle E. (1974): *Lordship and Community: Battle Abbey and its Banlieu, 1066–1538*, Pontifical Institute of Mediaeval Studies, Toronto.

Shaw R.C. (1956): *The Royal Forest of Lancaster*, Guardian Press, Preston.

Shiel R. (1991): 'Improving soil fertility in the pre-fertiliser era', in: B.M.S. Campbell and M. Overton eds, *Land, Labour and Livestock: Historical Studies in European Agricultural Productivity*, MUP, Manchester: 51–77.

Simmons I.G. (1974): *The Ecology of Natural Resources*, Arnold, London.

Smith R.A.L. (1943): *Canterbury Cathedral Priory: A Study in Monastic Administration*, CUP, Cambridge.

Smith R.M. (1991): 'Demographic developments in rural England 1300–1348: a survey', in: B.M.S. Campbell ed., *Before the Black Death: Studies in the 'Crisis' of the Early Fourteenth Century*, MUP, Manchester: 25–78.

Stephenson M.J. (1988): 'Wool yields in the medieval economy', *Economic History Review*, 2nd series, 41: 369–91.

Thirsk J. (1967): 'The farming regions of England', in: J. Thirsk ed, *The Agrarian History of England and Wales, IV, 1500–1640*, CUP, Cambridge: 1–112.

Trow-Smith R. (1957): *A History of British Livestock Husbandry to 1700*, Routledge and Kegan Paul, London.

Yaxley D. (1988): *The Prior's Manor-Houses: Inventories of Eleven of the Manor-Houses of the Prior of Norwich made in the Year 1352 A.D.*, Larks Press, Dereham.

VIII

Measuring the commercialisation of seigneurial agriculture c. 1300[1]

The issue

The years of European demographic and economic expansion between c. 1100 and c. 1300 represent an important stage in the evolution of commercial institutions and the transition to an economic system in which market trade assumed an increasingly important role. That transition was to be long drawn out and it was to be many centuries before the market attained the position of social and economic hegemony that it occupies today. During the centuries of European feudalism, according to Polanyi, the economic system remained enmeshed in customary social relationships and its potential for generating economic growth was consequently impeded. Not until fully fledged self-regulating and price-fixing markets were established, both throughout the greater part of the country and for a wide range of commodities, would production for gain supersede production for use as an objective and profit become the primary motive of most economic protagonists.[2] So long as feudal socio-property relations prevailed, places of trade, freedom of contract, mobility of labour, conditions of employment, quality of goods, spheres of market influence, and prices all remained regulated to a greater or lesser degree.[3] The market's capacity to organise and integrate society was thereby inhibited, as was its ability to achieve an

[1]Most of the research upon which this chapter is based was undertaken as part of the 'Feeding the City I' project, based at the Centre for Metropolitan History, University of London, and co-directed by Dr Derek Keene and myself. I am grateful to the Leverhulme Trust for providing funding, to Dr James Galloway and Dr Margaret Murphy for assistance, and Dr Keene for his helpful comments. Further assistance and advice has been given by Mr Ken Bartley, Dr Richard Britnell, Dr Harold Fox, Miss Marilyn Livingstone, Miss Olwen Myhill, and Mr John Power. Responsibility for the results presented and views expressed nevertheless remains my own.

[2]Polanyi (1945), 62, 73–82; Polanyi (1957). See also Dodgshon (1987), 223. For a useful critique of Polanyi's et al.' ideas on market development see C. A. Smith (1976).

[3]Britnell (above), 23–6; Britnell (1993a), 5–28, 79–101; Farmer (1991a), 324–58, 420–30; Farmer (1991b), 483–90; Hatcher (1981).

Measuring commercialisation

economically optimal allocation of resources, with all that this implies for economic progress.

Throughout this period many landholders, great and small, participated only partially and selectively in the market economy. In the first half of the thirteenth century one of the leading ecclesiastical magnates of the realm, Peter des Roches, bishop of Winchester, sold the bulk of the wool but little of the grain produced on his extensive estates.[4] Similarly, at the opening of the fourteenth century 'political reliance on consumption to conserve agrarian lordship and economic reliance on consumption to mitigate market dependence profoundly shaped production on the Peterborough Abbey estate'.[5] Such economic autarky, or 'householding' as Polanyi termed it, is above all one of the distinguishing features of peasantries: 'The peasant aims at subsistence, not reinvestment . . . he sells cash crops to get money, but this money is used in turn to buy goods and services which he requires to subsist and to maintain his social status, rather than to enlarge his scale of operations'.[6] According to Postan, medieval English peasants, 'though not wholly innocent of money and markets, could not be expected to expand or to contract their holdings, to take up land or to give it up, to sow more or to work harder in response to the stimuli of prices or under the influence of a pessimistic or optimistic view of future business prospects'.[7] So long as these attitudes and objectives prevailed, the English economy remained only partially commercialised.

Feudalism, by constituting a hierarchical social order dominated by an elite class of non-producers who required regular and efficient food provisioning, nevertheless provided an essential precondition for the fuller development of market exchange. Moreover, peasant producers generally only intensify production, specialise, and participate in market exchange when they have to, and feudalism – through the extraction of their surpluses in various forms of feudal rent – obliged them to do precisely this.[8] It is beyond doubt, therefore, that the twelfth and thirteenth centuries witnessed both a relative and an absolute increase in marketing activity.[9] The challenge to historians is to estimate the market sector's size and extent at the climax of its expansion *c.* 1300. In charting 'the rise of the market to a ruling force in the economy' Polanyi has stressed the importance of 'noting the extent to which land *and food* were mobilized through exchange, and labor was turned into a commodity free to be purchased in the market'.[10] Hilton concurs in identifying the production of agricultural surpluses for

[4]Biddick with Bijleveld (1991), 120.
[5]Biddick (1989), 129.
[6]Wolf (1955), 454, cited in Hodges (1988), 11.
[7]Postan (1959–60), 79.
[8]C. A. Smith (1976), 51.
[9]Britnell (above), 7–19.
[10]Polanyi (1957), 255 (emphasis added).

sale on the market as a key index of commercialisation, and thus of development within the predominantly agrarian economy of medieval England.[11] If by 1300 the market was not yet the single determining principle of production it was at least an increasingly powerful influence upon social and economic activity. Simple commodity production, whereby small-scale producers sold produce for money in order to buy other commodities for consumption, was firmly established as a feature of rural life, as, increasingly, were factor markets in labour and land.[12] Such was the apparent scale and vigour of the exchange thereby generated that in Dyer's view, lords and the state, by chartering markets, fairs and boroughs, were not so much creating trade as attempting to control and profit from it.[13]

Part of the impetus behind this upsurge in market exchange sprang from the growth of population, from the greater occupational specialisation and economic differentiation that it induced, and from the economic expediency and opportunism that induced mounting numbers of rural producers to exchange produce and services:[14] 'Almost half of peasants lacked enough land to feed their own households, and those with larger holdings found it convenient to buy their bread, ale, joints of meat, pies, and puddings from neighbours or from local markets'.[15] This was reinforced by a doubling in the per capita supply of coin, by rising rents and increasing taxation, and by a mounting demand from lords and the state that these rents and taxes be paid in cash rather than kind.[16] The very fact that by 1279 money rents exceeded in value payments in kind implies that a significant proportion of at least the rental component of production must have been marketed.[17] Moreover, as Biddick has argued, the more substantial peasant producers were far from insensitive to the financial advantages that could spring from such commercial activity. A lay subsidy return for parts of Bedfordshire in 1297 suggests that the larger rural producers were already specialising in certain branches of production according to distance from the market.[18] McIntosh has demonstrated how just over half a century later tenant farmers at Havering in Essex were alive to the commercial opportunities (especially for meat and other pastoral products) afforded by the London market, a mere 15 miles down the road.[19] Purveyance accounts, too, indicate the prominence in the market of large numbers of small sellers.[20]

[11]Hilton (1985b), 4.
[12]P. D. A. Harvey, ed. (1984a); R. M. Smith (1984b); Poos (1991), 207–28.
[13]Dyer (1992a), 152.
[14]Britnell (1993a), 104.
[15]Dyer (1992a), 142.
[16]Mann (1986), 424–30; Britnell (1993a), 105–8; Mayhew (above), 72.
[17]Kosminsky (1956), 152–96.
[18]Biddick (1985a, 1987).
[19]McIntosh (1986), 137–52.
[20]B. M. S. Campbell et al. (1993), 93–4.

Measuring commercialisation

About two-thirds of all land was occupied by such small producers, but it is a matter of debate whether their share of production was concomitant with their share of the soil.[21] Although there is much that may yet be learnt about the commercial activities and market involvement of this most numerous and important class of rural producer, the range and depth of that knowledge will always be circumscribed by the limited and haphazard survival of available evidence. By contrast, those parts of landed estates that were kept in hand and managed by reeves and bailiffs on behalf of their lords – the demesne lands – are altogether more accessible to research. The composition and management of agriculture in this smaller but relatively richly documented sector can be studied from the many surviving manorial extents and accounts. With the aid of these sources it is possible to establish quite systematically for the demesne sector, and for the demesne sector alone, which commodities were produced, how they were disposed of, and in what quantities. The picture thus obtained, while by no means representative of agriculture as a whole, can at least assist in providing a framework for assessing the more fragmentary evidence relating to the peasant sector.

The seigneurial sector undoubtedly had the potential to be the more commercialised of the two sectors. In the first place, its share of agricultural land was significantly greater than the share of total population (represented by the lord, his household, and his workforce) immediately dependent upon it. Demesne agriculture is therefore likely to have produced a substantial surplus over the immediate needs of consumption. Secondly, many estates were scattered in distribution, either obliging their lords to lead a peripatetic lifestyle and, with their households, eat their way round their estates (an option plainly not open to conventual communities), or inducing the adoption of management strategies whereby outlying manors sold their produce and transmitted cash to the household.[22] Thirdly, as medieval material culture grew in sophistication, the range of luxury goods obtained through international trade increased, and the rate and incidence of royal taxation rose, so landlords increasingly demanded cash rather than produce from their estates.[23] Historically, of course, landlords had always required part of their income in cash, which they obtained either through the sale of demesne produce or by demanding cash rents, so that the demesne sector had a longer and stronger tradition of market involvement than the peasant sector. In fact, Snooks considers seigneurial agriculture to have been the provenance of the bulk of all marketed produce in 1086.[24]

---

[21]Compare Postan (1966), 602, with B. M. S. Campbell (1983b), 39–41, and B. M. S. Campbell (1991a), 144–9.

[22]Davenport (1906), 22–4; Morgan (1946), 41–53; Dyer (1989a), 99–100; Biddick (1989), 76, 86–90.

[23]Dyer (1989a), 49–85; Biddick with Bijleveld (1991), 98–104; Britnell (1993a), 105–8.

[24]Snooks (above), 39–40.

For many landlords, however, especially major religious institutions, old habits died hard. On the most heavily manorialised estates, labour services and food farms subsidised management strategies geared towards consumption rather than exchange. For those with substantial households to support, local markets did not always offer a sufficiently reliable alternative source of provisions, nor was the supply of coin adequate for a high level of purchasing. Much, therefore, depended upon the size, type, composition, location, objectives and policy of individual estates, with the result that patterns of commercialisation can be expected to have varied considerably. This chapter is concerned with the reconstruction of those patterns at the culmination of medieval demographic and economic expansion within that part of England most fully exposed to the commercial influence of London.

Period and place

Great cities were one of the forcing grounds of commercial agriculture.[25] The more they grew, the wider was the area upon which they drew for their food and raw materials and the more complex and sophisticated were the commercial networks by which rural producers were linked to urban consumers. The largest cities drew food and raw materials traded in local and regional markets into national and even international orbits of exchange and thereby helped to forge a more integrated market economy. It was therefore in the hinterlands of such cities that agriculture may earliest have assumed its most commercialised forms. J. H. von Thünen's well known land-use model predicts greater commercialisation and intensification near the primate centre, with increasing self-sufficiency and extensive production away from it.[26] It is for this reason that historians often employ the relative size and structure of the urban sector as one indicator of commercialisation.[27]

Among English cities in 1300 none rivalled London in size and, among European cities north of the Alps, Paris alone was larger. During the twelfth and thirteenth centuries London had grown more rapidly than the national population as a whole, consolidating its status as England's primate city and developing its role as the political and commercial capital of a powerful

---

[25]'The important initiating condition or mechanism that propels market exchange is . . . the growth of hierarchical institutions *within* the internal or domestic economy that provide the regular concentrated demand that generates rural specialization and the local ability to supply. That is, central places are found to develop long before an internal marketing system – they are the *causes* rather than the *consequences* of market development': C. A. Smith (1976), 46.

[26]Von Thünen (1966).

[27]For example, Britnell (1989); Britnell (above), 9–12.

Measuring commercialisation

nation state.[28] The intensity of commercial activity attained by the city at the climax of its expansion may have remained unsurpassed until the final decades of the sixteenth century.[29] Sustaining that level of activity, and the population of 80,000 or more people that it supported, required food and raw materials in significant quantities. At minimum standards of living the city would have required each year approximately 175,000 quarters of assorted grains to satisfy its needs for food, drink, and fodder.[30] Fuelling the ovens and kilns that baked that grain into bread and brewed it into ale would have required in excess of 100,000 tons of firewood.[31] Fruit, vegetables, dairy produce, meat and fish would also have been consumed in significant quantities, especially by the social and political elites who resided within the city for periods or even the whole of the year.[32] Those elites also generated a significant demand for wine and other exotic imports, which were traded in return for the exports of wool and other primary agricultural products shipped through London. Artisans working in leather, textiles, and wood also drew upon agriculture for their raw materials and it was the surrounding countryside that supplied most of the stone, chalk, sand, and timber of which the city was built. Since many of these materials had to be brought over considerable distances, fodder and food were required in significant quantities to feed the horses, oxen, drovers, carriers, hauliers, boatmen, and seamen who transported produce to the city. In this way much business and traffic were brought to the many small towns that serviced the capital and had to be provisioned from the same hinterland.

At the beginning of the fourteenth century, in years of normal harvests, most towns of 10,000 inhabitants were capable of being provisioned with grain from a radius of ten to 20 miles, depending on the productivity of their hinterlands.[33] London, with at least eight times that population, drew its grain from market towns up to 20 miles from the city when only land transport was available, and up to 60 miles as the crow flies when water transport could be used, embracing an area more than 4,000 square miles in extent.[34] Livestock and livestock products were probably sent to the city from even further afield.[35] Within that hinterland the three elements identified by Polanyi as diagnostic of a commercialised economy (marketing institutions, trade for gain, and price-fixing mechanisms) were all recognisably in place by this date. Thünenesque patterns of production bear further

[28]Keene (1989).
[29]Keene (1985a), 19–20.
[30]B. M. S. Campbell *et al.* (1993), 31–6.
[31]Galloway and Murphy (1991), 3.
[32]Dyer (1989a), 55–70.
[33]Grantham (forthcoming).
[34]B. M. S. Campbell *et al.* (1993), 173.
[35]Keene (1989), 104–5; Farmer (1991a), 384.

testimony to the powerfulness of the trading nexus that focused on London.[36]

Insofar as London is representative of the kingdom of which it was the capital, it was in the final decade of the thirteenth and opening decade of the fourteenth century that demographic and economic growth peaked, before apparently giving way to decline and stagnation during the generation or so between the Great Famine of 1315–18 and the Black Death of 1348–9 (a contraction manifest in falling urban land values and a reduced intensity of commercial land-use).[37] Significantly, the one part of London's hinterland where demographic trends may be reconstructed with some confidence, a group of manors in rural Essex, seems to have shared the same trend.[38] Apart from the toll exacted by the Famine itself and the cattle plague which followed it, heavy taxation and the dislocation to trade that resulted from purveyancing and currency devaluation also contributed to a worsening in economic conditions.[39] At the same time a heightened incidence of warfare drove up transaction costs within international trade.[40] It was therefore in the decades immediately prior to the Famine that the quantity and intensity of market exchange in both London and its hinterland probably climaxed (although quantity per head may have been greater later). Certainly, mean land values within the London region, particularly of arable, were higher before 1300 than after (as revealed by an analysis of the valuations given in 1,966 IPM extents over the period 1270–1339).[41] Together with high prices and low wages, they encouraged landlords to maximise both the acreage and the productivity of land under cultivation and make increasing resort to the market for the disposal of produce and purchase of provisions. As Miller and Hatcher observe, '. . . the market demand for the produce of their land and the price that would be paid for it, or the demand for the land itself and the rent that would be offered for it . . . modified the objectives of estate management and the methods by which lords sought to realise them'.[42] Under the enterprising management of prior Henry of Eastry, for instance, the high farming practised on the Kentish estates of Canterbury Cathedral Priory was elevated to a new level of intensity while a drastic reorganisation of the food-farm system released a greater share of production for disposal on the market.[43] At much the same time the abbot and convent of Westminster Abbey were separately

[36]Von Thünen (1966); Chisholm (1962), 20–32; Grigg (1982), 135–40; B. M. S. Campbell *et al.* (1993), 111–44.
[37]Keene (1985a), 19–20.
[38]Poos (1985).
[39]B. M. S. Campbell, ed. (1991b); B. M. S. Campbell (forthcoming).
[40]Munro (1991).
[41]For comparable trends in the east midlands see Raftis (1974), 12–79.
[42]Miller and Hatcher (1978), 204.
[43]R. A. L. Smith (1943), 131; for comparable trends on the Norfolk estates of Norwich Cathedral Priory see B. M. S. Campbell (1991a), 154–6.

Measuring commercialisation

relaxing their dependence upon estate supplies of produce and placing increased reliance upon the market for provisions, although, significantly, that policy was to be reversed later in the fourteenth century as economic circumstances deteriorated.[44] The years around 1300 therefore represent a benchmark in the commercialisation of seigneurial agriculture.

The size and composition of seigneurial and manorial sales revenues

Individual estates differed considerably in the number and distribution of their constituent demesnes, just as individual demesnes varied in their size and composition. In managing those estates lords needed to cater for the reproductive requirements of an essentially organic system of agricultural production, the remuneration of their workforce in cash or in kind, the provisioning of their households either on the manor or elsewhere, and, finally, their own needs for cash. Most lords therefore combined production for use with production for sale. The balance struck between these two objectives differed, however, between lords, between manors on the same estate, between locations, and between different agricultural products.

Manorial accounts provide the principal source for evaluating these differences. These were rendered each year, usually at Michaelmas, by the reeve or bailiff of a manor and are a rich store of detailed and mostly reliable information.[45] Such accounts are rare before the mid-thirteenth century but survive thereafter in increasing numbers, and for a widening cross-section of estates, embracing properties of the crown, earls, barons, knights, archbishops and bishops, and greater and lesser conventual and collegiate institutions. Between 1288 and 1315 accounts have been identified for over 200 different manors and 41 different estates in the London region (defined here as the ten counties of Bedfordshire, Berkshire, Buckinghamshire, Essex, Hertfordshire, Kent, Middlesex, Northamptonshire, Oxfordshire, and Surrey).[46] For a few manors virtually complete annual series of accounts are extant, but most runs are shorter and more fragmentary and for a number of manors documentation is confined to a single year.[47] Limiting analysis to a sample of up to three accounts per

---

[44]B. F. Harvey (1977), 134–7, 142–7.

[45]On manorial accounts see *Manorial Records of Cuxham*; P. D. A. Harvey (1984b).

[46]Only 202 of these sampled manors have usable sales information; for their distribution see Figures 7.1 and 7.2. For a discussion and listing of the full sample of manorial accounts with appropriate manuscript references see B. M. S. Campbell *et al.* (1993), 18–22, 184–90. This sample of manorial accounts is henceforth referred to as the 'Feeding the City I, accounts database'.

[47]For a detailed listing of all known pre-1350 Kentish manorial accounts see Galloway *et al.* (1993).

Table 7.1 Comparison of the social distribution of landed income in the country as a whole *c.* 1300 with the institutional distribution of extant manorial accounts in the London region 1288–1315

Owner	Estimated annual income *c.* 1300 (whole country)		Number of manors with accounts 1288–1315 (London region only)	
	£	%	no.	%
Royal	30,000	4.7	20	9.9
Lay:				
earls	40,000	6.3	20	9.9
barons & knights[a]	82,300	12.9	13	6.5
lesser gentry	300,000	46.9	0	0.0
Sub-total	**422,300**	**66.1**	**33**	**16.3**
Ecclesiastical:				
episcopal	27,000	4.2	19	9.4
conventual & collegiate[b]	160,000	25.1	130	64.4
Sub-total	**187,000**	**29.3**	**168**	**73.8**
TOTAL	**639,300**	**100.0**	**202**	**100.0**

[a] Including lay manors in the king's hands.
[b] Including ecclesiastical manors in the king's hands.
Sources: Mayhew (above), 58; Feeding the City I, accounts database.

manor yields a database of some 460 accounts, providing a snapshot view of patterns of seigneurial production and sale at the turn of the thirteenth century. Institutionally, however, this sample is biased towards certain types and sizes of estate, as is revealed by Table 7.1. Thus, whereas lay estates accounted for approximately two-thirds of all landed revenues (with the numerous small holdings of the lesser gentry making up the lion's share), only one in six of documented manors was in lay hands. Conversely, although ecclesiastical estates of one sort or another contributed approximately 30 per cent of landed revenues they are represented by three out of four documented manors. In both cases it is also the largest estates that tend to be best documented. Manors belonging to the earldoms of Cornwall, Lincoln, and Norfolk, the archbishopric of Canterbury and the bishoprics of Winchester and London, the cathedral priories of Canterbury and Winchester, and the abbeys of Crowland, Peterborough, Ramsey, Waltham, and Westminster (convent and abbot), together with those of the crown and the confiscated lands of the knights templar under crown management, make up over 70 per cent of all those documented.

Measuring commercialisation

For all the ostensible detail and accuracy of the accounts, analysis of the abundant sales information that they contain is not without problems, nor can all of it be taken at face value. In some accounts, especially those of manors under royal management, income from sales of different products is lumped together, preventing any detailed breakdown of the figures. Sales of assorted grains and assorted livestock are quite often recorded in this way, which accounts for the categories 'unspecified/combined grains' and 'unspecified/combined livestock' in Table 7.3. Nor was all produce eventually destined for the market sold directly from the manor. Wool, in particular, was often transferred to a central depot – Wolvesey Castle at Winchester in the case of the estates of the bishopric of Winchester, Crowland in the case of those of Crowland Abbey – pending subsequent bulk sale.[48] Half of the sampled manors that disposed of wool did so partially or wholly by transfer, involving approximately 15 per cent of all wool by value. Since the bulk of that transferred wool was eventually sold this is a potential source of underestimation. Transfers of wool to estate headquarters or elsewhere have therefore been treated as *de facto* sales. Costing them and correcting the figures on wool sales to account for them is, however, far from straightforward, especially as wool transfers often tend to be recorded in numbers of fleeces whereas wool sales are more usually recorded in terms of the weight of wool sold. The problem is compounded by the fact that fleeces varied in weight and wool in quality and, therefore, in value. Fortunately, enough accounts record both the number and the weight of fleeces to allow the value of wool transfers to be estimated, using wool prices taken from Lloyd's regional series.[49]

Grain, too, was often transferred in quantity to central granaries, especially on conventual estates, but surviving granary accounts reveal little or no evidence of central selling.[50] Other products were also transferred centrally or to other manors, and although these were primarily for use rather than exchange it would be surprising if some were not subsequently sold off. Such post-transfer sales may, however, be partially or wholly offset by the convention, on some estates, of accounting for transfers 'for the lord's household' as sales. These fictitious 'sales' are distinguished in the accounts by the terms *ad hospicium domini*, *ut pro hospicio domini*, and *pro expensis hospicii domini*.[51] Yet, although a cash sum is recorded in the

[48]Farmer (1991a), 397, 399–400; Page (1926–9). The estates of Bec Abbey, Canterbury Cathedral Priory, Crowland Abbey, Oseney Abbey, Peterborough Abbey, Ramsey Abbey, Titchfield Abbey, Henry de Gray, and those in the king's hands formerly belonging to Walter de Langton, all transferred a majority of their wool for sale elsewhere. Conversely on the sampled properties of Merton College, Westminster Abbey (convent and abbot), Winchester Cathedral Priory, the bishop of Winchester, the earldom of Lincoln, and the confiscated properties of the knights templar most wool was sold directly from the manor.
[49]Lloyd (1973).
[50]B. M. S. Campbell *et al.* (1993), 205.
[51]B. M. S. Campbell *et al.* (1993), 148; Farmer (1991a), 359, 368.

accounts it is extremely unlikely that any cash changed hands and it is certain that the items concerned were not sold on the open market. This practice appears to have been most common on episcopal manors, where fictitious sales comprise 6.3 per cent of sales of crops and crop products and 4.0 per cent of all sales of agricultural produce. It was also followed on certain conventual and collegiate manors, where 4.1 per cent of sales of animals and animal products and 2.1 per cent of all sales of agricultural produce fall into this category. On some individual manors in particular years these proportions are significantly higher, but across all sampled manors income specifically identified as deriving from fictitious sales amounts to a modest 1.7 per cent of the total accounted income from sales of agricultural produce.

On average, correcting for wool transfers and discounting fictitious sales, each of the 201 sampled demesnes received £23 4s 8d per year from the sale of agricultural produce around the year 1300.[52] This mean figure nevertheless masks a wide range of individual experience, depending upon the size and location of the demesne and the management policy of the estate. At one extreme, for instance, sales of agricultural produce yielded less than £1 0s 0d on the Bicester Priory home demesne of Caversfield in Oxfordshire, the Peterborough Abbey home demesnes of Werrington and Torpel in Northamptonshire, and William de Fiennes's English base at Wendover in Buckinghamshire. At the other, sales of agricultural produce raised over £70 0s 0d on the royal manors of Eastwood in Essex, Langley Marish with Wraysbury in Buckinghamshire, Ospringe in Kent, and Merton in Oxfordshire (formerly a possession of the knights templar), as well as on the earl of Lincoln and earl of Norfolk's manors of Higham Ferrers in Northamptonshire and Weston in Hertfordshire. On John le Ferrers's large manor at Hampstead Norreys in Berkshire, however, sales raised well over £100 0s 0d. Significantly, four of these seven high-selling demesnes enjoyed ready access to the major trading artery of the Thames, and so to the metropolitan market.

Clearly, the demesne sector in the London region sold substantial quantities of agricultural produce and the income thereby generated represented an important source of revenue on many manors. Of the £4,670 actually raised in aggregate, 58 per cent derived from the sale of crops and crop products (including malt, straw, and garden produce); 32 per cent came from the sale of animals and animal products (including hides, wool, dairy produce, eggs, the farm of animals, fish, and game); and the remaining 10 per cent was contributed by various land-use products, especially wood and

---

[52]Wool transfers costed as sales account for £61 or 1.3 per cent of this figure. It would be even higher if revenues from the sale of herbage were included, but analysis is here confined to those agricultural products – crops, animals, animal products, grass, and wood etc. – actually produced under the direct management of the lord and his officials. Cows and dairies let at farm are the sole exception.

Measuring commercialisation

hay (Tables 7.2 and 7.3).[53] It is likely, however, that the institutional bias of the sample towards ecclesiastical manors tends to understate the sales contribution of crops and crop products and overstate the corresponding contributions of animals and animal products and the plant products of meadow and wood.

Unfortunately, few of the estates documented have been surveyed in their entirety, so the patterns of sale summarised in Table 7.2 should be interpreted with caution. Nevertheless, the 15 conventual and collegiate estates represented in the accounts database stand out as having derived on average a smaller proportion of their sales income from the disposal of crops and crop products, and a larger proportion from animals and animal products, than other classes of estate. The bias towards the sale of animals and animal products (together with hay and wood), and the consumption of crops and crop products, is most pronounced, as Biddick has demonstrated, on the 18 manors of Peterborough Abbey, which effectively sold no grain and made 43 per cent of their sales income from animals and animal products (particularly wool) and a further 48 per cent from hay and wood (only the solitary manor of St Catherine's Priory, Rouen made less of its income from crops and more from animals and their products). In contrast, the six manors of two other Fenland abbeys, Crowland and Ramsey, were greater sellers of crops than they were of animals and their products, and thereby generated on average higher cash revenues than their Peterborough neighbours.

The Fens were one of lowland England's greatest reservoirs of pasture, and it is perhaps surprising that conventual estates in and adjoining them did not exhibit a stronger commercial bias towards pastoralism. Paradoxically, the sale of animals and their products assumed greater relative importance on the twenty manors of Westminster Abbey, very differently distributed and far less favourably endowed with grassland. This is because significant proportions of these manors' crop production were consumed directly by the abbey. The Westminster manor of Birdbrook in Essex (which derived 61 per cent of its sales revenue from crops and 29 per cent from animals and animal products) is the exception that proves this rule: it is 45 miles as the crow flies from the abbey and was therefore in a weak position to serve as a home demesne.[54] Canterbury Cathedral Priory, by contrast, was better positioned to profit from the sale of crops. Its estate was large, concentrated in an area of generally productive agriculture, and favourably located relative to major markets both at home and overseas.

---

[53]This, and other aggregates, is the sum of the means at manorial level of the amounts recorded in individual accounts. All percentages have been calculated at an aggregate level: see Table 7.2.

[54]Staines in Middlesex derived 96 per cent of gross sales income from crops and crop products, but this was a property of the abbot rather than convent of Westminster and the overall volume of its sales was modest, amounting to £8 11s 0d.

In aggregate, 54 per cent of the sales revenue from its 34 documented manors (the single largest estate in the accounts database) came from crops, 40 per cent from animals and their products, and 6 per cent from land-use products. These aggregate figures, however, mask quite strong contrasts between those demesnes such as Barksore, Chartham, Ham, and Ickham in east Kent which sold mainly animals and animal products and sent most of their surplus crops to Canterbury to provision the household, and others at a further remove, such as Appledore, Copton, Cliffe, East Farleigh, Ebony, Fairfield, Farningham, and Leysdown in Kent, and Cheam, East Horsley, and Walworth in Surrey, whose revenues were dominated by the sale of crops. By the same token, among conventual and collegiate estates it was either those with no resident household to support, such as Bec Abbey, or those whose estates were too widely scattered for

Table 7.2 Components of aggregate gross agricultural sales income, by estate and ownership type, on manors in the London region, 1288–1315

Lord (by ownership type)	No. of manors[a]	Aggregate gross agricultural sales income per estate		
		Income received[a] (£)	*Percentage of sales income from:*	
			crops & crop products	*animals & animal products*	*land-use products*
Bec Abbey	6	186	51	29	20
Bicester Priory	4	8	48	38	14
Boxley Abbey	1	5	36	47	17
Canterbury Cathedral Priory	34	528	54	40	6
Crowland Abbey	3	20	79	20	1
Merton College, Oxford	8	142	68	28	4
Oseney Abbey	3	21	62	17	21
Peterborough Abbey	18	194	9	43	48
Ramsey Abbey	3	59	64	32	4
St Catherine's Priory, Rouen	1	6	1	99	0
Titchfield Abbey	1	16	40	46	14
Waltham Abbey	1	10	68	32	0
Westminster Abbey (abbot)	7	146	43	47	10
Westminster Abbey (convent)	20	345	44	44	12
Winchester Cathedral Priory	1	62	57	43	0
Conventual & collegiate	111	1,747	48	39	14
Archbishopric of Canterbury	4	89	66	30	4
Bishopric of London	1	20	36	58	6
Bishopric of Winchester	13	540	69	25	7
Episcopal	18	650	67	26	6

Measuring commercialisation

Table 7.2   Continued

Lord (by ownership type)	No. of manors[a]	Aggregate gross agricultural sales income per estate		
		Income received[a] (£)	Percentage of sales income from:		
			crops & crop products	animals & animal products	land-use products
D'Argentine	1	9	66	26	8
De Barlee	1	4	23	77	0
De Clare	2	57	55	42	3
De Cobham	1	27	68	32	0
De Fiennes	1	1	6	94	0
De Fortibus	1	21	50	26	24
De Gray	1	27	53	38	8
De Hamelton	1	34	72	28	0
De Seyton	1	8	43	31	26
Earldom of Cornwall	7	168	87	10	3
Earldom of Lincoln	9	403	67	21	12
Earldom of Norfolk	4	166	60	33	7
Le Ferrers	1	128	36	42	22
Lay	31	1,051	64	27	10
King	17	432	71	22	8
Late Earldom of Norfolk	1	66	61	29	10
Late Holy Trinity Abbey, Caen	1	64	88	11	<1
Late Knights Templar	17	491	56	37	7
Late Walter de Langton	5	194	48	47	5
Queen	3	55	73	26	1
Royal	44	1,301	62	31	7
All[a]	204	4,750	58	32	10

[a] Weston, Herts., is counted both as a possession of the Earldom of Norfolk and of the King; Isleworth, Middx., is counted both as a possession of the Earldom of Cornwall and of the King; Upper Heyford, Oxon., is counted both as a possession of Isabella de Fortibus and of the King.

Source: Feeding the City I, accounts database.

direct provisioning to be generally practicable, such as Merton College, which derived the largest shares of their sales income from the marketing of crops.

The features of a low mean revenue from agricultural sales, coupled with the prominence among sales of animals and their products, so characteristic of several conventual estates such as the abbeys of Boxley, Peterborough and Westminster (Table 7.2), were also common to several of the smaller lay estates whose lords similarly appear to have exploited them for consumption rather than revenue. The documentation is here much flimsier, but lords such as William de Fiennes at Wendover (Bucks.) and Roger de Barlee at Wicken Bonhunt (Essex) sold little agricultural produce and what they sold derived primarily from the pastoral sector. A few other lay manors – the de Clare manor of Standon (Herts.), John le Ferrers's large manor at Hampstead Norreys (Berks.) – likewise made more from their livestock than their crops but within a more commercialised context. Nevertheless, among lay manors and lay estates as a group it was crop sales that tended to predominate and to a much greater extent than on conventual and collegiate estates. Lay households presumably usually had fewer mouths to feed than conventual ones and fed fewer of those – servants and the poor – whose diets were dominated by grain rather than meat.

Half of the lay manors in the accounts database derived more than two-thirds of their sales revenue from crops; and on six of the seven database manors of the earldom of Cornwall and two of the nine of the earldom of Lincoln this proportion exceeded 80 per cent. Most manors of great but scattered lay estates were managed to yield revenue rather than produce, and on several of them the sums so raised were impressive. These were estates whose lords and attendant households were fairly constantly on the move and who consequently needed the liquidity of cash. The more important episcopal lords, too, were often similarly mobile while their prominent political and social role made heavy demands on their purse. The sales profiles of their manors therefore tended to resemble more those of estates belonging to their great lay counterparts than those of the major ecclesiastical institutions. The thirteen database manors of the bishopric of Winchester each raised on average £41 10s 9d from the sale of agricultural produce, 69 per cent of that coming from crops.[55] Similarly, the four database manors of the archbishopric of Canterbury each raised on average £22 5s 0d, with crops, in this case, accounting for 66 per cent of the total.[56] Crops also made a disproportionate contribution to agricultural revenues on the three manors of the queen and seventeen manors of the king:[57] on average the contributions of the arable, pastoral, and meadow/woodland

[55]Among the Winchester manors, 71 per cent of the £41 4s 5d received by Harwell, 72 per cent of the £67 7s 2d received by Brightwell, 77 per cent of the £69 19s 0d received by Wargrave, and 94 per cent of the £33 4s 7d received by Waltham St Lawrence, all in Berkshire, came from the sale of crops and crop products.

[56]Among the archiepiscopal manors, 77 per cent of the £20 7s 5d received by Maidstone and 79 per cent of the £20 14s 0d received by Northfleet, both in Kent, came from the sale of crops and crop products.

[57] Bray and Kennington (Berks.), Eastwood (Essex), Milton, Ospringe, Lessness and West Cliffe (Kent, the latter both possessions of the queen), Radstone (N'hants.), and Combe and Whitchurch (Oxon.) all exhibited a strong commercial bias towards crop sales, deriving over three-quarters of agricultural sales revenue from that source.

sectors to total revenues on these manors conformed remarkably closely to their respective shares of land-use on the properties of tenants-in-chief of the crown in the same region.

It is intriguing that the pastoral sector contributed less to agricultural sales on many royal, episcopal and lay estates than on most of those in conventual and collegiate ownership. In some cases this was because of local circumstances. Some conventual manors enjoyed substantial pastoral revenues simply because they were naturally well endowed with pasture; the Peterborough manors of the Biggin in Rockingham Forest and Cottingham in the lush Welland valley of Northamptonshire, and the Canterbury Cathedral Priory manors of Ebony in Romney Marsh and Lydden in the Ash Levels of Kent are cases in point. Others – the Westminster Abbey manors of Battersea in Surrey, Hampstead, Ebury and Laleham in Middlesex (the last two, possessions of the abbot), and the earl of Lincoln's manor of Colham also in Middlesex – owed the predominance of pastoral sales to their proximity to the London market, which stimulated dairying and fattening activities in its immediate environs. But such specific circumstances were not exclusive to conventual and collegiate estates and cannot adequately explain what appears to have been a general trait. More to the point, apparently, were the consumption requirements of conventual and collegiate institutions, which differed from the meat-eating households of most other lords.[58] This contrast shows up in the exceptionally high proportion of grain sent for household consumption on conventual and collegiate estates and the high proportion of animals slaughtered for consumption on lay estates (Tables 7.5 and 7.7). Conventual and collegiate estates, as perpetual institutions, were also less vulnerable to the expropriating activities of the crown to which periodic vacancies, minorities and wardships rendered episcopal and lay estates so susceptible.[59] Their higher stocking densities – 33 per cent higher than on episcopal estates, 86 per cent higher than on lay estates, and 140 per cent higher than on royal estates – may therefore reflect a greater long-term capacity to sustain investment in pastoral husbandry.

Measuring the commercialisation of different agricultural products

Hitherto grain and wool have received most attention in discussions of medieval agricultural commodity markets, the former because of its prominence in medieval diets and hence in local, regional and international trade, the latter because of its conspicuous importance in international

---

[58]Knowles (1950), 458–63; Dyer (1989a), 58–62.

[59]For the impact of episcopal vacancies upon livestock numbers on the estates of the bishops of Winchester see Titow (1962), 44–6; Biddick with Bijleveld (1991), 98–104.

trade.[60] On the 201 sampled manors in the London region, although sales of grain, malted and unmalted, were undoubtedly important, generating over half of gross agricultural sales income, wool sales (corrected for transfers) were much less so, contributing less than a tenth of sales income. Plainly, other products were often of equal or greater importance. In fact,

Table 7.3 Sales of individual agricultural products in the London region, 1288–1315

Agrarian product	% of manors selling product (N = 201)	Aggregate sales revenue (£)	% of aggregate sales revenue	% of aggregate sales sub-revenue
All agrarian products	100	4,670	100	
Crop & crop products	99	2,703	58	100
field crops	98	2,645	57	98
grains	93	2,471	53	91
unprocessed grains	90	2,382	51	88
wheat	78	828	18	31
rye	26	112	2	4
winter mixtures	23	129	3	5
barley	50	330	7	12
dredge	33	194	4	7
oats	56	228	5	8
unspecified/combined grains	29	561	12	21
processed grains	28	87	2	3
processed & unprocessed grains mixed/combined	<1	3	<1	<1
legumes	62	119	3	4
grains & legumes mixed/ combined	5	16	<1	1
chaff, straw & stubble	34	39	1	1
horticultural crops	61	59	1	2
Animals & animal products (including game & fish)	99	1,516	32	100
live animals	96	669	14	44
equines	58	48	1	3
bovines	74	133	3	9
ovines (including goats)	60	182	4	12

[60]On grain: Gras (1915); B. M. S. Campbell et al. (1993). On wool: Power (1941); Lloyd (1977a).

Measuring commercialisation

Table 7.3 Continued

Agrarian product	% of manors selling product (N = 201)	Aggregate sales revenue (£)	% of aggregate sales revenue	% of aggregate sales sub-revenue
porcines	58	125	3	8
unspecified/combined animals/poultry	12	150	3	10
poultry, swans, doves etc	82	32	1	2
animal products	94	807	17	53
eggs	49	5	<1	<1
dairy produce	61	130	3	9
farm/lactage of cows &/or ewes	37	192	4	13
wool (& some sheep skins) (including transfers costed as sales)	70	415	9	27
skins & hides	78	49	1	3
meat, carcasses, tallow, dung	14	15	<1	1
animals & animal products in combination	3	18	<1	1
game	3	8	<1	1
fish & fisheries	12	14	<1	1
Land-use products	72	450	10	100
wood & wood products	49	277	6	62
hay & meadow	44	159	3	35
heath, bracken, broom, rushes, turbary	4	9	<1	2
mineral products	1	4	<1	1
Miscellaneous or unidentifiable agrarian products	2	1	<1	

Source: Feeding the City I, accounts database.

the range of agricultural products sold was remarkably wide (Table 7.3), since almost everything, except horse meat, had a resale value in this resource-deficient age.[61] The motives for selling produce were similarly wide. Reeves, bailiffs and lords regularly sold off items that were surplus to the consumption requirements of the household or the reproductive requirements of husbandry, especially when there were windfalls of fish,

[61]Pig's innards, rotten pelts, old onions, chaff, nettles, and thorns all appear among the items sold, as do salmon, conger eels, and peacock's feathers.

game, pannage, and herbage, which the manor and estate were unable to absorb.[62] Every year there was a need to maintain and even upgrade the working stock of the manor, particularly its animals, entailing the removal of old, sterile, or sick beasts and their replacement with younger and healthier stock. Sometimes, too, the need for a substantial cash sum required the selling-off of capital stock, typically livestock or timber. The crown frequently employed this as a revenue-raising device on estates that were temporarily in its custody, and it was not unknown for the executors of bishops and lords in anticipation of a vacancy or wardship to resort to the same device in a ploy to pre-empt such expropriation.[63] Finally, there were items that were regularly and systematically produced and sold for profit and hence relied upon as one of the staple sources of cash income.

Does this mean that some agricultural products were intrinsically more commercialised than others? Farmer believes that it does, and has identified eleven criteria by which the extent of a product's commercialisation might be judged.[64] Unfortunately, few of these criteria are directly quantifiable, and most require a degree of detailed knowledge unattainable at the scale of analysis employed here. Certain more measurable indices do, however, come readily to hand. These include the frequency with which products were sold and the relative amounts of gross sales income that they generated, the quantities sold as a proportion of total output, and rates of sale per unit area and per unit livestock.

1) *Frequencies of sale and amounts of sales income*

A simple but crude way of assessing the degree of commercialisation of a commodity is in terms of the numbers and proportions of manors selling it and its contribution to mean gross income from sales (Table 7.3). Judged on these terms wheat was by far the most commercialised agricultural product, being sold by more manors and making a larger contribution to mean gross sales revenues than any other single commodity. It was also the most widely grown crop, occupied a larger share of the sown acreage than any other crop, and the vast majority of those manors that grew it also sold it: in aggregate, almost a fifth of all income from the sale of agricultural produce and almost a third of all income from the sale of crops and crop products came from the sale of wheat (more, if allowance is made for the fact that a substantial proportion of sales of unspecified grains is likely to have comprised wheat). This commercial prominence reflected wheat's status as both the preferred and the most highly-priced bread grain. Certainly, no

[62]Farmer (above), 106–7.
[63]Titow (1962), 44–5; Biddick with Bijleveld (1991), 98–104.
[64]These are listed in Farmer (above), 102–4.

Measuring commercialisation

other crop was sold in such quantities or with such frequency. Even though rye, and mixtures of rye with wheat or winter-barley, were the closest substitutes for wheat in bread-making, they were grown by far fewer demesnes, occupied a much smaller share of mean sown acreage, and were sold by less than half the demesnes that grew them. With certain notable exceptions, chiefly among demesnes in the lower Thames valley that specialised in producing these cheaper bread grains for the London market, rye and winter-mixtures were mostly produced for on-the-farm and on-the-estate consumption.[65]

Many of the oats, too, that were produced were destined for internal consumption on the demesne or estate (as fodder for livestock and pottage, ale, and an ingredient of the coarsest breads for manorial workers) rather than for sale. Oats, although grown as widely and occupying almost as large a share of the sown acreage as wheat, were less able to bear the costs of transport. This was because they commanded a poorer price and were characterised by lower extraction rates when milled.[66] Proximity to markets was therefore a prerequisite of those demesnes that specialised in its large-scale commercial production.[67] Since there were comparatively few of these, oats contributed, in aggregate, only 5 per cent of gross agricultural sales income and 8 per cent of gross income from the sale of crops. By contrast, barley and dredge (a mixture of barley and oats) together contributed over a tenth of gross agricultural sales income and almost a fifth of gross income from the sale of crops, even though they were grown by fewer demesnes and occupied, on average, a smaller share of the sown acreage than oats. They owed their ostensibly more commercial character to the fact that they were less likely to be consumed as fodder on the manor or estate and were capable of being marketed over a greater distance since they commanded a higher relative price and were characterised by marginally higher extraction rates when milled. They appear, however, to have been purchased principally for brewing rather than baking, and since brewing was itself already a relatively specialised and commercialised activity this ensured a comparatively buoyant demand.[68] Nevertheless, surprisingly few of the demesnes that produced barley and dredge sold them ready malted, even though this would have improved the price received, reduced their bulk, and improved their transportability.[69] Overall, only a quarter of demesnes sold malt and

---

[65]B. M. S. Campbell et al. (1993), 121–3.

[66]Conventional extraction rates in 1801 were for wheat 80 per cent, barley 78 per cent, and oats 56 per cent: Collins (1975), 108 n. Medieval rates are likely to have been somewhat higher. Corresponding mean prices per bushel, 1288–1315, were wheat 8.6d, barley 6.5d, and oats 3.7d: B. M. S. Campbell et al. (1993), 112.

[67]B. M. S. Campbell et al. (1993), 116–18, 160–1.

[68]On the organisation of urban brewing at this time see Keene (1985b), I, 265–9; B. M. S. Campbell et al. (1993), 79 n., 84–5.

[69]B. M. S. Campbell et al. (1993), 113, 164.

rarely in any quantity, while processed grains contributed only 2 per cent of aggregate sales income.

Finally, legumes (peas, beans, and vetches) contributed a modest but significant 4 per cent of gross income from the sale of crops. They occupied less than 10 per cent of the sown acreage but were sold by over 70 per cent of the demesnes that produced them, finding, no doubt, a ready market among the poor for whom they provided an important and nutritious food source. Collectively, the various grains, malted and unmalted, contributed in aggregate 53 per cent of gross agricultural sales income: the addition of legumes and grain and legume mixtures raises this to 56 per cent, and the inclusion of straw – a crop by-product essential for a variety of purposes and sold in generally modest quantities by two out of five manors – to 57 per cent. (The contribution of the horticultural products of garden and orchard was in proportion to their modest share of total land-use.)

Within the livestock sector no single animal type or animal product dominated both production and sale to the same extent that crop production and sale were dominated by wheat. Demesnes stocked varying combinations of horses, cattle, sheep (and, very occasionally, goats), swine, poultry, and, in some cases, game (principally rabbits and deer) and fish. With these they produced live animals for replacement, slaughter and sale – the source of roughly half of pastoral sales income – and a range of animal products, principally hides, wool and dairy produce – the source of the other half of pastoral sales income. Sales of meat, game, and fish can effectively be discounted as significant sources of income, since they contributed in aggregate barely 1 per cent of gross agricultural sales income. Over all, a third of gross agricultural sales income came from animals and animal products.

Over three out of five manors that stocked horses, and four out of five manors that stocked cattle, sheep, swine and poultry, sold them. (Since one in eight of all manors sold 'unspecified livestock' these proportions are probably a slight under-estimate.) These are high proportions, comparable with the proportion of demesnes that produced and sold wheat, and reflect management strategies aimed at the maintenance of healthy and productive flocks and herds through the selling off of worn-out, sick, old or superfluous animals and birds. In terms of the income they generated, sheep of varying types and conditions were the most important category of animal sold. They were followed in importance by cattle, swine, horses, and poultry; the horses mostly sold off towards the end of their working life when they had greatly depreciated in value, that depreciation being reflected in a mean sale price approximately 40 per cent lower than the purchase price.

Each of the various categories of animal yielded a variety of products, the aggregate sale of which raised more than as much again as the sale of live stock. Horses yielded traction (which in theory, but rarely in practice, could

Measuring commercialisation

be hired out) and hides (from dead animals). Cattle yielded traction (from oxen), hides and tallow, meat (frequently consumed on the manor but rarely sold there), and dairy produce (milk, butter and especially cheese) either directly from production on the demesne or indirectly from the farm (lease) of the dairy. Sheep yielded skins, fleeces, wool, meat (again, rarely sold), and dairy produce. Swine yielded skins and bacon (neither sold very often nor in significant quantity). Poultry yielded eggs and were sometimes included in the farm of the dairy or were farmed separately. Of these various products, skins and hides were the most widely sold, featuring among the sales of three out of four demesnes, but the revenues they raised were slight, amounting in aggregate to a mere 3 per cent of gross income from the sale of animals and animal products. Far more important were the fleeces and wool of sheep. If, as argued above, transfers of wool are regarded as *de facto* sales one stage removed, then virtually all manors that produced wool in effect sold it. The sums thereby raised were considerable, with over a quarter of the gross sales revenue of the pastoral sector coming from this source, and almost a tenth of total agricultural sales income. Nevertheless, the importance of wool sales should not be exaggerated and they certainly did not dominate manorial revenues or even pastoral revenues to the degree that has sometimes been suggested. In fact, more manors profited from the sale of dairy produce or lease of their dairies than sold or transferred wool. Robert Grosseteste's observation to the countess of Lincoln that 'the return of cows and of sheep in cheese is worth much money' is borne out by the fact that on the sampled manors cattle- and sheep-based dairying contributed over 22 per cent of gross pastoral revenues and 7 per cent of gross agricultural revenues.[70] Eggs, too, were a small but very reliable source of income, especially as so many of them were received as fixed rents in kind from tenants.

Together, crops and crop products and animals and animal products contributed 90 per cent of mean gross agricultural sales income: the remaining 10 per cent was made up by the sale of various land-use products, principally hay, wood and wood products. The latter proportion would, however, have been higher had income from the sale of pannage, herbage, and pasture been included, for this was an important source of income on those manors that opted to sell off and lease out pastures rather than extend flocks and herds to the limit of the available carrying capacity.[71] Such income has been excluded from consideration here partly because it did not fall within the remit of data collection and partly because leases of arable land have been similarly excluded.

[70]*Walter of Henley*, 398–9. For the contribution of dairying to revenues on the Winchester estate in the early thirteenth century see Biddick with Bijleveld (1991), 115–19. See also B. M. S. Campbell (1992).

[71]Peterborough Abbey sold herbage rather than maximise its demesne flocks and herds: Biddick (1989), 56–7, 131.

Hay and wood were both essential components of the manorial economy and IPM extents demonstrate that meadows and woods were among the scarcest and most highly prized resources. For the most part, therefore, as Farmer surmises, manors that sold these plant products were selling off produce which was surplus to their own needs. Roughly 40 per cent of manors sold hay and 50 per cent sold wood and wood products. Both commodities were low in value relative to their bulk, hence any fuller commercial specialisation was usually only possible for manors strategically placed for trade with major centres of demand. Hay and wood therefore tended to make their greatest relative and absolute contribution to gross sales revenues on manors readily accessible to major towns and actively engaged in provisioning them. This was the case on a notable concentration of manors to the north of London – including Edgware, Halliford, Ruislip and Hampstead (Mdx.), Aldenham and Great Amwell (Herts.), Theydon (Essex) and Iver (Bucks.) – where hay and wood often contributed a fifth or more of gross agricultural sales revenues; and a similar but smaller concentration of manors shows up around Oxford (the next largest urban centre in the region), including Clifton, Middleton Stoney, Oddington and Sandford-on-Thames. Other manors stand out as sellers of hay and wood more by default than by deliberate commercial specialisation. This was the case on several of the Northamptonshire manors of Peterborough Abbey, whose market participation was highly selective. In their case the relative prominence of hay and wood as sources of revenue derived from the corresponding unimportance of sales of crops and crop products.

2) *Proportions sold*

In practice only nine-tenths of the crops, animals and animal products produced by demesnes were actually available to them for use or sale since one-tenth of the annual increase of the produce of the soil – including field and garden crops, hay and wood, animals born, milk, wool, eggs and honey produced – was 'top sliced' and paid to the church as tithe. Tithes were collected with varying degrees of zeal according to a variety of arrangements and where possible were deducted at source, as, for instance, in the case of every tenth sheaf at harvest. Except in a few rare cases when the manorial lord and tithe owner were one and the same, accounts record crops net of tithe and explicit reference to the deduction of tithe only occurs in the context of animals and their products, most frequently lambs, wool and cheeses in the stock account.

That portion of production paid as tithe is therefore easily overlooked, yet its significance in the context of commercialisation is disproportionate to its 10 per cent share of gross output. The tithe came to the rector or his deputy net of seed, fodder, and the other reproductive requirements of husbandry and in absolute quantity was usually considerably in excess of the normal consumption requirements of the typical rectorial household. Its commercial potential was therefore high and much of it may indeed have been sold. Certainly, tithe owners feature prominently among those known to have been active in provisioning fourteenth-century Exeter with grain; rectors also show up as active participants in the grain trade of the London region at the beginning of the same century.[72] This needs to be taken into account when assessing the proportions of gross and net production that were eventually sold. The crops, animals, and animal products that remained to demesnes after deduction of tithe were either retained for consumption on the manor, transferred elsewhere, usually for consumption but sometimes for sale, or sold directly. Sales were made *in grosso* at the farm gate to merchants or their factors, in local markets, or directly at major centres of demand.[73] With most, but not all, agricultural products the accounts provide sufficient information for the amounts sold to be estimated as a proportion of total production.

a) Crops

The task of estimating sales as a proportion of total production is most straightforward in the case of crops, since the volumes disposed of (measured in quarters and bushels) and methods of their disposal are usually specified in the accounts (Table 7.4). Of the gross volume of grain received net of tithe – from harvest, by transfer from elsewhere on the estate, from purchase, and from other sources – a proportion had immediately to be set aside as seed for the following year.[74] That proportion varied according to both the rate at which the crop yielded and the rate at which it was customarily seeded. Roughly a quarter of gross receipts of wheat, rye, winter-mixtures, and barley was consumed as seed, in contrast to 28 per cent of dredge, 36 per cent of oats (the lowest yielding and most heavily seeded crop), and 44 per cent of legumes (a proportion possibly exaggerated by the practice of feeding legumes unthreshed to livestock). Of the crop that remained, between a third and two-thirds was retained on the manor either to be malted (in the case of grains), or consumed as fodder by livestock, food liveries by manorial workers (a useful expedient in a cash-deficient age), or household provisions by the lord and estate officials. Since the individual crops varied considerably both in the purposes to which they

---

[72]Kowaleski (forthcoming); B. M. S. Campbell *et al.* (1993), 74 n.
[73]Galloway and Murphy (1991), 6–7; B. M. S. Campbell *et al.* (1993), 98–9.
[74]Sometimes, as recommended by Walter of Henley, grain for seed was transferred from other manors or bought, but this is included in the gross total of grain receipts: *Walter of Henley*, 175. Very occasionally lords sold the entire standing crop, leaving no option but the purchase of seed for the following year: Biddick with Bijleveld (1991), 121; Farmer (1991a), 367; B. M. S. Campbell *et al.* (1993), 148.

were put and in their market potential (as reflected in their differing capacities to withstand transport costs), the proportions of total receipts net of seed that remained for disposal via transfer or sale differed a good deal from crop to crop (Table 7.4).

Wheat again stands out as the crop least likely to be consumed in quantity on the manor and most likely to be transferred elsewhere or sold, thus confirming its commercial pre-eminence. Except occasionally in the case of the *curallum*, or inferior wheat, it was never used as fodder. At this date it was usually considered too expensive to be fed to manorial workers (whose diet was dominated by the cheaper grains consumed as coarse bread or pottage), and it is rarely recorded as having been malted. When retained on the manor it was therefore almost invariably for consumption by the lord, his household and his officials. On-the-manor consumption of wheat accounted for 31 per cent of total receipts net of tithe and seed, and transfers of wheat, usually to estate headquarters for consumption by the household, accounted for a further 21 per cent. The latter were particularly important on the estates of major conventual landlords – notably Peterborough Abbey, Canterbury Cathedral Priory, Westminster Abbey – whose households regularly consumed substantial quantities of bread grain.[75] It was therefore on manors without resident lords and estates without fixed households that wheat was sold in greatest proportions: 45 of the 202 sampled demesnes sold at least 80 per cent of their wheat and prominent among these are properties of the king, the earls of Cornwall and Lincoln, the bishop of Winchester, the abbot of the alien abbey of Bec, and non-home manors of Canterbury Cathedral Priory.

After wheat, the crop disposed of and sold in greatest proportion was dredge. This, as already noted, was much less widely grown and was very much a minority crop except in parts of Oxfordshire, Bedfordshire, and Northamptonshire, where on some demesnes it eclipsed both oats and barley in importance.[76] Within the London region as a whole, 18 per cent of dredge was retained on the manor, a further 14 per cent was disposed of by transfer, and 39 per cent was sold. The remaining 29 per cent was malted and, since some dredge was almost certainly sold after malting, over half of the total receipt of dredge net of seed may eventually have been marketed (a proportion superior to that of any other crop). Surprisingly, the proportions sold of barley – more widely grown, higher priced, and increasingly preferred for brewing – were significantly lower, as the proportion retained for consumption on the manor was higher. Nor does much barley appear to have been sold after malting; only 49 database manors sold malt and the quantities sold were generally modest. On some demesnes in northern Kent and the lower Thames valley barley was grown in relatively

[75]B. M. S. Campbell *et al.* (1993), 203–6.
[76]B. M. S. Campbell *et al.* (1993), 119–20, 161–2.

Tabel 7.4 Aggregate disposal of crops (net of tithe) by manors in the London region, 1288–1315

Crop	No. of manors	Total receipt[a] (qtrs)	Sown as % of total receipt	Net receipt[b] (qtrs)	Percentage of net receipt:				
					malted	retained	transferred	sold	disposed of[c]
wheat	188	18,134	27	13,328	1	31	21	47	68
rye	99	3,436	23	2,640	0	65	6	28	35
winter mixtures	55	2,116	25	1,596	0	64	1	35	36
barley	156	10,482	24	7,971	21	39	12	27	40
dredge	111	5,366	28	3,866	30	18	14	39	53
oats	189	20,264	36	12,911	2	66	10	21	32
legumes	177	3,902	36	2,506	0	59	8	34	41

[a] net of tithe.
[b] net of tithe and seed.
[c] transferred plus sold.
Source: Feeding the City I, accounts database.

Table 7.5 Aggregate disposal of crops (net of tithe) in monetary value by lord and ownership type, 1288–1315

Lord (by owner-ship type)	No. of manors[a]	Total receipt[b] (£)	Sown as % of total receipt	Net receipt[c] (£)	Percentage of net receipt:				
					malted	retained	transferred	sold	disposed of[d]
Bec Abbey	6	142	19	116	11	54	1	34	35
Bicester Priory	5	26	31	18	1	35	56	8	64
Boxley Abbey	1	5	40	3	13	71	3	12	16
Canterbury Cathedral Priory	33	282	35	183	<1	41	22	37	58
Crowland Abbey	3	36	25	27	34	34	29	4	32
Merton College, Oxford	8	87	28	63	1	60	1	37	38
Oseney Abbey	2	12	35	8	13	44	30	13	43
Peterborough Abbey	18	301	22	234	25	41	34	<1	35
Ramsey Abbey	1	26	24	20	22	47	24	6	30
Titchfield Abbey	1	11	29	8	1	62	11	26	37
Waltham Abbey	1	16	28	11	1	58	33	8	41
Westminster Abbey (abbot)	7	61	35	40	3	69	12	16	28
Westminster Abbey (convent)	20	220	33	148	3	52	25	20	46

Winchester Cathedral Priory	1	11	22	9	0	45	3	52	55
Conventual & collegiate	**107**	**1,236**	**28**	**886**	**10**	**48**	**22**	**20**	**42**
Archbishopric of Canterbury	5	65	32	44	0	57	2	41	43
Bishopric of London	1	8	21	7	0	48	<1	51	52
Bishopric of Winchester	13	118	29	84	0	36	0	64	64
Episcopal	**19**	**192**	**30**	**135**	**0**	**43**	**1**	**56**	**56**
D'Argentine	1	20	27	14	14	67	7	12	19
De Barlee	1	1	54	1	0	90	6	4	10
De Clare	1	16	37	10	0	61	6	33	39
De Cobham	1	36	29	26	7	82	3	7	11
De Fortibus	1	13	24	10	12	23	1	64	65
De Hamelton	1	15	17	12	0	37	0	63	63
Earldom of Cornwall	7	62	32	42	0	41	0	59	59
Earldom of Lincoln	9	68	27	50	1	33	1	65	66
Earldom of Norfolk	4	69	30	48	5	48	3	44	47
Le Ferrers	1	31	12	28	27	28	0	45	45
Lay	**27**	**332**	**27**	**241**	**6**	**46**	**2**	**46**	**48**

Table 7.5 Continued

Lord (by owner-ship type)	No. of manors[a]	Total receipt[b] (£)	Sown as % of total receipt	Net receipt[c] (£)	Percentage of net receipt:				
					malted	retained	transferred	sold	disposed of[d]
King	16	150	36	96	0	42	3	55	58
Late Earldom of Norfolk	1	24	23	18	3	33	4	60	63
Late Holy Trinity Abbey, Caen	1	19	30	13	0	50	0	50	50
Late Knights Templar	15	119	39	73	0	46	1	53	54
Late Walter de Langton	3	35	32	23	0	41	0	59	59
Queen	3	34	40	20	0	47	4	49	53
Royal	39	381	36	244	<1	42	2	55	57
All[a]	190	12,747	28	9,136	7	42	15	36	51

[a] Weston, Herts., is counted both as a possession of the Earldom of Norfolk and of the King; Isleworth, Middx., is counted both as a possession of the Earldom of Cornwall and of the King; Upper Heyford, Oxon., is counted both as a possession of Isabella de Fortibus and of the King.
[b] net of tithe.
[c] net of tithe and seed.
[d] transferred plus sold.
Source: Feeding the City I, accounts database.

substantial quantities and several of these sold a majority of what they produced,[77] but elsewhere in the London region it was generally grown on a relatively small scale. As over half of the barley that remained after deduction of seed was normally retained on the manor, it is difficult to resist the conclusion that it was grown primarily to slake the immediate thirsts of the lord, his household, and his workers.

Production for consumption rather than exchange was even more pronounced in the case of rye, and winter-mixtures, oats, and the various legumes – peas, beans, and vetches – of which at least 60 per cent was generally retained on the manor and 40 per cent or less disposed of by transfer or sale. These crops were all grown as essential adjuncts of the manorial economy; to supply low-grade food liveries to manorial servants, fodder to livestock, and, in the case of legumes, nitrogen to the soil. In aggregate, 35 per cent of winter-mixtures, 34 per cent of legumes, 28 per cent of rye, and 21 per cent of oats were sold, on which criterion these crops rank as the least commercialised under cultivation. There were, of course, some notable exceptions to this, especially in the immediate vicinity of London which required the cheaper bread grains and fodder in exceptionally large quantities, but the inability of either crop to withstand high transport costs restricted most manors that grew and marketed rye and oats in quantity to within a 15-mile radius of that city.[78]

No manor in the London region concentrated on the production of any one of these crops to the exclusion of all others, for monoculture at this date was technologically irreconcilable with anything other than the most extensive cropping systems. On the contrary, the more intensive that husbandry systems became the more necessary it was to produce a mixture of food and fodder crops, to vary rotations through the combination of winter and spring cropping, and to make provision for the restoration of soil nitrogen through the cultivation of legumes.[79] To consider the relative 'commercialisation' of individual crops in isolation from the overall cropping system of which they formed part is therefore artificial. Cropping systems were, of course, partly a function of environmental and institutional factors, but in a commercialised economy the intensity of cultivation and choice of crops produced were also strongly influenced by market demand.[80] The proportion of total net grain and crop production sold is therefore a truer reflection of the relative commercialisation of cropping systems.

[77]B. M. S. Campbell *et al.* (1993), 119–21, 163–4.

[78]B. M. S. Campbell *et al.* (1993), 112–15, 160–1, 164–7.

[79]For the characteristics of the principal farming systems to be found at this date see B. M. S. Campbell and J. P. Power (1989), 24–39; J. P. Power and B. M. S. Campbell (1992), 227–45. For an account of medieval cropping systems at their most intensive and productive see B. M. S. Campbell (1983b).

[80]B. M. S. Campbell (forthcoming).

Total net grain and crop production are most conveniently analysed in monetary terms. This involves valuing the quantities and proportions of crops received and disposed of (including grain processed into malt and subsequently transferred or sold) using mean prices calculated for the London region as a whole. Monetary values are thereby ascribed to the total quantities of grain and crops received, sown, retained, transferred elsewhere on the estate, or sold on each manor.[81] The results are summarised in Table 7.5. Overall, 28 per cent by value of the aggregate gross receipt of crops net of tithe and excluding straw and garden produce was set aside as seed for the following year.[82] Of the crop that then remained, 42 per cent was retained and consumed on the manor and a further 7 per cent was malted. On some manors, particularly the home farms of resident lords, the latter proportion was significantly higher and occasionally, as at Wendover (Bucks.) in 1296–7, the entire crop might be consumed *in situ*, but on no estate was less than a quarter of the crop retained and on a majority of estates this proportion was significantly higher. Presumably this was the minimum proportion compatible with the on-going reproductive requirements of husbandry in the form of fodder for livestock and liveries for servants. The true net crop potentially available for consumption or disposal was therefore only two-thirds to three-quarters that which remained after deduction of seed, equivalent to 47–53 per cent of total receipts net of tithe or 42–7 per cent of total receipts gross of tithe. Tithes, however, should arguably be regarded as part of the disposable crop. On that assumption, 52–7 per cent of the gross output of crops produced by manors in the London region was potentially available for sale, of which at least 38 per cent and perhaps as much as 60 per cent was actually sold.[83] In other words, once the reproductive needs of husbandry had been satisfied, roughly half of the crop that remained was disposed of by sale.

Production for consumption and production for exchange were therefore fairly evenly balanced, that balance being tipped one way or the other by the use made of crops deducted as tithe. Approximately half of the total crop retained for consumption was consumed on the manor by lords, their officials, households, and labourers, and the other half was transferred for consumption elsewhere, the bulk of it at estate headquarters. Practice, however, differed considerably between estates. As will be seen from Table

[81]The method is described in B. M. S. Campbell *et al.* (1993), 145–7. For legumes mean prices have been employed: beans *5.9d*; peas *5.7d*; vetches *5.1d*.

[82]The aggregate value of that crop was £12,747.

[83]This was equivalent to just under a quarter of the crop net of tithes but gross of seed, fodder, and food liveries actually received by lords. On the assumption that two-thirds of all demesne arable was on average cropped each year in the London region, roughly one sown acre in four and one arable acre in six bore crops eventually destined for the market. In contrast, Britnell reckons that in England as a whole 'the share of the total arable acreage devoted to producing marketable demesne crops each year is unlikely to have exceeded 10 per cent': Britnell (1993a), 120.

Measuring commercialisation

7.4, those lords who consumed least and sold most were major magnates like the bishop of Winchester, the earl of Cornwall, and the earl of Lincoln, with far-flung estates, a mobile life-style, and major cash requirements. Conversely, those who consumed most and sold least were conventual lords in general with substantial fixed households to provision plus lords like Reginald d'Argentine, Roger de Barlee, and John de Cobham, who, on those of their manors for which information is available, placed a similarly high priority on management strategies geared towards consumption rather than exchange.

b) Animals

Within the pastoral sector the relative importance of sales as opposed to other forms of disposal or loss was somewhat different, although here a distinction must be drawn between the disposal of live animals and the disposal of their products, partly because of their intrinsically differing natures and partly because the information available for the former is more complete than that for the latter. Moreover, although manorial accounts record gains and losses of livestock during the year with as much precision as they record the receipt and disposal of crops, analysis of this information must first solve a basic problem of units. Losses of animals by death, slaughter, transfer, sale, or other means were selective by species, age, sex, and condition, but to measure the relative importance of these various forms of loss in terms of the raw number of animals involved is obviously misleading, for the sale of a calf is hardly to be equated, for instance, with the slaughter of an ox. The solution lies, as with crops, in measuring losses using a set of weightings based upon the mean sale price within the London region of each particular species and sub-types of animal concerned.[84]

A percentage breakdown of the composition of losses of live animals for the four principal livestock types – *equines, bovines, ovines,* and *porcines* – is given in Table 7.6 for the 173 database manors with usable livestock data (i.e. full details of livestock losses for all four principal livestock types). Among livestock as a whole, *ovines* accounted for 39 per cent of gross losses by value (34 per cent if deaths are discounted), *bovines* for 33 per

[84]These relative livestock weightings are as follows: cart horses, stallions, palfreys and rounceys 1.22; carthorses and horses 0.96; horses 0.72; horses and affers 0.65; stots 0.70; mares 0.60; affers, mill-horses and mules 0.59; three- and four-year-old horses 0.97; two-year-old horses 0.71; yearling and young horses 0.45; oxen 1.15; bulls 1.16; young bulls 0.87; cows 0.80; juvenile bulls 0.76; *bovecti* (male) 0.68; *bovecti* (female) 0.64; *bovecti* (unspecified) 0.66; *juvence* 0.64; *boviculi* (male) 0.60; *boviculi* (female) 0.58; *boviculi* (unspecified) and *bovecti* (two years old) 0.59; *juvencule* 0.58; young cattle 0.48; yearling cattle 0.36; calves 0.11; rams and wethers 0.13; ewes, gimmers and sheep 0.10; lambs 0.07; young rams and hoggets 0.11; adult goats 0.07; goats 0.05; young goats 0.02; boars 0.46; boars and sows 0.36; sows 0.26; pigs 0.25; pigs and hogasters 0.23; hogasters 0.20; piglets 0.10. For the mean sale price of animals in the London region see Murphy and Galloway (1992), 97.

Table 7.6 Aggregate disposal of animals by manors in the London region, 1288–1315

Livestock type	No. of manors disposing of livestock	Total disposal of livestock units[a]	Percentage of livestock disposal (in livestock units) resulting from:					
			death	slaughter	transfer	ad hospicium transfer	sale	other
A) Gross of deaths:								
Equines	156	311	38	0	14	0	43	4
Bovines	169	1,309	15	9	21	3	50	2
Ovines	134	1,538	35	2	20	<1	37	4
Porcines	135	765	13	17	21	7	38	4
All[b]	173	3,924	24	7	20	3	43	3
B) Net of deaths:								
Equines	131	193		0	23	0	70	7
Bovines	164	1,116		10	25	3	59	4
Ovines	127	999		3	31	1	59	5
Porcines	135	666		19	24	8	44	4
All[b]	168	2,974		9	27	3	56	4

[a] Individual sub-types of livestock have been weighted as follows according to mean sale prices in the London region: cart horses, stallions, palfreys and rounceys 1.22; carthorses and horses 0.96; horses 0.72; horses and affers 0.65; stots 0.70; mares 0.60; affers, mill-horses and mules 0.59; three- and four-year-old horses 0.97; two-year-old horses 0.71; yearling and young horses 0.45; oxen 1.15; bulls 1.16; young bulls 0.87; cows 0.80; juvenile bulls 0.76; *bovetti* (male) 0.68; *bovetti* (female) 0.64; *bovetti* (unspecified) 0.66; *juvence* 0.64; *boviculi* (male) 0.60; *boviculi* (female) 0.58; *boviculi* (unspecified) and *bovetti* (two-years-old) 0.59; *juvencule* 0.58; young cattle 0.48; yearling cattle 0.36; calves 0.11; rams and wethers 0.13; young rams and hoggets 0.11; ewes, gimmers and sheep 0.10; lambs 0.07; adult goats 0.07; goats 0.05; young goats 0.02; boars 0.46; boars and sows 0.36; sows 0.26; pigs 0.25; pigs and hogasters 0.23; hogasters 0.20; piglets 0.10.

[b] Including goats.

Source: Feeding the City I, accounts database.

Table 7.7 Aggregate disposal of animals in livestock units by lord and ownership type, 1288–1315

Lord (by ownership type)	No. of manors[a]	Gross disposal of livestock units[b]	Percentage of gross livestock disposal resulting from:						Net disposal of livestock units[b]	Percentage of net livestock disposal resulting from:				
			death	slaughter	transfer	ad hospicium transfer	sale	other		slaughter	transfer	ad hospicium transfer	sale	other
Bec Abbey	3	81	61	7	0	0	32	<1	32	17	0	0	82	1
Bicester Priory	4	34	13	20	26	0	38	3	29	23	30	0	44	3
Boxley Abbey	1	13	40	38	0	0	23	0	8	63	0	0	38	0
Canterbury Cathedral Priory	31	614	28	1	3	16	51	1	441	2	3	22	71	2
Crowland Abbey	3	42	32	6	54	0	7	2	29	8	79	0	10	3
Merton College, Oxford	2	64	55	3	7	0	35	<1	29	6	15	0	79	<1
Oseney Abbey	3	39	37	14	23	0	23	2	25	22	37	0	37	3
Peterborough Abbey	18	563	17	5	61	0	15	2	466	7	74	0	18	2
Ramsey Abbey	1	17	41	12	0	0	43	4	10	20	0	0	73	8
St Catherine's Priory, Rouen	1	21	56	18	15	0	10	1	9	41	35	0	22	2
Titchfield Abbey	1	31	31	22	19	0	25	4	21	32	28	0	35	5
Waltham Abbey	1	12	29	10	27	0	34	0	8	14	38	0	48	0
Westminster Abbey (abbot)	6	172	21	13	33	1	28	4	135	17	42	1	36	5
Westminster Abbey (convent)	20	342	21	3	6	0	64	6	269	4	8	0	81	7
Conventual & collegiate	95	2,044	26	5	24	5	37	2	1,511	7	33	7	50	3

Table 7.7 Continued

Lord (by ownership type)	No. of manors[a]	Gross disposal of livestock units[b]	Percentage of gross livestock disposal resulting from:						Net disposal of livestock units[b]	Percentage of net livestock disposal resulting from:				
			death	slaughter	transfer	ad hospicium transfer	sale	other		slaughter	transfer	ad hospicium transfer	sale	other
Archbishopric of Canterbury	4	64	35	0	9	1	53	1	41	0	14	1	83	2
Bishopric of London	1	26	21	7	37	0	35	0	20	8	47	0	44	0
Bishopric of Winchester	13	309	19	1	3	0	73	5	252	1	4	0	89	6
Episcopal	**18**	**399**	**21**	**1**	**6**	**<1**	**67**	**4**	**313**	**1**	**8**	**<1**	**85**	**5**
D'Argentine	1	41	4	91	0	0	3	2	40	95	0	0	3	2
De Barlee	1	6	58	13	0	0	27	2	2	31	0	0	64	5
De Clare	2	73	14	13	3	0	67	2	63	15	4	0	78	2
De Cobham	1	57	12	55	22	0	9	2	50	62	25	0	10	3
De Fiennes	1	4	71	0	0	0	15	15	1	0	0	0	50	50
De Gray	1	42	18	36	30	0	11	5	35	44	36	0	14	6
De Seyton	1	24	5	2	94	0	0	1	23	0	99	0	0	1
Earldom of Cornwall	7	59	17	<1	24	0	55	3	49	2	29	0	66	3
Earldom of Lincoln	9	122	27	28	18	0	53	3	90	<1	24	0	72	3
Earldom of Norfolk	4	107	20	28	17	0	25	11	86	34	21	0	31	14
Le Ferrers	1	215	15	12	33	0	34	7	182	14	38	0	40	8
Lay	**29**	**750**	**17**	**20**	**23**	**0**	**34**	**5**	**621**	**24**	**28**	**0**	**42**	**6**

King	16	305	24	3	14	0	56	3	231	4	19	0	74	4
Late Earldom of Norfolk	1	40	17	43	3	0	31	5	33	52	4	0	37	6
Late Holy Trinity Abbey, Caen	1	13	29	0	0	0	69	2	9	0	0	0	98	2
Late Knights Templar	16	316	33	0	17	0	44	5	211	0	26	0	66	8
Late Walter de Langton	3	78	18	0	0	0	80	2	64	0	0	0	97	3
Queen	2	31	28	0	37	0	28	7	22	0	52	0	39	9
Royal	**39**	**783**	**27**	**3**	**14**	**0**	**51**	**4**	**570**	**4**	**19**	**0**	**71**	**6**
All[a]	**181**	**3,976**	**24**	**7**	**20**	**2**	**42**	**3**	**3,016**	**10**	**27**	**3**	**56**	**4**

[a] Weston, Herts., is counted both as a possession of the Earldom of Norfolk and of the King; Isleworth, Middx., is counted both as a possession of the Earldom of Cornwall and of the King.

[b] Individual sub-types of livestock have been weighted according to mean sale prices in the London region: cart horses, stallions, palfreys and rounceys 1.22; carthorses and horses 0.96; horses 0.72; horses and affers 0.65; stots 0.70; mares 0.60; affers, mill-horses and mules 0.59; three- and four-year-old horses 0.97; two-year-old horses 0.71; yearling and young horses 0.45; oxen 1.15; bulls 1.16; young bulls 0.87; cows 0.80; juvenile bulls 0.76; *bovecti* (male) 0.68; *bovecti* (female) 0.64; *bovecti* (unspecified) 0.66; *juvence* 0.64; *boviculi* (male) 0.60; *boviculi* (female) 0.60; *bovicali* (unspecified) and *bovecti* (two-years-old) 0.59; *juvencule* 0.58; young cattle 0.48; yearling cattle 0.36; calves 0.11; rams and wethers 0.13; young rams and hoggets 0.11; ewes, gimmers and sheep 0.10; lambs 0.07; boars 0.46; boars and sows 0.36; sows 0.26; pigs 0.25; pigs and hogasters 0.23; hogasters 0.20; piglets 0.10.

Source: Feeding the City I, accounts database.

cent (38 per cent), *porcines* for 19 per cent (22 per cent), and *equines* for 8 per cent (6 per cent). The life-cycle of these different livestock types differed significantly: they matured at different rates, varied in the propensity with which they could be fattened and in the dietary value placed upon their meat, and differed in their susceptibility to disease. Horses were the slowest to mature, were among the costliest and most pampered of farm animals (being the most likely to be housed and fed on grain), and were the only animal not to be eaten. Rather than being fattened up and butchered when they began to outlive their working life as draught animals, manorial horses were evidently either worked until they dropped (38 per cent) or disposed of by transfer (14 per cent) or sale (43 per cent). Although horses were more likely to be purchased than any other type of animal, few manors actually aimed at producing surplus horses for sale; rather, the market was used to trade-in older animals for younger, fitter beasts.[85] Sheep exhibited a similar pattern of disposal, although they matured more quickly and were usually the most extensively managed of all livestock. These extensive methods are reflected in the relatively high proportion of losses from death (35 per cent), in this case due less to decrepitude than to disease and high rates of mortality among lambs and ewes. Nor were many sheep butchered, at least on the manor: only 2 per cent of sheep losses were accounted for by their consumption as meat.[86] The demographic structure of flocks coupled with the importance on many manors of ewes as a dairy animal nevertheless meant that more animals were reproduced than could be maintained (purchase accounted for only a third of all gains); these surplus animals were disposed of by transfer to other manors (31 per cent of net disposal) or sale (59 per cent of net disposal).

Cattle and swine, by contrast, exhibit very different disposal profiles. They were highly valued as meat animals and the aim of successful herd management was plainly to minimise natural losses from death through selective fattening and slaughter. Thus, compared with horses and sheep, fewer cattle and swine died from natural causes and more were butchered. Swine were also the animal most likely to be transferred to the lord's household *ad hospicium domini*.[87] High rates of consumption on the manor and estate meant, however, that, after exclusion of losses from death, fewer swine were sold than any other animal type. On this measure cattle were significantly more commercialised than swine, although no more so than sheep and horses (Table 7.6). The cattle disposed of were primarily old working or sterile dairy stock either fattened or ready for fattening, young calves produced as an adjunct of dairying (sometimes disposed of in

[85]Langdon (1986), 272–3.

[86]For archaeological evidence of social differences in the use of sheep as a meat animal see Grant (1988), 150–5. During the fifteenth century seigneurial flocks were increasingly managed for their meat: Mate (1987).

[87]Above, 141–2.

conjunction with the farm of the dairy and therefore excluded from these figures), and, less commonly, healthy oxen sold for draught. At this date the rearing of cattle for meat *per se* was comparatively unusual. Swine, however, were exclusively reared for their meat, either extensively on pannage and other forms of forage, or intensively, employing the techniques of sty husbandry.[88] They reproduced well, matured relatively quickly, and their flesh could be cured for long-term preservation.[89] They were the only animal for which losses from death were exceeded by losses from slaughter. Most swine herds were clearly managed with the object of producing surplus animals for consumption or sale, but, since fewer animals were acquired by purchase or transfer than any other livestock type, swine were also the animals most exclusively reliant upon on-the-manor reproduction for replacement. Most manors used the market to sell swine rather than to buy them (only 11 per cent of swine were gained by purchase). With cattle the market relationship was more symmetrical: sales accounted for 50 per cent of all losses and purchases for 38 per cent of all gains.

Manors therefore used the market selectively according to the type of livestock, employing it more to buy than to sell in the case of horses and more to sell than to buy in the case of swine. Sale was nevertheless an important means of disposal for all four principal types of livestock and much more consistently so than in the case of crops. Setting aside the 22 per cent of gross losses that resulted from death, sale accounted for 44 per cent of net swine losses, 59 per cent of net sheep losses, 59 per cent of net cattle losses, and 70 per cent of net horse losses. Taking all livestock together, in aggregate 56 per cent of net losses by value occurred from sale compared with 3 per cent from transfers *ad hospicium domini*, 27 per cent from transfers, 9 per cent from slaughter, and 4 per cent from other miscellaneous means. Interestingly, the ratio of sales to transfers at a little over two to one was almost identical to that for crops.

As with crops, the emphasis placed upon different forms of disposal varied from estate to estate (Table 7.7). Overall, excluding losses from death, sales of live animals assumed their greatest relative importance, accounting for at least two-thirds per cent of all losses, on the estates of Bec Abbey, Canterbury Cathedral Priory, Merton College, Oxford, Ramsey Abbey, Westminster Abbey (convent), the archbishopric of Canterbury, and the bishopric of Winchester, plus the two de Clare manors, the estates of the earldom of Cornwall and earldom of Lincoln, and on the former lands of Holy Trinity Abbey, Caen, the knights templar, and Walter de Langton in the king's hands: none of these estates transferred or butchered animals in significant numbers and all but Bec, the de Clare manors, and several of

---

[88]On sty husbandry see Searle (1974), 289–90; Biddick (1985b).

[89]Minimal sales of bacons by manors imply that peasant producers may have been the principal suppliers to the market.

those in the king's hands made above average use of the market to obtain replacement animals.[90] Livestock husbandry on these dozen or so estates stands out as particularly commercialised and although all were substantial estates there appears to have been little attempt to organise pastoral husbandry on an inter-manorial basis; instead, individual manors managed their flocks and herds more or less independently of others belonging to the same estate. This was the opposite of the policy pursued on the estates of Bicester Priory, Crowland Abbey, the abbot of Westminster, and, above all, Peterborough Abbey, which sold relatively few animals but transferred substantial numbers, either to other manors belonging to the same estate or to estate headquarters. Nor were these estates that purchased animals to any significant extent. By integrating livestock husbandry across the estate and transferring and exchanging animals between manors, as described so graphically by Biddick at Peterborough, they were able to circumvent the market.[91] Their scale of livestock husbandry was often considerable but it was relatively uncommercialised. Different again was the livestock husbandry of a third group of estates represented by the manors held by Reginald d'Argentine, John de Cobham, Henry de Gray, and John de Seyton. These all slaughtered a significant proportion of animals, sometimes transferred others to estate headquarters or elsewhere, but sold relatively few. The common denominator of livestock husbandry on this group of manors and estates appears to have been its orientation towards satisfying the consumption requirements of these respective seigneurial households for meat. Dyer has drawn attention to the great dietary reliance of lay households upon meat and this, along with the more peripatetic character of these households, is borne out by the fact that 24 per cent of net livestock losses on lay manors occurred from slaughter in contrast to only 7 per cent on conventual and collegiate manors.[92] Nor did episcopal or royal manors exhibit any greater propensity to slaughter animals. Nevertheless, if these mostly lay estates were not great sellers of animals the smallness of several of them precluded complete isolation from the market and Reginald d'Argentine and John de Cobham stand out as relatively significant purchasers of replacement animals. Most other estates fall somewhere between these three extremes, butchering, transferring, selling and buying animals according to their individual circumstances. Overall, it was manors in episcopal ownership that participated most actively in the market as sellers and buyers of animals, followed by those belonging to the king; lay manors participated least actively as sellers and conventual and collegiate manors least actively as buyers.

[90]Overall, 35 per cent of livestock gains arose from purchase. On the sampled manors of Canterbury Cathedral Priory, the archbishopric of Canterbury, and Ramsey Abbey the corresponding proportions were 38 per cent, 65 per cent, and 21 per cent respectively.
[91]Biddick (1989), 89.
[92]Dyer (1989a), 58–62.

Measuring commercialisation

These calculations make no allowance for the net expansion or depletion of animal stocks through the retention or deduction of livestock, as a result of which the relative importance of sales may be overstated. Nor do they take account of the production and sale of poultry, which were both widely produced and frequently sold but in aggregate cash terms generally realised only comparatively small sums, amounting in aggregate to 2 per cent of all sales income from animals and animal products. Omitted, too, are animals deducted as tithe and subsequently sold. The 56 per cent of net losses accounted for by sale is therefore a minimum figure (Table 7.6). By comparison, only 42–7 per cent of crops (net of tithe and on-the-farm requirements of seed, fodder and food liveries) were sold. By this measure, sale was a more important method of disposal for animals than it was for crops. It was, however, as a method of disposing of animal products – dairy produce, eggs, skins and hides, wool and meat – that sale appears to have assumed its greatest relative importance.

c) Animal products

Manorial accounts are much more sparing in the amount of information they give concerning the production and disposal of animal products. Income from produce sold is, of course, unfailingly recorded, and usually accompanied by a statement of the quantities involved (although the variety of methods and measures by which this is recorded tends to defy analysis), but corresponding information on the quantities of the same product disposed of in other ways is much less consistently given. Here, consequently, there is not just a problem of establishing the unit value of a product, when that was subject to significant variations in size, weight, and quality, but more seriously a problem of establishing the total volume of production.

The difficulties involved in costing wool transferred for sale at estate headquarters have already been referred to, and yet wool is generally accounted for in greater detail than most other animal products, with the total quantities produced, transferred, and sold recorded in some form or other. In aggregate the database demesnes sold wool and fleeces worth £355. In addition wool worth an estimated £61 was transferred either to estate headquarters or some other central depot usually pending sale in bulk. Not all of this wool would necessarily have been sold immediately and the proceeds of the sale would rarely have been enjoyed in any direct way by the manor or manors that produced the wool. It was also undoubtedly the case that a proportion, presumably small, of all wool transfers went to satisfy a genuine household demand for wool since some households manufactured their own cloth; hence to assume that *all* wool transfers were *de facto* sales is marginally to overstate the case.[93] Finally, a small proportion

---

[93]Dyer (1989a), 68.

of wool remained or was retained on the manor, either to satisfy the manor's own subsistence needs or to be carried over to the following year and sold or transferred on a later occasion. In aggregate 14 per cent of wool by quantity, less by value, was retained in this way. Total wool receipts thus amounted to approximately £475 by value, of which three-quarters was sold directly and an eighth transferred mostly to be sold subsequently: on these calculations, at least 80 and probably nearer 90 per cent of all wool was sold.

If the proportion of a product that was sold is taken as a measure of its 'commercialisation', wool was clearly one of the most commercialised of all agricultural products, but skins and hides were equally so. Skins and hides were inevitable by-products of animal husbandry and the numbers produced a simple function of the numbers of stock that died or were slaughtered. Hide production was not, therefore, something in which manors normally specialised, for all that leather manufacture was probably the country's second most important industry after textiles.[94] Curing and tanning were skilled and time-consuming tasks, hence skins and hides were invariably sold by rural producers in their raw unprocessed state. Prices recorded in the accounts show that hides, especially of the larger animals, were of some value and hence not something that a scrupulous auditor would allow a reeve to overlook.[95] In aggregate, however, skins and hides contributed only £49 to gross agricultural sales income, less than 1 per cent of the total. The smallness of this sum and proportion reflects the low rate at which skins and hides were produced by the database demesnes, since the number and type of carcasses that could be flayed was determined by the numbers of dead and slaughtered sheep, cattle, and horses. On average just over three-dozen skins and three hides were produced per manor per year. Valuing these skins and hides using mean prices calculated from those accounts where unit prices are recorded suggests an aggregate value of approximately £60. On this estimate over 80 per cent of available skins and hides were sold.

With dairy produce the problem of estimating and valuing total production is even greater since few accounts record the total numbers of cheeses and butters produced, as opposed merely to those that were sold, and fewer still provide sufficient information for the weights and values of both to be calculated;[96] much therefore hinges on the assumed milk yield of cows and ewes, relevant conversion rates to butter and cheese, and the effect of flavour and quality on the value of the latter. Although something is known about each of these elements, this is a minefield of uncertainty and

[94]Kowaleski (1990). Some estate complexes did, however, include tanneries: Searle (1974), 299–303.

[95]The mean price for the hide of an affer was 9.3*d*, for a stot 14.8*d*, for a cow 19.1*d*, and for an ox 40.4*d*. Sheep skins were generally worth ^{1}/$_2$*d* to 1*d* each.

[96]Biddick with Bijleveld (1991), 116–18.

the margins of error for any estimate thereby derived are inevitably wide.[97] A simpler approach is to estimate the income that cows and ewes would have generated if they had been let at farm. The leasing of demesne dairies was to become commonplace during the fourteenth century and was already the practice on many database demesnes at the beginning of the century. Indeed, aggregate income from the farm of dairies exceeded that obtained from the sale of dairy produce by almost 50 per cent. Ewes were generally farmed for their milk alone (at $1\frac{1}{2}d$ to $2\frac{1}{2}d$ per ewe and a mean rate of $2d$), whereas cows were farmed either for their milk alone (at 3s 0d to 4s 6d per cow and a mean rate of 4s 0d) or their milk and the calves that they produced (at 4s 6d to 5s 6d per cow and a mean rate of 5s $1\frac{1}{2}d$).[98] Immature cows just coming into milk were farmed at a correspondingly lower rate. The database demesnes stocked in aggregate an estimated 2,500 cows of varying degrees of maturity and 11,130 ewes which, if farmed for their lactage alone, would have yielded approximately £576. In fact, sales of dairy produce generated a total of £130 and the farm of cows and ewes a further £192. The latter figure, however, needs to be adjusted to correct for the value of the calves (approximately £29) included in combined farms of both milk and calves. The total income from the sale of dairy produce and farm of lactage was therefore approximately £293, equivalent to 51 per cent of the estimated income that would have been generated had the lactage of all cows and ewes been sold. Directly or indirectly, therefore, approximately half of total milk output was sold.[99] Of the other half, some was consumed by lords and their households on the manor or elsewhere, but the greater part was undoubtedly retained as an on-the-farm source of food liveries for manorial workers, within whose diets at this time cheese comprised a vital element.[100]

Together, sales of wool, hides, and dairy produce on the 201 database demesnes raised £757 (excluding the farm of calves). Sales of eggs (both produced on the demesne and received in rent), meat, carcasses, tallow, and dung together added another £20. The contributions of all other animal products were trifling and can safely be ignored. Had all available animal products been sold and nothing retained for consumption on the manor or estate the sum raised would have been approximately £1,130. Directly or indirectly, an estimated 70 per cent by value of all animal products was therefore disposed of on the market, a proportion that identifies this as by far the most commercialised branch of seigneurial agriculture.

[97]For some courageous estimates of animal output *c.* 1300 see G. Clark (1991), 214–17. For contemporary expectations of output see *Walter of Henley*, 179–82, 208–10.

[98]The difference of $13\frac{1}{2}d$ between the rates at which cows were farmed for their lactage alone and their lactage and calves corresponds to the mean sale price of a calf.

[99]Cf. B. M. S. Campbell (1992); Biddick with Bijleveld (1991), 115–19.

[100]Dyer (1988); Dyer (1989a), 63–4, 154–9.

Taking animals and animal products as a whole, sales of live animals yielded £669, the farm of calves approximately £29, sales of animal products £778, and sales of animal and animal products combined £18, giving a total income from the sale of animals and animal products (fish and game omitted) of £1,494. This may be compared with an estimated gross value of all animals and animal products potentially available for disposal of £2,360, made up of £1,200 from live animals, £29 from the farm of calves, and £1,130 from animal products. On these figures, almost two-thirds of the total output of animals and animal products was disposed of by sale. This, however, fails to take account of new-born animals and animal products deducted as tithe. Depending upon how systematically the latter were deducted and the extent to which they were subsequently sold by the tithe owner the final proportion of seigneurial livestock production gross of tithe that was eventually sold may have been slightly higher or lower.

d) All agricultural products

Together, the total receipts of crops, crop products, animals, and animal products were worth in aggregate approximately £15,100 net of tithe (84 per cent contributed by crops and 16 per cent by animals and animal products).[101] By comparison, the total revenue from the sale of all crops, crop products, animals, and animal products was £4,219, equivalent in value to just over a quarter of total receipts; deducting the value of seed from total receipts raises the proportion sold to over a third and deduction of fodder raises it still further to at least 40 per cent. Plainly, in estimating sales as a proportion of *net* seigneurial agricultural production, much hinges upon the definition of net product. If it is rigorously defined so as to exclude seed, fodder, and food liveries to manorial servants, then at least half of net manorial production may ultimately have been destined for the market; depending upon the use made of that 10 per cent of gross production deducted as tithe, the net proportion sold may have been even higher.

These aggregate figures obviously mask wide differences between individual manors and estates. In part these differences stem from the varying balance struck between arable and pastoral production with their differing degrees of commercialisation, but they also reflect genuine differences in market participation. At one extreme stood estates such as that of Peterborough Abbey which, as Biddick correctly diagnoses, 'strove to conserve the "costless" consumption of estate-produced subsistence goods' and

---

[101]Cf. G. Clark (1991), 234, who estimates that 'arable crops accounted for 80 per cent by value of total food output *c*. 1300, with a mere 20 per cent contributed by meat and dairy products'.

Measuring commercialisation

participated in the market only selectively.[102] Notwithstanding that the abbey's manors were concentrated in an area strongly penetrated by commercial influences, only a fraction of these manors' total production eventually entered the market. Production on the sampled portions of the estates of Bicester Priory and Crowland Abbey seems to have been similarly geared towards consumption rather than exchange.[103] At the other extreme, the far-flung manors of the king, the earls of Cornwall and Lincoln, and the bishop of Winchester, together with the non-home manors of Canterbury Cathedral Priory, all generally sold the greater part of what they produced.[104] The problem is that the latter highly commercialised manors are disproportionately represented within the sample of manorial accounts (Table 7.1). Whereas 23 per cent of sampled manors were in royal, comital, or episcopal ownership, nationally such estates accounted for only approximately 15 per cent of total landed income. In this context, considerable interest attaches to the handful of sampled manors that belonged to lay lords of baronial rank or below. Accounts for such manors are hard to find at this date, often survive in isolation, and rarely provide a comprehensive picture of the estate as a whole.[105] There is a very real danger, therefore, of generalising from a body of evidence that is itself small and unrepresentative. For what it is worth, however, that evidence indicates the continuing primacy of householding as a management objective on this class of estate. There is, of course, the possibility that were more evidence available for the non-home manors of lesser lay lords the picture that emerges might be rather different,[106] but on the currently available evidence, given that the estates of barons, knights, and the lesser lay gentry accounted for approximately 60 per cent of total landed income as compared with only 7 per cent of sampled manors, it is difficult to resist the conclusion that the true proportion of seigneurial agricultural production disposed of on the market was less than that indicated by the unweighted aggregate given above. Around the year 1300, lords in the London region sold perhaps nearer a quarter than a third of the agricultural output that remained to them after deduction of tithe and probably at most a half of

---

[102]Biddick (1989), 133.

[103]In 1258–9 the 14 demesnes of Crowland Abbey sold none of their wheat and legumes, virtually none of their oats, and only 2 per cent of their rye and maslin (mixed winter grain, usually wheat and rye), and their barley and dredge: Britnell (1993a), 121.

[104]In 1296–7 the eleven demesnes of the earl of Cornwall sold 73 per cent of their wheat, 17 per cent of their rye and maslin, 56 per cent of their barley and dredge, 41 per cent of their oats, and 68 per cent of their legumes: Britnell (1993a), 121. The estate of the bishop of Winchester comprised over 30 manors scattered through southern England, but with a concentration in Hampshire and immediately adjacent counties: Titow (1972), and Figure 6.1 above, 103.

[105]Britnell (1980b); Livingstone (1991). For an early account of a minor, lay, single-manor estate see B. M. S. Campbell (1986).

[106]Note Livingstone's speculations on the probably distinctive character of management policies on John Pulteney's home manor of Penshurst, Kent: Livingstone (1991), 33.

what remained after provision had been made for seed, fodder, and food liveries.

How would sales of hay, wood, and other related products affect this picture? In aggregate, sales of these products certainly made a modest contribution to income (10 per cent of the total), and on some manors they were the major money spinner, but to attempt to estimate the importance of sales as a proportion of total output of hay and wood is to venture onto ice that is increasingly thin. It is clear from an examination of those manors which made substantial sums from the sale of these products that their commercial potential was strongly circumscribed by distance from market, since these were among the bulkiest of agricultural products. If an analogy is drawn with oats, another bulky agricultural product widely consumed but expensive to transport over more than comparatively short distances, hay and wood are likely to have been among the least commercialised agricultural products, with the bulk of production destined for on-the-manor and on-the-estate consumption.[107] Only in the immediate hinterlands of Oxford and London, both of which would have required hay and wood in substantial quantities, does the picture appear to have been significantly different.[108] Overall, therefore, taking account of these residual agricultural products would tend marginally to depress the estimated proportion of seigneurial agricultural production that was disposed of by sale.

3) *Rates of sale per unit cropped and animal stocked*

Estimates of the proportions sold of different agricultural products may be instructive, but they are a by no means unambiguous index of commercialisation. The source of this ambiguity is the distinction which in principle it is necessary, but in practice difficult, to draw between sales as a proportion of gross and as a proportion of net production. In the modern highly commercialised age of post-organic agricultural technology farmers are able to obtain most of their inputs and dispose of virtually all of their output on the market and net and gross production are effectively the same. But in the Middle Ages, and for long afterwards, the relevant commodity and factor markets – in seed, fertiliser, capital, and labour – were imperfectly developed, cash was scarce and credit dear, and most farming systems had to be biologically self-sustaining. Maintaining the reproductive capacity of agriculture therefore consumed a significant proportion of output: animals supplied replacement stock together with traction and manure to the arable, the arable produced seed and provided fodder and pasturage for the animals, and both served as a source of food for workers. The more intensive

---

[107]Farmer (above), 108–10, 119.
[108]See note 78 above.

Measuring commercialisation

and productive that these mixed farming systems became, the greater was the volume of seed, fodder, traction, and labour required to sustain them, with all that this implies for the proportion of gross production absorbed by on-the-farm consumption.

In effect, by responding to commercial opportunity and intensifying their production, farmers raised the rate at which they were able to sell produce per unit area. J. H. von Thünen was aware of this tendency and it is an implicit feature of his well-known land-use model, with its pattern of farming systems and land-use zones of decreasing intensity and productivity with distance from a central market.[109] In only one of these farming systems, that closest to the central city, were off-the-farm inputs, in the form or purchases of urban manure, a major factor in the maintenance of productivity. This was because it was only closest to the city that economic rent was high enough to justify the expense involved.[110] At a greater distance all the farming systems that he describes were of necessity largely self-sustaining. Paradoxically, therefore, as distance from the market rose and the intensity of husbandry fell, so on-the-farm requirements of seed, fodder and food for workers should have diminished and the proportion of gross output available for sale may actually have risen. For this reason the *rate of sale* per unit area is a better guide to the commercialisation of agriculture than the *proportion* of total production sold.

Unfortunately, manorial accounts do not record the areas farmed with the same exhaustive detail with which they record cash receipts and expenditure. Details of the total arable area are rarely, and of the total farmed area never, stated; even details of the cropped area are sometimes lacking, although this can usually be rectified by interpolation from the recorded amounts of seed sown. For a few individual demesnes ancillary manorial sources can be used to establish the full extent of the arable, sown and unsown, and the quantities of other land-uses, but this is a time-consuming task and would fail to yield information for more than a fraction of the sample of manors with accounts. What may, however, be calculated simply and systematically for the bulk of manors with accounts is the gross income from crop sales per cropped acre and gross income from sales of animals and animal products per livestock unit. This at least provides some indication of the rate at which manors and localities used their cropped acreage and flocks and herds to generate gross sales revenues. What it does not, of course, take into account is the production costs involved, which could vary considerably with land quality, husbandry system, form of labour, and

---

[109]Von Thünen (1966); Chisholm (1962), 20–32; Grigg (1982), 135–40.

[110]At the end of the thirteenth century several demesnes in the immediate vicinity of Norwich made intensive use of manure and refuse from that city: B. M. S. Campbell (1983b), 34. However, a sharp distance-decay effect can be observed with transport costs from the city, and beyond a distance of five miles use of this important external source of fertiliser appears to have ceased.

choice of technology. High gross sales revenues per sown acre and per livestock unit should not therefore be mistaken for high profits per acre and per animal, although it may well be that there was often a close association between the two.

On average, manors in the London region realised £6 18s 10d per 100 cropped acres from the sale of crops, but rates on individual manors ranged from nothing to over £30 0s 0d. Plainly, on this criterion the extent to which crop production was commercialised was subject to wide variation. Underpinning these variations were the contrasting management objectives of different estates, differences in crop output per unit area, differences in the intensity of husbandry systems, differences in commercial opportunities, and differences in the unit price at which crops were sold.[111]

Fifty-seven manors sold crops at a rate of £2 10s 0d per 100 cropped acres or less. They occurred throughout the region irrespective of the intensity and productivity of husbandry, of the price of grain, or the strength of the commercial nexus and were predominantly those manors most actively engaged in the direct provisioning of seigneurial households (Figure 7.1). Included in this group are all 18 of the Peterborough Abbey manors, twelve of the Westminster Abbey manors (concentrated in Middlesex, Surrey, and Hertfordshire), two of the abbot of Westminster's, Canterbury Cathedral Priory's three home manors of Chartham, Ickham, and Eastry in east Kent, two low-yielding Bec manors, one Crowland Abbey manor and two of Bicester Priory, the royal manor of Sheen in Surrey, and the home manors of Oseney Abbey, Boxley Abbey, Reginald d'Argentine, Roger de Barlee, John de Seyton, and William de Fiennes. At the opposite extreme, 24 manors sold crops at a rate of £15 0s 0d or more per 100 cropped acres. Prominent among these are properties of the bishop of Winchester (seven manors), the crown (five manors), Canterbury Cathedral Priory (three manors), the earl of Lincoln (seven manors), the earl of Norfolk (one manor), and Merton College, Oxford (one manor); all of them either large and/or scattered estates noted in whole or in part for their strong market orientation. Nevertheless, the presence in both the lowest- and the highest-selling groups of manors belonging to the crown and to Canterbury Cathedral Priory highlights the contrasting commercial profiles that sometimes co-existed on the same estate according to a manor's location within that estate's production system.

Perhaps the most striking feature of the group of high-selling manors is, however, their distribution. They are largely absent from those parts of the region – Middlesex, Hertfordshire, Buckinghamshire, most of Surrey and much of Essex – on the face of it strategically best positioned to profit from

[111]For variations in wheat prices within the London region see B. M. S. Campbell *et al.* (1993), 63–9.

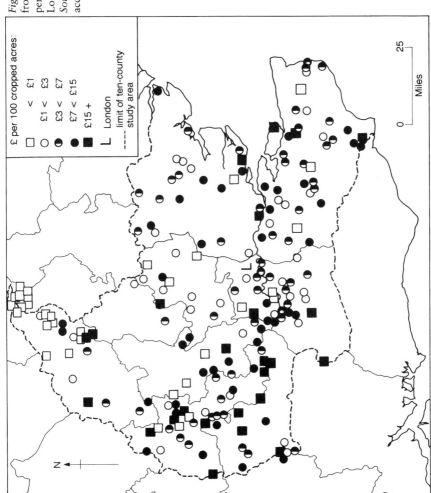

Figure 7.1 Gross income from the sale of field crops per 100 cropped acres in the London region, 1288–1315
Source: Feeding the City I, accounts database.

provisioning London (Figure 7.1). This is partly a figment of the pattern of account survival, but it is also a genuine reflection of relatively low yield levels prevailing within these counties and of the greater commercial importance attached in some parts of them to hay, wood, and livestock. It was also the case that London relied much more for its grain supplies upon areas that could provision it by water, especially those to which it was linked by the Thames, than upon those which were dependent upon transportation by road.[112] The key importance of the Thames must undoubtedly account in part for the concentration of nine high-selling manors upstream of the city and the presence of three others on the Kent and Essex shores at the mouth of the estuary, where the influence of overseas demand may also have been a factor. Within the former area Billingbear, Brightwell, Waltham St Lawrence, and Wargrave in Berkshire, Whitchurch in Oxfordshire, and Holmer in Buckinghamshire were all conveniently located relative to that part of the Thames served by the busy grain entrepot of Henley and known to have been one of the main sources of grain for London.[113] Harwell, also in Berkshire, lay at, or possibly just beyond, the limits of this zone of regular metropolitan supply and may have been as or more actively engaged in provisioning Oxford, the second largest urban concentration within the ten counties under consideration. Proximity to Oxford must certainly have helped to sustain the high rate of sale maintained by the Merton College manor of Holywell and the earl of Lincoln's manor of Middleton Stoney, both in Oxfordshire. A further feature of this western group of manors is that they tended to combine moderate yields per acre with two-course (Brightwell and Harwell) systems of cropping in which wheat – the most highly priced and commercialised of all crops – featured prominently.[114] Their rates of sale would therefore be much less impressive if calculated per arable acre rather than per cropped acre.[115] In contrast, many manors downstream of London employed more intensive rotational systems that featured a wider range of crops and catered for larger on-the-farm requirements of seed and fodder. Rates of sale calculated per 100 cropped acres fail to do these manors justice with the result that only Eastwood in Essex and Cliffe, Leysdown, and Ospringe in Kent stand out as highly commercialised, along with Appledore and Fairfield on the opposite side of the county, which appear to have taken advantage of the similar trading opportunities afforded by their proximity to the Channel ports. Analysing crop sales in terms of the gross revenue raised per 100 acres cropped therefore identifies two areas where crop

[112]B. M. S. Campbell et al. (1993), 46–77, 158–60, 172–5.

[113]B. M. S. Campbell et al. (1993), 47–9, 174–5.

[114]B. M. S. Campbell et al. (1993), 123–44; Titow (1962), 17–18; Biddick with Bijleveld (1991), 119; P. D. A. Harvey (1965), 39–46, 164–5.

[115]For an analysis of how frequency of fallowing affected rates of output per arable acre see Thornton (1991), 191–3.

Measuring commercialisation

production appears to have been particularly highly commercialised and hints at others on the edge of the study area that may have shared similar characteristics.[116] It also highlights a belt of country extending inland to the north and south of London with below average rates of sale by the standards of the region as a whole. As a true reflection of the pattern of commercialisation, however, this picture suffers from the distortions that arise from comparing cropping systems that fallowed land with different frequencies.[117]

Expressing the income received from the sale of animals and animal products per 100 livestock units at the start/end of the accounting year is subject to fewer spatial distortions.[118] By this measure well-stocked manors that sold animals and animal products at the highest rate – such as Weston, Hertfordshire, Sheen, Surrey, and Ebury, Middlesex – raised £18 0s 0d to £19 0s 0d per 100 livestock units. At the opposite extreme, as with crops, there were some manors that effectively sold no animals or animal products at all. Across all sampled manors within the London region the average sum received was £6 17s 3d per 100 livestock units.

At the bottom end of the sales spectrum, many of the estates whose cropping was most strongly orientated towards household consumption were similarly uncommercialised in their pastoral husbandry. Among manors which sold animals and animal products at a rate of less than £3 0s 0d per 100 livestock units were ten of the Northamptonshire manors of Peterborough Abbey, the three Northamptonshire manors of Crowland Abbey, two manors of the abbot of Westminster, two Oxfordshire manors of Oseney Abbey, the d'Argentine manor of Wymondley in Hertfordshire, and the home manors of John de Cobham and John de Seyton. In many cases, too, pastoral husbandry was relatively uncommercialised because it yielded little that could be sold. Many of the manors that received least from the sale of animals and animal products were those which carried fewest stock, often only the draught animals essential to the cultivation of the arable. Several manors under royal control fall into this category, as does the earl of Cornwall's manor of Watlington in Oxfordshire. But there are some conspicuous exceptions to this rule. The Peterborough Abbey home manor of Boroughbury in Northamptonshire and abbot of Westminster's manor of Islip in Oxfordshire both stocked over 100 units of livestock but sold little of the surplus animals and animal products that these yielded since most of what they produced was destined

---

[116]The most important non-metropolitan commercial foci were probably the Wash and Channel ports. An extensive system of navigable rivers allowed the former to penetrate deep into East Anglia and the east midlands: Langdon (1993), 1–11.

[117]For a discussion of differences in the intensity of cropping within the region see B. M. S. Campbell *et al.* (1993), 128–44.

[118]The livestock units are based on the mean purchase and sale price of each livestock type.

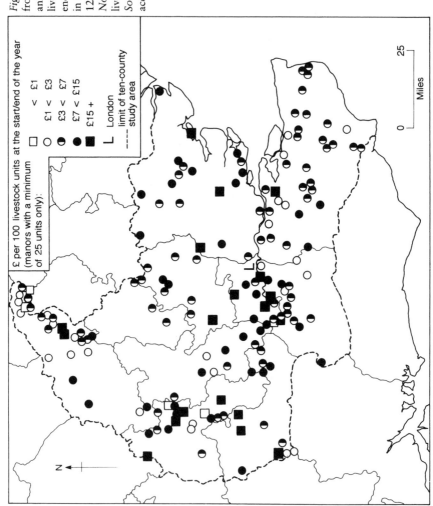

Figure 7.2 Gross income from the sale of animals and animal products per 100 livestock units at the start/end of the accounting year in the London region, 1288–1315

Note: for the caluclation of livestock units see note 84.

Source: Feeding the City I, accounts database.

Measuring commercialisation

for the household.[119] The rate of sale of pastoral products therefore tended to be low wherever there was a substantial seigneurial household to be fed, or where a lack of investment in animals or deficiency of pastoral resources restricted the numbers and types of animals that could be supported.

Among home manors ideally placed to provision seigneurial households the abbot of Westminster's Middlesex manors of Ebury, Laleham, and Yeoveney were almost alone in displaying a high rate of sale. They shared this feature with the properties of other large, far-flung, and relatively commercialised estates. Other moderately well-stocked manors that raised at least £8 0s 0d per 100 livestock units included four belonging to Westminster Abbey, three belonging to the bishopric of Winchester, three each of the earldoms of Cornwall and Norfolk, and six in royal hands. This illustrates the strong influence of institutional factors upon the commercialisation of the pastoral sector. Manors well-supplied with permanent grassland also possessed the potential to develop relatively commercialised pastoral husbandry. This appears to have been particularly the case with a group of manors – Adderbury, Bicester, Launton, Merton, Sibford Gower, and Upper Heyford, plus Turweston, Buckinghamshire – in the wold country of north Oxfordshire.[120] The prospects for commercialised pastoral farming were particularly good where favourable environmental opportunities were reinforced by strong urban demand.[121] Thus, several manors in the lower reaches of the Thames valley display highly commercialised pastoral regimes:[122] Ebury, Laleham, and Yeoveney in Middlesex and Battersea and Pyrford in Surrey belonging to Westminster Abbey, Acton and Colham in Middlesex belonging respectively to the bishop of London and earl of Lincoln, and the king's manors of Temple Bulstrode and Langley Marish with Wraysbury in Buckinghamshire and Sheen in Surrey. The commercial lure of the metropolis is also, probably, to be seen in the concentration of high-selling manors in Essex, the latter cutting across estates belonging to Westminster Abbey, Canterbury Cathedral Priory, the crown (formerly the knights templar), and the earl of Norfolk.[123] On this evidence, highly commercialised pastoral husbandry was characteristic of a significantly wider area than highly commercialised arable husbandry. Moreover, in several parts of the region the greater commercialisation

---

[119]On Boroughbury see Biddick (1989), 69, 82–4. Islip was used as a staging post between the western and eastern properties of Westminster Abbey; thirteenth-century abbots frequently stayed there and early the following century abbot William de Curtlington (1315–33) rebuilt the manor house there: B. F. Harvey (1977), 133.

[120]Extents contained in *inquisitiones post mortem* reveal parts of this area to have been relatively well-endowed with grassland: B. M. S. Campbell *et al.* (1992), 17–19.

[121]Cf. B. M. S. Campbell (1992).

[122]Murphy and Galloway (1992), 98–9.

[123]B. M. S. Campbell (1988b), 95–7.

of animals seems to have compensated in part for the lesser commercialisation of crops. This was particularly the case in the counties closest to
London.

Seventeen manors sold both crops and animals and animal products
at minimal rates (crops at less than £2 10s 0d per 100 cropped acres;
animals and animal products at less than £3 0s 0d per 100 livestock units)
and hence stand out as the least commercialised manors of all. They
include ten of the Northamptonshire manors of Peterborough Abbey,
one Northamptonshire manor of Crowland Abbey, and John de Seyton's
Northamptonshire manor of Maidwell, two Oxfordshire manors of
Oseney Abbey, the Titchfield Abbey manor of Inkpen in south Berkshire,
and the d'Argentine manor of Wymondley in Hertfordshire. Most of these
manors were at some remove from the commercial magnet of London
and 12 of the 17 were concentrated in Northamptonshire, the county
among the ten under study remotest from that city. Significantly, the
conventual houses evidently most strongly committed to a policy of
economic autarky – the abbeys of Peterborough, Crowland, and Oseney –
were similarly located at a considerable distance from that city and its
commercialising influence.[124]

Fifteen manors sold both crops and animals and animal products at a
high rate, the former at £12 10s 0d or more per 100 cropped acres, the
latter at £7 10s 0d or more per 100 livestock units (Figures 7.1 and 7.2).
All were properties of the largest and most commercialised estates and
comprised seven manors of the bishopric of Winchester, seven of the
earldom of Lincoln, one of the earldom of Norfolk, and one in royal hands.
Since the list includes the north-Oxfordshire manor of Adderbury and
the Northamptonshire manors of Long Buckby and Rushden it is apparent
that high rates of commercialisation were not necessarily precluded by
distance from London. Nevertheless, since at least six of these highly
commercialised manors enjoyed direct access to the London market, proximity to the metropolis was plainly an advantage. Significantly, these
manors lay upstream rather than downstream of the city in areas of extensive rather than intensive husbandry, where the pastoral sector was less
subservient to the arable.[125] In location they bear out von Thünen's
observation that the combination of commercialised arable and pastoral
husbandry was generally only found at some distance from a central
market, beyond the areas of highest economic rent and most intensive
husbandry. In the late thirteenth and early fourteenth centuries the areas
of highest economic rent lay downstream rather than upstream of London
and reflected the triple influences of local, metropolitan, and overseas

[124]Although St Paul's Cathedral, in the heart of the capital, long retained a reliance upon
food farms for its provisions: B. M. S. Campbell et al. (1993), 203–4.
[125]B. M. S. Campbell et al. (1993), 6.

Measuring commercialisation

demand. They are, however, partially masked from view by the dominance of the Kentish evidence by conventual estates. Twenty-seven of the 41 documented Kentish manors belonged to Canterbury Cathedral Priory (of the remainder, one belonged to Westminster Abbey, five to the arch-bishop of Canterbury, seven to the crown, and one to John de Cobham); like other conventual manors, their involvement in the market was selective and hence provides an imperfect guide to general levels and patterns of commercialisation.

Implications and conclusions

Within an agricultural context, commercialisation – the propensity with which agricultural goods were produced for sale – can be measured in a variety of ways. The ideal is either to measure the value of production sold as a proportion of total agricultural output inclusive of tithe but net of seed, fodder, and liveries to workers, or to calculate the income from agricultural sales (again, inclusive of tithes) per unit area of farmland. Unfortunately, these measures make demands on the available historical evidence that it is incapable of meeting. Instead, reliance has to be placed upon a variety of partial measures of commercialisation. These include the frequency with which individual products were sold and the proportions of gross sales income thereby generated; sales of crops, animals, and animal products as proportions of the respective totals produced (defined and measured in a variety of ways); and rates of sale per cropped acre and per livestock unit. None does adequate justice to agricultural production as a whole, although collectively they encapsulate most of its components; moreover, some are subject to distortion, especially rates calculated per unit area cropped rather than per unit area farmed, for these exaggerate rates of sale where fallowing was frequent and pasture was extensive. The intrinsic incompleteness or ambiguity of these measures is compounded by the spatial and institutional bias of extant sources; consequently, while much may be learnt about individual regions or localities, a balanced picture of both the seigneurial sector and the London region as a whole is unattainable. For some parts of the London region no accounts of the right date are extant at all. For others, evidence comes almost exclusively from a single estate which, if broadly representative of patterns of production, is unlikely to be equally representative of patterns of disposal. For the region as a whole certain types of estate are consistently under-represented: small lay estates in particular are badly served by accounts, which rarely survive in number and even more rarely document more than one manor on an estate. A lack of information on the use made of that 10 per cent of gross production 'top-sliced' as tithe is a further serious lacuna. Tithe owners were potentially important suppliers to the market and sys-tematic investigation of such evidence as relates to their activities is long overdue.[126] Some caution is therefore necessary in generalising from that sample of manors and estates represented by surviving sources, and even greater caution in extrapolating, on the basis of that evidence, from the London region to the country as a whole.

At the end of the thirteenth century it is plain that the basic consumption needs of seigneurial households still had first claim upon demesne production on many estates. A major conventual household such as Peterborough Abbey consumed almost exclusively produce supplied from its own estates.[127] Other conventual households augmented estate produce with market purchases and towards the end of the thirteenth century there are signs that some households, such as Canterbury Cathedral Priory and Westminster Abbey, were relaxing their dependence upon their estates and increasing their reliance upon the market. Nevertheless, even when, as at Canterbury and Westminster, households had convenient access to substantial and well-established markets they still tended to draw upon their estates for a substantial part of their needs. Canterbury Cathedral Priory purchased large quantities of grain in Canterbury market but drew even greater quantities from its intensively cultivated home manors in east Kent.[128] Westminster Abbey bought the majority of its brewing and fodder grains (presumably at Westminster or in one of the London markets) but obtained the greater part of its bread grain from its estates, with manors as far away as Ashwell in north-east Hertfordshire sending wheat over forty miles to the abbey.[129] Similarly, Oseney Abbey outside Oxford consumed much of the produce of its demesnes at Forest Hill, Kidlington and Little Tew. Most conservative and remarkable of all, the dean and chapter of St Paul's Cathedral in the heart of London continued to rely upon an old-established system of food farms for the bulk of their provisions and made only limited use of the major food market at their front doorstep.[130]

Lay lords with resident households to support appear to have acted no differently from their conventual counterparts and consumed their own produce in preference to purchasing provisions on the market. In the early 1240s when Robert Grosseteste, bishop of Lincoln, advised the countess of Lincoln on the management of her lands and household it was his clear expectation that she would draw upon her manors for her basic provisions.[131] By the end of the same century many lords were continuing to act

---

[126]Farmer (1991a), 376; Britnell (1993a), 122–3. The sources available for a study of tithes and tithe owners include some surviving tithe accounts as well as records of ecclesiastical taxation. For the latter, see, in particular, *Taxatio Ecclesiastica* and *Nonarum Inquisitiones*.

[127]Biddick (1989), 72–7, 132; B. M. S. Campbell *et al.* (1993), 203–5.

[128]B. M. S. Campbell *et al.* (1993), 203–5.

[129]B. M. S. Campbell *et al.* (1993), 203–5.

[130]B. M. S. Campbell *et al.* (1993), 24–5, 149, 203–5.

[131]*Walter of Henley*, 392–3.

Measuring commercialisation

in this way: substantial supplies were regularly sent by many of the East Anglian manors of the Bigod earls of Norfolk to the earls' principal East Anglian seat at Framlingham in Suffolk; when not at Framlingham the earls often descended with their retinue upon individual manors for periods at a time, often staying until that manor's store of provisions became exhausted.[132] Other lesser lords drew directly and heavily upon their home manors for supplies – John de Cobham of the prominent Kentish baronial family upon Cobham in Kent, William de Fiennes upon Wendover in Buckinghamshire, John de Seyton upon Maidwell in Northamptonshire, and Reginald d'Argentine upon Wymondley in Hertfordshire – thereby depressing these manors' propensities to sell.

Within estates the most important distinction was therefore that between manors whose prime role was the provisioning of households, and which therefore sold both little and selectively, and manors usually at some remove from estate headquarters which may have transferred some of their production to the household for consumption but disposed of the bulk of the remainder by sale. This selective policy of consumption, transfer and sale has been documented and discussed in some detail for the estate of Peterborough Abbey by Biddick.[133] Within the London region, however, it is best exemplified by the large and comprehensively documented estate of Canterbury Cathedral Priory. Thus, the priory's intensively managed home manors of Brook, Chartham, Eastry, and Ickham located within ten miles of Canterbury in east Kent transferred a majority of their grain direct to the household and sold mainly animals and animal products of which the priory had limited need; at a distance of ten to 25 miles manors such as Copton, Hollingbourne, and Ebony continued to send some grain to Canterbury but also made regular and substantial sales on the market; beyond 25 miles from Canterbury, little if anything was transferred to the priory and a majority of what was produced was often sold. Those Canterbury manors which show up as particularly highly commercialised in both their arable and pastoral husbandries were therefore those which were too remote from the priory for it to be worthwhile for them to supply it with produce while at the same time well placed to take advantage of commercial outlets elsewhere, especially the London market. On the arable side Cliffe on the Thames estuary thirty miles from Canterbury stands out in this respect, as to a lesser extent do East Farleigh in mid-Kent, convenient to the navigable River Medway and the busy market at Maidstone that is known to have been frequented by London cornmongers, and East Horsley in Surrey, twenty miles south-west of London and too distant to provision Canterbury.[134] On the pastoral side, Orpington in west Kent and the priory's

---

[132]Davenport (1906), 22–4; PRO, SC6/937/27–938/10.
[133]Biddick (1989).
[134]B. M. S. Campbell *et al.* (1993), 51–2, 60.

three Essex manors of Bocking, Mersea, and Middleton were all significant sellers.

Ideally, verdicts on the degree of commercialisation of a manor or estate should therefore be informed by knowledge of the size and composition of the estate concerned and the place of its component manors within the overall production system of that estate. Few of the estates surveyed in this chapter have been examined in their entirety and if evidence from a more representative cross-section of manors were available there is no doubt that their commercialisation profiles might appear somewhat different. On present evidence it is the far-flung manors and broad acres of such major episcopal and lay magnates as the bishop of Winchester, archbishop of Canterbury, and earls of Lincoln and Cornwall which emerge as the most exclusively geared towards production for sale.[135] Conventual estates, except that of the alien abbey of Bec which had no English household to support, were significantly less commercialised.[136] Indeed, the estates of abbeys such as Peterborough and Crowland stand out as among the least commercialised estates of all.[137] Yet it is conventual estates which, on account of their often abundant documentation and the historical interest that this has generated, tend to loom particularly large in perceptions of the period. By contrast, the evidence is flimsiest and the verdict to be returned least certain in the case of the estates of lay lords of sub-comital rank. Here, too often, conclusions have to be based upon evidence from a single manor often for a single year. John le Ferrers's and William de Hamelton's manors of Hampstead Norreys, Berkshire, and Little Baddow, Essex, emerge almost alone from the ranks of this group of manors and estates as relatively highly commercialised. The role as home farms of most of the other documented lesser lay manors conveys an overwhelming but probably exaggerated impression that production on this class of estate was geared primarily towards consumption. Nevertheless, finding minor lay estates with adequate documentation of all their component manors against which this impression might be tested is likely to prove elusive.[138] This is unfortunate, for the attitudes and objectives of this group of producers has important implications for those of landholders lower down the social scale of whose activities there is no direct evidence whatsoever.

If conventual and lesser lay households were alike in relying upon their estates for provisions, they nonetheless differed in the balance of provisions demanded. Dietary differences between predominantly vegetarian conventual households and non-vegetarian lay households, reinforced by differences in the size and composition of those households, ensured that

[135]This is broadly confirmed by Britnell's analysis of crop sales on six entire estates: Britnell (1993a), 121.

[136]Morgan (1946); Britnell (1993a), 121.

[137]Biddick (1989); Page (1934); Britnell (1993a), 121.

[138]For an example, see Livingstone (1991).

Measuring commercialisation

consumption of animals was least important on conventual and most important on lay estates. This placed conventual estates in a better position to dispose of animals on the market, hence it is on these estates that animals made their greatest relative contribution to sales income. Conversely, lesser lay estates were much more heavily reliant upon crop sales for their income. Reinforcing this difference was the apparently more developed character of pastoral husbandry on conventual estates, which may have derived from their greater capacity as perpetual institutions to conserve and build up the capital resources of flocks and herds. Irrespective of the type of estate, however, the pastoral sector appears to have been the most commercialised branch of seigneurial agriculture, and the production of animal products (wool, hides, and dairy produce) especially so. The proportions of animals and animal products sold were greater than the corresponding proportions of crops, and manors which sold animals and animal products at a high rate were geographically more widely distributed than those which sold crops at an equivalent rate. Other things being equal, therefore, the greater the relative importance of pastoral husbandry the more commercialised was agriculture. Moreover, it may have been through the trade in live animals and wool that commercial relationships were initially pioneered. Animals certainly had the inestimable advantage that they could be walked to market, while products such as wool and cheese were high in value relative to their bulk and hence less susceptible than crops to the limiting effects of high unit transport costs.[139] Nevertheless, although animals and animal products had the greater marketing range it was crops which in absolute terms dominated both production and sale: relative prices at a time of high population pressure dictated that this was so. Crops accounted for approximately three-quarters by value of total disposable agricultural output, net of tithes, seed, fodder, and food liveries, and over half of total gross income from the sale of agricultural products.

In aggregate the mean gross output of the 201 sampled manors within the London region was worth in excess of £16,750 *per annum*, but deduction of tithes, seed, fodder, and food liveries for workers left only about £9,200-worth of this available for disposal. On average approximately a quarter of that disposable output was retained for consumption on the manor, usually by resident lords and their households, a further quarter was transferred for consumption elsewhere, and the remainder – about 45 per cent – was sold. Sales of all crops, animals, and animal products yielded a gross income of £4,219, with crops being sold at a gross rate of £6 18s 10d per 100 cropped acres (16.6d an acre) and animals and animal products at a rate of £6 17s 3d per 100 livestock units at the start of the year (16.5d per livestock unit). Given the prominence of manors from highly commercialised estates among

---

[139]The distances over which live animals could be traded were often considerable: Blanchard (1986), 427–60.

those sampled, these rates should be regarded as upper-bound estimates. Particularly high proportions sold and rates of sale in those parts of the London region known to have been closely involved in the provisioning of the capital also suggest that in other parts of the country remote from such powerful commercial stimuli, levels of commercialisation are likely to have been lower. Nationally, therefore, less than half of net disposable seigneurial agricultural output probably reached the market. Yet, just over two centuries earlier, Snooks estimates on the evidence of Domesday Book that in England as a whole as much as 60 per cent of seigneurial production net of seed, fodder, and other on-the-farm deductions may have been sold.[140] Either the seigneurial sector was less commercialised *c.* 1300 than it had been at the time of Domesday or Snooks's estimate is too high. Historical retrogression is certainly not impossible but in this instance it runs counter to all known trends. In particular, several of the documented estates within the London region are known to have increased their dependence upon the market during the thirteenth century. Biddick's work shows that the manors of the bishops of Winchester were significantly less commercialised under bishop Peter des Roches at the beginning of the thirteenth century than, on the evidence of the 13 sampled manors within the London region, they were to be at the close of the thirteenth century.[141] R. A. L. Smith has described how Canterbury Cathedral Priory reorganised production on its demesnes to take advantage of buoyant market demand during the latter part of the thirteenth century,[142] and the implication of the increased market purchases described by B. F. Harvey at Westminster Abbey is that its manors were selling rather than transferring a higher proportion of their production.[143] The continued growth of London throughout the thirteenth century will also have increased commercial opportunities for seigneurial producers within its widening hinterland.

A stagnant or declining rate of commercialisation within the seigneurial sector between 1086 and 1300 is not, therefore, readily reconciled with what is known about developments during the thirteenth century. Nevertheless, this does not preclude the possibility, also implied by comparison of these two estimates, that it was within the non-demesne sector that commercialisation made its greatest progress during the intervening two centuries. Certainly, if the seigneurial sector accounted for a third of total agricultural production, if half of the net disposable product of that sector was sold, and if a proportion of what was sold was exported (principally in the form of grain and wool), then the amounts of demesne production reaching the market would have been unequal to the needs of a non-

---

[140]Snooks includes the product of free peasants within his definition of the seigneurial (demesne) sector: above, 28.

[141]Biddick with Bijleveld (1991), 106–15.

[142]R. A. L. Smith (1943), 131–5.

[143]B. F. Harvey (1977), 131–48.

agricultural sector which *c.* 1300 contained a quarter or more of the national population.[144] In this context it is significant that patterns of production on seigneurial demesnes at this date tended to conform to local rather than estate practice and may therefore reflect the preferred husbandry traits of non-demesne producers, whose labours accounted for the larger share of agricultural production.[145] Moreover, those patterns of production and local husbandry preferences bear every sign of having been strongly influenced by market demand, regardless of whether the demesnes in question were producing for the market. Commercialisation, in fact, implies a great deal more than production for sale, for the very presence of markets influences prevailing levels of economic rent and thereby affects what is produced and how it is produced. Direct management of demesnes by landlords would not have been economically rational unless the value that landlords thereby derived from their estates, whether in revenue earned or produce sold, was at least equivalent to the income they would have obtained had they leased the land and lived off the rents. That meant producing the crops and animals and pitching the intensity of production at levels that were broadly consistent with prevailing levels of economic rent. This is borne out by the overall spatial coherence of patterns of demesne production and associated valuations placed upon demesne resources, almost regardless of the estates to which those demesnes belonged or the specific needs of their households.[146] In other words, the market's influence upon patterns of seigneurial production was more profound than its influence upon patterns of disposal.

When – to ponder the question posed by Farmer – lords and their officials did choose to sell all or some of what was produced, does it follow that their motive was a desire for gain and profit rather than a simple need for cash?[147] At one level they were plainly not indifferent to commercial opportunity nor deficient in knowledge about prevailing price levels and market trends, but it has yet to be convincingly demonstrated that in responding to those opportunities and price levels they were acting as proto-capitalists. The essence of capitalist behaviour is the application of capital to production and the management of resources with the prime objective of making a profit, taking account of both production and depreciation costs: lords certainly do not appear to have been so consciously entrepreneurial, for in managing their estates they were as much concerned with considerations of status and patronage as they were with profit. Moreover, insofar as they had a concept of 'profit' it was a relatively unsophisticated one.[148] Widespread

---

[144]Dyer (1992a), 152.

[145]B. M. S. Campbell (1983a), 397–8; Mate (1985), 31; B. M. S. Campbell *et al.* (1993), 141–3, 176–8.

[146]B. M. S. Campbell *et al.* (1993), 121–3, 164–7.

[147]Farmer (above), 102–4.

[148]E. Stone (1962), 25–48; Postles (1986), 12–28.

as manorial accounts had become by the end of the thirteenth century, as an instrument of estate administration they did not readily admit of calculations of profit. They take the form of simple charge and discharge accounts and although excellent for detecting fraud and embezzlement by manorial officials and ensuring that the lord received everything that was due to him, they are deficient in the information necessary for a true calculation of the return on capital invested.[149] Commercialisation is not, therefore, necessarily synonymous with the development of capitalism. On the contrary, there are those who would argue that the growth of the market and of market production merely transformed and extended the means of feudal exploitation without fundamentally altering the socio-property relations of feudalism.[150] But, of course, the market and marketing institutions once created acquired a momentum of their own which lords were to find themselves incapable of controlling and in the very long term the growth of commerce was to be truly revolutionary.

The amount of time that it took for the market to evolve to a stage when it could provide a viable alternative to customary relationships should not be under-estimated. For many lords, the tried and tested customary methods of recruiting a labour-force, provisioning their households, and securing a revenue remained the best and certainly the most reliable. Change was slow, almost imperceptibly so by modern standards, and lords as controllers of rural resources were particularly well placed to insulate themselves from it. Individual lords responded to the new economic opportunities afforded by the growth of commerce in their own ways, according to inclination, need, and circumstance. Most of them, except perhaps the mightiest, still practised a policy of 'householding' and drew upon their estates, and especially their home farms, for many of their immediate consumption needs. Agriculture, too, remained heavily reliant upon on-the-farm reproduction of seed, fodder, fertiliser, and replacement animals, although estate-based sometimes superseded manor-based systems of reproduction. In part this reflected the constraints of a predominantly organic and animate technology but it also demonstrates the absence or imperfect development of relevant commodity markets in seed, fodder, fertiliser, and, to a lesser extent, animals. Various non-financial means of recruiting and remunerating labour, with labour being substituted for rent and food for wages, were similarly means of compensating for inadequate supplies of cash.[151]

Yet, at the same time, markets were well established for many commodities and the prices of the principal foodstuffs were largely determined by the interaction of supply and demand. By 1300 a sufficient proportion of

---

[149]*Walter of Henley*, 213–22; Noke (1991).
[150]Brenner (1982), 33–6; Dunford and Perrons (1983), 104–8.
[151]Mayhew (above), 69–70.

agricultural production was entering the market for perhaps one in four of the population to be exclusively dependent upon the market for its consumption needs.[152] During the thirteenth century major concentrations of market demand began to emerge, and the commercial opportunities that these offered clearly induced many producers to become more actively and selectively involved in the market. Rates of market participation were conspicuously higher, for instance, on manors within areas known to have been actively engaged in the provisioning of London than on those further afield. Within the hinterlands of these emergent centres of demand even those estates preoccupied with consumption rather than exchange were strongly influenced by the market in their patterns and methods of production. Elsewhere, however, it was in the countryside rather than the towns that the bulk of demand was concentrated, with the result that the market for agricultural products remained fragmented and dispersed.[153] Rates of production and sale per unit area therefore remained relatively low and the commercialisation of agriculture remained imperfect. The market had yet to become the universal instrument of transfer and exchange. Nevertheless, the twelfth and thirteenth centuries saw the creation of much of the infrastructure that was necessary for the fuller elaboration of market forces and the wider social diffusion of market participation. Although it would be many centuries before the market ceased, in Polanyi's phrase, to be 'embedded in society', that breakthrough would have been much longer coming but for the foundations laid during these formative centuries of economic expansion and commercial growth.

[152]Dyer (1992a), 152–3.

[153]'It was in the villages and small towns that lords and peasants found most of the customers for their surplus corn and cheese, livestock and poultry. Markets in the larger towns left the better records, but the local markets and the communities around them were the more important outlets for the produce of the countryside': Farmer (1991a), 329.

BIBLIOGRAPHY
CHAPTER VIII

Biddick, K. (1985a), 'Medieval English peasants and market involvement', *Journal of Economic History*, XLV, 823–31.

Biddick, K. (1985b), 'Pig husbandry on the Peterborough Abbey estate from the twelfth to the fourteenth century', in J. Clutton-Brock and C. Grigson, eds., *Animals and Archaeology*, British Archaeological Reports, International Ser., CCXXVII, Oxford, 161–77.

Biddick, K. (1987), 'Missing links: taxable wealth, markets, and stratification among medieval English peasants', *Journal of Interdisciplinary History*, XVIII, 277–98.

Biddick, K. (1989), *The Other Economy: Pastoral Husbandry on a Medieval Estate*, Berkeley and Los Angeles.

Biddick, K. with Bijleveld, C.C.J.H. (1991), 'Agrarian productivity on the estates of the bishopric of Winchester in the early thirteenth century: a managerial perspective', in B.M.S. Campbell and M. Overton, eds., *Land, Labour and Livestock: Historical Studies in European Agricultural Productivity*, Manchester, 95–123.

Blanchard, I.S.W. (1986), 'The continental European cattle trade, 1400–1600', *Economic History Review*, 2nd ser., XXXIX, 427–60.

Brenner, R. (1982), 'The agrarian roots of European capitalism', *Past and Present*, XCVII, 16–113, reprinted in T.H. Aston and C.H.E. Philpin, eds., (1985), *The Brenner Debate: Agrarian Class Structure and Economic Development in Pre-industrial Europe*, Cambridge, 213–327.

Britnell, R.H. (1980b), 'Minor landlords and medieval agrarian capitalism', *Past and Present*, LXXXIX, 3–22, reprinted in T.H. Aston, ed., (1987), *Landlords, Peasants and Politics in Medieval England*, Cambridge, 227–46.

Britnell, R.H. (1989), 'England and northern Italy in the early fourteenth century: the economic contrasts', *Transactions of the Royal Historical Society*, 5th ser., XXXIV, 167–83.

Britnell, R.H. (1993a), *The Commercialisation of English Society, 1000–1300*, Cambridge.

Britnell, R.H. (above/1995), 'Commercialisation and economic development in England, 1000–1300', in R.H. Britnell and B.M.S. Campbell, eds., *A Commercialising Economy: England 1086–c.1300*, Manchester, 7–26.

Campbell, B.M.S. (1983a), 'Arable productivity in medieval England: some evidence from Norfolk', *Journal of Economic History*, XLIII, 379–404.

Campbell, B.M.S. (1983b), 'Agricultural progress in medieval England: some evidence from eastern Norfolk', *Economic History Review*, 2nd ser., XXXVI, 26–46.

Campbell, B.M.S. (1986), 'The complexity of manorial structure in medieval Norfolk: a case study', *Norfolk Archaeology*, XXXIX, 225–61.

Campbell, B.M.S. (1988b), Towards an agricultural geography of medieval England', *Agricultural History Review*, XXXVI, 87–98.

Campbell, B.M.S. (1991a), 'Land, labour, livestock, and productivity trends in English seignorial agriculture, 1208–1450', in *idem* and M. Overton, eds., *Land, Labour and Livestock: Historical Studies in European Agricultural Productivity*, Manchester, 144–82.

Campbell, B.M.S., ed., (1991b), *Before the Black Death: Studies in the 'Crisis' of the Early Fourteenth Century*, Manchester.

Campbell, B.M.S. (1992), 'Commercial dairy production on medieval English demesnes: the case of Norfolk, *Anthropozoologica*, XVI, 107–18.

Campbell, B.M.S. (forthcoming/1995), 'Ecology versus economics in late thirteenth- and early fourteenth-century English agriculture', in D. Sweeney, ed., *Agriculture in the Middle Ages: Technology, Practice, and Representation*, Philadelphia, 76–108.

Campbell, B.M.S. and Power, J.P. (1989), 'Mapping the agricultural geography of medieval England', *Journal of Historical Geography*, XV, 24–39.

Campbell, B.M.S., Galloway, J.A., and Murphy, M., (1992), 'Rural land-use in the metropolitan hinterland, 1270–1339: the evidence of the *inquisitiones post mortem*', *Agricultural History Review*, XL, 1–22.

Campbell, B.M.S., Galloway, J.A., Keene, D., and Murphy, M., (1993), *A Medieval Capital and its Grain Supply: Agrarian Production and Distribution in the London Region circa 1300*, Historical Geography Research Ser., XXX.

Chisholm, M. (1962), *Rural Settlement and Land-use: An Essay on Location*, London.

Clark, G. (1991), 'Labour productivity in English agriculture, 1300–1860', in B.M.S. Campbell and M. Overton, eds., *Land, Labour and Livestock: Historical Studies in European Agricultural Productivity*, Manchester, 211–35.

Collins, E.J.T. (1975), 'Dietary change and cereal consumption in Britain in the nineteenth century', *Agricultural History Review*, XXIII, 97–115.

Davenport, F.G. (1906), *The Economic Development of a Norfolk Manor 1086–1565*, Cambridge.

Dunford, M., and Perrons, D. (1983), *The Arena of Capital*, London.

Dyer, C. (1988), 'Changes in diet in the late Middle Ages: the case of harvest workers', *Agricultural History Review*, XXXVI, 21–37.

Dyer, C. (1989a), *Standards of Living in the Later Middle Ages: Social Change in England, c.1200–1520*, Cambridge.

Dyer, C. (1992a), 'The hidden trade of the Middle Ages: evidence from the west midlands of England', *Journal of Historical Geography*, XVIII, 141–57.

Farmer, D.L. (1991a), 'Marketing the produce of the countryside, 1200–1500', in E. Miller, ed., *The Agrarian History of England and Wales, III: 1348–1500*, Cambridge, 324–430.

Farmer, D.L. (1991b), 'Prices and wages, 1350–1500', in E. Miller, ed., *The Agrarian History of England and Wales, III: 1348–1500*, Cambridge, 431–525.

Farmer, D.L. (above/1995), 'Woodland and pasture sales on the Winchester manors in the thirteenth century: disposing of a surplus, or producing for the market?', in R.H. Britnell and B.M.S. Campbell, eds., *A Commercialising Economy: England 1086–c.1300*, Manchester, 102–31.

Galloway J.A., and Murphy M. (1991), 'Feeding the city: medieval London and its agrarian hinterland', *London Journal*, XVI, 3–14.

Galloway, J.A., Murphy, M., and Myhil, O. (1993), *Kentish Demesne Accounts up to 1350: A Catalogue*, London.

Grant, A. (1988), 'Animal resources', in G. Astill and A. Grant, eds., *The Countryside of Medieval England*, Oxford, 149–87.

Grantham, G. (forthcoming/1997), 'Espaces privilégés: productivité agraire et zones d'approvisionnement des villes dans l'Europe preindustrielle', *Annales. Histoire, Sciences Socials*, 52, 3, 695–725.

Gras, N.S.B. (1915), *The Evolution of the English Corn Market from the Twelfth to the Eighteenth Century*, Cambridge, Mass.

Grigg, D. (1982), *The Dynamics of Agricultural Change: The Historical Experience*, London.

Harvey, B.F. (1977), *Westminster Abbey and its Estates in the Middle Ages*, Oxford.

Harvey, P.D.A. (1965), *A Medieval Oxfordshire Village: Cuxham 1240–1400*, Oxford.

Harvey, P.D.A. (1984b), *Manorial Records*, British Records Association, London.

Hatcher, J. (1981), 'English serfdom and villeinage: towards a reassessment', *Past and Present*, XC, 3–39, reprinted in T.H. Aston, ed., (1987), *Landlords, Peasants and Politics in Medieval England*, Cambridge, 247–84.

Hilton, R.H. (1985b), 'Medieval market towns and simple commodity production', *Past and Present*, CIX, 3–23.

Hodges, R. (1988), *Primitive and Peasant Markets*, Oxford.

Keene, D.J. (1985a), *Cheapside Before the Great Fire*, London.

Keene, D.J. (1985b), *Survey of Medieval Winchester*, 2 vols., Winchester Sudies, II, Oxford.

Keene, D.J. (1989), 'Medieval London and its region', *London Journal*, XIV, 99–111.

Knowles,D. (1950), *The Monastic Order in England: A History of its Development from the Times of Saint Dunstan to the Fourth Lateran Council, 943–1216*, Cambridge.

Kosminsky, E.A. (1956), *Studies in the Agrarian History of England in the Thirteenth century*, ed. R.H. Hilton, trans. R. Kisch, Oxford, 1956.

Kowaleski, M. (1990), 'Town and country in late medieval England: the hide and leather trade', in P. Corfield and D.J. Keene, eds., *Work in Towns 850–1850*, Leicester, 57–73.

Kowaleski, M. (forthcoming/1995), 'The grain trade in fourteenth-century Exeter', in E.B. Dewindt, ed., *The Salt of Common Life: Individuality and Choice in the Medieval Town, Countryside and Church. Essays Presented to J. Ambrose Raftis*, Kalamazoo, 1–52.

Langdon, J.L. (1986), *Horses, Oxen and Technological Innovation: The Use of Draught Animals in English Farming from 1066 to 1500*, Cambridge.

Langdon, J.L. (1993), 'Inland water transport in medieval England', *Journal of Historical Geography*, XIX, 1–11.

Livingstone, M. (1991), 'Sir John Pulteney's landed estates: the acquisition and management of land by a London merchant', unpublished University of London M.A. thesis.

Lloyd, T.H. (1973), *The Movement of Wool Prices in Medieval England*, Economic History Review Supplements, VI, Cambridge.

Lloyd, T.H. (1977a), *The English Wool Trade in the Middle Ages*, Cambridge.

Mann, M. (1986), *The Sources of Social Power, I: A History of Power from the Beginning to A.D. 1760*, Cambridge.

Manorial Records of Cuxham, Oxfordshire, c.1200–1359, ed., P.D.A. Harvey (1976), Oxfordshire Record Society, L, and Royal Commission on Historical Manuscripts joint publication, XXIII, London.

Mate, M. (1985), 'Medieval agrarian practices: the determining factors?', *Agricultural History Review*, XXXIII, 22–31.

Mate, M. (1987), 'Pastoral farming in south-east England in the fifteenth century', *Economic History Review*, 2nd ser., XL, 523–36.

Mayhew, N.J. (above/1995), 'Modelling medieval monetisation', in R.H. Britnell and B.M.S. Campbell, eds., *A Commercialising Economy: England 1086–c.1300*, Manchester, 55–77 and 195–6.

McIntosh, M.K. (1986), *Autonomy and Community: The Royal Manor of Havering, 1200–1500*, Cambridge.

Miller, E., and Hatcher, J. (1978), *Medieval England: Rural Society and Economic Change, 1086–1348*, London.

Morgan, M. (1946), *The English Lands of the Abbey of Bec*, Oxford.

Munro, J.H. (1991), 'Industrial transformations in the north-west European textile trades, c.1290–c.1340: economic progress or economic crisis?', in B.M.S. Campbell, ed., *Before the Black Death: Studies in the 'Crisis' of the Early Fourteenth Century*, Manchester, 110–48.

Murphy, M., and Galloway, J.A. (1992), 'Marketing animals and animal products in London's hinterland circa 1300', *Anthropozoologica*, XVI, 93–100.

Noke, C. (1991), 'Agency and the *excessus* balance in manorial accounts', *Accounting and Business Research*, LXXXIV, 339–48.

Nonarum Inquisitiones in Curia Scaccarii Tempore Regis Edwardi III, ed. G. Vanderzee (1807), Record Commission, London.

Page, F.M. (1926–9), 'Bidentes Hoylandie (a medieval sheep farm)', *Economic History*, I, 603–13.

Page, F.M. (1934), *The Estates of Crowland Abbey: A Study in Manorial Organisation*, Cambridge.

Polanyi, K. (1945), *Origins of our Time: The Great Transformation*, London.

Polanyi, K. (1957), 'The economy as instituted process', in *idem*, C.M. Arensberg, and H.W. Pearson, *Trade and Market in the Early Empires: Economies in History and Theory*, Glencoe, Ill., 243–69.

Poos, L.R. (1985), The rural population of Essex in the later Middle Ages, *Economic History Review*, 2nd ser., XXXVIII, 515–30.

Poos, L.R. (1991), *A Rural Society After the Black Death: Essex, 1350–1525*, Cambridge.

Postan, M.M. (1959-60), 'Note', *Economic History Review*, 2nd ser., XII, 77–82.

Postan, M.M. (1966), 'Medieval agrarian society in its prime: England', in *idem*, ed., *The Cambridge Economic History of Europe, I: The Agrarian Life of the Middle Ages*, Cambridge, 2nd edn, 548–632.

Postles, D. (1986), 'The perception of profit before the leasing of demesnes', *Agricultural History Review*, XXXIV, 12–28.

Power, E. (1941), *The Wool Trade in English Medieval History*, London.

Power, J.P., and Campbell, B.M.S. (1992), 'Cluster analysis and the classification of medieval demesne-farming systems', *Transactions of the Institute of British Geographers*, new ser., XVII, 227–45.

Raftis, J.A. (1974), *Assart Data and Land Values: Two Studies in the East Midlands 1200–1350*, Pontifical Institute of Mediaeval Studies, Subsidia Mediaevalia, III, Toronto.

Searle, E. (1974), *Lordship and Community: Battle Abbey and its Banlieu, 1066–1538*, Pontifical Institute of Mediaeval Studies, Studies and Texts, XXVI, Toronto.

Smith, C.A. (1976), 'Introduction: the regional approach to economic systems', in *idem*, ed., *Regional Analysis, I: Economic Systems*, New York, San Francisco, and London, 44–51.

Smith, R.A.L. (1943), *Canterbury Cathedral Priory: A Study in Monastic Administration*, Cambridge.

Smith, R.M. (1984b), 'Some issues concerning families and their property in rural England 1250–1800', in *idem*, ed., *Land, Kinship and Life-cycle*, Cambridge, 1–86.

Snooks, G.D. (above/1995), 'The dynamic role of the market in the Anglo-Norman economy and beyond, 1086–1300', in R.H. Britnell and B.M.S. Campbell, eds., *A Commercialising Economy: England 1086–c.1300*, Manchester, 27–54 and 194–5.

Stone, E. (1962), 'Profit-and-loss accountancy at Norwich Cathedral Priory', *Transactions of the Royal Historical Society*, 5th ser., XII, 25–48.

Taxatio Ecclesiastica Angliae et Walliae Auctoritate P. Nicholai IV, circa A.D. 1291, ed. S. Ayscough and J. Caley (1802), Record Commission, London.

Thornton, C. (1991), 'The determinants of land productivity on the bishop of Winchester's demesne of Rimpton, 1208 to 1403', in B.M.S. Campbell and M. Overton, eds., *Land, Labour and Livestock: Historical Studies in European Agricultural Productivity*, Manchester, 183–210.

Titow, J.Z. (1962), 'Land and population on the bishop of Winchester's estates 1209–1350', unpublished University of Cambridge Ph.D. thesis.

Titow, J.Z. (1972), *Winchester Yields: A Study in Medieval Agricultural Productivity*, Cambridge.

von Thünen, J.H. (1966), *Von Thünen's Isolated State: An English Edition of Der Isolierte Staat by Johann Heinrich von Thünen*, ed. P. Hall, trans. C.M. Wartenberg, London.

Walter of Henley and Other Treatises on Estate Management and Accountancy, ed., D. Oschinsky (1971), Oxford.

Wolf, E.R.(1955), 'Types of Latin American peasantry', *American Anthropologist*, LVII, 452–71.

IX

Matching Supply to Demand: Crop Production and Disposal by English Demesnes in the Century of the Black Death

To what extent did market forces shape and determine the development of the medieval English economy? Formative as the twelfth and thirteenth centuries were for the foundation of marketing institutions—fairs, markets, and boroughs—and improvement of transport infrastructure, the market occupies only a secondary role in the dominant explanatory models of the period, which attach greater weight to population, technology, and socio-property relations.[1] Within the dominant agrarian sector, autarky, it is held, still prevailed over exchange as the objective of most producers, whether great or small. Consequently, as R. H. Hilton once observed, "everyone had to produce, on the whole, the same type of crop and tend the same sort of domesticated animals for meat, wool, and pulling power."[2] This was not a rural landscape "forged in the market-place."[3] On the contrary,

This article builds upon the labor and advice of others, notably Ken Bartley, Jim Galloway, George Grantham, Derek Keene, John Langdon, Margaret Murphy, Olwen Myhil, Jenitha Orr, and John Power. I am also grateful for the comments of three anonymous referees and the editors. Responsibility for the views expressed nevertheless remains my own. The research upon which it is based would not have been possible without funding from the Leverhulme Trust, the Economic and Social Research Council (grant ref. R000 23 3157), and The Queen's University of Belfast. An earlier version of the paper was presented to Session 5B, *A precocious infant: the market in medieval England,* at the 1996 Annual Conference of the Economic History Association, Berkeley, California.

[1]Britnell, *Commercialisation*; Harrison, "Bridges"; Masschaele, "Transport Costs"; Postan, "Medieval Agrarian Society"; and Aston and Philpin, *Brenner Debate.*

[2]Hilton, "Medieval Agrarian History", p. 145.

[3]Dodgshon, *European Past*, p. 239.

without much specialization and exchange, "the pattern of agriculture in early fourteenth-century England reflected the broad physical controls of soils, climate, and topography."[4] Custom rather than commerce bound society, as reflected in the persistence of serfdom and a partial reliance by many lords upon forced, servile labor for the cultivation of their estates.[5] Hence the preoccupation of most analyses of the period with the constraints to growth; hence, too, the predominance of explanations that emphasize supply- rather than demand-side factors. Nemesis, in its fourteenth-century forms of war, famine, and pestilence, is thus interpreted as the penalty inevitably incurred for demographic and economic expansion under feudal socio-property relations. Here, it would seem, is a classic instance of the operation of the law of diminishing returns.[6]

Such views sit increasingly unhappily with a mounting body of historical evidence which suggests that greater numbers of medieval producers were finding it increasingly expedient and possibly even profitable to entrust their fortunes in whole or in part to the market.[7] Encouragement to do so was provided by a twelfth-century surge in English bullion output reinforced by a positive trade balance.[8] This bore fruit in a 24-fold increase in money supply during the twelfth and thirteenth centuries and sustained price inflation from the 1180s.[9] The former oiled the wheels of exchange and enabled crown and magnates alike to demand more of their revenues in cash rather than kind; the latter created an expectation of higher prices which helped induce progressively greater market participation. That trade expanded at all levels is implicit in the growing number and size of towns and the probability that a greater share of the population came to live in towns and rely in one way or another upon exchange for a living.[10] It is also explicit in the estimated trebling in the real value of English overseas trade that occurred during the thirteenth century.[11] At this rate trade almost certainly grew per capita. Agricultural products—unprocessed, semi-processed, and processed —bulked large in English trade, both domestic and overseas, and there is now good evidence to show that agriculture responded to the expanding market opportunities by becoming more differentiated and specialized.[12] Gains from wider application of the division of labor thus acted to counteract the losses from diminishing returns. Hence Persson's verdict that "the evolution of the mediaeval economy will be related to the extent of the

[4]Glasscock, "England circa 1334", p. 167.
[5]But see the revisions of Hatcher, "English Serfdom"; and Britnell, "Commerce and Capitalism."
[6]Grigg, *Population Growth*, pp. 64–82.
[7]Britnell, *Commercialisation*; and Britnell and Campbell, *Commercialising Economy*.
[8]Blanchard, *Middle Ages*.
[9]Mayhew, "Modelling."
[10]Dyer, *Everyday Life*, pp. 241–55 and "How Urbanized."
[11]Miller and Hatcher, *Towns, Commerce and Crafts*, p. 214.
[12]Power and Campbell, "Cluster Analysis."

diminishing returns, to what extent such tendencies were countervailed by increasing specialization and the capacity of the system to generate techno- logical change."[13]

Nevertheless, the evidence and the argument should not be pushed too far. Marketing institutions and the market economy still had a long way to evolve. Many legal impediments to their efficient operation remained. Alter- native values and relationships still persisted. Although much of what was produced was intended for the market, rather more was not. Transaction costs, although falling, remained high.[14] Trade was still a risky activity. Major centers of concentrated demand were few and far between; London, by far the largest, had a population of approximately 60,000 to 80,000 in 1300.[15] The dilemma, therefore, is to know just how much importance to attach to the market in accounting for the production and distribution of goods.

The dilemma is the more profound because it is not easily resolved. Studying markets and market relationships is one approach, but it inevitably overlooks those goods that did not enter the market and those relationships that were noncontractual in nature. Another, is to study production itself, but here there are serious evidential problems, particularly on the crucial agrar- ian front, where the smaller seignorial sector is conspicuously better docu- mented than the larger nondemesne/peasant sector. Nevertheless, the task is far from hopeless. An obvious place to begin is with the copiously docu- mented seignorial sector about which much remains to be learned. This can then serve as an analogue for evaluating the less direct and more disparate evidence relating to other classes of producer. Accordingly, this article offers some preliminary gleanings from an investigation of seignorial arable production during that most eventful of centuries, the fourteenth.

Sometime after 1315 expansion, demographic and economic, finally and decisively gave way to contraction. By 1375 England's population had been reduced by perhaps 40 percent, with profound consequences for prices, wages, and living standards.[16] Factor costs were transformed and production and consumption both changed accordingly.[17] If the market was important it should have shaped the responses of agricultural producers to these changes. Fortunately, this is the century for which the demesne sector is best documented, thanks to the creation and survival of large numbers of annual manorial accounts. Using three complementary samples of manorial ac- counts—at the scales of the country as a whole, the ten metropolitan coun- ties of Bedfordshire, Hertfordshire, Middlesex, Essex, Kent, Surrey, Berk-

[13]Persson, *Pre-Industrial Economic Growth,* p. 73.
[14]On relatively favorable unit transport costs see, Masschaele, "Transport Costs."
[15]Keene, "New Study"; and Nightingale, "Growth."
[16]Smith, "Human Resources," pp. 191–93; and Farmer, "Prices."
[17]Dyer, *Standards of Living.*

shire, Oxfordshire, Buckinghamshire, and Northamptonshire (the Feeding the City counties [FTC]) that collectively focus upon London, and the single county of Norfolk (England's then most populous county)—this article infers the influence of the market upon the production decisions of lords.[18] It then examines the extent to which lords utilized the market to dispose of their produce.

CROP PRODUCTION

An economic sea change occurred during the course of the fourteenth century. At the beginning, demand for foodstuffs was approaching its medieval maximum. As the population pressed ever harder on the land not only was more food in aggregate required but grain consumption in various forms increasingly dominated diets. High and rising land values also offered more favorable returns to investment and encouraged many demesne lords to make the most of what was often their greatest asset. A century later land scarcity had been transformed by population decline into land abundance. Less food was required by a population now 60 percent its former size and there was more scope for that population to indulge its dietary preferences. Changes in the scale, composition, and configuration of demand elicited corresponding changes in production.

---

[18]The National Accounts Database, Feeding the City I [hereafter FTC1] and Feeding the City II [hereafter FTC2] Accounts Databases; and Norfolk Accounts Database. The bulk of the data contained in the National Accounts Database was generously made available by Professor John L. Langdon of the Department of History, University of Edmonton. The manorial accounts that he sampled are listed in Langdon, "Horses," appendix C, part 2. Data for some additional demesnes have also been incorporated. The two Feeding the City accounts databases were created by James A. Galloway and Margaret Murphy (with some assistance from Olwen Myhil) and derive from the projects Feeding the City I, funded by the Leverhulme Trust, and Feeding the City II, funded by the Economic and Social Research Council (Award No. R000233157). Both were collaborative projects between the Centre for Metropolitan History, Institute of Historical Research, University of London and the Department of Economic and Social History, The Queen's University of Belfast, the former co-directed by Derek Keene and Bruce Campbell, the latter by Keene, Campbell, Galloway, and Murphy. The FTC1 accounts are listed in Campbell, et al., *Medieval Capital*, app. 1; a handlist of the FTC2 accounts is available from the Centre for Metropolitan History. The FTCII Accounts Database has been deposited at the ESRC Data Archive, University of Essex. The Norfolk Accounts Database was finalized by Bruce Campbell while in receipt of a personal research grant from the Social Science Research Council. The database contains information extracted from accounts in the following public and private archives: Bodleian Library, Oxford, British Library, Cambridge University Library, Canterbury Cathedral Library, Chicago University Library, Christ's College Cambridge, Elveden Hall (Suffolk), Eton College, Harvard Law Library, Holkham Hall (Norfolk), King's College Cambridge, Lambeth Palace Library, Magdalen College Oxford, Norfolk Record Office, North Yorkshire Record Office, Nottinghamshire Record Office, Nottingham University Library, Pomeroy & Sons, Wymondham, Public Record Office, Raynham Hall (Norfolk), John Ryland's Library, Manchester, St George's Chapel, Windsor, and the West Suffolk Record Office. A handlist of these accounts is available from Professor Campbell. I am grateful to all the authorities concerned for access to these materials. Listings of the manors in all three databases will be included as an appendix in my forthcoming book, *Seignorial Agriculture in England, 1250–1450.*

TABLE 1

TRENDS IN THE MEAN SOWN ACREAGE OF DEMESNES RETAINED IN HAND, 1250–1449: ENGLAND, NORFOLK, AND THE FTC COUNTIES

Years	Mean Sown Acreage		
	England[a]	Norfolk[b]	FTC Counties[c]
1275–1324	193.4	171.1	223.7[d]
1300–1349	172.1	146.0	
1325–1374	156.4	132.8	
1350–1399	147.1	126.8	
1375–1424	144.7	136.9	178.4[e]
Percentage decline, c.1300–c.1400	25.2	20.0	20.2

[a]Weighted mean derived from six regional submeans
[b]Weighted mean derived from four subcounty means
[c]Unweighted mean
[d]1288–1315
[e]1375–1400
Source: National Accounts Database; Norfolk Accounts Database; and FTC1 and FTC2 Accounts Databases.

The Scale of Cultivation

Over the second half of the fourteenth century all arable producers were confronted by a major contraction in demand. Changes in production costs further exacerbated the situation. By the close of the fourteenth century wage rates had risen by approximately one-third relative to grain prices. Profit margins for arable producers were thus seriously eroded. Poor land and expensive land became unprofitable to work. Meanwhile, lower production costs in pastoral husbandry coupled with a more buoyant market for pastoral products, as per capita purchasing power increased, encouraged the conversion of tillage to grass.[19] Lords responded by leasing many of their demesnes wholesale to tenants and curtailing the scale of their arable operations on those of their demesnes that they still retained in hand (Table 1).

In Norfolk, England's most arable county, mean cropped acreages on demesnes cultivated by the prior of Norwich shrank by 25 percent over the course of the fourteenth century.[20] On 61 demesnes common to both FTC samples (most of them in conventual or collegiate ownership) the contraction was the same.[21] Less controlled comparisons between all Norfolk, FTC, and national demesnes at the opening and close of the fourteenth century confirm a 20 to 25 percent reduction in mean cropped acreages (Table 1).

---

[19]Campbell, "Fair Field."

[20]These observations are based upon a detailed analysis of all extant accounts relating to the prior's manors: Norfolk Record Office [hereafter NRO], DCN 40/13, 60/4, 60/8, 60/10, 60/13, 60/14, 60/15, 60/18, 60/20, 60/23, 60/26, 60/28; 60/29, 60/30, 60/33, 60/35, 60/37, 61/35-6, 62/1-2; l'Estrange IB 1/4 & 3/4; NNAS 20 D1-3; Raynham Hall, Townshend Manuscripts; Bodleian Library, Oxford, MS Rolls Norfolk 29–45.

[21]On the estate of the bishopric of Winchester the equivalent contraction was 26 percent: Farmer, "Grain Yields," p. 562.

Why, at a time when the population probably fell by 40 percent and diets became less rather than more dependent upon grain, was the contraction in mean demesne cropped acreage not greater, especially given that it was achieved in part by leasing portions of demesne arable piecemeal to tenants? The selective nature of arable contraction provides part of the explanation. The retreat from arable production may have been most pronounced on soils and in terrains where demesne agriculture had never been well developed. A reluctance to forego customary labor services at a time when labor was appreciating in value may also have endowed seignorial arable production with a degree of inertia. For all producers it made sense to substitute land which was falling in price for labor which was rising. Many demesnes were being cultivated less intensively at the end of the century than they had been at the beginning.[22] Crop yields consequently tended to decline with the result that arable output fell by more than the reduction in cultivated area.[23] But the crop mix also changed as land-extensive drink and fodder crops expanded their respective shares of the cultivated area (Table 3). These kinds of developments endowed the arable sector with a degree of resilience in the face of demographic decline and ensured that there was no simple direct relationship between the population to be supported and the area under crop.

The Composition of Production

The rising per capita purchasing power which was the concomitant of population decline empowered consumers with greater dietary choice. C. C. Dyer's analysis of the diets of agricultural laborers confirms that most social groups took full advantage of this opportunity.[24] The upshot was that demand for some crops proved more buoyant than for others. As producers responded a fresh balance was struck between supply and demand, expressed in changing relative prices (Table 2).

Bread, the staff of life, formed the foundation of medieval diets. Rich and poor alike ate it, combining it with other foodstuffs according to their means.[25] It is a measure of its central dietary importance that the grains grown principally for bread—wheat, rye, and maslin/mancorn—consistently occupied at least 40 percent of the national demesne grain acreage and, until 1400, at least one- third of the national demesne cropped acreage (Table 3). Within the FTC counties bread grains assumed an even greater importance, for these counties had to feed London as well as themselves, and London's appetite for bread was voracious.[26] At the opening of the fourteenth century,

[22]Campbell, "Agricultural Progress", pp. 38–39; and Thornton, "Determinants," pp. 205–07.
[23]Campbell, "Land," pp. 160–65, 171; and Overton and Campbell, "Production."
[24]Dyer, "Changes."
[25]Dyer, *Standards of Living*, pp. 55–57, 153, 157–59.
[26]Campbell et al., *Medieval Capital*, pp. 24–36.

TABLE 2
TRENDS IN CROP PRICES RELATIVE TO WHEAT, C.1300–1400:
ENGLAND, NORFOLK, AND THE FTC COUNTIES

	Price Relative to Wheat (wheat = 1.00)			
	Rye	Barley	Oats	Peas
England				
1275–1324	0.78	0.71	0.40	0.68
1300–1349	0.77	0.72	0.42	0.67
1325–1374	0.72	0.72	0.42	0.64
1350–1399	0.69	0.72	0.42	0.62
1375–1424	0.70	0.68	0.40	0.61
Norfolk				
1275–1324	0.72	0.77	0.44	0.71
1300–1349	0.67	0.74	0.49	0.72
1325–1374	0.61	0.65	0.46	0.67
1350–1399	0.68	0.55	0.36	0.53
1375–1424	0.71	0.56	0.43	0.60
FTC counties				
1288–1315	0.83	0.76	0.43	0.66
1375–1400	0.52	0.76	0.43	0.67

Source: Farmer, "Prices and Wages," pp. 797–805; Farmer, "Prices and Wages, 1350–1500," pp. 502–04; Lord Beveridge, unpublished price data; and FTC1 and FTC2 Accounts Databases.

when the city attained its medieval peak in commercial activity, demesnes in the FTC counties devoted 47 percent of their grain acreage and 43 percent of their cropped acreage to bread grains. A century later these grains still occupied 43 percent of the grain acreage and 37 percent of the cropped acreage in these counties. This contrasts with the situation in Norfolk. Here, because barley - grown in abundance in the county - was widely used as a bread grain, the conventional bread grains never accounted for more than 30 percent of the grain acreage and 26 percent of the cropped acreage, shares which contracted quite markedly as the fourteenth century drew to a close.[27]

Barley bread, like maslin bread, rye bread, and breads which incorporated assorted grains and legumes, were all much cheaper than pure wheaten bread. People had tended to trade down to them whenever they could no longer afford the superior wheaten variety. Conversely, demand for them withered once purchasing power improved. From 1325, and especially from 1350, fewer demesnes cultivated rye and maslin, which occupied dwindling shares of both the cropped acreage and that proportion of it devoted to bread grains.[28] In the FTC counties rye and maslin's share of the bread-grain acreage was halved from 24 percent in the period from 1288 to 1315 to 12 percent in the period from 1375 to 1400. In the country as a whole cultivation of these two crops contracted even more dramatically, from 17 percent

[27]Dyer, "Changes," p. 28.
[28]The proportion of demesnes growing rye shrank from one-third in the period from 1250 to 1349 to one-fifth from 1350 to 1449.

TABLE 3
TRENDS IN SEIGNORIAL CROP PRODUCTION, C.1300–1400: ENGLAND, NORFOLK, AND THE FTC COUNTIES

Years	Bread Grains as a Percentage of Total Cropped Area			Brewing Grains as a Percentage of Total Cropped Area			Pottage/Fodder Grains as a Percentage of Total Cropped Area		
	England	Norfolk	FTC counties	England	Norfolk	FTC counties	England	Norfolk	FTC counties
1275–1324	40.3	24.9	43.1[a]	18.2	45.4	17.8[a]	40.6	29.7	39.2[a]
1300–1349	42.9	25.9		19.3	46.9		37.2	27.2	
1325–1374	39.4	25.6		22.0	47.3		37.6	27.1	
1350–1399	35.6	21.5		25.5	51.3		37.9	27.2	
1375–1424	33.6	18.5	36.6[b]	27.3	54.0	26.5[b]	36.6	27.4	37.0[b]

Years	Rye and Winter Mixtures as a Percentage of Bread-Grain Area			Barley as Percentage of Brewing-Grain Area			Legumes as a Percentage of Pottage/Fodder Grain Area		
	England	Norfolk	FTC counties	England	Norfolk	FTC counties	England	Norfolk	FTC counties
1275–1324	17.2	44.6	23.9[a]	82.1	99.5	62.9[a]	19.1	46.1	23.5[a]
1300–1349	17.7	50.2		77.9	99.4		26.6	49.0	
1325–1374	15.0	41.4		72.5	98.8		35.8	48.8	
1350–1399	12.4	30.4		74.4	99.1		35.7	47.0	
1375–1424	7.3	29.9	12.3[b]	75.7	99.9	69.1[b]	41.8	44.8	38.9[b]

[a]Figure is for the years 1288 to 1315.
[b]Figure is for the years 1375 to 1400.
Notes: Bread grains are wheat, winter mixtures, and rye; brewing grains are barley and dredge; pottage/fodder grains are oats, legumes, and legume-grain mixtures. Data for England are weighted means derived from six regional submeans. Data for Norfolk are weighted means derived from four subcounty means. Data for the FTC counties are the unweighted means.
Source: National Accounts Database; Norfolk Accounts Database; and FTC1 and FTC2 Accounts Databases.

of the bread-grain area c.1300 to 7 percent c.1400 (Table 3). Notwith-standing this pronounced cutback in production, the relative price of rye deteriorated more than that of any other grain (Table 2), which suggests that the cutback was demand driven.

Unlike rye and maslin, wheat was much more successful in maintaining both its price and its share of the cropped acreage. After the Black Death it remained in demand as consumers substituted wheaten bread for that made from rye, maslin, and other grains. As the modest but expanding proportions of wheat fed as liveries to manorial workers indicate, wheat was increasingly being consumed by socioeconomic groups hitherto unable to afford it.[29] Within the FTC counties the proportion of net aggregate wheat receipts retained for on-the-manor consumption rose from 31 percent to 48 percent over the course of the fourteenth century. Nevertheless, the stability of demand for wheat was insufficient to offset the steadily diminishing impor-tance of the cheaper bread grains. By the close of the fourteenth century the principal bread grains' share of the cropped acreage had been reduced by 15 percent in the FTC counties, 22 percent in the country as a whole, and 29 percent in Norfolk from their respective pre-plague peaks (Table 3).

Per capita demand for ale was altogether more elastic than that for bread. Where the output of bread grains contracted that of the principal brewing grains—barley and dredge—expanded (although partly at the expense of oats). Growing grain exclusively for ale was extravagant of land since 70 percent of potential kilocalories were lost in the brewing process. Before 1350 high land values and declining purchasing power had depressed per capita ale consumption and caused a trading down, both to cheaper and weaker ales (brewed increasingly from dredge and oats rather than the more expensive barley) and to milk and water, with all the potential health prob-lems associated with the latter.[30] After 1350 both these constraints were relaxed and the demand for barley and dredge proved stronger than that for any other grain. Increasingly, too, it was quality as well as quantity that was wanted. Hence the progressive elimination of oats as a brewing grain in many parts of the country and its replacement with either dredge or barley. But whereas before 1350 it was dredge, the cheaper of these two brewing grains, which had fared best, it was now barley whose cultivation expanded most vigorously since it brewed the better ale.

Barley production grew both in Norfolk and the southeast, where barley had long been a prominent crop, and in several new areas—the valleys of the Thames and Severn and the east coast from the Humber to the Tweed—where it had formerly been of limited significance. By the close of the four-teenth century it had expanded to occupy over two-thirds of the brewing-

[29]Dyer, "English Diet," pp. 213–14 and *Standards of Living,* pp. 158–59.
[30]Dyer,"English Diet," pp. 203–04; and Campbell et al., *Medieval Capital,* p. 33.

grain acreage in the FTC counties, three-quarters of that acreage in the country as a whole, and, effectively, the entire brewing-grain acreage in Norfolk, the country's greatest malt-producing county now producing well in excess of its own needs (Table 3).[31] Simultaneously, the brewing grains increased their share of the cropped acreage by approximately one-fifth in Norfolk and a half in both the FTC counties and the country as a whole. So great a relative increase suggests that, against the prevailing arable trend, the absolute acreage sown with barley and dredge may have been greater at the close of the fourteenth century than at the beginning.[32] Suppliers were obviously playing to the most buoyant component of arable demand. It is a measure of the strength of that demand that until almost the very end of the fourteenth century the relative price of barley proved remarkably resilient to the massive growth in supply (Table 2). Norfolk is the exception. Formerly unique in its concentration upon malting barley, its barley producers now had to face much stiffer competition in regional, national, and international markets and consequently had to accept relative barley prices in the second half of the fourteenth century that were substantially down on those to which they had hitherto been accustomed.[33]

The remaining 37 to 41 percent of the cropped area (27 to 30 percent in Norfolk) was consistently devoted to crops that might be used interchangeably for human or animal consumption. These included oats, legumes (peas, beans, and vetches), and various oat and legume mixtures. As human food these were staple ingredients of pottage and the cheaper forms of bread, while oats could also be used for brewing. These were nutritious foodstuffs whose coarseness and association with fodder nevertheless gave them a low dietary status. Consequently, it was their cheapness which chiefly commended them to consumers. Demand for them was strong in the early fourteenth century when living standards were low but waned in the second half of the century as living standards improved. Only where the supply of alternative grains remained scarce, in parts of the extreme north and west of the country, did oats retain a prominent place in diets. Elsewhere it was as a source of fodder rather than foodstuffs that these crops were increasingly to be cultivated, as an adjunct of the expanding pastoral sector.[34]

Oats were already in retreat as a crop well before the fourteenth century opened and they continued to lose ground to legumes throughout that century. As pottage and fodder crops they were more-or-less interchange-

[31]Saul, "Great Yarmouth", pp. 226, 368–71.

[32]For example, Bailey, *Marginal Economy*, p. 237.

[33]Lord Beveridge's unpublished Norfolk grain price series indicates a 31 percent fall in mean barley prices between the 1350s and the 1400s, compared with only an 18 percent fall in the country as a whole over the same period: Lord Beveridge, unpublished price data; and Farmer, "Marketing the Produce," p. 444.

[34]Campbell, "Land," pp. 153–59.

Matching Supply to Demand 837

TABLE 4
NATIONAL CLASSIFICATION OF CROPPING TYPES, 1250–1349

Demesne sample	National Cropping Type							
	1	2	3	4	5	6	7	All
England, 1250–1349								
Mean percentage of total sown area								
Wheat	25.3	8.6	28.2	35.3	44.1	70.4	12.2	33.7
Rye	2.6	28.3	2.0	3.1	1.3	0.0	11.3	4.9
Barley	38.0	34.4	6.1	18.4	4.1	8.8	3.3	15.0
Oats	11.2	19.8	17.4	28.1	44.9	12.2	67.9	31.3
Grain mixtures	1.3	1.9	36.9	4.1	1.8	4.3	3.3	6.4
Legumes	21.7	7.0	9.5	11.0	3.7	4.4	2.0	8.7
Mean total sown acres	171.4	193.3	172.6	222.1	192.2	143.3	159.6	188.6
Number of demesnes	65	35	51	117	131	30	44	473
Percentage of total classified area	12.5	7.6	9.9	29.1	28.2	4.8	7.9	100.0
FTC counties, 1288–1315								
Mean percentage of total sown area								
Wheat	26.2	7.5	30.2	34.4	44.4	58.3	10.2	32.9
Rye	5.1	37.9	3.2	4.2	1.6	0.0	17.1	6.1
Barley	29.8	17.7	6.9	14.8	2.2	13.7	6.1	10.7
Oats	12.4	28.1	19.7	27.2	43.2	9.1	59.1	30.4
Grain mixtures	1.5	3.5	33.4	5.6	4.9	11.5	2.2	10.5
Legumes	24.9	5.4	6.5	13.8	3.8	7.5	5.5	9.4
Mean total sown acres	194.3	217.5	207.7	222.2	278.4	133.1	139.7	224.9
Number of demesnes	17	12	40	58	53	4	12	196
Percentage of total classified area	7.5	5.9	18.8	29.2	33.5	1.2	3.8	100.0
Norfolk, 1250–1349								
Mean percentage of total sown area								
Wheat	17.4	7.2		29.7	44.2			15.7
Rye	5.0	24.2		4.4	8.2			11.9
Barley	46.1	44.1		20.6	7.9			41.4
Oats	12.6	15.8		27.2	33.3			16.1
Grain mixtures	1.7	1.2		2.0	0.0			1.5
Legumes	17.3	7.5		16.1	6.4			13.5
Mean total sown acres	137.4	148.2		199.5	366.5			152.3
Number of demesnes	63	47		19	1			130
Percentage of total classified area	43.7	35.2		19.1	1.9			100.0

Source: National Accounts Database; FTC1 Accounts Database; and Norfolk Accounts Database. For an explanation of the method of calculation, see Campbell and Power, "Mapping," pp. 24–39.

able, with the exception that legumes, unlike oats, were restorative of soil nitrogen. Substituting legumes for oats therefore made sound agricultural sense. Significantly, at the climax of demand for arable produce in the first half of the fourteenth century legumes' share of the pottage/fodder-crop acreage was greater in the more intensively cropped FTC counties than the country as a whole, and greater still in Norfolk, arguably the most intensively cropped county of all. Moreover, it was on the most intensively cropped Norfolk demesnes that oats occupied their smallest and legumes their greatest share of the cropped acreage (Table 4).[35] On these demesnes

[35]Campbell, "Arable Productivity," pp. 392–95. For instance, at Hemsby in the 1320s a mere 3 percent of the cropped area was sown with oats compared with 22 percent sown with legumes. Of the oats, 36 percent of the net receipt was consumed as food liveries, 54 percent as fodder, and the remain-

enough oats were grown to feed the work horses and no more.

After 1350, although there was a general shift towards more land-extensive forms of arable husbandry, legumes continued their inexorable advance. The brunt of that advance now occurred not in areas of intensive arable production (where, on the contrary, the legume acreage tended to contract) but in localities and regions traditionally associated with more extensive methods of production. Thus, they became a major crop in many parts of the midlands which had long been ecologically straight-jacketed by a shortage of permanent grassland.[36] Here in the heartland of the common-field system the opportunity of sowing more land with legumes solved many interrelated problems. Legumes also began to be grown in substantial quantities in both the northwest and northeast. In fact, on a few demesnes they became the single largest crop in terms of acreage.[37] Their appeal lay as a source of fodder to support the growing numbers of animals now being stocked, for whose meat and dairy produce there was a steadily strengthening demand. Converting crops into pastoral foodstuffs has the lowest kilocalorie extraction rate of all and is therefore even more extravagant in its land-use requirements than ale production.[38] The doubling in legumes' share of the pottage/fodder-grains acreage thus bears testimony to the falling unit value of land. So great was this expansion that by the end of the fourteenth century the relative price of peas was beginning to sag. Oats, too, suffered a lowering in relative price, notwithstanding a massive cutback in supply. When times had been hard they had been much in demand as a cheap, nutritious and versatile foodstuff but as living standards improved demand for them progressively narrowed until they were chiefly cultivated in lowland England as a fodder crop for horses.

At the beginning of the fourteenth century bread grains, brewing grains, and pottage/fodder crops were grown in the ratio 41:18:41. A century later the equivalent ratio was 35:28:38. Less land was being devoted to bread grains, significantly more to brewing grains, and the slight contraction in pottage/fodder crops was accompanied by a marked increase in the proportions fed to animals rather than humans. The fortunes of individual crops changed even more markedly, with the higher quality bread and brewing grains faring conspicuously better than their lower quality alternatives. Amidst such changes the comparative stability of relative prices over the course of the century is remarkable (Table 2). It implies that demesne

---

ing 10 percent was sold: of the legumes, 1 percent was consumed as food liveries, 8 percent as fodder, and 91 percent was sold: NRO, DCN 60/15/12-15.

[36]Hilton, *Economic Development*, pp. 65–66; Howell, *Land*, pp. 96–99; Hogan, "Clays," pp. 117–31; and Miller, *Agrarian History*, pp. 213–14, 215, 229–30.

[37]Miller, *Agrarian History*, pp. 178, 187; Morimoto, "Arable Farming"; Durham, Dean and Chapter, Cell accounts; Public Record Office, SC6/1083/4, SC6/1144/10.

[38]Simmons, *Ecology*, pp. 170–73.

managers were sufficiently market sensitive to keep what they produced more or less in line with what was in demand. With wheat that meant holding output reasonably steady, with rye and oats it entailed cutting output back hard, and with barley and peas it entailed expanding production. These, however, are aggregate trends and as such the outcome of many separate production decisions, each taken in the context of the husbandry system peculiar to each demesne. Collectively, these decisions transformed the configuration of production.

The Configuration of Cropping

Demesne land-use was most rational when it was attuned to the prevailing level of economic rent.[39] In an agrarian economy where market influences were strong, as J. H. von Thünen demonstrated, economic rent declined with distance from the market as transport costs rose.[40] The decline was steepest for perishable products and for those with a high bulk content, such as fresh milk, flour, fat animals and firewood. The decline was not as sharp for those such as cheese and grain, which traveled better, and especially for those that, like wool, had a high unit value or, like lean animals on the hoof, were cheap to transport. For von Thünen market-determined economic rent structured not only what farmers produced but also how they produced it, since it was necessary to offset increases in economic rent with more intensive methods of land-use. Nevertheless, as Ricardo showed, economic rent also varied with the type and quality of land and the strength of local demand for it. This was especially the case where market demand was remote and weak. In such situations the best land in strongest demand would command the highest economic rent and accordingly be the most intensively cultivated. In practice, of course, both aspects of economic rent exercised some influence upon demesne production decisions, the balance struck between them depending upon the strength of the market's gravitational pull relative to local environmental and institutional factors. Since those charged with the day-to-day management of demesnes were those most closely acquainted with available opportunities it made sense for lords with far-flung estates to delegate to them the precise choice of crops and methods of cropping. It was these many separate decisions, each informed by prevailing levels of economic rent, which determined the overall configuration of demesne cropping systems.

Analyzing the changing configuration of cropping systems poses a considerable methodological challenge. The solution adopted here has been to generate directly comparable national classifications of cropping types by

---

[39]Campbell, "Economic Rent."
[40]*Von Thünen's Isolated State.*

TABLE 5
NATIONAL CLASSIFICATION OF CROPPING TYPES, 1350–1449

Demesne sample	National Cropping Type						
	1	2	3	4	5	8	All
England, 1350–1449							
Mean percentage of total sown area							
Wheat	14.7	12.2	23.7	36.4	36.9	31.9	30.4
Rye	3.9	22.2	2.1	1.3	1.2	1.5	2.9
Barley	53.9	20.0	9.6	29.1	7.8	17.8	22.6
Oats	11.9	34.6	10.6	17.7	43.9	9.0	23.5
Grain mixtures	2.2	0.5	39.6	2.2	2.1	4.4	6.2
Legumes	13.3	4.7	14.4	13.3	8.2	35.4	14.1
Mean total sown acres	150.6	123.4	152.3	161.6	142.2	161.7	151.6
Number of demesnes	42	17	32	94	87	36	308
Percentage of total classified area	13.5	4.5	10.4	32.5	26.5	12.5	100.0
FTC counties, 1375–1400							
Mean percentage of total sown area							
Wheat	16.0	16.8	22.5	36.7	40.8	27.2	32.1
Rye	4.7	19.8	2.5	0.2	0.9	0.2	2.2
Barley	44.8	12.6	9.4	29.7	5.6	20.7	18.4
Oats	15.3	39.9	10.6	13.0	40.4	11.6	22.5
Grain mixtures	4.6	4.1	41.8	5.6	3.2	5.7	10.2
Legumes	14.6	6.9	13.3	14.8	9.0	34.7	14.6
Mean total sown acres	143.2	160.6	196.8	175.1	182.9	173.8	177.5
Number of demesnes	9	7	19	38	38	14	125
Percentage of total classified area	5.8	5.1	16.9	30.0	31.3	11.0	100.0
Norfolk, 1350–1449							
Mean percentage of total sown area							
Wheat	12.2	8.3	10.5	29.4	33.2	26.3	15.1
Rye	5.5	27.6	2.8	3.3	0.0	2.5	6.9
Barley	55.4	35.9	13.4	32.3	12.4	14.7	47.9
Oats	12.9	20.1	26.6	19.1	39.5	15.8	15.2
Grain mixtures	0.9	2.3	33.8	1.4	4.7	0.0	2.1
Legumes	13.0	5.9	13.1	14.6	10.2	25.4	12.8
Mean total sown acres	129.7	136.0	127.3	143.6	104.4	134.9	131.3
Number of demesnes	79	10	2	17	2	2	112
Percentage of total classified area	69.7	9.2	1.7	16.6	1.4	1.8	100.0

Source: National Accounts Database; FTC2 Accounts Database; and Norfolk Accounts Database. For an explanation of the method of calculation, see Campbell and Power, "Mapping," pp. 24–39.

applying cluster analysis (Relocation method) to the pre-1350 and post-1349 national samples of demesnes, using as the basis of classification the percentage share of the sown acreage occupied by each of the six principal crops (wheat, rye, barley, oats, grain mixtures, and legumes).[41] These same classifications have then been applied to the FTC and Norfolk samples of demesnes using discriminant functions calculated on each national cluster grouping.[42] The results are set out in Tables 4 and 5.

Seven basic cropping types are distinguishable before 1350 and six thereafter. Five of these cropping types are basically common to both periods

[41]Campbell and Power, "Mapping," pp. 24–39; and Power and Campbell, "Cluster Analysis."
[42]Bartley, "Classifying the Past."

(types 1 to 5), although each naturally displays some change in character over time. Cropping-types 6 and 7, specializing respectively in the extensive production of wheat and oats, are specific to the earlier period when arable husbandry was at fullest stretch. They effectively disappear thereafter as, with certain notable exceptions, cropping systems became more diversified and it became increasingly unusual for any one crop to dominate production. In their place a new cropping type appears—cropping-type 8—distinguished by the large-scale cultivation of legumes.

Before 1350 the seven basic cropping types range from the simple to the complex, from those extensive in their use of land to those that exploited it intensively. At the intensive extreme cropping-types 1 and 2 were practiced by just over one-fifth of the sampled demesnes. Both types were characterized by a strong emphasis upon spring-sown crops, especially barley, and, on the most intensively cropped demesnes of all, substantial sowings of legumes. A further one-third of demesnes operated cropping regimes of intermediate complexity and intensity, represented by cropping-types 3 and 4. These appear to have been the demesnes most actively engaged in modifying conventional cropping regimes and adopting new methods. Finally, over two-fifths of demesnes employed relatively simple and extensive systems of cropping—cropping-types 5, 6, and 7—featuring some combination of winter-corn and oats, with few legumes, only minor quantities of other crops, and, usually, biennial or triennial fallows.

The predominance of extensive over intensive cropping systems is consistent with the predictions of the von Thünen model and implies the existence of an agrarian landscape characterized by limited and highly specific areas of high economic rent.[43] Thus, the most intensive systems were almost exclusively confined to the extreme east and southeast of England (the few exceptions are attributable to specific economic, environmental, and institutional circumstances), from which the most extensive systems were conspicuously absent. Within this broad area cropping intensity attained its fullest development where agrarian institutions, in the form of field systems and manorial structures, allowed individuals greatest freedom and enterprise in the management of their land, and especially where cultivators enjoyed the triple advantage of naturally fertile and easily cultivated soils, an abundant labor force, and cheap and convenient access to concentrated centers of demand both at home and overseas. Eastern Norfolk and eastern Kent stand out in this regard and on the evidence of their cropping systems were the localities where levels of economic rent attained their pre–Black Death maxima, mirroring neighboring areas across the North Sea which shared many of the same agricultural characteris-

---

[43]Campbell, "Economic Rent"; and Campbell et al., *Medieval Capital*, pp. 141–44.

tics.[44] Cropping types of intermediate intensity occupied a complementary distribution and in the vicinity of London, in the Thames valley, and the southeast midlands represented market-induced specialization in the cheaper bread and brewing grains. The same may also be true of the many demesnes of this type in Kent, East Anglia, and northeastern Northamptonshire.[45] The more extensive cropping systems were altogether more widely distributed throughout the country. They show up strongly in the immediate hinterland of London where they may have benefited from the substantial metropolitan demand for wheat and oats and were also the typical cropping type of many lowland areas of heavy soil and moderate population density. Above all, they were the characteristic cropping type of much of the north, west, and southwest of the country where there were either environmental or economic constraints upon the development of more intensive and diversified cropping regimes.

Superimposed upon these broad regional patterns was much local variation in cropping systems, best exposed by the denser spatial coverage of the FTC and Norfolk samples of demesnes. The juxtaposition of wold and vale, of light land and heavy land, and of upland and reclaimed marshland almost everywhere found expression in some differentiation of cropping regime.[46] The home demesnes of seignorial households also sometimes developed particular specialisms.[47] Nevertheless, some of the greatest variation over the shortest distances plainly arose from the selective penetration of market demand. The wide array of cropping systems to be found within the middle and lower Thames Valley, upstream of London, is a case in point.[48] Likewise, the wide hinterland of the busy grain entrepot of Kings Lynn contained many different cropping types. Neither hinterland, however, was yet extensive enough to generate spatial differentiation on a grander scale, with the result that the bulk of the country remained outside their respective von Thünen "fields of force." It took the massive metropolitan growth of the seventeenth century to transform the situation and generate a nationally more integrated geography of cropping systems.[49]

After 1349 the picture changes significantly. The trend towards a selective intensification of cropping systems was reversed. A general lowering of Ricardian and von Thünen economic rent—as subsistence pressures receded and urban populations contracted—in conjunction with altered factor costs

[44]Campbell, "Agricultural Progress"; Campbell, "Economic Rent"; Verhulst, "L'intensification"; and Thoen, "Technique agricole."

[45]Campbell et al., Medieval Capital, pp. 138–42; and Campbell, "Economic Rent."

[46]Many of these contrasts are to be seen in Norfolk; see Campbell, "Medieval Arable and Pastoral Husbandry."

[47]Campbell et al., Medieval Capital, p. 151.

[48]Ibid., pp. 111–44.

[49]Langton and Hoppe, Town, pp. 30–41; and Wrigley, "Urban Growth," pp. 683–728. Compare Bieleman, "Dutch Agriculture."

encouraged a return to more extensive forms of land-use and a search for more efficient and cost-effective forms of production. Henceforth the vast majority of demesnes operated cropping systems that were neither intensive nor extensive but of an intermediate character, and it is this proliferation of "intermediate" systems that most distinguishes the post-plague period. In a few localities this represented a downgrading of existing systems whose intensity it was impossible to sustain, but in many more instances it constituted a diversification of existing practice. Often it was associated with the cultivation of a wider range of crops and the allocation of a larger share of the cropped acreage to barley and legumes, usually at the expense of oats. The upshot was a narrower range of cropping types, variants of each of which might be found in quite contrasting geographical contexts often cutting across differences in economic rent and types of field system.

Symptomatic of the times is the fact that London—smaller in population than it had been before the decimation of plague but per caput thirstier and better fed—appears to have exercised a less pronounced impact upon the configuration of cropping types within the Thames basin than formerly. Similarly, there is less evidence that overseas demand was structuring agricultural production along England's North Sea littoral, notwithstanding that the country was in a stronger position to produce and export grain surpluses. By national standards cropping systems were less distinctive than previously in both the southeast and those counties of the east midlands that focused on the Wash and its extensive network of navigable rivers. Norfolk alone retained and enhanced its already distinctive arable identity. All of this points to a flattening of the contours of economic rent as the main centers of concentrated urban demand contracted. As the influence of market-generated von Thünen economic rent waned so the importance of Ricardian economic rent—reflecting differences in land quality and population density—waxed.[50] Demesne managers seem increasingly to have attuned their cultivation to those crops best suited to prevailing environmental circumstances, subject to the estate's own consumption needs and local and regional (rather than national and international) market opportunities. Production was pitched at a level consistent with local land values, themselves a function of land quality and the demand for land. The overall pattern may consequently be interpreted as a reversion to one less structured by wider and more powerful market forces.[51]

CROP DISPOSAL

For demesne managers, producing what was consistent with prevailing relative prices and levels of economic rent involved one set of decisions,

[50]Grigg, *Dynamics,* pp. 50–51, 134–40.
[51]Campbell et al., "Demesne-Farming Systems."

while selling or otherwise disposing of what was produced involved another. Whereas the former were most sensibly taken at a demesne level, the latter were much more a matter of estate policy. The size, nature, and location of the seignorial household and place of the individual demesne within the overall estate structure all affected whether a lord drew upon a demesne for provisions or cash. Transaction costs also exercised a bearing upon the extent to which production for exchange was a more profitable, efficient, and reliable alternative to production for consumption where the estates in question had high internal consumption needs to satisfy. For many lords it always made good sense to provision their workers and their households, in part at least, from the produce of their own estates. The market had yet to attain a level of development where it was advantageous for them to sell all that they produced and purchase all that they consumed.[52]

Measuring the Importance of Crop Sales

There are two important dimensions to the sale of produce, neither entirely straightforward of measurement. First, there is the proportion of net disposable produce that was sold; second, there is the income such sales yielded per unit area. At one extreme, in areas of low economic rent and extensive methods of production the sale of even large proportions of produce are unlikely to have yielded more than a modest cash income per unit area. At the other, the high rates of sale that arose from intensive methods of production close to markets were only sustainable if significant proportions of output were recycled on the manor as fodder and food liveries. Developing commercial considerations had implications for the entire production system far beyond the specific crops intended for sale.

Costing the quantities of each crop sold and unsold poses immediate problems. Discontinuities in account survival mean that it is necessary to use relative rather than absolute prices. Although relative prices unique to each location are to be preferred, only mean relative prices for the FTC counties as a whole are available. These are most misleading close to London where rye and oats—cheap and bulky crops demanded in quantity by that great city—commanded a higher relative price than at a distance.[53] Defining and measuring the "net disposable crop" poses even greater problems. For instance, within the FTC counties crop sales represented 27 percent of gross receipts, 38 percent of gross receipts net of seed, and 50 percent of gross receipts net of seed, fodder, and food liveries to farm workers. The last is the most precise of these three measures but makes the most exacting demands on the evidence. The second is more readily calculated but understates the

[52]Harvey, "Aristocratic Consumer."
[53]Campbell et al., *Medieval Capital*, pp. 111–25. For example, at Fulham, within a few miles of London, rye was valued above wheat in 1304; ibid., p. 124, fn. 36.

significance of sales on those demesnes that made fullest use of fodder and farm labor. In all three cases allowance has to be made for that 7 to 11 percent of grain consumed, transferred, or sold subsequent to malting.[54] No such allowance can however be made for that tenth of gross output "top-sliced" as tithe, whose commercial potential was considerable.[55]

Calculating income per unit area from crop sales is equally problematic. Some accounts record internal transfers as proxy sales. As these are not true sales they need to be discounted, nevertheless, it is only possible to do so when they are explicitly recorded as such. Customary acres are even more elusive of detection and introduce a mostly unquantifiable margin of error. A more systematic bias arises from the failure of all but a handful of accounts to record the total arable area. Without such information only the sales income per *cropped* acre can usually be calculated, even though this exaggerates rates of sale on those demesnes that made greatest use of fallows. Substantial sales of nondemesne grain are a further potential source of inflation; accounts that record 25 percent or more of gross receipts from such sources have therefore been excluded from analysis.

The Geography of Crop Sales

The dichotomy that existed between the rationales of production and disposal is well brought out by Table 6. This analyzes whether there was any connection between choice of cropping type and levels of commercialization within the FTC counties. Unfortunately, not all cropping types are equally well represented within the two samples of demesnes, hence direct comparison is difficult. Certainly, the mostly high standard deviations warn against attaching undue significance to mean figures of the percentages sold and rates of sale. As the maximum and minimum figures indicate, in the period from 1288 to 1315 all cropping types bar cropping-type 6 (of which there are only three examples) furnish examples of demesnes at opposite extremes of the commercialization spectrum.

The same is true respecting minimally commercialized demesnes in the period from 1375 to 1400 but not of strongly commercialized demesnes, which were now comparatively rare (partly because revenues per acre were depressed by falling prices). Nevertheless, cropping types 3, 4, 5, and 6 do all furnish examples of moderately strongly commercialized demesnes which sold at least 40 percent of their net receipts and received at least £10 per 100 sown acres from crop sales. Plainly, no one cropping type was

---

[54]Campbell et al., *Medieval Capital*, pp. 146–47.

[55]Tithe owners feature prominently among those known to have been active in provisioning fourteenth-century Exeter with grain, and rectors were active participants in the grain trade of the London region in much the same period: Kowaleski, "Grain Trade"; and Campbell et al., *Medieval Capital*, pp. 74 n.

TABLE 6
PROPORTIONS SOLD AND RATES OF SALE BY CROPPING TYPE WITHIN THE FTC COUNTIES, 1288–1315 AND 1375–1400

National Cropping Type	Number of Demesnes	Percentage of Aggregate Net Crop Receipt (£) Sold				Income from Sale of Field Crops (£) per 100 Sown Acres			
		Mean	Standard Deviation	Minimum	Maximum	Mean	Standard Deviation	Minimum	Maximum
FTC counties, 1288–1315									
Cropping-type 1	12	43.1	24.5	3.7	75.8	11.5	7.5	1.2	24.9
Cropping-type 2	8	41.2	30.7	2.9	92.7	7.0	6.3	0.8	19.5
Cropping-type 3	26	50.7	26.5	0.0	89.9	11.0	8.5	0.4	28.2
Cropping-type 4	41	37.1	22.3	0.2	93.0	8.0	6.8	0.0	28.3
Cropping-type 5	37	36.6	19.5	0.0	82.4	7.1	5.1	0.0	21.0
Cropping-type 6	3	67.2	15.4	46.0	82.1	24.7	8.5	13.8	34.5
Cropping-type 7	8	42.6	18.8	12.0	71.7	8.2	6.6	1.2	22.8
FTC counties, 1375–1400									
Cropping-type 1	7	23.6	12.9	3.5	41.0	5.3	2.9	1.2	10.8
Cropping-type 2	4	35.7	10.0	19.8	47.2	5.8	2.5	1.9	8.6
Cropping-type 3	13	34.3	14.9	6.1	53.9	11.6	6.3	0.5	24.3
Cropping-type 4	29	38.7	22.7	0.0	77.5	9.2	10.8	0.2	54.9
Cropping-type 5	36	35.4	18.3	5.9	70.5	6.1	3.7	0.2	16.2
Cropping-type 8	12	40.1	29.1	0.5	100.0	8.9	6.2	0.0	20.4

Source: FTC1 and FTC2 Accounts Databases.

associated with intrinsically higher or lower levels of commercialization than any other. The intensively cultivated demesnes of cropping-type 1 were no more commercialized than the more extensively cultivated demesnes of cropping-type 5, which grew mostly wheat and oats. Likewise, the specialized pottage- and fodder-producing demesnes of cropping-types 7 and 8 and the cheap-bread-grain producing demesnes of cropping-type 2 were neither more nor less highly commercialized than others. On this evidence a demesne's choice of cropping type was of little moment in determining the extent of its involvement in the market, even though the market was of considerable moment in determining the choice of cropping type.

Nor was close proximity to urban markets a precondition for a disposal strategy based upon sale. Highly commercialized Avington in southwest Berkshire, Broadwell in west Oxfordshire, Adderbury and Middleton Stoney in north Oxfordshire, and Birdbrook in Essex (20 miles from both Cambridge and Colchester, 30 miles from Ipswich, and almost 50 miles from London) all demonstrate that commercial opportunities were widely available when lords chose to exploit them.[56] Concentrated commercial opportunities did nevertheless encourage some demesnes to become more actively involved in supplying the market. For the Romney Marsh demesnes of Appledore and Fairfield the lure of the coastal and cross-Channel grain trades may have provided the necessary focus for strongly commercialized arable production.[57] For Brightwell, Harwell, and Wantage in Berkshire the Thames provided the vital commercial artery, linking them to both Oxford and London. Lower down the river, Billingbear, Waltham St. Lawrence, and Wargrave also in Berkshire were even better placed to provision London due to their proximity to the major grain entrepot of Henley, much frequented by London cornmongers.[58] Several of these Thames-side manors are known to have engaged directly in the metropolitan grain trade.[59] Downstream of the city, Eastwood and West Thurrock in south Essex and Cliffe and Ospringe in north Kent appear to have taken similar advantage of the lively grain trade—partly metropolitan and partly national and international—that focused upon the Thames estuary.[60] Other less strongly commercialized demesnes reinforce this pattern and define the Thames Valley both upstream and downstream of London as the major axis of commercialization within the southeast. Within the more immediate environs of London, however, sales of wood and pastoral products tended to eclipse those of field crops,

[56]Rates of sale on these demesnes remain impressive even when allowance is made for the fallowing of one-third to one-half of the arable.

[57]For an early analysis of those trades see, Gras, *Evolution*. See also, Farmer, "Marketing," pp. 358–77.

[58]Campbell et al., *Medieval Capital*, pp. 47–49, 51–55, 76–77, 92–93, 101–02.

[59]Farmer, "Marketing," pp. 367–68, 371.

[60]Campbell et al., *Medieval Capital*, pp. 68–69, 92–94, 169, 181–82.

as was consistent with prevailing patterns of land-use and levels of economic rent.[61] Here a weakly commercialized arable sector was a concomitant of other more strongly commercialized areas of activity.

Evidently there were certain localities where the commercial pulse beat faster and drew a greater proportion and volume of production to market. True, most of the demesnes which took greatest advantage of those opportunities belonged to those lords most interested in exploiting their estates as a source of cash rather than provisions, hence it was clearly not good enough merely to be in the right location. It was being in the right location *and* belonging to the right estate that made the difference. That is why neighboring demesnes sharing effectively the same location and physical characteristics and employing much the same cropping system nevertheless often displayed fundamentally different commercialization profiles depending on the estate to which they belonged and their role within it. This is most readily illustrated with reference to Essex and Hertfordshire, two counties close to London whose predominantly heavy soils supported a strikingly uniform pattern of cropping. In the period from 1375 to 1400 no less than 30 documented demesnes in these two counties practiced some version of three-course cropping with wheat and oats (cropping-type 5). Ten were possessions of Westminster Abbey, the other 20 were divided between 15 different conventual, collegiate, and lay lords. Significantly, disposal strategies mirrored this diversity of ownership rather than the uniformity of production or gradations of cost-distance from London. Individual demesnes sold anything from 6 to 63 percent of their net crop receipts, generating (with one exception) a sales income per 100 sown acres of £0.1 to £9.2. Even the ten Westminster Abbey demesnes sold variously 9 to 57 percent of their net crop receipts at rates ranging from £1.0 to £8.8 per 100 sown acres. The four Hertfordshire demesnes of Aldenham, Kinsbourne, Stevenage, and Wheathampstead were the least commercialized of this group, no doubt because they were geographically best placed to send provisions to Westminster.[62] Feering, Kelvedon, and Moulsham in mid-Essex were further removed and consequently more actively involved in supplying the market. Most commercialized of all, however, were Bekeswell, a close neighbor of Moulsham in mid Essex, Sawbridgeworth in Hertfordshire, convenient to the navigable River Lea and thence both London and Westminster, and Birdbrook in north Essex, remotest of all from Westminster. The co-existence of strongly and weakly commercialized demesnes on this one large and geographically extensive estate highlights the role of estate managers in determining which demesnes yielded provisions, which cash, and which a combination of the two. Nor was the

---

[61]Campbell, "Measuring," pp. 177–84; Galloway et al., "Fuelling the City."
[62]For a case study of Kinsbourne, see Stern, "Hertfordshire Manor."

Westminster estate unique. The place of the individual demesne within the overall estate production system was almost always a matter of considerable commercial consequence.

Trends in Crop Sales

Over the course of the fourteenth century seignorial arable production tended to become less rather than more commercialized (Table 7). Sale gained relative to intra-estate transfer as a method of disposal but declined in absolute importance. Proportionately, there were as many weakly commercialized demesnes at the end of the fourteenth century as at the beginning, but fewer that were strongly commercialized. Whereas in the period from 1288 to 1315 demesnes in the ten FTC counties sold 40 percent of their net crop receipt and received a gross mean income of £8.8 per 100 sown acres, in the period from 1375 to 1400 they sold on average 36 percent of their net crop receipt and received £8.1 from crop sales. On 54 demesnes common to both databases the mean proportion sold slipped from 38 to 36 percent, while their mean sales income sank from £10.2 to £9.3 per 100 sown acres. The lower prices prevailing in the final quarter of the fourteenth century compounded this trend.

At the beginning of the fourteenth century—on the evidence of Table 7—just over one-third of FTC demesnes were heavily involved in selling their crops on the market, and on one in three of these levels of commercialization were particularly high. Yet by the close of the century less than a quarter of demesnes may be classified as strongly commercialized, and on only two of these 23 demesnes was commercialization maintained at the very highest level. In both periods a striking common denominator of these most market-orientated demesnes is that they invariably belonged to major lay or ecclesiastical magnates—the crown, the earl of Lincoln, and the bishop of Winchester—as much, if not more, in need of cash than provisions. Conversely, all 32 of the demesnes that in the period from 1288 to 1315 sold less than 20 percent of their net crop receipt and received less than £5 per 100 sown acres from crop sales belonged to conventual estates, which were perpetual institutions with substantial fixed households to provision. The list includes properties of the abbeys of Boxley, Crowland, Oseney, Peterborough (13 demesnes), Waltham, and Westminster (eight demesnes) and the priories of Bicester and Canterbury. In the period from 1375 to 1400 20 of the 26 demesnes that were similarly least commercialized were likewise in conventual hands. They are joined by one property of New College, Oxford, and five demesnes in the ownership of such lay lords as John Doget, John de Gildeburgh, Edmund de la Pole, and William Wanton. The appearance of so many lay demesnes on the later list is a reminder that many a lay

TABLE 7
SALE OF CROPS BY DEMESNES IN THE FTC COUNTIES, 1288–1315 AND 1375–1400
(by ownership type)

Number of Manors

	FTC1, 1288–1315 Ownership Type					FTC2, 1375–1400 Ownership Type				
	All	Conventual / Collegiate	Episcopal	Lay	Royal	All	Conventual / Collegiate	Episcopal	Lay	Royal
A. Sales as a Percentage of Aggregate Net Crop Receipt (£)										
80 percent and over	9	2	3	2	2	1	1	0	0	0
60 to less than 80 percent	20	6	4	1	9	11	8	0	3	0
40 to less than 60 percent	51	27	7	6	11	36	21	6	9	0
20 to less than 40 percent	23	14	1	2	6	33	17	6	9	1
less than 20 percent	33	32	0	0	1	28	23	0	5	0
Mean percentage	39.8	31.4	63.1	49.0	52.1	36.1	34.5	42.3	37.2	39.5
Standard deviation	23.5	21.5	17.1	17.9	18.2	20.4	22.2	8.7	19.1	0.0
B. Income from Sale of Field Crops per 100 Acres Sown										
£15.0 and over	23	8	8	3	4	8	4	2	2	0
£12.5 to less than £15.0	9	3	3	0	3	8	6	2	0	0
£10.0 to less than £12.5	17	10	2	2	3	18	9	6	3	0
£ 7.5 to less than £10.0	18	13	1	1	3	15	9	1	5	0
£ 5.0 to less than £ 7.5	18	8	0	2	8	22	15	0	6	1
£ 2.5 to less than £ 5.0	20	10	1	2	7	19	13	1	5	0
less than £2.5	31	29	0	1	1	19	14	0	5	0
Mean £	8.8	6.8	18.9	9.8	8.9	8.1	6.9	16.8	7.1	7.0
Standard deviation	7.3	6.3	7.3	5.8	5.4	7.1	4.8	13.4	5.2	0.0

TABLE 7—continued

Number of Manors

C. Combined Commercialization Index

Level of Commercialization	FTC 1, 1288–1315 Ownership Type					FTC2, 1375–1400 Ownership Type				
	All	Conventual / Collegiate	Episcopal	Lay	Royal	All	Conventual / Collegiate	Episcopal	Lay	Royal
Very strong	17	5	6	2	4	2	2	0	0	0
Strong	30	14	7	3	6	23	13	6	4	0
Intermediate	35	18	1	4	12	32	19	4	9	0
Weak	22	12	1	2	7	26	15	2	8	1
Very weak	32	32	0	0	0	26	21	0	5	0
Total	136	81	15	11	29	109	70	12	26	1

Notes: The number of manors excludes those deriving less than 75 percent of gross receipts (net of tithe) from the harvest. Very strongly commercialized is defined as selling at least 60 percent and receiving at least £15 per 100 sown acre. Strongly commercialized is defined as selling at least 40 percent and receiving at least £10 per 100 sown acre. Intermediate is defined as either selling at least 40 percent and receiving less than £10 per 100 sown acre or selling less than 40 percent and receiving at least £10 per 100 sown acre. Weakly commercialized is selling less than 40 percent and receiving less than £10.0 per 100 sown acre. Very weakly commercialized is selling less than 20 percent and receiving less than £5.0 per 100 sown acre.

Source: FTC1 and FTC2 Accounts Databases.

household remained as dependent upon its own estates, or at least its home farm, for its provisions as its conventual counterparts. On the other hand, it is often only for these home demesnes that manorial accounts are extant, conveying a misleading impression of the limited market involvement by this class of producer.[63]

If in the twilight of direct management economic autarky remained a cherished principle on at least one in four of demesnes that remained in hand, it was also true that fewer demesnes were exclusively dedicated to the direct provisioning of seignorial and especially conventual households than had been the case at the beginning of the fourteenth century. At the same time the more extreme forms of commercial specialization were also less in evidence (Table 7). The kinds of institutional distinction so apparent at the beginning of the century were far less sharply etched by its close. While differences between individual estates remained important, contrasts between broad ownership types were more muted. Cropping systems, too, became less commercialized over the course of the century (Table 6) and locationally the Thames valley upstream and downstream of London ceased to be the focus of heightened commercial activity which it had once been, at least so far as grain was concerned. Instead, it is the vale country north of the Chiltern scarp that emerges most strongly, together with parts of Kent.[64] This mirrors the changing scale and structure of market demand and underscores the dynamic character of arable husbandry throughout this period. None of this is surprising for by 1400 the grain trade was flowing down fewer, smaller arteries and hence provided a weakening incentive to commit a greater volume of seignorial production to the market. Animals rather than crops now offered the best commercial opportunities and expanding fodder consumption may be one reason why a greater share of net crop production was now being retained and consumed on the manor.

CONCLUSION

These observations imply that market forces exercised a profound influence upon the production decisions of demesne managers. Changes in the scale, composition, and configuration of crop production all point to an agrarian economy which was demand led and therefore responsive to factor and commodity prices and levels of economic rent. Relative prices show that supply and demand remained more or less in equilibrium throughout the dramatic demographic and economic changes which characterized the fourteenth century. Until these setbacks the potential for market-generated growth undoubtedly existed but remained less than completely fulfilled for reasons largely external to the agrarian sector. Part of the explanation may

---

[63]Compare Livingstone, "Sir John Pulteney's Landed Estates."
[64]Galloway, "London's Grain Supply."

lie in the dispersed nature of demand and lack of really major urban centers capable of generating agricultural specialization over a wide area. Low levels of economic rent must consequently have lain like a shadow across much of the country, justifying the relatively unspecialized and extensive cropping systems of so many demesnes.

Since demesnes conformed in the main with the prevailing husbandry practice of their localities, estates as institutions can have exercised only a limited and selective influence upon production. Disposal strategies, in contrast, were much more a matter of estate policy. Lords had a choice of provisioning their households either directly from their estates or by purchase on the market, with the consequence that demesne surpluses might either be retained for consumption on the estate (on the manor, at headquarters, or elsewhere) or sold. In practice most lords appear to have pursued a dual policy, providing part of their needs from their estates and part from the market. Strikingly, even within the FTC counties, in the immediate hinterland of the country's greatest single grain market, more produce appears to have been transferred within estates than was transferred off them. As metropolitan a household as Westminster Abbey preferred to supply a substantial part of its needs from its own estates, sometimes transferring produce a significant distance overland in order to do so. Nor do central accounts suggest that produce was being transferred with the intention of selling it centrally, although more work remains to be done on this potentially revealing class of evidence.[65]

The abiding adherence of many estates, especially those supporting major conventual communities, to a policy of at least partial autarky is one of the most striking features of the evidence. It implies that direct provisioning continued to offer certain real or perceived advantages over market purchase. Relevant factors probably include the transaction-cost differential between obtaining provisions from the market or the estate, the nature and scale of the seignorial households to be provisioned, the corresponding scale and reliability of markets and risks involved in relying upon them, and the hidden subsidies of customary labor and carrying services.[66] Market participation by individual demesnes thus depended upon their place within the estate production system as a whole, the commercial pull of the most accessible markets, and the importance of arable production within the overall production strategy of the demesne. These are all issues that would repay further enquiry. Although few of the sampled demesnes sold little or none of their net crop output, highly commercialized demesnes were always very much the exception. In this respect, markets, although highly developed and all pervasive, had a lot of ground yet to gain. Nor is there much evidence to

[65]Campbell, "Measuring," p. 141; and *Household Accounts*.
[66]Harvey, "Aristocratic Consumer."

suggest that much if any of that ground was gained during the fourteenth century. On the contrary, there is a case for arguing that in the face of economic recession and demographic collapse market development lost much of its existing momentum, at least as far as the majority arable sector was concerned.

By any definition, seignorial estates and their constituent demesnes were major enterprises. They had an inherent tendency to produce more than their dependent households could consume and hence were potentially substantial suppliers of the market. Yet, paradoxically, lords were better placed to isolate themselves from the market and live off their estates than almost any other class of producer. These results from the seignorial sector thus raise intriguing questions about levels of market involvement among nondemesne producers. Did the preoccupation of most small agricultural producers with subsistence rather than profit cause them to shun the market as much as possible? Or did the absence of an estate-based supply system or its equivalent foster a far greater dependence upon the market? The answers, as in the case of the seignorial sector, are likely to depend upon the type, location, enterprise, and institutional characteristics of the producer.[67]

[67]For approaches to peasant involvement in the market see, Biddick, "Medieval English Peasants" and "Missing Links"; Harvey, "Introduction", pp. 12–16; and Dyer, "Hidden Trade."

REFERENCES

Aston, T. H., and Philpin, C. H. E., eds. *The Brenner Debate: Agrarian Class Structure and Economic Development in Pre-Industrial Europe.* Cambridge: Cambridge University Press, 1985.

Bailey, Mark. *A Marginal Economy? East-Anglian Breckland in the Later Middle Ages.* Cambridge: Cambridge University Press, 1989.

Bartley, Ken. "Classifying the Past: Discriminant Analysis and its Application to Medieval Farming Systems." *History and Computing*, 8, 1 (1996): 1–10.

Bennett, Judith. *Ale, Beer, and Brewsters in England: Women's Work in a Changing World, 1300–1600.* Oxford: Oxford University Press, 1996.

Lord Beveridge. Unpublished price data. Box G9. London School of Economics Library.

Biddick, Kathleen. "Medieval English Peasants and Market Involvement." This JOURNAL 45, no. 4 (1985): 823–31.

_____. "Missing Links: Taxable Wealth, Markets, and Stratification among Medieval English Peasants." *Journal of Interdisciplinary History* 18, no. 2 (1987): 277–98.

Bieleman, Jan. "Dutch Agriculture in the Golden Age, 1570–1660." In *The Dutch Economy in the Golden Age: Nine Studies*, edited by K. Davids and L. Noordegraaf, 159–83. Amsterdam: Netherlands Economic History Archives, 1993.

Blanchard, Ian. *The Middle Ages: A Concept too Many?*. Avonbridge: Newlees Press, 1996.

Bodleian Library. MS Rolls Norfolk. Oxford.

Britnell, R. H. "Commerce and Capitalism in Late Medieval England: Problems of Description and Theory." *Journal of Historical Sociology*, 6, no. 4 (1993): 359–76.

_____. *The Commercialisation of English Society 1000–1500.* Cambridge: Cambridge

University Press, 1993.

Britnell, R. H., and Campbell, Bruce M. S., eds. *A Commercialising Economy: England 1086–1300*. Manchester: Manchester University Press, 1995.

Campbell, Bruce M. S. "Agricultural Progress in Medieval England: Some Evidence from Eastern Norfolk." *Economic History Review*, 2d ser. 36, no. 1 (1983): 26–46.

_____. "Arable Productivity in Medieval England: some Evidence from Norfolk." This JOURNAL 43, no. 2(1983): 379–404.

_____. "Land, Labour, Livestock, and Productivity Trends in English Seignorial Agriculture, 1208–1450." In *Land, Labour and Livestock: Studies in European Agricultural Productivity*, edited by Bruce M. S. Campbell and Mark Overton, 144–82. Manchester: Manchester University Press, 1991.

_____. "A Fair Field once Full of Folk: Agrarian Change in an Era of Population Decline, 1348–1500." *Agricultural History Review*, 41, no. 1 (1993): 60–70.

_____. "Medieval Arable and Pastoral Husbandry 1250–1349." In *An Historical Atlas of Norfolk*, edited by Peter Wade-Martins, 50–1. Norwich: Norfolk Museums Service, 1993.

_____. "Measuring the Commercialisation of Seigneurial Agriculture c. 1300." In *A Commercialising Economy: England 1086 to c. 1300*, edited by R. H. Britnell and Bruce M. S. Campbell, 132–93. Manchester: Manchester University Press, 1995.

_____. "Economic Rent and the Intensification of English Agriculture, 1086–1350." In *Agricultural Technology in North-Western Europe in the Middle Ages*, edited by Grenville Astill and John Langdon, 225–50. Leiden: Brill, 1997.

Campbell, Bruce M. S., et al. *A Medieval Capital and its Grain Supply: Agrarian Production and its Distribution in the London Region c.1300*. Historical Geography Research Series, 30. 1993.

Campbell, Bruce M. S., Bartley, Ken, and Power, John P. "The Demesne-Farming Systems of Post Black Death England: A Classification." *Agricultural History Review*, 44, no. 2 (1996): 131–79.

Campbell, Bruce M. S., and Power, J. P. "Mapping the Agricultural Geography of Medieval England." *Journal of Historical Geography*, 15, no. 1 (1989): 24–39.

Chisholm, M. *Rural Settlement and Land-use: An Essay on Location*. London: Hutchinson, 1962.

Dodgshon, R. A. *The European Past: Social Evolution and Spatial Order*. London: Macmillan, 1987.

Dyer, C. C. "English Diet in the Later Middle Ages." In *Social Relations and Ideas: Essays in Honour of R. H. Hilton*, edited by T. H. Aston, et al., 191–216. Cambridge: Cambridge University Press, 1983.

_____. "Changes in Diet in the Late Middle Ages: The Case of Harvest Workers." *Agricultural History Review*, 36, no. 1 (1988): 21–38.

_____. *Standards of Living in the Later Middle Ages: Social Change in England c.1200–1520*. Cambridge: Cambridge University Press, 1989.

_____. "The Hidden Trade of the Middle Ages: Evidence from the West Midlands of England." *Journal of Historical Geography*, 18, no. 2 (1992): 141–57.

_____. *Everyday Life in Medieval England*. London: Hambledon, 1994.

_____. "How Urbanized was Medieval England?" In *Peasants and Townsmen in Medieval Europe: Studia in honorem Adriaan Verhulst*, edited by J.-M. Duvosquel and Erik Thoen, 169–83. Ghent: Snoeck-Ducaju and Zoon, 1995.

Farmer, D. L. "Grain Yields on the Winchester Manors in the Later Middle Ages." *Economic History Review*, 2d ser. 30, no. 4 (1977): 555–66.

_____. "Prices and Wages." In *The Agrarian History of England and Wales, II,*

1042–1350, edited by H. E. Hallam, 716–817. Cambridge: Cambridge University Press, 1988.

———. "Marketing the Produce of the Countryside, 1200–1500." In *The Agrarian History of England and Wales, III, 1348–1500*, edited by Edward Miller, 324–430. Cambridge: Cambridge University Press, 1991.

———. "Prices and wages, 1350–1500." In *The Agrarian History of England and Wales, III, 1348–1500*, edited by Edward Miller, 431–525. Cambridge: Cambridge University Press, 1991.

Galloway, James A. "London's Grain Supply: Changes in Production, Distribution and Consumption during the Fourteenth Century." *Franco-British Studies: Journal of the British Institute in Paris*, 20 (1995): 23–34.

Galloway, James A., Keene, Derek, and Murphy, Margaret. "Fuelling the City: Production and Distribution of Firewood and Fuel in London's Region 1290–1400." *Economic History Review*, 2d ser. 49, no. 3 (1996): 447–72.

Glasscock, R. E. "England circa 1334." In *A New Historical Geography of England*, edited by H. C. Darby, 136–85. Cambridge: Cambridge University Press, 1973.

Gras, N. S. B. *The Evolution of the English Corn Market from the Twelfth to the Eighteenth Century*. Cambridge, Mass.: Harvard University Press, 1915.

Grigg, D. B. *Population Growth and Agrarian Change: An Historical Perspective*. Cambridge: Cambridge University Press, 1980.

———. *The Dynamics of Agricultural Change: The Historical Experience*. London: Hutchinson, 1982.

Harrison, D. F. "Bridges and Economic Development, 1300–1800." *Economic History Review*, 2nd series, 45, no. 2 (1992): 240–61.

Harvey, B. F. "Introduction: The 'Crisis' of the Early Fourteenth Century." In *Before the Black Death: Studies in the 'Crisis' of the Early Fourteenth Century*, edited by Bruce M. S. Campbell, 1–24. Manchester: Manchester University Press, 1991.

———. "The Aristocratic Consumer in England in the Long Thirteenth Century." In *Thirteenth Century England VI*, 17–37. Woodbridge: Boydell, 1997.

Hatcher, John. "English Serfdom and Villeinage: Towards a Reassessment." *Past and Present*, 90 (1981): 247–84.

Hilton, R. H. *The Economic Development of some Leicestershire Estates in the Fourteenth and Fifteenth Centuries*. London: Oxford University Press, 1947.

———. "Medieval Agrarian History." In *The Victoria History of the County of Leicester, II*, edited by William Page, 145–98. The Victoria History of the Counties of England. London: Constable, 1954.

Hogan, M. P. "Clays, *Culturae* and the Cultivator's Wisdom: Management Efficiency at Fourteenth-Century Wistow." *Agricultural History Review*, 36, no. 2 (1988): 117–31.

Household Accounts from Medieval England. 2 vols. Edited by C. M. Woolgar. Oxford: Oxford University Press for The British Academy, 1992–93.

Howell, Cicely. *Land, Family and Inheritance in Transition: Kibworth Harcourt 1280–1700*. Cambridge: Cambridge University Press, 1983.

Keene, Derek. "A New Study of London before the Great Fire." *Urban History Yearbook 1984*: 11–21.

Kowaleski, Maryanne. "The Grain Trade in Fourteenth-century Devon." In *The Salt of Common Life: Individuality and Choice in the Medieval Town, Countryside and Church. Essays Presented to J. Ambrose Raftis on the Occasion of his 70th Birthday*, edited by Edwin Brezette DeWindt, 1–52. Kalamazoo: Medieval Institute, Western Michigan University, 1996.

Langdon, John. "Horses, Oxen, and Technological Innovation: The Use of Draught

Animals in English Farming from 1066 to 1500." Ph.D. diss., University of Birmingham, 1983.

Langton, John, and Hoppe, Göran. *Town and Country in the Development of Early Modern Western Europe*. Historical Geography Research Series, 11, Norwich, 1983.

Livingstone, Marilyn. "Sir John Pulteney's Landed Estates: The Acquisition and Management of Land by a London Merchant." M.A. diss., University of London, 1991.

Masschaele, James. "Transport Costs in Medieval England." *Economic History Review*, 2d ser. 46, no. 2 (1993): 266-79.

Mayhew, Nicholas. "Modelling Medieval Monetisation." In *A Commercialising Economy: England 1086 to c.1300*, edited by R. H. Britnell and Bruce M. S. Campbell, 55–77. Manchester: Manchester University Press, 1995.

Miller, Edward, ed. *The Agrarian History of England and Wales, III, 1348–1500*. Cambridge: Cambridge University Press, 1991.

Miller Edward, and Hatcher, John. *Medieval England: Towns, Commerce and Crafts 1086–1348*. London: Longmans, 1995.

Morimoto, N. "Arable Farming of Durham Cathedral Priory in the Fourteenth Century." *Nagoya Gakuin University Review*, 11, no. 3.4 (1975): 137–331.

Nightingale, Pamela. "The Growth of London in the Medieval English Economy." In *Progress and Problems in Medieval England: Essays in Honour of Edward Miller*, edited by R. H. Britnell and John Hatcher, 89–106. Cambridge: Cambridge University Press, 1996.

Norfolk Record Office (NRO). Dean and Chapter Collection (DCN), l'Estrange Collection, and Norfolk and Norwich Antiquaries' Society Collection (NNAS). Norwich, Norfolk.

Overton, Mark, and Campbell, Bruce M. S. "Production et productivité dans l'agriculture anglais, 1086–1871." *Histoire et Mesure*, XI-3/4 (1996): 255–97.

Persson, Karl Gunnar. *Pre-Industrial Economic Growth: Social Organization and Technological Progress in Europe*. Oxford: Basil Blackwell, 1988.

Postan, M. M. "Medieval Agrarian Society in its Prime: England." In *The Cambridge Economic History of Europe*, Vol. 1. *The Agrarian Life of the Middle Ages*, edited by M. M. Postan, 549–632. Cambridge: Cambridge University Press, 2d ed. 1966.

Power, John P., and Campbell, Bruce M. S. "Cluster Analysis and the Classification of Medieval Demesne-farming Systems." *Transactions of the Institute of British Geographers*, new series, 17 (1992), pp 232–42.

Public Record Office (PRO). London.

Saul, Andrew. "Great Yarmouth in the Fourteenth Century: A Study in Trade, Politics and Society." D.Phil. diss., University of Oxford, 1975.

Simmons, I. G. *The Ecology of Natural Resources*. London: Edward Arnold, 2d ed. 1981.

Smith, R. M. "Human Resources." In *The Countryside of Medieval England*, edited by Grenville Astill and Annie Grant, 188–212. Oxford: Basil Blackwell, 1988.

Stern, D. V. "A Hertfordshire Manor of Westminster Abbey: An Examination of Demesne Profits, Corn Yields, and Weather Evidence." Ph.D. diss., University of London, 1978.

Thoen, Erik. "Technique agricole, cultures nouvelles et economie rurale en Flandre au bas moyen âge." In *Flaran 12 (1990): Plantes et cultures nouvelles en Europe occidentale, au moyen age et à l'époque moderne*: 51–67. Centre Belge d'histoire rurale, publication 107. Gent 1993.

Thornton, Christopher. "The Determinants of Land Productivity on the Bishop of Winchester's Demesne of Rimpton, 1208 to 1403." In *Land, Labour and Livestock: Studies in European Agricultural Productivity*, edited by Bruce M. S. Campbell and Mark Overton, 183–210. Manchester: Manchester University Press, 1991.

858

Townshend Manuscripts. Raynham Hall, Norfolk.

Verhulst, Adriaan. "L'intensification et la commercialisation de l'agriculture dans les Pays-Bas méridionaux au XIIIᵉ siècle." In *La Belgique rurale du moyen-âge à nos jours. Mélanges offerts à J. J. Hoebanx*: 89–100. Brussels: Editions de l'Université de Bruxelles, 1985.

Von Thünen's Isolated State. Translated by Carla M. Wartenberg, edited by Peter Hall. London: Pergamon, 1966.

Wrigley, E. A. "Urban Growth and Agricultural Change: England and the Continent in the Early Modern Period." *Journal of Interdisciplinary History*, 15, no. 4 (1985), 683–728.

X

Constraint or constrained? Changing perspectives on medieval English agriculture[1]

1. Introduction

Agriculture was by far the largest sector within the medieval English economy, accounting for at least 60 percent of GDP in 1300.[2] It was agriculture, too, which furnished the bulk of English exports, notably wool (in processed and unprocessed form) plus hides and grain. At least three-quarters of the population lived on the land and in most cases they made all or part of their living by working the land. Even for the elite, landed wealth constituted the foundation of social status and political power. Nevertheless, medieval English agriculture has traditionally received a bad press. For instance, according to D.L. Farmer: 'The struggle to grow grain used most of the labour resources, most of the land, most of the capital, and most of the management talent in the medieval rural economy - and to such little success that poorish harvests brought famine and death'.[3] Farmer takes his cue from M.M. Postan, for whom 'the inertia of medieval agricultural technology is unmistakable'.[4] Nor, on this point, does the Marxist historian Robert Brenner disagree: 'There

1. This paper would not have been written without the encouragement of Jan Bieleman. Figure 1 was generated by Ken Bartley using data collected by Roger Dickinson and Marilyn Livingstone. Funding for this component of the research upon which this paper is based was provided by the Leverhulme Trust and The Queen's University of Belfast. The data upon which Table 1 is based were largely contributed by John Langdon. Additional data were collected with the financial assistance of the Social Science Research Council.
2. N. Mayhew, 'Modelling Medieval Monetisation', in: R.H. Britnell and B.M.S. Campbell (eds.), *A Commercialising Economy: England 1086 to c.1300* (Manchester, 1995) 57-60; B.M.S. Campbell, *English Seigniorial Agriculture 1250-1450* (Cambridge, forthcoming).
3. D.L. Farmer, 'Grain Yields on Westminster Abbey Manors, 1271-1410', *Canadian Journal of History,* XVIII: 3 (1983) 331.
4. M.M. Postan, *The Medieval Economy and Society: An Economic History of Britain in the Middle Ages* (London, 1972) 44.

were, in fact, known and available agricultural improvements - including the ultimately revolutionary "convertible husbandry" - which could have brought significant improvements in demesne output. ....[But these] were almost totally ignored
by English landlords'.[5]

Postan and Brenner concur in attributing the root of agriculture's perceived un-
der-performance to supply-side constraints. For Postan these constraints were
essentially Ricardian in nature and arose from the difficulty of avoiding diminishing
returns to both land and labour as population growth led more and more land of
inferior quality to be brought into production.[6] For Brenner, more serious was the
chronic under-investment which arose from feudal socio-property relations.[7] Rather than invest, lords preferred to spend 'up to the hilt on personal display, on
extravagant living, on the maintenance of a numerous retinue, and on war'.[8] Nor
could peasants make good this deficiency for they were deprived of capital by a
combination of excessive feudal exactions, arbitrary royal purveyancing, and puni-
tive taxation. The upshot in both cases was technological inertia. Agriculture - the
producer of vital food and raw materials - thus remained within a low productivity
trap, with increments in output depending upon a process of *extensification* (to
which the supply of land set finite limits) rather than one of *intensification* and
productivity growth. Under these circumstances headlong population growth was
bound sooner or later to precipitate demographic crisis. This in turn triggered the
breakdown of feudal socio-property relations and opened the way to the emergence of agrarian capitalism in the ensuing early modern period, with all that this
implies for increased investment levels, higher productivity, and eventually agricultural revolution.[9]

Traditional accounts of medieval agriculture are thus more preoccupied with
supply than demand and tend to stress the primacy of socio-political and institutional considerations over market forces. Thus, it is political power, socio-property
relationships and class conflict, which provide the key to change (or the lack of it),
and manorial structures and field systems which provide the essential framework

5. R. Brenner, 'Agrarian Class Structure and Economic Development in Pre-Industrial
Europe', in: T.H. Aston and C.H.E. Philpin (eds.), *The Brenner Debate: Agrarian Class
Structure and Economic Development in Pre-Industrial Europe* (Cambridge, 1987) 32-3.
6. M.M. Postan and J. Hatcher, 'Population and Class Relations in Feudal Society', in:
Aston and Philpin, *Brenner Debate*, 69-70.
7. R. Brenner, 'The Agrarian Roots of European Capitalism', in: Aston and Philpin, *Brenner Debate*, 232-6.
8. R.H. Hilton, *The English Peasantry in the Later Middle Ages: The Ford Lectures for
1973 and Related Studies* (Oxford, 1975) 177.
9. For an early exposition of this traditional view see, R.E. Prothero, *English Farming
Past and Present* (London, 1912). For a recent reassessment of the decline of feudalism see
R.H. Britnell, 'Commerce and Capitalism in Late Medieval England: Problems of Description and Theory', *Journal of Historical Sociology*, 6: 4 (1993) 359-76.

within which change took place. A further sub-plot emphasizes the potential ecological shortcomings and productivity constraints of organic husbandry systems. This has led to claims that soil exhaustion rendered even existing levels of productivity impossible to sustain.[10] As J.D. Chambers observed 'It was not merely that agricultural techniques were unable to respond to the challenge of increased demand; it was worse than this. The techniques that had sufficed to enable the population to reach the existing limit began to recede'.[11] Indeed, the very knowledge that the entire socio-economic system eventually succumbed to demographic disaster in the form of famine and plague lends appeal to explanatory models - be they Malthusian, Ricardian, or Marxist - which see nemesis as the eventual price paid for expansion. The chronological bias of surviving historical evidence towards the troubled half century or so before the Black Death reinforces this tendency.

Such gloomy and negative verdicts nevertheless fail to do justice to the genuine achievements of English agriculture during the 250 years between the making of Domesday Book in 1086 and the outbreak of the Black Death in 1348. By c.1300 English agriculture was feeding at least twice as many people as in 1086. It was also provisioning a greatly enlarged urban population, whose share of the total had approximately doubled from a tenth to a fifth.[12] Several major urban centres had also come into being. London, by far the largest, contained 70-75,000 inhabitants at the climax of its medieval growth c.1300 and drew upon a greatly extended rural hinterland for food and fuel.[13] As the medieval economy expanded so did the de-

10. Postan, *Medieval Economy and Society*, 57-72. For the historiography of this hypothesis see N. Hybel, *Crisis or Change. The Concept of Crisis in the Light of Agrarian Structural Reorganization in Late Medieval England*, trans. J. Manley (Aarhus, 1989). For a recent scientific contribution to the debate see E. I. Newman and P.D.A. Harvey, 'Did Soil Fertility Decline in Medieval English Farms? Evidence from Cuxham, Oxfordshire, 1320-1340, *Agricultural History Review*, 45: II (1997) 119-36.

11. J.D. Chambers, *Population, Economy, and Society in Pre-industrial England* (London, 1972) 24. Cf B.M.S. Campbell, 'Ecology Versus Economics in Late Thirteenth- and Early Fourteenth-Century English Agriculture' in: D. Sweeney (ed.), *Agriculture in the Middle Ages: Technology, Practice, and Representation* (Philadelphia, 1995) 76-110.

12. M. Overton and B.M.S. Campbell, 'Production et productivité dans l'agriculture anglaise, 1086-1871', *Histoire & Mesure*, XI: 3/4, *Prix, production, productivité agricoles* (1996) 290.

13. B.M.S. Campbell, J.A. Galloway, D.J. Keene, and M. Murphy, *A Medieval Capital and its Grain Supply: Agrarian Production and its Distribution in the London Region c.1300*, Historical Geography Research Series, 30 (1993) 9-11; P. Nightingale, 'The Growth of London in the Medieval English Economy', in: R.H. Britnell and J. Hatcher (eds.) *Progress and Problems in Medieval England: Essays in Honour of Edward Miller* (Cambridge, 1996) 35-8; J.A. Galloway, D.J. Keene, and M. Murphy, 'Fuelling the City: Production and Distribution of Firewood and Fuel in London's Region, 1290-1400', *Economic History Review*, 2nd series, XLIX: 3 (1996), 447-72.

mand for agriculturally produced raw materials. By 1300 agriculture was supplying flax, hemp, wool, dye plants, hides, skins, tallow, grain, straw, timber and wood to a greatly enlarged and diversified manufacturing sector. Increasing quantities of primary products were also being exported overseas. Wool and cloth contributed the lion's share of the growing volume of English exports and by the early fourteenth century the equivalent of 8m. fleeces were leaving the country annually.[14]

Never again would dependence upon domestic agricultural production for food, raw materials and exports be so complete. In later centuries general economic progress would derive as much from the relaxation of this domestic dependence as from productivity growth within the agricultural sector *per se*. In particular, more use would be made of fossil fuels, inorganic raw materials and inanimate sources of energy and ever greater quantities of foodstuffs and organic raw materials (processed and unprocessed) would be imported.[15] This is not to deny the contribution of rising domestic agricultural production to post-medieval economic expansion and growth, but the sources of that increased agricultural output were essentially the same as those which had applied between 1086 and 1348. Developments in English agriculture before 1348 thus anticipated in several key respects the more celebrated achievements of later centuries.[16]

2. Sources of output growth in English agriculture 1086-1350

Expansion of the agricultural area
The single most immediate source of increased agricultural output was a greatly enlarged agricultural area.[17] On the evidence of Domesday Book there were just under 6m. acres (2.43m. hectares) of arable in 1086.[18] By c.1300 reclamation and the conversion of grassland to tillage had probably increased this to just short of the

14. A. R. Bridbury, *The English Economy from Bede to the Reformation* (Woodbridge, 1992) 185-6.
15. E. A. Wrigley, 'The Supply of Raw Materials in the Industrial Revolution', *Economic History Review*, 2nd series, XV: 1 (1962) 1-16; G. Clark, *A Revolution too Many: The Agricultural Revolution, 1700-1850*, Agriculture History Center, University of California, Davis, Working Paper Series 91 (1997) 25-9.
16. For a case study of these continuities and discontinuities see B.M.S. Campbell and M. Overton, 'A New Perspective on Medieval and Early Modern Agriculture: Six Centuries of Norfolk Farming c.1250-c.1850', *Past and Present*, 141 (1993), 38-105.
17. R. A. Donkin, 'Changes in the Early Middle Ages', in: H.C. Darby (ed.), *A New Historical Geography of England* (Cambridge, 1973) 98-106.
18. This figure is a recomputation of the estimate made by F. Seebohm, *The English Village Community: Examined in its Relations to the Manorial and Tribal Systems and to the Common or Open Field System of Husbandry* (London, 1883) 102-03. It is more plausible, in terms of implied levels of food output and the size of the population to be supported

10.5m. acres (4.24m. hectares) under the plough in 1800 (the climax of the plough-ing-up campaign which resulted from the Napoleonic War).[19] In other words, the arable area grew by up to two-thirds. In many lowland arable-farming regions this expansion was at the expense of permanent pasture of one sort or another. Never-theless, at a national scale, and contrary to what is usually assumed, these lowland pastoral losses were undoubtedly more than compensated for by pastoral gains elsewhere.

It was pasture rather than arable that was the principal beneficiary from the clearance of woodland and forest, the drainage of fenland and marshland, and the enclosure and upgrading of upland 'waste'. In fact, most reclamation around Eng-land's extensive upland margins, especially that undertaken by the many newly-founded Cisterican abbeys which received extensive land grants in these areas, was aimed primarily at the creation of pasture farms.[20] A national sheep flock in excess of 12m. animals *circa* 1300 is unaccountable unless permanent grassland remained abundant. Rather than grassland, it was woodland which bore the brunt of the expansion of the agricultural area, with the result that timber and wood became the land-use products often in scarcest supply.[21] By 1300 few areas pos-sessed arable, grassland and woodland in adequate measure. Local, regional and national trade thus performed an increasingly important role in rectifying deficien-cies in particular land-uses and their products.[22]

Increased labour and capital inputs:
Reclamation was a labour-intensive task and invariably involved upgrading land-use from an extensive to a more intensive form. At Podimore in Somerset, for example, H.S.A. Fox has demonstrated how marshland was upgraded first to rough pasture and then, by further ditching and draining, to meadow.[23] Arable was the most labour-intensive land-use of all and between 1086 and 1300, great as was the increase in the arable area, the growth of population was greater. The potential therefore existed to cultivate the land more intensively. This process undoubtedly went furthest on peasant smallholdings, since they were characterised by the high-est ratios of labour to land. For example, at the close of the thirteenth century

than the more commonly cited total of 8m. acres, based on an estimate made by R.V. Lennard, *Rural England 1086-1135* (Oxford, 1959) 393.

19. Overton and Campbell, 'Production et productivité', 290-1.

20. R. A. Donkin, *The Cistercians: Studies in the Geography of Medieval England and Wales* (Toronto, 1978) 104-34.

21. Galloway, Keene, and Murphy, 'Fuelling the City', 449.

22. D.L. Farmer 'Marketing the Produce of the Countryside, 1200-1500', in: in E. Miller, (ed.), *The Agrarian History of England and Wales*, III, *1348-1500* (Cambridge, 1991) 324-430.

23. H.S.A. Fox, 'The Alleged Transformation from Two-field to Three-field Systems in Medieval England', *Economic History Review*, 2nd series, XXXIX: 4 (1986) 544.

peasants at Martham in Norfolk had at least six times the available labour resources per unit of land as the the prior of Norwich on his 210 acre demesne.[24] It is on seignorial demesnes that the trend toward increased labour inputs per unit area can be most explicitly demonstrated. On the bishop of Winchester's demesne at Rimpton in Somerset, for instance, labour inputs per acre increased by 40 percent over the course of the thirteenth century.[25] Adoption of written accounting here as elsewhere facilitated more careful management and closer supervision of the workers. As labour inputs rose, so they became more specialised, with increased differentiation by task. Partial or complete substitution of waged for servile labour, as the former became abundant and cheap, also improved the quality of labour inputs.[26] New forms of labour process encouraged greater seasonal use of casual labour, for weeding, mowing and harvesting, and it became the norm for certain types of labour to be remunerated by the task.[27]

In the eleventh century low land values, borne of under-population and limited commerce, discouraged investment. Thereafter, rising population and expanding commerce drove up land-values and rendered capital investment more worthwhile (although high interest rates remained an obstacle).[28] By far the most spectacular capital investments of the age were the great drainage schemes – involving cooperation between several communities and the digging of drains and construction of dykes and sluices - which brought vast areas of potentially fertile marshland into agricultural use. Nowhere was the transformation greater than in the East Anglian fens.[29] By the 1330s land that had been of little value in 1086 supported the greatest concentrations of taxable wealth and tax-paying population in the country.[30] Meanwhile, throughout the land, fixed capital investment in improved farm buil-

24. B.M.S. Campbell, 'Agricultural Progress in Medieval England: some Evidence from Eastern Norfolk', *Economic History Rewview*, 2nd series, XXXVI: 1 (1983) 39.

25. C. Thornton, 'The Determinants of Land Productivity on the Bishop of Winchester's Demesne of Rimpton, 1208 to 1403' in: B.M.S. Campbell, and M. Overton (eds.), *Land, Labour and Livestock: Historical Studies in European Agricultural Productivity* (Manchester, 1991) 205.

26. D. Stone, 'The Productivity of Hired and Customary Labour: Evidence from Wisbech Barton in the Fourteenth Century', *Economic History Review*, 2nd series, L: 4 (1997), 640-56.

27. D.L. Farmer, 'Prices and Wages', in: H. E. Hallam (ed.), *The Agrarian History of England and Wales*, II, *1042-1350* (Cambridge, 1988) 760-72.

28. G. Clark, 'The Cost of Capital and Medieval Agricultural Technique', *Explorations in Economic History*, 25 (1988) 265-92.

29. H. E. Hallam, *Settlement and Society: A Study of the Early Agrarian History of South Lincolnshire* (Cambridge, 1965).

30. H.C. Darby, *The Medieval Fenland* (Cambridge, 1940); H.C. Darby, R.E. Glasscock, J. Sheail, and G.R. Versey, 'The Changing Geographical Distribution of Wealth in England 1086-1334-1525', *Journal of Historical Geography*, 5: 3 (1979) 249-56.

dings, notably barns, byres, stables, sties and cotes, steadily rose.[31] Although there was an element of prestige and display in this, livestock became better housed and the storage capacity of grain was improved. Higher rent levels also encouraged heavier seeding rates, which were one of the surest ways of raising yields per unit area. Such rates attained their maxima in eastern Norfolk and eastern Kent, both strongly commercialised areas of fertile soil and high population density.[32] Lords and peasants alike could afford to invest in higher seeding rates. Mill construction, in contrast, required the kinds of substantial capital sums which only lords could muster. Mills were built and rebuilt in large numbers throughout the twelfth and thirteenth centuries. In particular, invention of the windmill c.1180 allowed mills to be erected where there had been none before.[33] Mills enhanced the processing rather than the production of grain and as such represented an infra-structural improvement. Similarly, seignorial investment in bridge construction – another largely unsung achievement of the age - gave all classes of producer improved access to markets.[34]

Changes in the composition of production:
As the population rose and the relative scarcity of land increased, significant changes were made to the composition of agricultural production (Table 1). Certain crops and animals were more productive of cash, food and/or energy than others. Industrial and horticultural crops, for instance, yielded particularly high cash returns per unit area and hence gained in favour as holdings shrank in size and the demand from craftworkers rose. Cultivation of flax and hemp is widely recorded in the returns of the *Nonarum Inquisitiones* of 1340-41 and appears to have been almost exclusively associated with peasant rather than seignorial producers.[35] Processing grain into ale is far more extravagant of available kilocalories than milling it and baking it into bread or dehusking it and consuming it as pottage. Over

31. J. G. Hurst, 'Rural Building in England and Wales: England', in: Hallam, *Agrarian History,* 888-98; C. Dyer, 'Sheepcotes: Evidence for Medieval Sheepfarming', *Medieval Archaeology*, XXXIX: 1 (1995) 136-64.
32. B.M.S. Campbell, 'Arable Productivity in Medieval England: Some Evidence from Norfolk', *Journal of Economic History*, XLIII: 2 (1983) 386-8; Campbell *et al., Medieval Capital*, 131, 136-8.
33. R. Holt, *The Mills of Medieval England* (Oxford, 1988) 20-22, 171-5; J.L. Langdon, 'Water-mills and Windmills in the West Midlands, 1086-1500', *Economic History Review*, 2nd series, XLIV: 3 (1991) 424-44.
34. D. F. Harrison, 'Bridges and Economic Development, 1300-1800', *Economic History Review*, 2nd series, XLV: 2 (1992), 240-61; R.H. Britnell, 'Commercialisation and Economic Development in England, 1000-1300', in: Britnell and Campbell, *Commercialising Economy*, 17-18.
35. N. Evans, *The East Anglian Linen Industry: Rural Industry and Local Economy, 1500-1850*, Pasold Studies in Textile History 5 (Aldershot, 1985), 41-6.

Table 1. *National trends in demesne husbandry, 1250-99 to 1325-74*

Component of demesne husbandry	Years			
	1250-1299	1275-1324	1300-1349	1325-1374
Crops:				
Mean sown acreage per demesne	189	193	172	156
% of cropped area devoted to:				
bread grains[1]	39	40	43	39
brewing grains[2]	17	18	19	22
pottage & fodder grains[3]	44	41	37	38
Rye & winter mixtures as % bread grains[1]	17	17	18	15
Barley as % brewing grains[2]	85	82	78	73
Legumes as % pottage & fodder grains[3]	14	19	27	36
Livestock:				
Mean livestock units[4] per demesne	64	68	65	64
a) Working animals:				
Working animals[5] as % of livestock units[4]	44	41	40	36
Oxen per 100 horses	498	448	404	396
Cart horses per 1,000 horses	105	131	137	200
b) Non-working animals:				
% of non-working livestock units[6] from:				
adult cattle[7]	36	33	33	34
immature cattle[8]	23	21	18	17
all cattle	59	53	51	50
sheep	36	41	43	44
swine	4	5	6	6
Immature cattle[8] per 100 adults[7]	119	110	102	95
Sheep per 100 cattle	71	83	86	90
Stocking densities:				
Mean livestock units[4] per 100 grain acres:				
all livestock	42	44	48	56
non-working livestock[6] only	21	23	25	30

1 wheat + rye + winter mixtures
2 barley + dredge
3 legumes + oats
4 (horses x 1.0) + (oxen & adult cattle x 1.2) + (immature cattle x 0.8) + (swine & cattle x 0.1)
5 horses + oxen
6 cattle + sheep + swine
7 bulls + cows
8 calves + heifers + steers
Source: B.M.S. Campbell, *English seigniorial agriculture 1250-1450* (Cambridge, forth-
    coming)

time, therefore, the food grains gained relative to the brewing grains and the cheaper food and brewing grains – rye mixtures, oats, and dredge – gained relative to those of highest value (i.e. wheat and barley) (Table 1).[36] Such simple production shifts delivered significant gains in the rate of food output per unit area. Substituting legumes for bare fallows had much the same effect. They provided a nutritious food source for humans and draught animals alike and had the further merit that they helped fix atmospheric nitrogen within the soil.

Once the decision was taken to cultivate fodder crops the decision to substitute horses for oxen, either partially or wholly, tended to follow, since horses convert fodder into work with greater efficiency. Over the course of the twelfth and thirteenth centuries horses came into more general use for farm work of all kinds, but especially for carting. Their adoption made greatest progress in the more commercialised and urbanised east and south-east of England, especially on peasant rather than seignorial holdings.[37] Increased cultivation of legumes was also associated with a switch from pannage-fed to sty-fed pigs.[38] No other domesticated animal was as efficient a producer of meat and the pig, like the horse, occupied an especially prominent place on peasant holdings. Milk was an even more productive food source and producers who substituted horses for oxen often did so with the aim of specialising more exclusively in cattle-based dairying.[39] Dairying was certainly a more efficient use of scarce meadows and pastures and on many lowland demesnes it gained in relative importance throughout the period 1250-1350, as witnessed by the decline of immature cattle relative to adults (Table 1). Sheep were the most land-extensive animal of all and, other things being equal, should have lost out to their more food productive rivals over this period. But other things were not equal. Rising international prices for English wool ensured that sheep remained important on holdings and in locations where dairy cattle and swine were not more profitable. Overall, sheep became more important over the period 1250-1349, not less (Table 1).

36. B.M.S. Campbell, 'Matching Supply to Demand: Crop Production and Disposal by English Demesnes in the Century of the Black Death', *Journal of Economic History*, 57: 4 (1997) 830-39.

37. J.L. Langdon, *Horses, Oxen and Technological Innovation: The Use of Draught Animals in English Farming from 1066-1500* (Cambridge, 1986).

38. K. Biddick, *The Other Economy: Pastoral Husbandry on a Medieval Estate* (Berkeley and Los Angeles, 1989) 121-5; J.P. Power and B.M.S. Campbell, 'Cluster Analysis and the Classification of Medieval Demesne-farming Systems', *Transactions of the Institute of British Geographers*, new series, 17: 3 (1992) 237.

39. B.M.S. Campbell, 'Towards an Agricultural Geography of Medieval England', *Agricultural History Review*, 36: I (1988) 95-7; B.M.S. Campbell, 'Commercial Dairy Production on Medieval English Demesnes: The Case of Norfolk', *Anthropozoologica*, 16, *Animals and their Products in Trade and Exchange* (1992) 107-18.

Many specific changes in the composition of production were associated with the adoption of agricultural food-chains which were more productive of food and energy per unit area. Especially notable was the emergence of mixed-farming systems geared towards the intensive production of grain supported by the rapid recycling of nutrients through livestock partially fed on fodder. Within the pastoral sector the growing practice of feeding animals on a combination of grazing and produced fodder rather than grazing alone, represented a significant step forwards.[40] Systems of woodland management based upon systematic coppicing similarly delivered significantly higher returns per unit area.[41] These broad shifts in production systems were reflected in a progressively greater emphasis upon fodder cropping, managed hay meadows, and coppiced woodland, all of which required higher factor inputs per unit area.

In all these ways the aggregate value of agricultural output was raised per unit area. That rise was, however, contingent upon a concomitant change in diets. Ale and meat, especially beef, dwindled in their relative contribution to diets, whereas bread, particularly of the coarser sort, pottage and dairy produce all grew.[42]

Technological innovation:
The writings of Lynn White Jnr apart, technological innovation is not something which has generally received much attention in accounts of medieval agriculture.[43] After all, introduction of potentially revolutionally new crops and new breeds of animals mostly lay in the future. Nevertheless, innovations there were: the most conspicuous were the most novel. Improved methods of harnessing facilitated the substitution of horses for oxen, an innovation which made significantly greater progress in road haulage than in farm traction.[44] Greater use of horses placed

40. B.M.S. Campbell, 'The Livestock of Chaucer's Reeve: Fact or Fiction?', in: E. B. Dewindt (ed.), *The Salt of Common Life: Individuality and Choice in the Medieval Town, Countryside and Church. Essays Presented to J. Ambrose Raftis on the Occasion of his 70th Birthday* (Kalamazoo, 1995) 290; I. G. Simmons, *The Ecology of Natural Resources* (London, 1974).

41. O. Rackham, *The History of the Countryside* (London, 1986) 62-118; K. P. Witney, 'The Woodland Economy of Kent, 1066-1348', *Agricultural History Review*, 38: I (1990) 20-39.

42. C. Dyer, *Standards of Living in the Later Middle Ages: Social Change in England c.1200-1520* (Cambridge, 1989) 151-60.

43. L. White Jr, *Medieval Technology and Social Change* (Oxford, 1962); G. E. Fussell, 'Social Change but Static Technology: Rural England in the Fourteenth Century', *History Studies*, 1 (1968) 23-32. Recent reassessments include, J. Mokyr, *The Lever of Riches: Technological Creativity and Economic Progress* (Oxford, 1990) 31-56; G. Astill and J. Langdon (eds.), *Medieval Farming and Technology: The Impact of Agricultural Change in Northwest Europe* (Leiden, 1997).

44. Langdon, *Horses, Oxen*; J.L. Langdon, 'Horse Hauling: A Revolution in Vehicle Transport in Twelfth- and Thirteenth-Century England?', *Past and Present*, 103 (1984) 37-66.

greater demands on fodder, in response to which vetches were reintroduced as a field crop.[45] They were especially favoured by those farmers who had made the changeover to horsepower but lacked an adequate supply of hay. Greater use of horses was one way of harnessing more energy; constructing windmills was another. Widespread windmill construction in the period 1180-1300 is one of the most striking examples of the rapid diffusion of an important new innovation and demonstrates that there was no reluctance to adopt new technology when it proved advantageous.[46] Simultaneous adoption of improved record keeping and accounting on seignorial demesnes is an equally striking example of the same phenomenon, creating in the manorial account the single most vital source for the analysis of technological change in medieval agriculture.[47] The great barns constructed on many demesnes during the twelfth and thirteenth centuries are an equally tangible legacy.[48] They represented a radical new approach to the need for greater and better storage and provided an improved environment for carrying out those agricultural tasks best undertaken under cover.[49] Finally, it was during the twelfth and thirteenth centuries that the rabbit was introduced and acclimatised. Production of rabbit meat and fur provided a lucrative means of turning poor sandy soils to financial advantage.[50]

The true significance of these individual innovations lay less in their separate impacts than in the new and more productive technological complexes which they helped bring into being.[51] Here, one of the key achievements of the age was the development of more intensive and complex rotations. In areas of regular commonfields this often entailed the creation of extra field divisions in order to accommodate a greater diversity and flexibility of cropping. Sometimes, when the frequency of fallowing was permanently reduced and two-course cropping was replaced by three-, even greater structural reorganisation was required.[52] The latter was, however, less common than has sometimes been claimed and generally speaking the greatest changes were made to rotations in areas of irregular and

45. B.M.S. Campbell, 'The Diffusion of Vetches in Medieval England', *Economic History Review*, 2nd series, XLI: 2 (1988), 193-208.

46. Holt, *Mills*, 17-35.

47. P.D.A. Harvey (ed.), *Manorial Records of Cuxham, Oxfordshire circa 1200-1359*, Oxfordshire Record Society, 50 (1976) 12-71; M. Clanchy, *From Memory to Written Record: England 1066 to 1307* (London, 1979).

48. Hurst, 'Rural Building'.

49. D. M. McCloskey and J. Nash, 'Corn at Interest: The Extent and Cost of Grain Storage in Medieval England', *American Economic Review* LXXIV (1984) 174-87.

50. J. Sheail, *Rabbits and their History* (Newton Abbot, 1971); M. Bailey, 'The Rabbit and the Medieval East Anglian Economy', *Agricultural History Review*, 36 (1988), 1-20.

51. J. Myrdal, 'The Agricultural Transformation of Sweden, 1000-1300': I in: Astill and Langdon, *Medieval Farming and Technology*, 151-3.

52. D. Hall, *Medieval Fields* (Aylesbury, 1982) 44-55; G. Astill, 'Fields', in G. Astill and A.

more flexible field systems. In such areas, by the close of the thirteenth century, rotations had evolved in which (a) fallows took place as and when required, (b) cropping was virtually continuous, and (c) land was either sown or unsown for several consecutive years at a time (i.e. convertible husbandry).[53] Lest the sustainability of cropping be jeopardised, it became necessary as a corollary to pay greater attention to several related aspects of cultivation. These included more thorough preparation of the seed-bed via repeated ploughings, use of greater quantities of higher quality seed, and more effective weed control via systematic weeding, heavier seeding rates, and multiple summer ploughings of bare fallows. Greater effort was also expended on the maintenance and improvement of soil structure and fertility through the cultivation of nitrogen-fixing legumes, systematic folding of sheep, and applications of farmyard manure, marl, lime, night-soil and the like.[54]

An associated and more striking achievement of the period was the evolution of integrated mixed-farming systems, which combined arable with pastoral husbandry in such a way that their respective land-use requirements became complementary rather than competitive.[55] In other words, the arable supplied fodder and temporary fallow grazing to the livestock while the livestock supplied manure, traction and haulage to the arable. This symbiosis was crucial if the resultant arable-based mixed-farming systems were to prove ecologically sustainable in more than the short term (an issue which has loomed large in assessments of the agricultural achievements of this period).[56] It was achieved via better control of fallow grazing and folding, the development of convertible-farming systems in which land alternated between arable and temporary pasture, a greater reliance upon fodder crops (principally legumes and oats) in conjunction with the stall- and sty-feeding of animals (especially in winter), and a more systematic recycling of nitrogen via the collection of animal wastes and their application to the arable fields. Fully fledged, integrated, mixed-farming systems had emerged in the most advanced regions of

Grant (eds.), *The Countryside of Medieval England* (Oxford, 1988 75-80; Fox, 'Alleged Transformation'.

53. T. A. M. Bishop, 'The Rotation of Crops at Westerham, 1297-1350', *Economic History Review*, IX (1938) 38-44; P. Brandon, 'Farming Techniques in Southeast England', in Hallam, *Agrarian History*, 312-25; B.M.S. Campbell, 'The Regional Uniqueness of English Field Systems? Some Evidence from Eastern Norfolk', *Agricultural History Review*, 29: 1 (1981) 21-2; E. Searle, *Lordship and Community: Battle Abbey and its Banlieu, 1066-1538* (Toronto, 1974) 272-91; Campbell and Overton, 'New Perspective', 62.

54. R. A. L. Smith, *Canterbury Cathedral Priory: A Study in Monastic Administration* (Cambridge, 1943) 135-7; Campbell, 'Agricultural Progress', 31-6.

55. M. Overton and B.M.S. Campbell, 'Productivity Change in European Agricultural Development', in: Campbell and Overton, *Land, Labour and Livestock*, 42-3.

56. J. Pretty, 'Sustainable Agriculture in the Middle Ages: The English Manor', *Agricultural History Review*, 38: I (1990) 1-19.

England by the mid thirteenth century.[57] Their great achievement was to reconcile intensive methods of production with sustained high levels of both arable and pastoral productivity. In Norfolk, England's most populous county and the county most in the vanguard of these developments, mean grain yields displayed a modest upward trend over the period 1275-1349: proof positive that high population densities and intensive and innovative methods of production were capable of raising land productivity.[58] Here, in embryo, was the 'Norfolk system of husbandry' whose diffusion five centuries later in an improved and more developed form constituted a key element of the so-called 'agricultural revolution'.[59]

Greater specialisation:
Greater farm specialisation was the fifth avenue by which aggregate agricultural output was raised.[60] As more farmers capitalised upon their comparative advantage, land productivity as a whole was enhanced. Additional efficiency gains accrued from a fuller spatial division of labour. Pastoral husbandry was particularly open to specialisation due to the ease with which animals and certain of their products - wool, hides, cheese and butter - could be transported over long distances. Farmers increasingly specialised in different types of livestock, different stages of livestock production, and different types of livestock product.[61] Growing numbers of markets and fairs were established to service this trade, which enabled pasture-deficient farms to take advantage of those with a relative abundance of pasture. One aspect of this trade was the rearing of replacement draught oxen on upland farms for sale to lowland arable farms. Another, was the sale of surplus calves by specialist dairying demesnes in the south and east. Such dairying demesnes also sold significant quantities of cheese and butter.[62] Wool production was even more highly commercialised. Wool, sometimes produced in the remotest loca-

57. In eastern Norfolk documentation is provided by a set of grouped manorial accounts relating to demesnes operated by St Benet's Abbey during the period 1239-46: Norfolk Record Office (Norwich) Diocesan Est/1 & 2,1.
58. B.M.S. Campbell, 'Land, Labour, Livestock, and Productivity Trends in English Seignorial Agriculture, 1208-1450', in: Campbell and Overton, *Land, Labour and Livestock*, 144-82.
59. Campbell and Overton, 'New Perspective', 88-95.
60. Overton and Campbell, 'Productivity Change', 19-22.
61. M. Overton and B.M.S. Campbell, Norfolk Livestock Farming 1250-1740: A Comparative Study of Manorial Accounts and Probate Inventories', *Journal of Historical Geography*, 18: 4 (1992) 377-96; Campbell, 'Livestock of Chaucer's Reeve', 271-306.
62. Campbell, 'Commercial Dairy Production' 113-14; B.M.S. Campbell, 'Measuring the Commercialisation of Seigneurial Agriculture c.1300', in: Britnell and Campbell, *Commercialising Economy*, 172-73.

tions, was the one agricultural commodity regularly to be traded in local, regional, national and international markets.[63]

Within the arable sector the opportunities for specialising were equally real but geographically more circumscribed, due to the higher unit transport costs of grain, especially overland. Access to cheap bulk transport by river and sea thus shaped patterns of arable specialisation.[64] The concentrated demand of major urban centres was a spur to specialisation within their hinterlands, especially on demesnes whose grain output was, on average, well in excess of seignorial consumption requirements. By the close of the thirteenth century London's normal grain provisioning hinterland encompassed over 4,000 square miles. Within that hinterland the choice of grains produced was consistent with the cost-distance of transporting them to the metropolis. Thus, the cheapest fodder and bread grains were produced in greatest quantity close to the city, high quality brewing grains at an intermediate distance, and wheat – the most highly prized bread grain – at the greatest distance of all.[65] Specialist production of firewood, charcoal and timber bore a similar cost-distance relationship to the London market.[66]

It was once thought that 'technology and exchange had not progressed far enough by the early fourteenth century to allow much [agricultural] specialisation'.[67] Such a view is no longer tenable. Within the demesne sector alone seven different types of mixed-farming system may be distinguished at a national scale c.1300, differentiated from one another in the character, intensity and composition of their husbandry. Each of these seven farming types in its distribution reflects the wider forces - environmental, institutional, and economic - shaping agricultural production.[68] It would be surprising if the non-demesne sector did not display at least as wide a range of specialisms.

The relative importance of these sources of output growth:
By 1300 English agriculture had yet to achieve its full output potential. Although the agricultural area had been greatly expanded much potential farmland remained in reserve as royal forest and private hunting grounds.[69] Institutional obstacles had

63. E. Power, *The Wool Trade in English Medieval History* (Oxford, 1941); T.H. Lloyd, *The English Wool Trade in the Middle Ages* (Cambridge, 1977).

64. B.M.S. Campbell and J.P. Power, 'Mapping the Agricultural Geography of Medieval England', *Journal of Historical Geography*, 15: 1 (1989) 24-39; Campbell, 'Ecology versus Economics', 81-91.

65. Campbell *et al*, *Medieval Capital*, 76-7, 111-44.

66. Galloway, Keene and Murphy, 'Fuelling the City'.

67. R.E. Glasscock, 'England circa 1334', in: Darby, *New Historical Geography*, 167.

68. Power and Campbell, 'Cluster Analysis'.

69. C. R. Young, *The Royal Forests of Medieval England* (Leicester, 1979); L. Cantor, 'Forests, Chases, Parks and Warrens', in: L. Cantor (ed.), *The English Medieval Landscape* (London, 1982) 56-85.

to be removed before this land could be brought into more productive use. The same applied to the often considerable areas of common pasture and waste. True, these did yield a range of agricultural products, but rates of productivity were bound to remain low until more effective means of managing and exploiting these land-use resources were put in place. In later centuries enclosure would transform these areas. Enclosure facilitated the substitution of more intensive methods of production, requiring greater unit inputs of labour and capital. Reclamation and land-use change during the twelfth and thirteenth centuries had much the same effect. Whether land was upgraded from natural to coppiced woodland, from marsh to pasture, from pasture to meadow, or from grassland or woodland to arable, the intensity of production rose. Nevertheless, methods of managing woodland, grassland and arable themselves remained predominantly extensive. The intensive extremes of coppiced woodland, enclosed grassland, and more-or-less continuously cropped arable were confined in their adoption to relatively limited areas of high population density, resource scarcity and strong market demand in the east midlands, East Anglia and parts of the south-east. Elsewhere, scope for fuller adoption of these methods remained largely unfulfilled and had to await the far-reaching socio-economic changes of the seventeenth and eighteenth centuries.

Significant gains in food and energy output could nevertheless be achieved without altering the nature or intensity of land-use. The broad shifts in the composition of agricultural production which can be observed within the demesne sector after 1250 greatly extended the subsistence base of society, albeit at the sacrifice of certain food preferences (Table 1). Indeed, the shift to a predominantly grain-based diet, composed of increasing proportions of coarse bread and pottage and decreasing proportions of ale and meat, had been taken almost as far as was realistically possible by the early fourteenth century. This was especially the case in the areas of greatest population pressure and strongest market demand where there is abundant evidence that consumers were trading down to the cheaper bread and brewing grains. For instance, it was in response to the concentrated demand from the urban poor that farmers in the immediate hinterlands of London and Norwich specialised in the cultivation of rye, rye mixtures, oats and barley.[70]

Technological innovation was far more limited and selective in its impact. None of the key innovations of the age was universal in its adoption. Most were limited in their geographical spread and restricted to certain categories of producer. Written accounting was exclusive to the seignorial sector and in the remoter parts of the country appears only to have been adopted on the greatest estates. Horse haulage was adopted by a far wider cross-section of producers, but remained the exception rather than the rule in the remoter parts of the south-west and north-west. In fact, the more commercialised and populous parts of the east and south-

70. B.M.S. Campbell, 'Economic Rent and the Intensification of English Agriculture, 1086-1350', in: Astill and Langdon, *Medieval Farming,* 239-40.

Figure 1. *The unit value of agricultural land in England, 1300-49, according to the* Inquisitiones Post Mortem

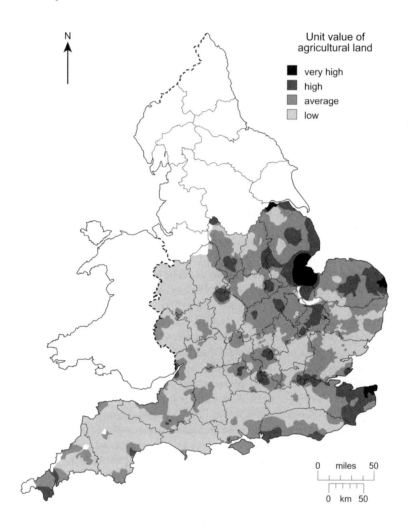

Source: all extant and legible IPM extents dated 1300-49 and preserved in the Public Record Office, London.
Method: K. Bartley and B.M.S. Campbell, 'Inquisitiones Post Mortem, G.I.S., and the Creation of a Land-use Map of Pre Black Death England', Transactions in G.I.S., 2 (1997).
Variables: (unit value grassland: unit value arable) x 2.0; (unit value meadow: unit value arable) x 1.5; (unit value meadow: unit value pasture) x 1.5; (unit value arable) x 1.2

Definition:

Land category	Mean unit value of arable (pence)	Mean ratio (unit value: unit value) of:		
		grassland to arable	meadow to arable	meadow to pasture
Very high	16.2	1.1	1.3	2.9
High	7.0	2.2	2.8	3.3
Average	4.3	3.6	4.3	3.9
Low	2.6	5.7	6.5	5.3
All	3.9	4.5	5.3	4.5

east consistently proved themselves to be most receptive to the adoption of new technology. It was here, by the early fourteenth century, that written accounting, horse traction as well as horse haulage, vetches, windmills, barns and rabbit warrens were all most likely to be encountered. It was here, too, that agricultural systems attained their fullest development. Technologically sophisticated, complex and productive agricultural systems emerged in only a few key areas where environmental, locational, economic and institutional factors combined to nurture the evolution of uniquely progressive methods. Eastern Kent, eastern Norfolk, and parts of the East Anglian Fenland stand out in these respects. The high unit land values which their advanced agricultural methods sustained provide a striking contrast with much of the rest of the country, where production methods were uniformly less precocious and unit land values were almost monotonously low (Figure 1). Not surprisingly, these technologically more conservative parts of the country were also less differentiated and specialised in their husbandry. Specialisation, like innovation, was most pronounced where market demand was strongest and most differentiated.[71]

In England the story of medieval agricultural change is therefore one of uneven development. Although change of one sort or another can be found almost everywhere, intensification, innovation and specialisation went very much further in some areas than others. The gap between the least and most progressive and productive husbandry systems steadily widened. In a few privileged parts of the country the best English methods were practically on a par with those to be found in the more developed parts of the continent, especially in northern France and Flanders.[72]

71. Power and Campbell, 'Cluster Analysis', 232-42.
72. B. H. Slicher Van Bath, 'The Rise of Intensive Husbandry in the Low Countries', in: J. S. Bromley and E. H. Kossmann (eds.), *Britain and the Netherlands: Papers delivered to the Oxford-Netherlands Historical Conference 1959*, I (London, 1960), 130-53; E. Thoen, 'The Birth of "The Flemish Husbandry": Agricultural Technology in Medieval Flanders', in: Astill and Langdon, *Medieval Farming*, 69-88.

Such localities mostly faced the continent and were distinguished by high unit values of land. They were, however, very much the exception rather than the rule (as, indeed, were their counterparts in Europe) and comprised no more than an eighth of the total agricultural area within England south of the River Trent (Figure 1). From these early beginnings manure-intensive mixed-farming systems would eventually develop and diffuse until, by the nineteenth century, they had become the norm throughout the greater part of the country.

3. Markets and agriculture - the demand side of the equation

Spurring medieval agricultural change on was not merely the growth of population (as Postan argued) or the ever growing consumption requirements of lords and their households (as Georges Duby claimed), but the need to service a commercialising economy in which trade was growing at all levels and urban centres were expanding.[73] The production decisions of farmers became increasingly influenced by the relative price of agricultural products, rent of land and cost of labour.[74] Indeed, as opportunities for extending the agricultural area dwindled, specialisation and exchange became the principal means of averting diminishing returns and offsetting environmental limitations.[75] Trade enabled land-deficient areas to draw upon the resources of land-abundant areas and encouraged individual farmers to concentrate upon what they could best produce. The extent to which specialisation resulted was determined by the size of the market: during the twelfth and thirteenth centuries local, regional, national and international markets for agricultural produce all grew. Demand became more concentrated. Farmers almost everywhere were influenced in some way by these expanding opportunities, although their capacity to exploit them was constrained by the cost of delivering their produce to market.[76]

Proliferating markets, fairs, and boroughs during the twelfth and thirteenth centuries testify to the vigour with which internal trade was then expanding.[77] Towns not only increased in number but grew in size, doubling their share of the population

---

73. Postan, 'Medieval Agrarian Society'; G. Duby, *The Early Growth of the European Economy: Warriors and Peasants from the Seventh to the Twelfth Century* (London, 1974), trans. H. B. Clarke, 177-80; K. G. Persson, *Pre-industrial Economic Growth, Social Organization and Technological Progress in Europe* (Oxford, 1988); R.H. Britnell, *The Commercialisation of English Society 1000-1500* (Cambridge, 1993); E. Miller and J. Hatcher, *Medieval England: Towns, Commerce and Crafts* (London, 1995).

74. Campbell, 'Matching Supply'.

75. Persson, *Pre-Industrial Economic Growth*, 71-3.

76. Campbell, 'Ecology versus Economics', 91-4; Campbell, 'Economic Rent', 235-42; Campbell *et al, Medieval Capital*, 46-75.

77. Miller and Hatcher, *Medieval England*, 135-80.

from perhaps 10 percent in 1086 to 20 percent in 1300.[78] Greater economic and market integration delivered disproportionate benefits to the cities at the top of the urban hierarchy. In 1086 London alone contained at least 10,000 inhabitants; by 1300 at least fourteen other towns were of this size. London consolidated its primacy over this period, trebling in size to 70-75,000 inhabitants in 1300, by which time it was the second largest city north of the Alps. Where in 1086 possibly one in ninety English people had lived in London, by 1300 this had narrowed to approximately one in sixty. London grew in part because during the thirteenth century its role as a capital city was enhanced. The king and his court spent more and more of their time in London, and Westminster became the more-or-less permanent seat for the Exchequer, Chancery, and Royal Courts of Law, attracting governmental, administrative and legal business to the city. The metropolis benefited even more from the enhancement of its role as a regional, national and international centre of commerce. Denizen merchants were more active in its overseas trade than that of any other English port. Due to their initiative, London's share of English overseas trade doubled to about 35 percent of the total, at a time when the total value of trade trebled. Specialist groups emerged within the city dependent upon trade and commerce for a living and to service that trade London became a manufacturing and distribution centre. The finest London-made goods commanded a national market.[79]

Great cities like London were the forcing ground of agricultural change as levels and contours of economic rent within their hinterlands were reconfigured in response to expanding urban demand. Analysis of land-use and farming systems within London's hinterland reveals that they were strongly influenced by the provisioning needs of the capital. Nevertheless, at this early stage in the city's history London's 'von Thünen field of force' embraced - for all commodities - no more than perhaps a fifth of the total national land area. Of this, less than half was engaged in the regular supply of grain to the city. Even within this area of regular grain supply relatively low levels of economic rent prevailed over high, with the result that extensive systems of production prevailed over intensive. This is consistent with the von Thünen model which predicts that within the provisioning hinterland of a major city high-yielding, intensive systems will occupy 6 percent of the arable, moderately productive and intensive systems a further 54 percent, and low-yielding extensive systems 40 percent of the arable.[80] The provisioning hinterlands

78. C. Dyer, 'How Urbanized was Medieval England?', in: J.-M. Duvosquel and E. Thoen (eds.), *Peasants and Townsmen in Medieval Europe: studia in honorem Adriaan Verhulst* (Ghent, 1995) 169-83.

79. D.J. Keene, 'Medieval London and its Region', *London Journal*, 14: 2 (1989) 99-111; Nightingale, 'Growth of London'; Miller and Hatcher, *Medieval England*, 181-254.

80. South of the Trent high unit land values accounted for 12 percent, average unit land values for 35 percent, and low unit land values for 52 percent of the agricultural area: see Figure 1.

of lesser urban centres were even smaller. Exeter drew its grain from within a 20 mile radius and Winchester from within a 12 mile radius.[81] Little wonder, therefore, that at a national scale low economic rent and extensive farming systems remained very much the order of the day. Low unit land values accounted for half of the total agricultural area south of the River Trent and were predominant throughout those southern and western parts of the country most remote from London and the leading entrepots of the east coast (Figure 1). For producers in these areas 'the local markets and the communities around them were the more important outlets for the produce of the countryside'.[82] Such markets were, however, incapable of stimulating economic rent and agricultural intensification to the same extent as major urban concentrations of demand. Consequently, low economic rent lay like a shadow across the land, discouraging intensification, innovation and specialisation. It is hardly surprising that evidence drawn from estates located in such areas conveys a powerful impression of technological inertia. Until substantial growth occurred in the non-agricultural sector and there was a quantum leap in the scale of urban centres the incentives to intensify, specialise and innovate would remain selective in nature and geographically circumscribed in impact. Surplus labour would also remain trapped on the land, depressing labour productivity in agriculture.

The crucial historical lesson to be drawn from this is that technology was not the limiting factor upon agricultural productivity and output which it has so often been represented as being. In the increasingly commercialised world of the thirteenth century factor costs and economic rent were more important. It was these that determined in the main how land was used, what was produced, and whether it was worth adopting more intensive and innovative methods. When and where circumstances were propitious medieval English farmers were as innovative and productive as their seventeenth-century successors.[83] The vital difference between the thirteenth and the seventeenth centuries was therefore less the available agricultural technology than the size, composition and concentration of the market. London, for instance, was over three times larger at the beginning of the seventeenth century than it had been at the end of the thirteenth.[84]

Recent research into medieval English agriculture thus emphasizes the demand rather than supply side of the equation and interprets the state of agricultural deve-

81. J.H. von Thünen, *Der isolierte staat* (Hamburg, 1826), English edn. trans. C.M. Wartenberg, *Von Thünen's Isolated State*, (ed.) P. Hall (Oxford, 1966); Campbell, *Medieval Capital*, 172-74; Campbell, 'Economic Rent', 241-44.

82. Farmer, 'Marketing', 329.

83. J. Langdon, G. Astill, and J. Myrdal, 'Introduction', in: Astill and Langdon, *Medieval Farming*, 2-3.

84. F. J. Fisher, 'The Development of the London Food Market, 1540-1640', *Economic History Review*, V: 1 (1935) 46-64; E. A. Wrigley, 'A Simple Model of London's Importance in Changing English Society and Economy, 1650-1750', *Past and Present,* 37 (1967) 44-70;

lopment as a largely rational response to the prevailing scale, composition and configuration of demand. On this reading it was not agriculture that impeded economic development: on the contrary, it was the limited and selective nature of viable commercial opportunities that constrained agricultural progress. The great achievement of subsequent centuries was to liberate agriculture from those constraints thereby allowing a fuller articulation of agricultural productive forces.

INDEX

Abel, Wilhelm: V 42
Acle (Norfolk): II 28 n., 29, 30, 33, 34, 37,
    38, 40, 44; III 393, 400, 401;
    VII 7, 11
Acre, size of: III 380, 385; V 68; IX 845
Acton (Middx.): VIII 183
Adderbury (Oxon.): VIII 183, 184; IX 847
Adisham (Kent): II 42n.
Agricultural:
    area: I 544; X 18–19, 28–9
    exports: V 93; X 15
    output: V 39–42, 45–7, 67; VI 378;
        VII 2; X 15
    revolution: I 543, 558; II 27; IV 146,
        148; V 38–9, 40, 44–8, 75, 88–95;
        VI 392; VII 2; X 16, 27
    sales: VIII 139–47, 174–6, 189–90
    specialisation: viii; I 553–4; V 104–05;
        VI 385, 393–4; VII 3; IX 828–9;
        X 27–8, 31, 32
    statistics: V 41, 49, 51–3, 59, 69–70,
        76–7; VI 378, 386–7
    treatises: VII 1
Albemarle, see Aumale
Alby (Norfolk): II 28n.
Alciston (Sussex): II 42n.
Aldborough (Norfolk): II 45; III 401
Aldeby (Norfolk): III 385, 393, 401
Aldeby Priory & its estate: III 382, 401
Aldenham (Herts.): VIII 154; IX 848
Alderford (Norfolk): V 59n.
All Hallows Hoo (Kent): II 41n.
Allen, Robert C.: IV 150; V 46, 68, 74
Animal ratio, see Stocking density
Animals, see Livestock
Antingham (Norfolk): II 45; III 401
Appledore (Kent): VIII 144, 180; IX 847
Arable
    area: VI 391; VIII 177
    unit value: II 28, 41
Argentine, Reginald d', & his estate:
        VIII 145, 159, 163, 166, 170, 178,
        181, 184, 187
Arminghall (Norfolk): II 30, 33, 44; III 401;

VII 12
Artois (France): IV 145
Ashby (Norfolk): II 36, 45; III 393, 401;
    V 57n.
Ashill (Norfolk): V 62n., 63n.
Ashwell (Herts.): VIII 186
Asset stripping: VII 2; VIII 147, 150
Attleborough (Norfolk): III 401; VII 7
Attlebridge (Norfolk): II 30, 33, 44; III 401;
    VII 10
Aumale (*alias* Albemarle), countess of, &
    her estate: II 42; III 381, 398;
    VIII 145, 159
Autarky: VIII 133, 184; IX 852–3
Avington (Berks.): IX 847
Aylmerton (Norfolk): II 30, 33, 44; III 401;
    V 57n.
Aylsham (Norfolk): V 57n.

Bacon: VIII 169n.
Badlesmere, Giles de, & his estate: II 41
Bailey, Mark: I 551–2
Barlee, Roger de, & his estate: VIII 145,
    146, 159, 163, 166, 178
Barley: IV 166–8; VIII 148, 151–2, 155–8;
    IX 833–40; X 22–3:
    rents: II 40; V 54–66, 102–03
    seeding rate: III 387, 388
    yields: I 556–7;
        per seed (yield ratio): II 38–9, 42n.;
            III 382–4, 390–1, 395; IV 161,
            163–4
        per unit area: II 30–31, 38–9, 42n.;
            III 388-91, 395, 398–9;
            IV 174–6, 179–80; V 70–76
Barns: X 25, 31
Bastwick (Norfolk): II 45
Battersea (Surrey): VIII 147, 183
Battle Abbey & its estate: II 42; III 380, 398
Bawburgh (*alias* Bauburgh) (Norfolk):
    II 44; III 401; VII 10
Bec Abbey & its estate: III 382, 403;
    VIII 141n., 144, 156, 158, 165, 169,
    178, 188